CCNA®:
Cisco® Certified Network Associate

Fast Pass

Third Edition

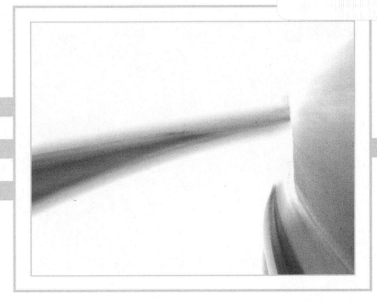

CCNA®:
Cisco® Certified
Network Associate
Fast Pass
Third Edition

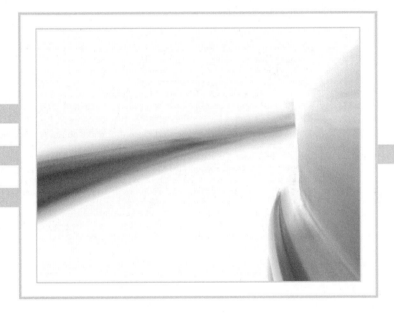

Todd Lammle

BICENTENNIAL
1807
WILEY
2007
BICENTENNIAL

Wiley Publishing, Inc.

Acquisitions Editor: Jeff Kellum
Development Editor: Lisa Thibault
Production Editor: Christine O'Connor
Copy Editor: Foxxe Editorial Services
Production Manager: Tim Tate
Vice President and Executive Group Publisher: Richard Swadley
Vice President and Executive Publisher: Joseph B. Wikert
Vice President and Publisher: Neil Edde
Media Associate Project Manager- Laura Atkinson
Media Assistant Producer- Kit Malone
Media Quality Assurance- Angie Denny
Compositor: Craig Woods, Happenstance Type-O-Rama
Proofreader: Christopher M. Jones
Indexer: Robert Swanson
Anniversary Logo Design: Richard Pacifico
Cover Designer: Richard Miller, Calyx Design; Ryan Sneed

Library of Congress Cataloging-in-Publication Data

Lammle, Todd.

  CCNA : Cisco Certified Network Associate fast pass / Todd Lammle. -- 3rd ed.

    p. cm.

  ISBN 978-0-470-18571-1 (pbk. : cd-rom)

  1. Electronic data processing personnel--Certification. 2. Computer networks--Examinations--Study guides. I. Title. II. Title: CCNA fast pass. III. Title: Cisco Certified Network Associate fast pass.

  QA76.3.L3485 2007

  004.6--dc22

                              2007038333

Dear Reader,

Thank you for choosing *CCNA: Cisco Certified Network Associate Fast Pass, Third Edition*. This book is part of a family of premium quality Sybex books, all written by outstanding authors who combine practical experience with a gift for teaching.

Sybex was founded in 1976. More than thirty years later, we're still committed to producing consistently exceptional books. With each of our titles we're working hard to set a new standard for the industry. From the paper we print on, to the authors we work with, our goal is to bring you the best books available.

I hope you see all that reflected in these pages. I'd be very interested to hear your comments and get your feedback on how we're doing. Feel free to let me know what you think about this or any other Sybex book by sending me an email at `nedde@wiley.com`, or if you think you've found a technical error in this book, please visit `http://sybex.custhelp.com`. Customer feedback is critical to our efforts at Sybex.

Best regards,

Neil Edde
Vice President and Publisher
Sybex, an Imprint of Wiley

About the Author

Todd Lammle, CCSI, CCNA/CCNP/CCSP, MCSE, CEH/CHFI, FCC RF Licensed, is the authority on Cisco Certification internetworking. He is a world renowned author, speaker, trainer and consultant. Todd has over 25 years of experience working with LAN's, WAN's and large licensed and unlicensed Wireless networks. He is president of GlobalNet Training and Consulting, inc, a network integration and training firm based in Dallas. You can reach Todd through his forum at www.lammle.com.

Acknowledgments

Thanks to Jeff Kellum, who always keeps me working hard and makes sure I am headed in the right direction. This is no easy task for Jeff!

And thanks to Christine O'Connor, who somehow made sense of my work and helped me put it together in a great, easy to study format.

Thank you both!

Contents at a Glance

Contents

Introduction

Welcome to the exciting world of Cisco certification! You have picked up this book because you want something better; namely, a better job with more satisfaction. Rest assured that you have made a good decision. Cisco certification can help you get your first networking job, or more money and a promotion if you are already in the field.

Cisco certification can also improve your understanding of the internetworking of more than just Cisco products: You will develop a complete understanding of networking and how different network topologies work together to form a network. This is beneficial to every networking job and is the reason Cisco certification is in such high demand, even at companies with few Cisco devices.

Cisco is the king of routing and switching, the Microsoft of the internetworking world. The Cisco certifications reach beyond the popular certifications, such as the MCSE, to provide you with an indispensable factor in understanding today's network—insight into the Cisco world of internetworking. By deciding that you want to become Cisco certified, you are saying that you want to be the best—the best at routing and the best at switching. This book will lead you in that direction.

How Is This Book Organized?

This book is organized according to the official objectives list prepared by Cisco for the CCNA exam. The chapters correspond with the eight broad categories:

- Describe how a network works.

- Configure, verify and troubleshoot a switch with VLANs and interswitch communications.

- Implement an IP addressing scheme and IP Services to meet network requirements in a medium-size Enterprise branch office network.

- Configure, verify, and troubleshoot basic router operation and routing on Cisco devices.

- Explain and select the appropriate administrative tasks required for a WLAN.

- Identify security threats to a network and describe general methods to mitigate those threats.

- Implement, verify, and troubleshoot NAT and ACLs in a medium-size Enterprise branch office network.

- Implement and verify WAN links.

Within each chapter, the individual exam objectives are each addressed. Each section of a chapter covers one exam objective. For each objective, the critical information for that exam objective is first presented, and then there are several Exam Essentials for each exam objective. Additionally, each chapter ends with a section of Review Questions. Here is a closer look at each of these components:

Exam Objective   The individual exam objective sections present the greatest level of detail on information that is relevant to the CCNA exam. This is the place to start if you're unfamiliar with or uncertain about the technical issues related to the objective.

Exam Essentials   Here you are given a short list of topics that you should explore fully before taking the test. Included in the Exam Essentials areas are notations of the key information you should take out of the exam objective section.

Review Questions   This section ends every chapter and provides 10 questions to help you gauge your mastery of the chapter.

Cisco—A Brief History

Many readers may already be familiar with Cisco and what they do. However, those of you who are new to the field, just coming in fresh from your MCSE, and those of you who maybe have 10 or more years in the field but wish to brush up on the new technology may appreciate a little background on Cisco.

In the early 1980s, Len and Sandy Bosack, a married couple who worked in different computer departments at Stanford University, were having trouble getting their individual systems to communicate (like many married people). So in their living room they created a gateway server that made it easier for their disparate computers in two different departments to communicate using the IP protocol. In 1984, they founded cisco Systems (notice the small *c*) with a small commercial gateway server product that changed networking forever. Some people think the name was intended to be San Francisco Systems but the paper got ripped on the way to the incorporation lawyers—who knows? In 1992, the company name was changed to Cisco Systems, Inc.

The first product the company marketed was called the Advanced Gateway Server (AGS). Then came the Mid-Range Gateway Server (MGS), the Compact Gateway Server (CGS), the Integrated Gateway Server (IGS), and the AGS+. Cisco calls these "the old alphabet soup products."

In 1993, Cisco came out with the amazing 4000 router and then created the even more amazing 7000, 2000, and 3000 series routers. These are still around and evolving (almost daily, it seems).

Cisco has since become an unrivaled worldwide leader in networking for the Internet. Its networking solutions can easily connect users who work from diverse devices on disparate networks. Cisco products make it simple for people to access and transfer information without regard to differences in time, place, or platform.

In the big picture, Cisco provides end-to-end networking solutions that customers can use to build an efficient, unified information infrastructure of their own or to connect to someone else's. This is an important piece in the Internet/networking–industry puzzle because a common architecture that delivers consistent network services to all users is now a functional imperative. Because Cisco Systems offers such a broad range of networking and Internet services and capabilities, users who need to regularly access their local network or the Internet can do so unhindered, making Cisco's wares indispensable.

Cisco answers this need with a wide range of hardware products that form information networks using the Cisco Internetwork Operating System (IOS) software. This software provides network services, paving the way for networked technical support and professional services to maintain and optimize all network operations.

Along with the Cisco IOS, one of the services Cisco created to help support the vast amount of hardware it has engineered is the Cisco Certified Internetwork Expert (CCIE) program, which was designed specifically to equip people to effectively manage the vast quantity of installed Cisco networks. The business plan is simple: If you want to sell more Cisco equipment and have more Cisco networks installed, ensure that the networks you install run properly.

Clearly, having a fabulous product line isn't all it takes to guarantee the huge success that Cisco enjoys—lots of companies with great products are now defunct. If you have complicated products designed to solve complicated problems, you need knowledgeable people who are fully capable of installing, managing, and troubleshooting them. That part isn't easy, so Cisco began the CCIE program to equip people to support these complicated networks. This program, known colloquially as the Doctorate of Networking, has also been very successful, primarily due to its extreme difficulty. Cisco continuously monitors the program, changing it as it sees fit, to make sure that it remains pertinent and accurately reflects the demands of today's internetworking business environments.

Building upon the highly successful CCIE program, Cisco Career Certifications permit you to become certified at various levels of technical proficiency, spanning the disciplines of network design and support. So, whether you're beginning a career, changing careers, securing your present position, or seeking to refine and promote your position, this is the book for you!

Cisco's Network Support Certifications

Initially, to secure the coveted Cisco CCIE certification, you took only one test and then you were faced with the (extremely difficult) hands-on lab, an all-or-nothing approach that made it tough to succeed.

In response, Cisco created a series of new certifications to help you get the coveted CCIE as well as aid prospective employers in measuring skill levels. With these new certifications, which make for a better approach to preparing for that almighty lab, Cisco opened doors that few were allowed through before.

 This book covers everything CCNA related. For up-to-date information on Todd Lammle Cisco Authorized CCNA CCNP, CCSP, CCVP, and CCIE bootcamps, please see www.lammle.com and/or www.globalnettraining.com.

Cisco Certified Network Associate (CCNA)

The CCNA certification was the first in the new line of Cisco certifications and was the precursor to all current Cisco certifications. Now you can become a Cisco Certified Network Associate for the meager cost of this book and either one test at $150 or two tests at $125 each—although the CCNA exams are extremely hard and cover a lot of material, so you have to really know your stuff! Taking a Cisco class or spending months with hands-on experience is not out of the norm.

And once you have your CCNA, you don't have to stop there—you can choose to continue with your studies and achieve a higher certification, called the Cisco Certified Network

Professional (CCNP). Someone with a CCNP has all the skills and knowledge he or she needs to attempt the Routing and Switching CCIE lab. Just becoming a CCNA can land you that job you've dreamed about.

Why Become a CCNA?

Cisco, not unlike Microsoft and Novell (Linux), has created the certification process to give administrators a set of skills and to equip prospective employers with a way to measure skills or match certain criteria. Becoming a CCNA can be the initial step of a successful journey toward a new, highly rewarding, and sustainable career.

The CCNA program was created to provide a solid introduction not only to the Cisco Internetwork Operating System (IOS) and Cisco hardware, but also to internetworking in general, making it helpful to you in areas that are not exclusively Cisco's. At this point in the certification process, it's not unrealistic that network managers—even those without Cisco equipment—require Cisco certifications for their job applicants.

If you make it through the CCNA and are still interested in Cisco and internetworking, you're headed down a path to certain success.

What Skills Do You Need to Become a CCNA?

To meet the CCNA certification skill level, you must be able to understand or do the following:

A CCNA certified professional can install, configure, and operate LAN, WAN, and wireless access services securely, as well as troubleshoot and configure small to medium networks (500 nodes or fewer) for performance.

This knowledge includes, but is not limited to, use of these: IP, IPv6, EIGRP, RIP, RIPv2, OSPF, serial connections, Frame Relay, cable, DSL, PPPoE, LAN switching, VLANs, Ethernet, security, and access lists.

Be sure and check my web site at www.lammle.com for the latest Cisco CCNA objectives and other Cisco exams, objectives and certifications that can change on a moments notice.

How Do You Become a CCNA?

The way to become a CCNA is to pass one little test (CCNA Composite exam 640-802). Then—poof!—you're a CCNA. True, it can be just one test, but you still have to possess enough knowledge to understand what the test writers are saying.

However, Cisco has a two-step process that you can take in order to become a CCNA that may or may not be easier than taking one longer exam (this book is based on the one-step method 640-802; however, this book has all the information you need to pass all three exams.

The two-step method involves passing the following:

- Exam 640-822: Interconnecting Cisco Networking Devices 1(ICND1)

- Exam 640-816: Introduction to Cisco Networking Devices 2 (ICND2)

I can't stress this enough: It's critical that you have some hands-on experience with Cisco routers. If you can get a hold of some 1841 or 2800 series routers, you're set. But if you can't, I've worked hard to provide hundreds of configuration examples throughout this book to help network administrators (or people who want to become network administrators) learn what they need to know to pass the CCNA exam.

Since the new 640-802 exam is so hard, Cisco wants to reward you for taking the two test approach. Or so it seems anyways. If you take the ICND1 exam, you actually receive a certification called the CCENT (Cisco Certified Entry Networking Technician). This is one step towards your CCNA. To achieve your CCNA, you must still pass your ICND2 exam.

Again, this book was written for the CCNA 640-802 Composite exam – one exam and you get your certification.

> For Cisco Authorized hands-on training with CCSI Todd Lammle, please see www.globalnettraining.com. Each student will get hands-on experience by configuring at least three routers and two switches—no sharing of equipment!

Where Do You Take the Exams?

You may take the CCNA exam at any Pearson VUE authorized center (www.vue.com) or call (877) 404-EXAM (3926).

To register for a Cisco Certified Network Associate exam:

1. Determine the number of the exam you want to take. (The CCNA exam number is 640-802.)

2. Register with the nearest Pearson VUE testing center. At this point, you will be asked to pay in advance for the exam. At the time of this writing, the exams are $125 each and must be taken within one year of payment. You can schedule exams up to six weeks in advance or as late as the same day you want to take it—but if you fail a Cisco exam, you must wait five days before you will be allowed to retake the exam. If something comes up and you need to cancel or reschedule your exam appointment, contact Pearson VUE at least 24 hours in advance.

3. When you schedule the exam, you'll get instructions regarding all appointment and cancellation procedures, the ID requirements, and information about the testing-center location.

Tips for Taking Your CCNA Exam

The CCNA test contains about 55 questions or more, to be completed in about 90 minutes or less. This can change per exam. You must get a score of about 85% to pass this exam, but again, each exam can be different.

Many questions on the exam have answer choices that at first glance look identical—especially the syntax questions! Remember to read through the choices carefully, because close doesn't cut it. If you get commands in the wrong order or forget one measly character, you'll get the question wrong. So, to practice, do the hands-on exercises at the end of the chapters over and over again until they feel natural to you.

Also, never forget that the right answer is the Cisco answer. In many cases, more than one appropriate answer is presented, but the *correct* answer is the one that Cisco recommends. On the exam, it always tells you to pick one, two or three, never "choose all that apply".

The CCNA 640-802 exam includes the following test formats:

- Multiple-choice single answer
- Multiple-choice multiple answer
- Drag-and-drop
- Fill-in-the-blank
- Router simulations
- In addition to multiple choice. fill-in-the-blank and drag and drop response questions, Cisco Career Certifications exams may include performance simulation exam items.

Here are some general tips for exam success:

- Arrive early at the exam center, so you can relax and review your study materials.
- Read the questions *carefully*. Don't jump to conclusions. Make sure you're clear about *exactly* what each question asks.
- When answering multiple-choice questions that you're not sure about, use the process of elimination to get rid of the obviously incorrect answers first. Doing this greatly improves your odds if you need to make an educated guess.
- You can no longer move forward and backward through the Cisco exams, so double-check your answer before clicking Next since you can't change your mind.

After you complete an exam, you'll get immediate, online notification of your pass or fail status, a printed Examination Score Report that indicates your pass or fail status, and your exam results by section. (The test administrator will give you the printed score report.) Test scores are automatically forwarded to Cisco within five working days after you take the test, so you don't need to send your score to them. If you pass the exam, you'll receive confirmation from Cisco, typically within two to four weeks.

How to Contact the Author

You can reach CCSI Todd Lammle through GlobalNet Training Solutions, Inc. (www .globalnettraining.com), his training and systems Integration Company in Dallas, Texas—or through his online forum at www.lammle.com.

The CCNA Exam Objectives

Cisco has posted eight categories with specific objectives within each category. As was mentioned, these exam objectives form the outline for this book. Following are Cisco's objectives for the CCNA:

Describe how a network works

- Describe the purpose and functions of various network devices
- Select the components required to meet a network specification

- Use the OSI and TCP/IP models and their associated protocols to explain how data flows in a network
- Describe common networked applications including web applications
- Describe the purpose and basic operation of the protocols in the OSI and TCP models
- Describe the impact of applications (Voice Over IP and Video Over IP) on a network
- Interpret network diagrams
- Determine the path between two hosts across a network
- Describe the components required for network and Internet communications
- Identify and correct common network problems at layers 1, 2, 3 and 7 using a layered model approach
- Differentiate between LAN/WAN operation and features

Configure, verify and troubleshoot a switch with VLANs and interswitch communications

- Select the appropriate media, cables, ports, and connectors to connect switches to other network devices and hosts
- Explain the technology and media access control method for Ethernet networks
- Explain network segmentation and basic traffic management concepts
- Explain basic switching concepts and the operation of Cisco switches
- Perform and verify initial switch configuration tasks including remote access management
- Verify network status and switch operation using basic utilities (including: ping, traceroute, telnet, SSH, arp, ipconfig), SHOW & DEBUG commands
- Identify, prescribe, and resolve common switched network media issues, configuration issues, auto negotiation, and switch hardware failures
- Describe enhanced switching technologies (including: VTP, RSTP, VLAN, PVSTP, 802.1q)
- Describe how VLANs create logically separate networks and the need for routing between them
- Configure, verify, and troubleshoot VLANs
- Configure, verify, and troubleshoot trunking on Cisco switches
- Configure, verify, and troubleshoot interVLAN routing
- Configure, verify, and troubleshoot VTP
- Configure, verify, and troubleshoot RSTP operation
- Interpret the output of various show and debug commands to verify the operational status of a Cisco switched network
- Implement basic switch security (including: port security, trunk access, management vlan other than vlan1, etc.)

Implement an IP addressing scheme and IP Services to meet network requirements in a medium-size Enterprise branch office network.

- Describe the operation and benefits of using private and public IP addressing
- Explain the operation and benefits of using DHCP and DNS
- Configure, verify and troubleshoot DHCP and DNS operation on a router.(including: CLI/SDM)
- Implement static and dynamic addressing services for hosts in a LAN environment
- Calculate and apply an addressing scheme including VLSM IP addressing design to a network
- Determine the appropriate classless addressing scheme using VLSM and summarization to satisfy addressing requirements in a LAN/WAN environment
- Describe the technological requirements for running IPv6 in conjunction with IPv4 (including: protocols, dual stack, tunneling, etc.)
- Describe IPv6 addresses
- Identify and correct common problems associated with IP addressing and host configurations

Configure, verify, and troubleshoot basic router operation and routing on Cisco devices

- Describe basic routing concepts (including: packet forwarding, router lookup process)
- Describe the operation of Cisco routers (including: router bootup process, POST, router components)
- Select the appropriate media, cables, ports, and connectors to connect routers to other network devices and hosts
- Configure, verify, and troubleshoot RIPv2
- Access and utilize the router to set basic parameters.(including: CLI/SDM)
- Connect, configure, and verify operation status of a device interface
- Verify device configuration and network connectivity using ping, traceroute, telnet, SSH or other utilities
- Perform and verify routing configuration tasks for a static or default route given specific routing requirements
- Manage IOS configuration files. (including: save, edit, upgrade, restore)
- Manage Cisco IOS
- Compare and contrast methods of routing and routing protocols
- Configure, verify, and troubleshoot OSPF
- Configure, verify, and troubleshoot EIGRP
- Verify network connectivity (including: using ping, traceroute, and telnet or SSH)
- Troubleshoot routing issues
- Verify router hardware and software operation using SHOW & DEBUG commands.
- Implement basic router security

Explain and select the appropriate administrative tasks required for a WLAN

- Describe standards associated with wireless media (including: IEEE WI-FI Alliance, ITU/FCC)
- Identify and describe the purpose of the components in a small wireless network (Including: SSID, BSS, ESS)
- Identify the basic parameters to configure on a wireless network to ensure that devices connect to the correct access point
- Compare and contrast wireless security features and capabilities of WPA security (including: open, WEP, WPA-1/2)
- Identify common issues with implementing wireless networks. (Including: Interface, Miss configuration)

Identify security threats to a network and describe general methods to mitigate those threats

- Describe today's increasing network security threats and explain the need to implement a comprehensive security policy to mitigate the threats
- Explain general methods to mitigate common security threats to network devices, hosts, and applications
- Describe the functions of common security appliances and applications
- Describe security recommended practices including initial steps to secure network devices

Implement, verify, and troubleshoot NAT and ACLs in a medium-size Enterprise branch office network

- Describe the purpose and types of ACLs
- Configure and apply ACLs based on network filtering requirements.(including: CLI/SDM)
- Configure and apply an ACLs to limit telnet and SSH access to the router using (including: SDM/CLI)
- Verify and monitor ACLs in a network environment
- Troubleshoot ACL issues
- Explain the basic operation of NAT
- Configure NAT for given network requirements using (including: CLI/SDM)
- Troubleshoot NAT issues

Implement and verify WAN links

- Describe different methods for connecting to a WAN
- Configure and verify a basic WAN serial connection
- Configure and verify Frame Relay on Cisco routers
- Troubleshoot WAN implementation issues
- Describe VPN technology (including: importance, benefits, role, impact, components)
- Configure and verify a PPP connection between Cisco routers

CCNA®:
Cisco® Certified
Network Associate

Fast Pass

Third Edition

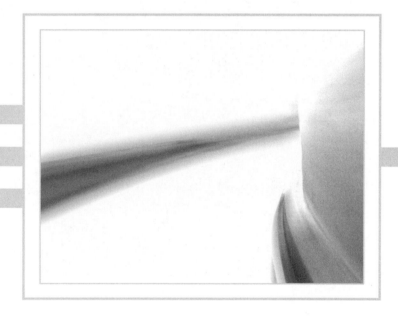

Chapter

1

Describe how a network works

THE CISCO CCNA EXAM OBJECTIVES COVERED IN THIS CHAPTER INCLUDE:

- 1.1 Describe the purpose and functions of various network devices
- 1.2 Select the components required to meet a network specification
- 1.3 Use the OSI and TCP/IP models and their associated protocols to explain how data flows in a network
- 1.4 Describe common networked applications including web applications
- 1.5 Describe the purpose and basic operation of the protocols in the OSI and TCP models
- 1.6 Describe the impact of applications (Voice over IP and Video Over IP) on a network
- 1.7 Interpret network diagrams
- 1.8 Determine the path between two hosts across a network
- 1.9 Describe the components required for network and Internet communications
- 1.10 Identify and correct common network problems at layers 1, 2, 3 and 7 using a layered model approach
- 1.11 Differentiate between LAN/WAN operation and features

Welcome to the exciting world of internetworking. This first chapter will really help you understand the basics of internetworking by focusing on how to connect networks using Cisco routers and switches. First, you need to know exactly what an internetwork is. You create an internetwork when you connect two or more LANs or WANs via a router and configure a logical network addressing scheme with a protocol such as the Internet Protocol (IP).

I'm also going to dissect the Open Systems Interconnection (OSI) model and describe each part to you in detail because you need a good grasp of it for the solid foundation you'll build your networking knowledge upon. The OSI model has seven hierarchical layers that were developed to enable different networks to communicate reliably between disparate systems. Since this book is centering upon all things CCNA, it's crucial for you to understand the OSI model as Cisco sees it.

Since there are a bunch of different types of devices specified at the different layers of the OSI model, it's also very important to understand the many types of cables and connectors used for connecting all those devices to a network. We'll go over cabling Cisco devices, discussing how to connect to a router or switch (along with Ethernet LAN technologies) and even how to connect a router or switch with a console connection.

NOTE For up-to-the-minute updates on the CCNA objectives covered by this chapter, please see www.lammle.com and/or www.sybex.com.

1.1 Describe the purpose and functions of various network devices

It is likely that at some point you'll have to break up one large network into a bunch of smaller ones because user response will have dwindled to a slow crawl as the network grows and grows. And with all that growth, your LAN's traffic congestion has reached epic proportions. The answer to this is breaking up a really big network into a number of smaller ones—something called *network segmentation*.

You do this by using devices like *routers*, *switches*, and *bridges*. Figure 1.1 displays a network that's been segmented with a switch so each network segment connected to the switch is now a separate collision domain. But make note of the fact that this network is still one broadcast domain.

FIGURE 1.1   A switch can replace the hub, breaking up collision domains.

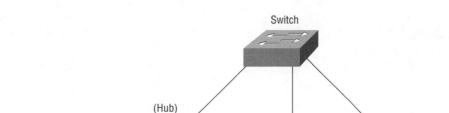

Keep in mind that the hub used in Figure 1.1 just extended the one collision domain from the switch port. Here's a list of some of the things that commonly cause LAN traffic congestion:

- Too many hosts in a broadcast domain
- Broadcast storms
- Multicasting
- Low bandwidth
- Adding hubs for connectivity to the network
- A bunch of ARP or IPX traffic (*IPX* is a Novell protocol that is like IP but really, really chatty. Typically, it is not used in today's networks.)

Now routers are used to connect networks together and route packets of data from one network to another. Cisco became the de facto standard of routers because of its high-quality router products, great selection, and fantastic service. Routers, by default, break up a *broadcast domain*—the set of all devices on a network segment that hear all the broadcasts sent on that segment. Figure 1.2 shows a router in our little network that creates an internetwork and breaks up broadcast domains.

The network in Figure 1.2 shows that each host is connected to its own collision domain, and the router has created two broadcast domains. And don't forget that the router provides connections to WAN services as well! The router uses something called a *serial interface* for WAN connections, specifically, a V.35 physical interface on a Cisco router.

FIGURE 1.2   Routers create an internetwork.

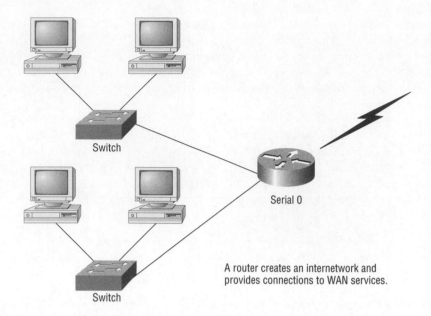

Switch

Serial 0

A router creates an internetwork and
provides connections to WAN services.

Switch

Breaking up a broadcast domain is important because when a host or server sends a network broadcast, every device on the network must read and process that broadcast—unless
you've got a router. When the router's interface receives this broadcast, it can respond by basically saying, "Thanks, but no thanks," and discard the broadcast without forwarding it on
to other networks. Even though routers are known for breaking up broadcast domains by
default, it's important to remember that they break up collision domains as well.

There are two advantages of using routers in your network:

- They don't forward broadcasts by default.

- They can filter the network based on layer 3 (Network layer) information (e.g.,
  IP address).

Four router functions in your network can be listed as follows:

- Packet switching

- Packet filtering

- Internetwork communication

- Path selection

Remember that routers are really switches; they're actually what we call layer 3 switches
(we'll talk about layers later in this chapter). Unlike layer 2 switches, which forward or filter
frames, routers (layer 3 switches) use logical addressing and provide what is called *packet
switching*. Routers can also provide packet filtering by using access lists, and when routers
connect two or more networks together and use logical addressing (IP or IPv6), this is called

an *internetwork*. Last, routers use a *routing table* (map of the internetwork) to make path selections and to forward packets to remote networks.

Conversely, switches aren't used to create internetworks (they do not break up broadcast domains by default); they're employed to add functionality to a network LAN. The main purpose of a switch is to make a LAN work better—to optimize its performance—providing more bandwidth for the LAN's users. And switches don't forward packets to other networks as routers do. Instead, they only "switch" frames from one port to another within the switched network.

By default, switches break up *collision domains*. This is an Ethernet term used to describe a network scenario wherein one particular device sends a packet on a network segment, forcing every other device on that same segment to pay attention to it. At the same time, a different device tries to transmit, leading to a collision, after which both devices must retransmit, one at a time. Not very efficient! This situation is typically found in a hub environment where each host segment connects to a hub that represents only one collision domain and only one broadcast domain. By contrast, each and every port on a switch represents its own collision domain.

Switches create separate collision domains but a single broadcast domain. Routers provide a separate broadcast domain for each interface.

The term *bridging* was introduced before routers, switches and hubs were implemented, so it's pretty common to hear people referring to bridges as switches. That's because bridges and switches basically do the same thing—break up collision domains on a LAN (in reality, you cannot buy a physical bridge these days, only LAN switches, but they use bridging technologies, so Cisco still calls them multiport bridges).

So what this means is that a switch is basically just a multiple-port bridge with more brainpower, right? Well, pretty much, but there are differences. Switches do provide this function, but they do so with greatly enhanced management ability and features. Plus, most of the time, bridges only had 2 or 4 ports. Yes, you could get your hands on a bridge with up to 16 ports, but that's nothing compared to the hundreds available on some switches!

You would use a bridge in a network to reduce collisions within broadcast domains and to increase the number of collision domains in your network. Doing this provides more bandwidth for users. And keep in mind that using hubs in your network can contribute to congestion on your Ethernet network. As always, plan your network design carefully!

Exam Essentials

Understand the different terms used to describe a LAN.   A LAN is basically the same thing as a VLAN, subnet or network, broadcast domain, or data link. These terms all describe roughly the same concept in a different context.

Remember the possible causes of LAN traffic congestion.   Too many hosts in a broadcast domain, broadcast storms, multicasting, and low bandwidth are all possible causes of LAN traffic congestion.

Understand the difference between a collision domain and a broadcast domain.   *Collision domain* is an Ethernet term used to describe a network collection of devices in which one particular device sends a packet on a network segment, forcing every other device on that same segment to pay attention to it. On a broadcast domain, a set of all devices on a network segment hears all broadcasts sent on that segment.

1.2 Select the components required to meet a network specification

As mentioned in the previous objectives, we use routers, bridges, and switches in an internetwork.

Figure 1.3 shows how a network would look with all these internetwork devices in place. Remember that the router will not only break up broadcast domains for every LAN interface, it will break up collision domains as well.

When you looked at Figure 1.3, did you notice that the router is found at center stage and that it connects each physical network together? We have to use this layout because of the older technologies involved—bridges and hubs.

On the top internetwork in Figure 1.3, you'll notice that a bridge was used to connect the hubs to a router. The bridge breaks up collision domains, but all the hosts connected to both hubs are still crammed into the same broadcast domain. Also, the bridge only created two collision domains, so each device connected to a hub is in the same collision domain as every other device connected to that same hub. This is actually pretty lame, but it's still better than having one collision domain for all hosts.

Notice something else: The three hubs at the bottom that are connected also connect to the router, creating one collision domain and one broadcast domain. This makes the bridged network look much better indeed!

 Although bridges/switches are used to segment networks, they will not isolate broadcast or multicast packets.

The best network connected to the router is the LAN switch network on the left. Why? Because each port on that switch breaks up collision domains. But it's not all good—all devices are still in the same broadcast domain. Do you remember why this can be a really bad thing? Because all devices must listen to all broadcasts transmitted, that's why. And if your broadcast domains are too large, the users have less bandwidth and are required to process more broadcasts, and network response time will slow to a level that could cause office riots.

Once we have only switches in our network, things change a lot! Figure 1.4 shows the network that is typically found today.

FIGURE 1.3 Internetworking devices

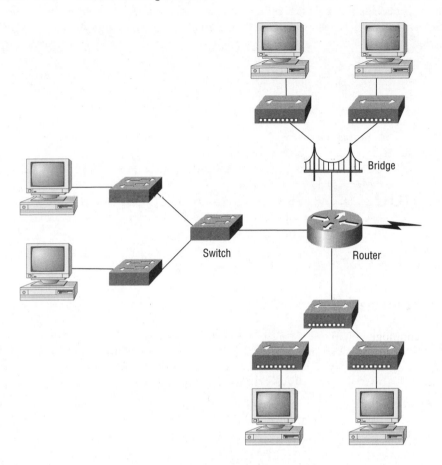

FIGURE 1.4 Switched networks creating an internetwork

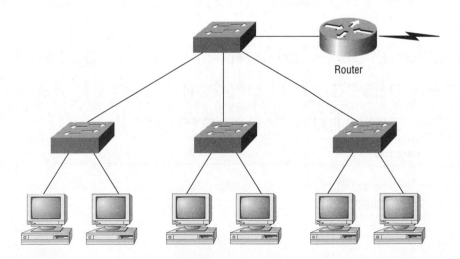

Here, I've placed the LAN switches at the center of the network world so that the routers are connecting only logical networks together. If I implemented this kind of setup, I've created virtual LANs (VLANs). But it is really important to understand that even though you have a switched network, you still need a router to provide your inter-VLAN communication, or internetworking.

Obviously, the best network is one that's correctly configured to meet the business requirements of the company it serves. LAN switches with routers, correctly placed in the network, are the best network design. This book will help you understand the basics of routers and switches, so you can make tight, informed decisions on a case-by-case basis.

Let's go back to Figure 1.3. Looking at the figure, how many collision domains and broadcast domains are in this internetwork? Hopefully, you answered nine collision domains and three broadcast domains! The broadcast domains are definitely the easiest to see because only routers break up broadcast domains by default. And since there are three connections, that gives you three broadcast domains. But do you see the nine collision domains? Just in case that's a no, I'll explain. The all-hub network is one collision domain; the bridge network equals three collision domains. Add in the switch network of five collision domains—one for each switch port—and you've got a total of nine.

So now that you've gotten an introduction to internetworking and the various devices that live in an internetwork, it's time to head into internetworking models.

Exam Essentials

Understand which devices create a LAN and which separate and connect LANs.   Switches and bridges are used to create LANs. While they do separate collision domains, they do not create separate LANs (collision domain and LAN are not the same concept). Routers are used to separate LANs and connect LANs (broadcast domains).

Understand the difference between a hub, a bridge, a switch, and a router.   Hubs create one collision domain and one broadcast domain. Bridges break up collision domains but create one large broadcast domain. They use hardware addresses to filter the network. Switches are really just multiple-port bridges with more intelligence. They break up collision domains but create one large broadcast domain by default. Switches use hardware addresses to filter the network. Routers break up broadcast domains (and collision domains) and use logical addressing to filter the network.

1.3 Use the OSI and TCP/IP models and their associated protocols to explain how data flows in a network

The Department of Defense (DoD) model is basically a condensed version of the OSI model—it's composed of four, instead of seven, layers:

- Process/Application layer
- Host-to-Host layer

- Internet layer
- Network Access layer

Figure 1.5 shows a comparison of the DoD model and the OSI reference model. As you can see, the two are similar in concept, but each has a different number of layers with different names.

FIGURE 1.5   The DoD and OSI models

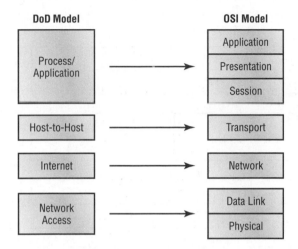

 When the different protocols in the IP stack are discussed, the layers of the OSI and DoD models are interchangeable. In other words, the Internet layer and the Network layer describe the same thing, as do the Host-to-Host layer and the Transport layer.

A vast array of protocols combine at the DoD model's *Process/Application layer* to integrate the various activities and duties spanning the focus of the OSI's corresponding top three layers (Application, Presentation, and Session). We'll be looking closely at those protocols in the next part of this chapter. The Process/Application layer defines protocols for node-to-node application communication and also controls user-interface specifications.

The *Host-to-Host layer* parallels the functions of the OSI's Transport layer, defining protocols for setting up the level of transmission service for applications. It tackles issues such as creating reliable end-to-end communication and ensuring the error-free delivery of data. It handles packet sequencing and maintains data integrity.

The *Internet layer* corresponds to the OSI's Network layer, designating the protocols relating to the logical transmission of packets over the entire network. It takes care of the addressing of hosts by giving them an IP (Internet Protocol) address, and it handles the routing of packets among multiple networks.

At the bottom of the DoD model, the *Network Access layer* monitors the data exchange between the host and the network. The equivalent of the Data Link and Physical layers of the

OSI model, the Network Access layer oversees hardware addressing and defines protocols for the physical transmission of data.

The DoD and OSI models are alike in design and concept and have similar functions in similar layers. Figure 1.6 shows the TCP/IP protocol suite and how its protocols relate to the DoD model layers.

FIGURE 1.6   The TCP/IP protocol suite

DoD Model

| Process/
Application | Telnet | FTP | LPD | SNMP |
| | TFTP | SMTP | NFS | X Window |

| Host-to-Host | TCP | | UDP | |

| Internet | ICMP | ARP | | RARP |
| | IP | | | |

| Network
Access | Ethernet | Fast
Ethernet | Token
Ring | FDDI |

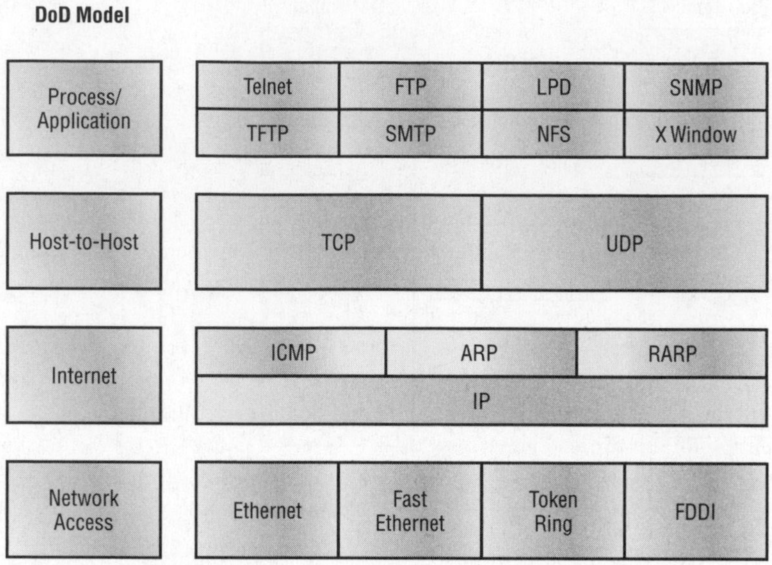

In the following sections, we will look at the different protocols in more detail, starting with the Process/Application layer protocols.

Exam Essentials

Remember that the OSI/DoD model is a layered approach.   Functions are divided into layers, and the layers are bound together. This allows layers to operate transparently to each other, that is, changes in one layer should not impact other layers.

1.4 Describe common networked applications including web applications

In this section, I'll describe the different applications and services typically used in IP networks. The following protocols and applications are covered in this section:

- Telnet
- FTP

- TFTP
- NFS
- SMTP
- LPD
- X Window
- SNMP
- DNS
- DHCP/BootP

Telnet

Telnet is the chameleon of protocols—its specialty is terminal emulation. It allows a user on a remote client machine, called the *Telnet client*, to access the resources of another machine, the *Telnet server*. Telnet achieves this by pulling a fast one on the Telnet server and making the client machine appear as though it were a terminal directly attached to the local network. This projection is actually a software image—a virtual terminal that can interact with the chosen remote host.

These emulated terminals are of the text-mode type and can execute refined procedures such as displaying menus that give users the opportunity to choose options and access the applications on the duped server. Users begin a Telnet session by running the Telnet client software and then logging in to the Telnet server.

The problem with Telnet is that all data, even login data, is sent in clear text. This can be a security risk. And if you are having problems telnetting into a device, you should verify that both the transmitting and receiving device have telnet services enabled. Lastly, by default, Cisco devices allow five simultaneous telnet sessions.

File Transfer Protocol (FTP)

File Transfer Protocol (FTP) is the protocol that actually lets us transfer files, and it can accomplish this between any two machines using it. But FTP isn't just a protocol; it's also a program. Operating as a protocol, FTP is used by applications. As a program, it's employed by users to perform file tasks by hand. FTP also allows for access to both directories and files and can accomplish certain types of directory operations, such as relocating into different ones. FTP teams up with Telnet to transparently log you in to the FTP server and then provides for the transfer of files.

Accessing a host through FTP is only the first step, though. Users must then be subjected to an authentication login that's probably secured with passwords and usernames implemented by system administrators to restrict access. You can get around this somewhat by adopting the user-name *anonymous*—though what you'll gain access to will be limited.

Even when employed by users manually as a program, FTP's functions are limited to listing and manipulating directories, typing file contents, and copying files between hosts. It can't execute remote files as programs.

Trivial File Transfer Protocol (TFTP)

Trivial File Transfer Protocol (TFTP) is the stripped-down, stock version of FTP, but it's the protocol of choice if you know exactly what you want and where to find it, plus it's so easy to use and it's fast too! It doesn't give you the abundance of functions that FTP does, though. TFTP has no directory-browsing abilities; it can do nothing but send and receive files. This compact little protocol also skimps in the data department, sending much smaller blocks of data than FTP, and there's no authentication as with FTP, so it's insecure. Few sites support it because of the inherent security risks.

Network File System (NFS)

Network File System (NFS) is a jewel of a protocol specializing in file sharing. It allows two different types of file systems to interoperate. It works like this: Suppose that the NFS server software is running on an NT server and the NFS client software is running on a Unix host. NFS allows for a portion of the RAM on the NT server to transparently store Unix files, which can, in turn, be used by Unix users. Even though the NT file system and Unix file system are unlike—they have different case sensitivity, filename lengths, security, and so on—both Unix users and NT users can access that same file with their normal file systems, in their normal way.

Simple Mail Transfer Protocol (SMTP)

Simple Mail Transfer Protocol (SMTP), answering our ubiquitous call to email, uses a spooled, or *queued*, method of mail delivery. Once a message has been sent to a destination, the message is spooled to a device—usually a disk. The server software at the destination posts a vigil, regularly checking the queue for messages. When it detects them, it proceeds to deliver them to their destination. SMTP is used to send mail; POP3 is used to receive mail.

Line Printer Daemon (LPD)

The Line Printer Daemon (LPD) protocol is designed for printer sharing. The LPD, along with the Line Printer (LPR) program, allows print jobs to be spooled and sent to the network's printers using TCP/IP.

X Window

Designed for client/server operations, *X Window* defines a protocol for writing client/server applications based on a graphical user interface (GUI). The idea is to allow a program, called a *client*, to run on one computer and have it display things through a window server on another computer.

Simple Network Management Protocol (SNMP)

Simple Network Management Protocol (SNMP) collects and manipulates valuable network information. It gathers data by polling the devices on the network from a management station at fixed or random intervals, requiring them to disclose certain information. When all is well, SNMP receives something called a *baseline*—a report delimiting the operational traits of a healthy network. This protocol can also stand as a watchdog over the network, quickly notifying managers of any sudden turn of events. These network watchdogs are called *agents*, and when aberrations occur, agents send an alert called a *trap* to the management station.

Domain Name Service (DNS)

Domain Name Service (DNS) resolves hostnames—specifically, Internet names, such as www.lammle.com. You don't have to use DNS; you can just type in the IP address of any device you want to communicate with. An IP address identifies hosts on a network and the Internet as well. However, DNS was designed to make our lives easier. Think about this: What would happen if you wanted to move your web page to a different service provider? The IP address would change, and no one would know what the new one was. DNS allows you to use a domain name to specify an IP address. You can change the IP address as often as you want, and no one will know the difference.

DNS is used to resolve a *fully qualified domain name (FQDN)*—for example, www.lammle .com or todd.lammle.com. An FQDN is a hierarchy that can logically locate a system based on its domain identifier.

If you want to resolve the name *todd*, you either must type in the FQDN of todd.lammle .com or have a device such as a PC or router add the suffix for you. For example, on a Cisco router, you can use the command ip domain-name lammle.com to append each request with the lammle.com domain. If you don't do that, you'll have to type in the FQDN to get DNS to resolve the name.

Dynamic Host Configuration Protocol (DHCP)/Bootstrap Protocol (BootP)

Dynamic Host Configuration Protocol (DHCP) assigns IP addresses to hosts. It allows easier administration and works well in small to even very large network environments. All types of hardware can be used as a DHCP server, including a Cisco router.

DHCP differs from BootP in that BootP assigns an IP address to a host but the host's hardware address must be entered manually in a BootP table. You can think of DHCP as a dynamic BootP. But remember that BootP is also used to send an operating system that a host can boot from. DHCP can't do that.

But there is a lot of information a DHCP server can provide to a host when the host is requesting an IP address from the DHCP server. Here's a list of the information a DHCP server can provide:

- IP address
- Subnet mask
- Domain name

- Default gateway (routers)
- DNS
- WINS information

A DHCP server can give us even more information than this, but the items in the list are the most common.

A client that sends out a DHCP Discover message in order to receive an IP address sends out a broadcast at both layer 2 and layer 3. The layer 2 broadcast is all *F*s in hex, which looks like this: FF:FF:FF:FF:FF:FF. The layer 3 broadcast is 255.255.255.255, which means all networks and all hosts. DHCP is connectionless, which means that it uses User Datagram Protocol (UDP) at the Transport layer, also known as the Host-to-Host layer, which we'll talk about next.

In case you don't believe me, here's an example of output from my trusty OmniPeak analyzer:

```
Ethernet II, Src: 192.168.0.3 (00:0b:db:99:d3:5e), Dst: Broadcast
➡(ff:ff:ff:ff:ff:ff)
Internet Protocol, Src: 0.0.0.0 (0.0.0.0), Dst: 255.255.255.255
➡(255.255.255.255)
```

The Data Link and Network layers are both sending out "all hands" broadcasts saying, "Help—I don't know my IP address!"

To dive further into this, we now know that a broadcast is determined to be all 1's or 255.255.255.255 at the Network layer and FF:FF:FF:FF:FF:FF at the Data Link layer, meaning all hosts on the local LAN. If a DHCP client sends an all-hands broadcast looking for a DHCP server and there is no DHCP server on the local LAN, a router can route this packet through the network to where the DHCP server is located. This packet is now called a Unicast packet.

Exam Essentials

Remember the Process/Application layer protocols.   Telnet is a terminal emulation program that allows you to log in to a remote host and run programs. File Transfer Protocol (FTP) is a connection-oriented service that allows you to transfer files. Trivial FTP (TFTP) is a connectionless file transfer program. Simple Mail Transfer Protocol (SMTP) is a send-mail program.

Remember the difference between connection-oriented and connectionless network services.   Connection-oriented services use acknowledgments and flow control to create a reliable session. More overhead is used than in a connectionless network service. Connectionless services are used to send data with no acknowledgments or flow control. This is considered unreliable.

Understand DNS and DHCP.   *Domain Name Service (DNS)* resolves hostnames—specifically, Internet names, such as www.lammle.com. You don't have to use DNS; you can just type in the IP address of any device you want to communicate with. An IP address identifies hosts on a network and the Internet as well. *Dynamic Host Configuration Protocol (DHCP)* assigns IP addresses to hosts. It allows easier administration and works well in small to even very large network environments.

1.5 Describe the purpose and basic operation of the protocols in the OSI and TCP models

When networks first came into being, computers could typically communicate only with computers from the same manufacturer. For example, companies ran either a complete DECnet solution or an IBM solution—not both together. In the late 1970s, the *Open Systems Interconnection (OSI) reference model* was created by the International Organization for Standardization (ISO) to break this barrier.

The OSI model was meant to help vendors create interoperable network devices and software in the form of protocols so that different vendor networks could work with each other. Like world peace, it'll probably never happen completely, but it's still a great goal.

The OSI model is the primary architectural model for networks. It describes how data and network information are communicated from an application on one computer through the network media to an application on another computer. The OSI reference model breaks this approach into layers.

In the following section, I am going to explain the layered approach and how we can use this approach to help us troubleshoot our internetworks.

The Layered Approach

A *reference model* is a conceptual blueprint of how communications should take place. It addresses all the processes required for effective communication and divides these processes into logical groupings called *layers*. When a communication system is designed in this manner, it's known as *layered architecture*.

Think of it like this: You and some friends want to start a company. One of the first things you'll do is sit down and think through what tasks must be done, who will do them, the order in which they will be done, and how they relate to each other. Ultimately, you might group these tasks into departments. Let's say that you decide to have an order-taking department, an inventory department, and a shipping department. Each of your departments has its own unique tasks, keeping its staff members busy and requiring them to focus on only their own duties.

In this scenario, I'm using departments as a metaphor for the layers in a communication system. For things to run smoothly, the staff of each department will have to trust and rely heavily upon the others to do their jobs and competently handle their unique responsibilities. In your planning sessions, you would probably take notes, recording the entire process to facilitate later discussions about standards of operation that will serve as your business blueprint, or reference model.

Once your business is launched, your department heads, each armed with the part of the blueprint relating to their own department, will need to develop practical methods to implement their assigned tasks. These practical methods, or protocols, will need to be compiled into a standard operating procedures manual and followed closely. Each of the various procedures in your manual will have been included for different reasons and have varying degrees of importance and implementation. If you form a partnership or acquire another company, it will be imperative that its business protocols—its business blueprint—match yours (or at least be compatible with it).

Similarly, software developers can use a reference model to understand computer communication processes and see what types of functions need to be accomplished on any one layer. If they are developing a protocol for a certain layer, all they need to concern themselves with is that specific layer's functions, not those of any other layer. Another layer and protocol will handle the other functions. The technical term for this idea is *binding*. The communication processes that are related to each other are bound, or grouped together, at a particular layer.

Advantages of Reference Models

The OSI model is hierarchical, and the same benefits and advantages can apply to any layered model. The primary purpose of all such models, especially the OSI model, is to allow different vendors' networks to interoperate.

Advantages of using the OSI layered model include, but are not limited to, the following:

- It divides the network communication process into smaller and simpler components, thus aiding in component development, design, and troubleshooting.

- It allows multiple-vendor development through the standardization of network components.

- It encourages industry standardization by defining what functions occur at each layer of the model.

- It allows various types of network hardware and software to communicate.

- It prevents changes in one layer from affecting other layers, so it does not hamper development.

The OSI Reference Model

One of the greatest functions of the OSI specifications is to assist in data transfer between disparate hosts—meaning, for example, that they enable us to transfer data between a Unix host and a PC or a Mac.

The OSI isn't a physical model, though. Rather, it's a set of guidelines that application developers can use to create and implement applications that run on a network. It also provides a framework for creating and implementing networking standards, devices, and internetworking schemes.

The OSI has seven different layers, divided into two groups. The top three layers define how the applications within the end stations will communicate with each other and with users. The bottom four layers define how data is transmitted from end to end. Figure 1.7 shows the three upper layers and their functions, and Figure 1.8 shows the four lower layers and their functions.

When you study Figure 1.7, understand that the user interfaces with the computer at the Application layer and also that the upper layers are responsible for applications communicating between hosts. Remember that none of the upper layers knows anything about networking or network addresses. That's the responsibility of the four bottom layers.

In Figure 1.8, you can see that it's the four bottom layers that define how data is transferred through a physical wire or through switches and routers. These bottom layers also determine how to rebuild a data stream from a transmitting host to a destination host's application.

FIGURE 1.7   The upper layers

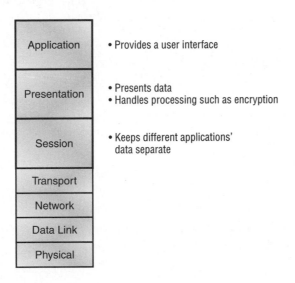

Application	• Provides a user interface
Presentation	• Presents data • Handles processing such as encryption
Session	• Keeps different applications' data separate
Transport	
Network	
Data Link	
Physical	

FIGURE 1.8   The lower layers

Transport	• Provides reliable or unreliable delivery • Performs error correction before retransmit
Network	• Provides logical addressing, which routers use for path determination
Data Link	• Combines packets into bytes and bytes into frames • Provides access to media using MAC address • Performs error detection not correction
Physical	• Moves bits between devices • Specifies voltage, wire speed, and pin-out of cables

The following network devices operate at all seven layers of the OSI model:

- Network management stations (NMSs)
- Web and application servers
- Gateways (not default gateways)
- Network hosts

Basically, the ISO is pretty much the Emily Post of the network protocol world. Just as Ms. Post wrote the book setting the standards—or protocols—for human social interaction, the ISO developed the OSI reference model as the precedent and guide for an open network protocol set. Defining the etiquette of communication models, it remains today the most popular means of comparison for protocol suites.

The OSI reference model has seven layers:

- Application layer (layer 7)
- Presentation layer (layer 6)
- Session layer (layer 5)
- Transport layer (layer 4)
- Network layer (layer 3)
- Data Link layer (layer 2)
- Physical layer (layer 1)

Figure 1.9 shows a summary of the functions defined at each layer of the OSI model. With this in hand, you're now ready to explore each layer's function in detail.

FIGURE 1.9   Layer functions

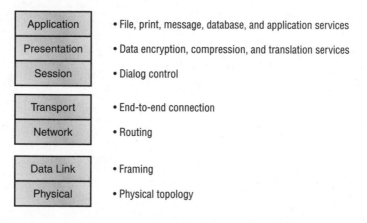

In the next section, I'll dive deeper into TCP and UDP that reside at the Transport layer.

Exam Essentials

Understand the advantages of using layered models.   The OSI model is hierarchical, and the same benefits and advantages can apply to any layered model. The primary purpose of all such models, especially the OSI model, is to allow different vendors' networks to interoperate.Remember that the OSI/DoD model is a layered approach.

Functions are divided into layers, and the layers are bound together. This allows layers to operate transparently to each other, that is, changes in one layer should not impact other layers.

1.6 Describe the impact of applications (Voice over IP and Video over IP) on a network

The main purpose of the Host-to-Host layer is to shield the upper-layer applications from the complexities of the network. This layer says to the upper layer, "Just give me your data stream, with any instructions, and I'll begin the process of getting your information ready to send."

The following sections describe the two protocols at this layer:

- Transmission Control Protocol (TCP)
- User Datagram Protocol (UDP)

By understanding how TCP and UDP work, you can interpret the impact of applications on networks when using Voice and Video Over IP.

Transmission Control Protocol (TCP)

Transmission Control Protocol (TCP) takes large blocks of information from an application and breaks them into segments. It numbers and sequences each segment so that the destination's TCP stack can put the segments back into the order the application intended. After these segments are sent, TCP (on the transmitting host) waits for an acknowledgment of the receiving end's TCP virtual circuit session, retransmitting those that aren't acknowledged.

Before a transmitting host starts to send segments down the model, the sender's TCP stack contacts the destination's TCP stack to establish a connection. What is created is known as a *virtual circuit*. This type of communication is called *connection-oriented*. During this initial handshake, the two TCP layers also agree on the amount of information that's going to be sent before the recipient's TCP sends back an acknowledgment. With everything agreed upon in advance, the path is paved for reliable communication to take place.

TCP is a full-duplex, connection-oriented, reliable, and accurate protocol, but establishing all these terms and conditions, in addition to error checking, is no small task. TCP is very complicated and, not surprisingly, costly in terms of network overhead. And since today's networks are much more reliable than those of yore, this added reliability is often unnecessary.

TCP Segment Format

Since the upper layers just send a data stream to the protocols in the Transport layers, I'll demonstrate how TCP segments a data stream and prepares it for the Internet layer. When the Internet layer receives the data stream, it routes the segments as packets through an internetwork. The segments are handed to the receiving host's Host-to-Host layer protocol, which rebuilds the data stream to hand to the upper-layer applications or protocols.

Figure 1.10 shows the TCP segment format. The figure shows the different fields within the TCP header.

FIGURE 1.10 TCP segment format

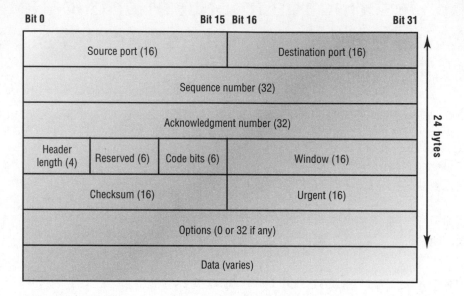

The TCP header is 20 bytes long, or up to 24 bytes with options. You need to understand what each field in the TCP segment is:

Source port The port number of the application on the host sending the data. (Port numbers will be explained a little later in this section.)

Destination port The port number of the application requested on the destination host.

Sequence number A number used by TCP that puts the data back in the correct order or retransmits missing or damaged data, a process called *sequencing*.

Acknowledgment number The TCP octet that is expected next.

Header length The number of 32-bit words in the TCP header. This indicates where the data begins. The TCP header (even one including options) is an integral number of 32 bits in length.

Reserved Always set to zero.

Code bits   Control functions used to set up and terminate a session.

Window   The window size the sender is willing to accept, in octets.

Checksum   The cyclic redundancy check (CRC), because TCP doesn't trust the lower layers and checks everything. The CRC checks the header and data fields.

Urgent   A valid field only if the Urgent pointer in the code bits is set. If so, this value indicates the offset from the current sequence number, in octets, where the first segment of non-urgent data begins.

Options   May be 0 or a multiple of 32 bits, if any. What this means is that no options have to be present (option size of 0). However, if any options are used that do not cause the option field to total a multiple of 32 bits, padding of 0s must be used to make sure the data begins on a 32-bit boundary.

Data   Handed down to the TCP protocol at the Transport layer, which includes the upper-layer headers.

Let's take a look at a TCP segment copied from a network analyzer:

```
TCP - Transport Control Protocol
  Source Port:       5973
  Destination Port: 23
  Sequence Number:   1456389907
  Ack Number:        1242056456
  Offset:            5
  Reserved:          %000000
  Code:              %011000
      Ack is valid
      Push Request
  Window:            61320
  Checksum:          0x61a6
  Urgent Pointer:    0
  No TCP Options
  TCP Data Area:
  vL.5.+.5.+.5.+.5   76 4c 19 35 11 2b 19 35 11 2b 19 35 11
   2b 19 35 +. 11 2b 19
Frame Check Sequence: 0x0d00000f
```

Did you notice that everything I talked about earlier is in the segment? As you can see from the number of fields in the header, TCP creates a lot of overhead. Application developers may opt for efficiency over reliability to save overhead, so the User Datagram Protocol was also defined at the Transport layer as an alternative.

User Datagram Protocol (UDP)

If you were to compare the *User Datagram Protocol (UDP)* with TCP, the former is basically the scaled-down economy model that's sometimes referred to as a *thin protocol*. Like a thin person on a park bench, a thin protocol doesn't take up a lot of room—or in this case, much bandwidth on a network.

UDP doesn't offer all the bells and whistles of TCP either, but it does do a fabulous job of transporting information that doesn't require reliable delivery—and it does so using far fewer network resources. (UDP is covered thoroughly in Request for Comments 768.)

> The *Requests for Comments* (RFCs) form a series of notes, started in 1969, about the Internet (originally the ARPAnet). The notes discuss many aspects of computer communication; they focus on networking protocols, procedures, programs, and concepts but also include meeting notes, opinion, and sometimes humor.

There are some situations in which it would definitely be wise for developers to opt for UDP rather than TCP. Remember the watchdog SNMP up there at the Process/Application layer? SNMP monitors the network, sending intermittent messages and a fairly steady flow of status updates and alerts, especially when running on a large network. The cost in overhead to establish, maintain, and close a TCP connection for each one of those little messages would reduce what would be an otherwise healthy, efficient network to a dammed-up bog in no time!

Another circumstance calling for UDP over TCP is when reliability is already handled at the Process/Application layer. Network File System (NFS) handles its own reliability issues, making the use of TCP both impractical and redundant. But ultimately, it's up to the application developer to decide whether to use UDP or TCP, not the user who wants to transfer data faster.

UDP does *not* sequence the segments and does not care in which order the segments arrive at the destination. But after that, UDP sends the segments off and forgets about them. It doesn't follow through, check up on them, or even allow for an acknowledgment of safe arrival—complete abandonment. Because of this, it's referred to as an unreliable protocol. This does not mean that UDP is ineffective, only that it doesn't handle issues of reliability.

Further, UDP doesn't create a virtual circuit, nor does it contact the destination before delivering information to it. Because of this, it's also considered a *connectionless* protocol. Since UDP assumes that the application will use its own reliability method, it doesn't use any. This gives an application developer a choice when running the Internet Protocol stack: TCP for reliability or UDP for faster transfers.

So if you're using Voice over IP (VoIP), for example, you really don't want to use UDP, because if the segments arrive out of order (very common in IP networks), they'll just be passed up to the next OSI (DoD) layer in whatever order they're received, resulting in some seriously garbled data. On the other hand, TCP sequences the segments so they get put back together in exactly the right order—something that UDP just can't do.

UDP Segment Format

Figure 1.11 clearly illustrates UDP's markedly low overhead as compared to TCP's hungry usage. Look at the figure carefully—can you see that UDP doesn't use windowing or provide for acknowledgments in the UDP header?

It's important for you to understand what each field in the UDP segment is:

Source port   Port number of the application on the host sending the data

Destination port   Port number of the application requested on the destination host

Length   Length of UDP header and UDP data

Checksum   Checksum of both the UDP header and UDP data fields

Data   Upper-layer data

FIGURE 1.11   UDP segment

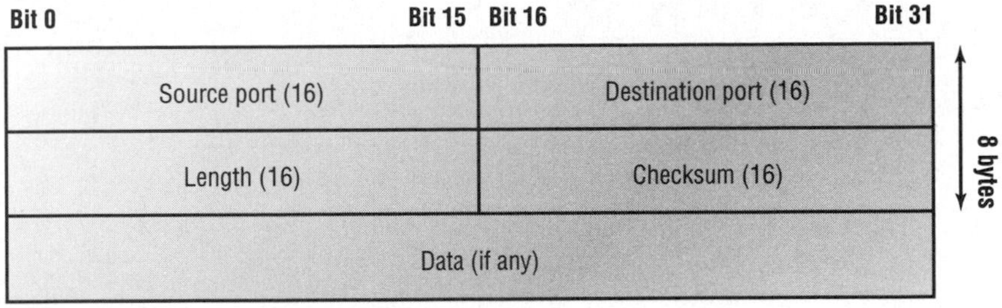

UDP, like TCP, doesn't trust the lower layers and runs its own CRC. Remember that the Frame Check Sequence (FCS) is the field that houses the CRC, which is why you can see the FCS information.

The following shows a UDP segment caught on a network analyzer:

```
UDP - User Datagram Protocol
 Source Port:       1085
 Destination Port: 5136
 Length:            41
 Checksum:          0x7a3c
 UDP Data Area:
 ..Z......00 01 5a 96 00 01 00 00 00 00 00 11 0000 00
 ...C..2._C._C  2e 03 00 43 02 1e 32 0a 00 0a 00 80 43 00 80
Frame Check Sequence: 0x00000000
```

Notice that low overhead! Try to find the sequence number, ack number, and window size in the UDP segment. You can't because they just aren't there!

Key Concepts of Host-to-Host Protocols

Since you've seen both a connection-oriented (TCP) and connectionless (UDP) protocol in action, it would be good to summarize the two here. Table 1.1 highlights some of the key concepts that you should keep in mind regarding these two protocols. You should memorize this table.

TABLE 1.1   Key Features of TCP and UDP

TCP	UDP
Sequenced	Unsequenced
Reliable	Unreliable
Connection-oriented	Connectionless
Virtual circuit	Low overhead
Acknowledgments	No acknowledgment
Windowing flow control	No windowing or flow control

A telephone analogy could really help you understand how TCP works. Most of us know that before you speak to someone on a phone, you must first establish a connection with that other person—wherever they are. This is like a virtual circuit with the TCP protocol. If you were giving someone important information during your conversation, you might say, "You know?" or ask, "Did you get that?" Saying something like this is a lot like a TCP acknowledgment—it's designed to get you verification. From time to time (especially on cell phones), people also ask, "Are you still there?" They end their conversations with a "Goodbye" of some kind, putting closure on the phone call. TCP also performs these types of functions.

Alternately, using UDP is like sending a postcard. To do that, you don't need to contact the other party first. You simply write your message, address the postcard, and mail it. This is analogous to UDP's connectionless orientation. Since the message on the postcard is probably not a matter of life or death, you don't need an acknowledgment of its receipt. Similarly, UDP does not involve acknowledgments.

Exam Essentials

Remember the Host-to-Host layer protocols.   Transmission Control Protocol (TCP) is a connection-oriented protocol that provides reliable network service by using acknowledgments and flow control. User Datagram Protocol (UDP) is a connectionless protocol that provides low overhead and is considered unreliable.

Remember the Internet layer protocols.   Internet Protocol (IP) is a connectionless protocol that provides network address and routing through an internetwork. Address Resolution Protocol (ARP) finds a hardware address from a known IP address. Reverse ARP (RARP) finds an IP address from a known hardware address. Internet Control Message Protocol (ICMP) provides diagnostics and destination unreachable messages.

1.7 Interpret network diagrams

The best way to look at, build, and troubleshoot network diagrams is to use CDP. *Cisco Discovery Protocol* (CDP) is a proprietary protocol designed by Cisco to help administrators collect information about both locally attached and remote devices. By using CDP, you can gather hardware and protocol information about neighbor devices, which is useful info for troubleshooting and documenting the network.

In the following sections, I am going to discuss the CDP timer and CDP commands used to verify your network.

Getting CDP Timers and Holdtime Information

The **show cdp** command (**sh cdp** for short) gives you information about two CDP global parameters that can be configured on Cisco devices:

- *CDP timer* is how often CDP packets are transmitted out all active interfaces.

- *CDP holdtime* is the amount of time that the device will hold packets received from neighbor devices.

Both Cisco routers and Cisco switches use the same parameters.

 For this section, my 2811 used in this next example will have a hostname of Corp, and it will have four serial connections to ISR routers named R1, R2, and R3 (there are two connections to R1) and one FastEthernet connection to a 1242 access point with a hostname of just ap.

The output on the Corp router looks like this:

```
Corp#sh cdp
Global CDP information:
        Sending CDP packets every 60 seconds
        Sending a holdtime value of 180 seconds
        Sending CDPv2 advertisements is  enabled
```

Use the global commands **cdp holdtime** and **cdp timer** to configure the CDP holdtime and timer on a router:

```
Corp(config)#cdp ?
  advertise-v2      CDP sends version-2 advertisements
  holdtime          Specify the holdtime (in sec) to be sent in packets
  log               Log messages generated by CDP
  run               Enable CDP
  source-interface  Insert the interface's IP in all CDP packets
```

```
timer            Specify rate (in sec) at which CDP packets are sent  run
Corp(config)#cdp holdtime ?
 <10-255> Length of time (in sec) that receiver must keep this packet
Corp(config)#cdp timer ?
 <5-254>  Rate at which CDP packets are sent (in  sec)
```

You can turn off CDP completely with the no cdp run command from the global configuration mode of a router. To turn CDP off or on for an interface, use the no cdp enable and cdp enable commands. Be patient—I'll work through these with you in a second.

Gathering Neighbor Information

The **show cdp neighbor** command (**sh cdp nei** for short) delivers information about directly connected devices. It's important to remember that CDP packets aren't passed through a Cisco switch and that you only see what's directly attached. So this means that if your router is connected to a switch, you won't see any of the devices hooked up to that switch.

The following output shows the **show cdp neighbor** command used on my ISR router:

```
Corp#sh cdp neighbors [Should this be neighbor (singular)?]no
Capability Codes: R - Router, T - Trans Bridge, B - Source Route Bridge
                  S - Switch, H - Host, I - IGMP, r - Repeater
Device ID    Local Intrfce   Holdtme   Capability  Platform  Port ID
ap           Fas 0/1         165          T I      AIR-AP124 Fas 0
R2           Ser 0/1/0       140         R S I     2801      Ser 0/2/0
R3           Ser 0/0/1       157         R S I     1841      Ser 0/0/1
R1           Ser 0/2/0       154         R S I     1841      Ser 0/0/1
R1           Ser 0/0/0       154         R S I     1841      Ser 0/0/0
Corp#
```

Okay, we are directly connected with a console cable to the Corp ISR router, and the router is directly connected to four devices. We have two connections to the R1 router. The device ID shows the configured hostname of the connected device, the local interface is our interface, and the port ID is the remote devices' directly connected interface. All you get to view are directly connected devices.

Table 1.2 summarizes the information displayed by the show cdp neighbor command for each device.

TABLE 1.2   Output of the show cdp neighbor Command

Field	Description
Device ID	The hostname of the device directly connected.
Local Interface	The port or interface on which you are receiving the CDP packet.

TABLE 1.2   Output of the show cdp neighbor Command *(continued)*

Field	Description
Holdtime	The amount of time the router will hold the information before discarding it if no more CDP packets are received.
Capability	The capability of the neighbor, such as the router, switch, or repeater. The capability codes are listed at the top of the command output.
Platform	The type of Cisco device directly connected. In the previous output, a Cisco 2500 router and Cisco 1900 switch are attached directly to the 2509 router. The 2509 only sees the 1900 switch and the 2500 router connected through its serial 0 interface.
Port ID	The neighbor device's port or interface on which the CDP packets are multicast.

It is imperative that you can look at the output of a show cdp neighbors command and decipher the neighbor's device (capability, i.e., router or switch), model number (platform), your port connecting to that device (local interface), and the port of the neighbor connecting to you (port ID).

Another command that'll deliver the goods on neighbor information is the **show cdp neighbors detail** command (**show cdp nei de** for short). This command can be run on both routers and switches, and it displays detailed information about each device connected to the device you're running the command on. Check out this router output for an example:

```
Corp#sh cdp neighbors detail
-------------------------
Device ID: ap
Entry address(es): 10.1.1.2
Platform: cisco AIR-AP1242AG-A-K9   , Capabilities: Trans-Bridge IGMP
Interface: FastEthernet0/1,  Port ID (outgoing port): FastEthernet0
Holdtime : 122 sec

Version :
Cisco IOS Software, C1240 Software (C1240-K9W7-M), Version 12.3(8)JEA,
    RELEASE SOFTWARE (fc2)
Technical Support: http://www.cisco.com/techsupport
Copyright (c) 1986-2006 by Cisco Systems, Inc.
Compiled Wed 23-Aug-06 16:45 by kellythw
```

```
advertisement version: 2
Duplex: full
Power drawn: 15.000 Watts
-------------------------
Device ID: R2
Entry address(es):
  IP address: 10.4.4.2
Platform: Cisco 2801,  Capabilities: Router Switch IGMP
Interface: Serial0/1/0,  Port ID (outgoing port): Serial0/2/0
Holdtime : 135 sec

Version :
Cisco IOS Software, 2801 Software (C2801-ADVENTERPRISEK9-M),
    Experimental Version 12.4(20050525:193634) [jezhao-ani 145]
Copyright (c) 1986-2005 by Cisco Systems, Inc.
Compiled Fri 27-May-05 23:53 by jezhao

advertisement version: 2
VTP Management Domain: ''
-------------------------
Device ID: R3
Entry address(es):
  IP address: 10.5.5.1
Platform: Cisco 1841,  Capabilities: Router Switch IGMP
Interface: Serial0/0/1,  Port ID (outgoing port): Serial0/0/1
Holdtime : 152 sec

Version :
Cisco IOS Software, 1841 Software (C1841-IPBASE-M), Version 12.4(1c),
    RELEASE SOFTWARE (fc1)
Technical Support: http://www.cisco.com/techsupport
Copyright (c) 1986-2005 by Cisco Systems, Inc.
Compiled Tue 25-Oct-05 17:10 by evmiller

advertisement version: 2
VTP Management Domain: ''
-------------------------
[output cut]
Corp#
```

First, we're given the hostname and IP address of all directly connected devices. In addition to the same information displayed by the show cdp neighbor command (see Table 1.5), the show cdp neighbor detail command gives us the IOS version of the neighbor device.

Remember that you can see only the IP address of directly connected devices.

The **show cdp entry** * command displays the same information as the **show cdp neighbor details** command. Here's an example of the router output using the **show cdp entry** * command:

```
Corp#sh cdp entry *
-------------------------
Device ID: ap
Entry address(es):
Platform: cisco AIR-AP1242AG-A-K9   , Capabilities: Trans-Bridge IGMP
Interface: FastEthernet0/1,  Port ID (outgoing port): FastEthernet0
Holdtime : 160 sec

Version :
Cisco IOS Software, C1240 Software (C1240-K9W7-M), Version 12.3(8)JEA,
    RELEASE SOFTWARE (fc2)
Technical Support: http://www.cisco.com/techsupport
Copyright (c) 1986-2006 by Cisco Systems, Inc.
Compiled Wed 23-Aug-06 16:45 by kellythw

advertisement version: 2
Duplex: full
Power drawn: 15.000 Watts
-------------------------
Device ID: R2
Entry address(es):
  IP address: 10.4.4.2
Platform: Cisco 2801,  Capabilities: Router Switch IGMP
 --More-
[output cut]
```

There isn't any difference between the **show cdp neighbors detail** and **show cdp entry** * commands. However, the **sh cdp entry** * command has two options that the **show cdp neighbors detail** command does not:

```
Corp#sh cdp entry * ?
  protocol  Protocol information
  version   Version information
  |         Output modifiers
  <cr>
```

```
Corp#show cdp entry * protocols
Protocol information for ap :
  IP address: 10.1.1.2
Protocol information for R2 :
  IP address: 10.4.4.2
Protocol information for R3 :
  IP address: 10.5.5.1
Protocol information for R1 :
  IP address: 10.3.3.2
Protocol information for R1 :
  IP address: 10.2.2.2
```

The preceding output of the **show cdp entry * protocols** command can show you just the IP addresses of each directly connected neighbor. The show cdp entry * version will show you only the IOS version of your directly connected neighbors:

```
Corp#show cdp entry * version
Version information for ap :
  Cisco IOS Software, C1240 Software (C1240-K9W7-M), Version
    12.3(8)JEA, RELEASE SOFTWARE (fc2)
Technical Support: http://www.cisco.com/techsupport
Copyright (c) 1986-2006 by Cisco Systems, Inc.
Compiled Wed 23-Aug-06 16:45 by kellythw

Version information for R2 :
  Cisco IOS Software, 2801 Software (C2801-ADVENTERPRISEK9-M),
    Experimental Version 12.4(20050525:193634) [jezhao-ani 145]
Copyright (c) 1986-2005 by Cisco Systems, Inc.
Compiled Fri 27-May-05 23:53 by jezhao

Version information for R3 :
  Cisco IOS Software, 1841 Software (C1841-IPBASE-M), Version 12.4(1c),
    RELEASE SOFTWARE (fc1)
Technical Support: http://www.cisco.com/techsupport
Copyright (c) 1986-2005 by Cisco Systems, Inc.
Compiled Tue 25-Oct-05 17:10 by evmiller

 --More-
[output cut]
```

Although the **show cdp neighbors detail** and **show cdp entry** commands are very similar, the **show cdp entry** command allows you to display only one line of output for each directly connected neighbor, whereas the **show cdp neighbor detail** command does not. Next, let's look at the **show cdp traffic** command.

Documenting a Network Topology Using CDP

As the title of this section implies, I'm now going to show you how to document a sample network by using CDP. You'll learn to determine the appropriate router types, interface types, and IP addresses of various interfaces using only CDP commands and the **show running-config** command. And you can only console into the Lab_A router to document the network. You'll have to assign any remote routers the next IP address in each range. Figure 1.12 is what you'll use to complete the documentation.

FIGURE 1.12   Documenting a network topology using CDP

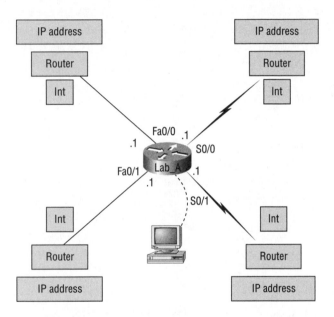

In this output, you can see that you have a router with four interfaces: two FastEthernet and two serial. First, determine the IP addresses of each interface by using the **show running-config** command:

```
Lab_A#sh running-config
Building configuration...

Current configuration : 960 bytes
!
version 12.2
service timestamps debug uptime
service timestamps log uptime
no service password-encryption
!
```

```
hostname Lab_A
!
ip subnet-zero
!
!
interface FastEthernet0/0
 ip address 192.168.21.1 255.255.255.0
 duplex auto
!
interface FastEthernet0/1
 ip address 192.168.18.1 255.255.255.0
 duplex auto
!
interface Serial0/0
ip address 192.168.23.1 255.255.255.0
!
interface Serial0/1
ip address 192.168.28.1 255.255.255.0
!
ip classless
!
line con 0
line aux 0
line vty 0 4
!
end
```

With this step completed, you can now write down the IP addresses of the Lab_A router's four interfaces. Next, you need to determine the type of device on the other end of each of these interfaces. It's easy to do this—just use the **show cdp neighbors** command:

```
Lab_A#sh cdp neighbors
Capability Codes: R - Router, T - Trans Bridge, B - Source Route Bridge
S - Switch, H - Host, I - IGMP, r - Repeater
Device ID   Local Intrfce   Holdtme   Capability Platform  Port ID
Lab_B        Fas 0/0         178         R         2501      E0
Lab_C        Fas 0/1         137         R         2621      Fa0/0
Lab_D        Ser 0/0         178         R         2514      S1
Lab_E        Ser 0/1         137         R         2620      S0/1
Lab_A#
```

You've got a good deal of information now! By using both the **show running-config** and **show cdp neighbors** commands, you know about all the IP addresses of the Lab_A router plus the types of routers connected to each of the Lab_A router's links and all the interfaces of the remote routers.

And by using all the information gathered from **show running-config** and **show cdp neighbors**, we can now create the topology in Figure 1.13.

FIGURE 1.13   Network topology documented

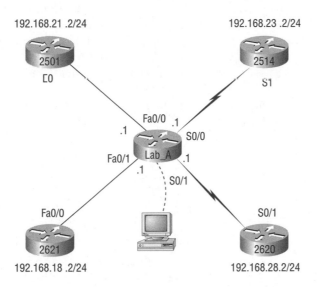

If we needed to, we could've also used the **show cdp neighbors detail** command to view the neighbor's IP addresses. But since we know the IP addresses of each link on the Lab_A router, we already know what the next available IP address is going to be.

Exam Essentials

Understand when to use CDP.   Cisco Discovery Protocol can be used to help you document as well as troubleshoot your network.

Remember what the output from the show cdp neighbors command shows.   The show cdp neighbors command provides the following information: device ID, local interface, holdtime, capability, platform, and port ID (remote interface).

1.8 Determine the path between two hosts across a network

Once you create an internetwork by connecting your WANs and LANs to a router, you'll need to configure logical network addresses, such as IP addresses, to all hosts on the internetwork so that they can communicate across that internetwork.

The term *routing* is used for taking a packet from one device and sending it through the network to another device on a different network. Routers don't really care about hosts—they only care about networks and the best path to each network. The logical network address of the destination host is used to get packets to a network through a routed network, and then the hardware address of the host is used to deliver the packet from a router to the correct destination host.

If your network has no routers, then it should be apparent that you are not routing. Routers route traffic to all the networks in your internetwork. To be able to route packets, a router must know, at a minimum, the following:

- Destination address

- Neighbor routers from which it can learn about remote networks

- Possible routes to all remote networks

- The best route to each remote network

- How to maintain and verify routing information

The router learns about remote networks from neighbor routers or from an administrator. The router then builds a routing table (a map of the internetwork) that describes how to find the remote networks. If a network is directly connected, then the router already knows how to get to it.

If a network isn't directly connected to the router, the router must use one of two ways to learn how to get to the remote network: *static routing*, meaning that someone must hand-type all network locations into the routing table, or something called dynamic routing. In *dynamic routing*, a protocol on one router communicates with the same protocol running on neighbor routers. The routers then update each other about all the networks they know about and place this information into the routing table. If a change occurs in the network, the dynamic routing protocols automatically inform all routers about the event. If *static routing* is used, the administrator is responsible for updating all changes by hand into all routers. Typically, in a large network, a combination of both dynamic and static routing is used.

Before we jump into the IP routing process, let's take a look at a simple example that demonstrates how a router uses the routing table to route packets out of an interface. We'll be going into a more detailed study of the process in the next section.

Figure 1.14 shows a simple two-router network. Lab_A has one serial interface and three LAN interfaces.

Looking at Figure 1.14, can you see which interface Lab_A will use to forward an IP datagram to a host with an IP address of 10.10.10.10?

FIGURE 1.14   A simple routing example

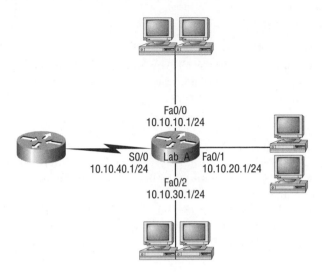

By using the command show ip route, we can see the routing table (map of the internetwork) that Lab_A uses to make forwarding decisions:

```
Lab_A#sh ip route
[output cut]
Gateway of last resort is not set
C       10.10.10.0/24 is directly connected, FastEthernet0/0
C       10.10.20.0/24 is directly connected, FastEthernet0/1
C       10.10.30.0/24 is directly connected, FastEthernet0/2
C       10.10.40.0/24 is directly connected, Serial 0/0
```

The C in the routing table output means that the networks listed are "directly connected," and until we add a routing protocol—something like RIP, EIGRP, or the like—to the routers in our internetwork (or use static routes), we'll have only directly connected networks in our routing table.

RIP and EIGRP are routing protocols and are covered in chapters 6 and 7 of the Sybex CCNA Study Guide 6th edition as well as in chapter x of this FastPass book.

So let's get back to the original question: By looking at the figure and the output of the routing table, can you tell what IP will do with a received packet that has a destination IP address of 10.10.10.10? The router will packet-switch the packet to interface FastEthernet 0/0, and this interface will frame the packet and then send it out on the network segment.

Because we can, let's do another example: Based on the output of the next routing table, which interface will a packet with a destination address of 10.10.10.14 be forwarded from?

```
Lab_A#sh ip route
[output cut]
Gateway of last resort is not set
C      10.10.10.16/28 is directly connected, FastEthernet0/0
C      10.10.10.8/29 is directly connected, FastEthernet0/1
C      10.10.10.4/30 is directly connected, FastEthernet0/2
C      10.10.10.0/30 is directly connected, Serial 0/0
```

First, you can see that the network is subnetted and each interface has a different mask. And I have to tell you—you just can't answer this question if you can't subnet! 10.10.10.14 would be a host in the 10.10.10.8/29 subnet connected to the FastEthernet0/1 interface. If you don't understand, just go back and reread Chapter 3 of the Sybex CCNA Study Guide 6th Edition if you're struggling, and this should make perfect sense to you afterward.

I really want to make sure you understand IP routing because it's super-important. So I'm going to use this section to test your understanding of the IP routing process by having you look at a couple of figures and answer some very basic IP routing questions.

Figure 1.15 shows a LAN connected to RouterA, which is, in turn, connected via a WAN link to RouterB. RouterB has a LAN connected with an HTTP server attached.

FIGURE 1.15   IP routing example 1

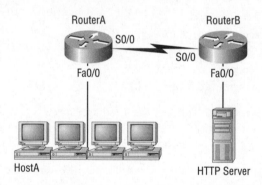

The critical information you need to glean from this figure is exactly how IP routing will occur in this example. Okay—we'll cheat a bit. I'll give you the answer, but then you should go back over the figure and see if you can answer example 2 without looking at my answers.

1.   The destination address of a frame, from HostA, will be the MAC address of the F0/0 interface of the RouterA router.

2.   The destination address of a packet will be the IP address of the network interface card (NIC) of the HTTP server.

3.   The destination port number in the segment header will have a value of 80.

That example was a pretty simple one, and it was also very to the point. One thing to remember is that if multiple hosts are communicating to the server using HTTP, they must all use a different source port number. That is how the server keeps the data separated at the Transport layer.

Let's mix it up a little and add another internetworking device into the network and then see if you can find the answers. Figure 1.16 shows a network with only one router but two switches.

FIGURE 1.16   IP routing example 2

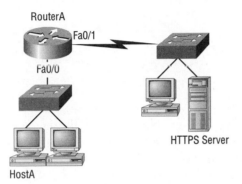

What you want to understand about the IP routing process here is what happens when HostA sends data to the HTTPS server:

1. The destination address of a frame, from HostA, will be the MAC address of the F0/0 interface of the RouterA router.

2. The destination address of a packet will be the IP address of the network interface card (NIC) of the HTTPS server.

3. The destination port number in the segment header will have a value of 443.

Notice that the switches weren't used as either a default gateway or another destination. That's because switches have nothing to do with routing. I wonder how many of you chose the switch as the default gateway (destination) MAC address for HostA? If you did, don't feel bad—just take another look with that fact in mind. It's very important to remember that the destination MAC address will always be the router's interface—if your packets are destined for outside the LAN, as they were in these last two examples.

Before we move into some of the more advanced aspects of IP routing, let's discuss ICMP in more detail, as well as how ICMP is used in an internetwork. Take a look at the network shown in Figure 1.17. Ask yourself what will happen if the LAN interface of Lab_C goes down.

Lab_C will use ICMP to inform Host A that Host B can't be reached, and it will do this by sending an ICMP destination unreachable message. Lots of people think that the Lab_A router would be sending this message, but they would be wrong because the router that sends the message is the one with that interface that's down is located.

FIGURE 1.17 ICMP error example

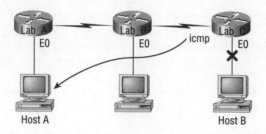

Let's look at another problem: Look at the output of a corporate router's routing table:

```
Corp#sh ip route
[output cut]
R    192.168.215.0 [120/2] via 192.168.20.2, 00:00:23, Serial0/0
R    192.168.115.0 [120/1] via 192.168.20.2, 00:00:23, Serial0/0
R    192.168.30.0 [120/1] via 192.168.20.2, 00:00:23, Serial0/0
C    192.168.20.0 is directly connected, Serial0/0
C    192.168.214.0 is directly connected, FastEthernet0/0
```

What do we see here? If I were to tell you that the corporate router received an IP packet with a source IP address of 192.168.214.20 and a destination address of 192.168.22.3, what do you think the Corp router will do with this packet?

If you said, "The packet came in on the FastEthernet 0/0 interface, but since the routing table doesn't show a route to network 192.168.22.0 (or a default route), the router will discard the packet and send an ICMP destination unreachable message back out interface FastEthernet 0/0," you're a genius! The reason it does this is because that's the source LAN where the packet originated from.

Exam Essentials

Understand the basic IP routing process. You need to remember that the frame changes at each hop but that the packet is never changed or manipulated in any way until it reaches the destination device.

Understand that MAC addresses are always local. A MAC (hardware) address will only be used on a local LAN. It will never pass a router's interface.

Understand that a frame carries a packet to only two places. A frame uses MAC (hardware) addresses to send a packet on a LAN. The frame will take the packet to either a host on the LAN or a router's interface if the packet is destined for a remote network

1.9 Describe the components required for network and Internet communications

When a host transmits data across a network to another device, the data goes through *encapsulation*: It is wrapped with protocol information at each layer of the OSI model. Each layer communicates only with its peer layer on the receiving device.

To communicate and exchange information, each layer uses *Protocol Data Units (PDUs)*. These hold the control information attached to the data at each layer of the model. They are usually attached to the header in front of the data field but can also be in the trailer, or end, of it.

Each PDU attaches to the data by encapsulating it at each layer of the OSI model, and each has a specific name depending on the information provided in each header. This PDU information is read only by the peer layer on the receiving device. After it's read, it's stripped off and the data is then handed to the next layer up.

Figure 1.18 shows the PDUs and how they attach control information to each layer. This figure demonstrates how the upper-layer user data is converted for transmission on the network. The data stream is then handed down to the Transport layer, which sets up a virtual circuit to the receiving device by sending over a synch packet. Next, the data stream is broken up into smaller pieces, and a Transport layer header (a PDU) is created and attached to the header of the data field; now the piece of data is called a *segment*. Each segment is sequenced so the data stream can be put back together on the receiving side exactly as it was transmitted.

FIGURE 1.18   Data encapsulation

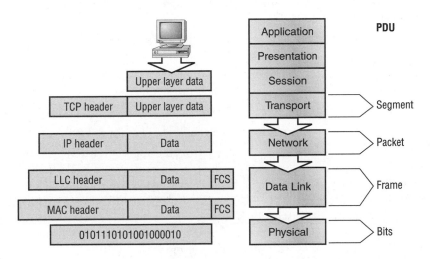

Each segment is then handed to the Network layer for network addressing and routing through the internetwork. Logical addressing (for example, IP) is used to get each segment to the correct network. The Network layer protocol adds a control header to the segment handed down from the Transport layer, and what we have now is called a *packet* or *datagram*. Remember that the Transport and Network layers work together to rebuild a data stream on a receiving host, but it's not part of their work to place their PDUs on a local network segment—which is the only way to get the information to a router or host.

It's the Data Link layer that's responsible for taking packets from the Network layer and placing them on the network medium (cable or wireless). The Data Link layer encapsulates each packet in a *frame*, and the frame's header carries the hardware address of the source and destination hosts. If the destination device is on a remote network, then the frame is sent to a router to be routed through an internetwork. Once it gets to the destination network, a new frame is used to get the packet to the destination host.

To put this frame on the network, it must first be put into a digital signal. Since a frame is really a logical group of 1s and 0s, the Physical layer is responsible for encoding these digits into a digital signal, which is read by devices on the same local network. The receiving devices will synchronize on the digital signal and extract (decode) the 1s and 0s from the digital signal. At this point, the devices build the frames, run a CRC, and then check their answer against the answer in the frame's FCS field. If it matches, the packet is pulled from the frame and what's left of the frame is discarded. This process is called *de-encapsulation*. The packet is handed to the Network layer, where the address is checked. If the address matches, the segment is pulled from the packet and what's left of the packet is discarded. The segment is processed at the Transport layer, which rebuilds the data stream and acknowledges to the transmitting station that it received each piece. It then happily hands the data stream to the upper-layer application.

At a transmitting device, the data encapsulation method works like this:

1. User information is converted to data for transmission on the network.

2. Data is converted to segments and a reliable connection is set up between the transmitting and receiving hosts.

3. Segments are converted to packets or datagrams, and a logical address is placed in the header so each packet can be routed through an internetwork.

4. Packets or datagrams are converted to frames for transmission on the local network. Hardware (Ethernet) addresses are used to uniquely identify hosts on a local network segment.

5. Frames are converted to bits, and a digital encoding and clocking scheme is used.

6. To explain this in more detail using the layer addressing, I'll use Figure 1.19.

Remember that a data stream is handed down from the upper layer to the Transport layer. As technicians, we really don't care who the data stream comes from because that's really a programmer's problem. Our job is to rebuild the data stream reliably and hand it to the upper layers on the receiving device.

Before we go further in our discussion of Figure 1.19, let's discuss port numbers and make sure we understand them. The Transport layer uses port numbers to define both the virtual circuit and the upper-layer process, as you can see from Figure 1.20.

FIGURE 1.19   PDU and layer addressing

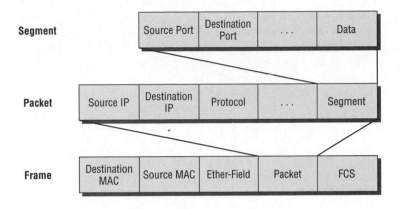

Bit   1011011100011110000

FIGURE 1.20   Port numbers at the Transport layer

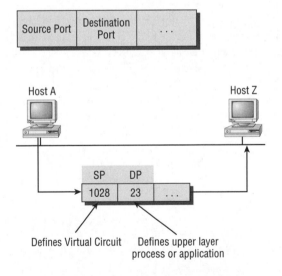

The Transport layer takes the data stream, makes segments out of it, and establishes a reliable session by creating a virtual circuit. It then sequences (numbers) each segment and uses acknowledgments and flow control. If you're using TCP, the virtual circuit is defined by the source port number. Remember, the host just makes this up starting at port number 1024 (0 through 1023 are reserved for well-known port numbers). The destination port number defines the upper-layer process (application) that the data stream is handed to when the data stream is reliably rebuilt on the receiving host.

Now that you understand port numbers and how they are used at the Transport layer, let's go back to Figure 1.20. Once the Transport layer header information is added to the piece of data, it becomes a segment and is handed down to the Network layer along with the destination IP address. (The destination IP address was handed down from the upper layers to the Transport layer with the data stream, and it was discovered through a name resolution method at the upper layers—probably DNS.)

The Network layer adds a header, and adds the logical addressing (IP addresses), to the front of each segment. Once the header is added to the segment, the PDU is called a packet. The packet has a protocol field that describes where the segment came from (either UDP or TCP) so it can hand the segment to the correct protocol at the Transport layer when it reaches the receiving host.

The Network layer is responsible for finding the destination hardware address that dictates where the packet should be sent on the local network. It does this by using the Address Resolution Protocol (ARP). IP at the Network layer looks at the destination IP address and compares that address to its own source IP address and subnet mask. If it turns out to be a local network request, the hardware address of the local host is requested via an ARP request. If the packet is destined for a remote host, IP will look for the IP address of the default gateway (router) instead.

The packet, along with the destination hardware address of either the local host or default gateway, is then handed down to the Data Link layer. The Data Link layer will add a header to the front of the packet and the piece of data then becomes a frame. (We call it a frame because both a header and a trailer are added to the packet, which makes the data resemble bookends or a frame, if you will.) This is shown in Figure 1.19. The frame uses an Ether-Type field to describe which protocol the packet came from at the Network layer. Now a CRC is run on the frame, and the answer to the CRC is placed in the FCS field found in the trailer of the frame.

The frame is now ready to be handed down, one bit at a time, to the Physical layer, which will use bit timing rules to encode the data in a digital signal. Every device on the network segment will synchronize itself with the clock and extract the 1s and 0s from the digital signal and build a frame. After the frame is rebuilt, a CRC is run to make sure that the frame is okay. If everything turns out to be all good, the hosts will check the destination address to see if the frame is for them.

Exam Essentials

Remember the encapsulation method.   The encapsulation method is data, segment, packet, frames, and bits.

Remember the Transport port numbers that are reserved.   Hosts can create a session to another host by using any number from 1024 to 65535. Ports 0 through 1023 are well known port numbers and are reserved.

1.10 Identify and correct common network problems at layers 1, 2, 3, and 7 using a layered model approach

Troubleshooting IP addressing is obviously an important skill because running into trouble somewhere along the way is pretty much a sure thing, and it's going to happen to you. No— I'm not a pessimist; I'm just keeping it real. Because of this nasty fact, it will be great when you can save the day because you can both figure out (diagnose) the problem and fix it on an IP network whether you're at work or at home!

So this is where I'm going to show you the "Cisco way" of troubleshooting IP addressing. Let's go over the troubleshooting steps that Cisco uses first. These are pretty simple, but important nonetheless. Pretend that you're at a customer host and they're complaining that their host cannot communicate to a server, which just happens to be on a remote network. Here are the four troubleshooting steps that Cisco recommends:

1. Open a DOS window and ping 127.0.0.1. This is the diagnostic or loopback address, and if you get a successful ping, your IP stack is then considered to be initialized. If it fails, then you have an IP stack failure and need to reinstall TCP/IP on the host.

2. From the DOS window, ping the IP address of the local host. If that's successful, then your network interface card (NIC) card is functioning. If it fails, then there is a problem with the NIC card. This doesn't mean that a cable is plugged into the NIC, only that the IP protocol stack on the host can communicate to the NIC.

3. From the DOS window, ping the default gateway (router). If the ping works, it means that the NIC is plugged into the network and can communicate on the local network. It also means the default router is responding and configured with the proper IP address on its local interface. If it fails, then you have a local physical network problem that could be happening anywhere from the NIC to the router.

4. If steps 1 through 3 were successful, try to ping the remote server. If that works, then you know that you have IP communication between the local host and the remote server. You also know that the remote physical network is working.

If the user still can't communicate with the server after steps 1 through 4 are successful, then you probably have some type of name resolution problem, and need to check your Domain Name Service (DNS) settings. But if the ping to the remote server fails, then you know you have some type of remote physical network problem, and need to go to the server and work through steps 1 through 3 until you find the snag.

Once you've gone through all these steps, what do you do if you find a problem? How do you go about fixing an IP address configuration error? Let's move on and discuss how to determine the IP address problems and how to fix them.

Let's use Figure 1.21 as an example of your basic IP trouble—poor Sally can't log in to the Windows server. Do you deal with this by calling the Microsoft team to tell them their server is a pile of junk and causing all your problems? Probably not such a great idea—let's first double-check our network instead.

FIGURE 1.21   Basic IP troubleshooting

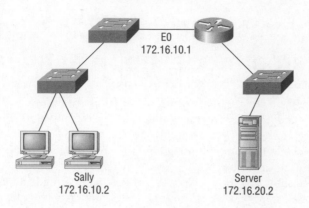

Sally
172.16.10.2

Server
172.16.20.2

EO
172.16.10.1

Okay let's get started by going over the troubleshooting steps that Cisco follows. They're pretty simple, but important nonetheless. Pretend that you're with a customer and they're complaining that they're host can't communicate to a server that just happens to be on a remote network. Here are the four troubleshooting steps Cisco recommends:

1. Open a DOS window and ping 127.0.0.1. This is the diagnostic, or *loopback*, address, and if you get a successful ping, your IP stack is considered to be initialized. If it fails, then you have an IP stack failure and need to reinstall TCP/IP on the host.

```
C:\>ping 127.0.0.1
Pinging 127.0.0.1 with 32 bytes of data:
Reply from 127.0.0.1: bytes=32 time<1ms TTL=128
Reply from 127.0.0.1: bytes=32 time<1ms TTL=128
Reply from 127.0.0.1: bytes=32 time<1ms TTL=128
Reply from 127.0.0.1: bytes=32 time<1ms TTL=128
Ping statistics for 127.0.0.1:
    Packets: Sent = 4, Received = 4, Lost = 0 (0% loss),
Approximate round trip times in milli-seconds:
    Minimum = 0ms, Maximum = 0ms, Average = 0ms
```

2. From the DOS window, ping the IP address of the local host. If that's successful, your NIC is functioning. If it fails, there is a problem with the NIC. Success here doesn't mean that a cable is plugged into the NIC, only that the IP protocol stack on the host can communicate to the NIC (via the LAN driver).

```
C:\>ping 172.16.10.2
Pinging 172.16.10.2 with 32 bytes of data:
Reply from 172.16.10.2: bytes=32 time<1ms TTL=128
Reply from 172.16.10.2: bytes=32 time<1ms TTL=128
Reply from 172.16.10.2: bytes=32 time<1ms TTL=128
```

```
Reply from 172.16.10.2: bytes=32 time<1ms TTL=128
Ping statistics for 172.16.10.2:
    Packets: Sent = 4, Received = 4, Lost = 0 (0% loss),
Approximate round trip times in milli-seconds:
    Minimum = 0ms, Maximum = 0ms, Average = 0ms
```

3. From the DOS window, ping the default gateway (router). If the ping works, it means that the NIC is plugged into the network and can communicate on the local network. If it fails, you have a local physical network problem that could be anywhere from the NIC to the router.

```
C:\>ping 172.16.10.1
Pinging 172.16.10.1 with 32 bytes of data:
Reply from 172.16.10.1: bytes=32 time<1ms TTL=128
Reply from 172.16.10.1: bytes=32 time<1ms TTL=128
Reply from 172.16.10.1: bytes=32 time<1ms TTL=128
Reply from 172.16.10.1: bytes=32 time<1ms TTL=128
Ping statistics for 172.16.10.1:
    Packets: Sent = 4, Received = 4, Lost = 0 (0% loss),
Approximate round trip times in milli-seconds:
    Minimum = 0ms, Maximum = 0ms, Average = 0ms
```

4. If steps 1 through 3 were successful, try to ping the remote server. If that works, then you know that you have IP communication between the local host and the remote server. You also know that the remote physical network is working.

```
C:\>ping 172.16.20.2
Pinging 172.16.20.2 with 32 bytes of data:
Reply from 172.16.20.2: bytes=32 time<1ms TTL=128
Reply from 172.16.20.2: bytes=32 time<1ms TTL=128
Reply from 172.16.20.2: bytes=32 time<1ms TTL=128
Reply from 172.16.20.2: bytes=32 time<1ms TTL=128
Ping statistics for 172.16.20.2:
    Packets: Sent = 4, Received = 4, Lost = 0 (0% loss),
Approximate round trip times in milli-seconds:
    Minimum = 0ms, Maximum = 0ms, Average = 0ms
```

If the user still can't communicate with the server after steps 1 through 4 are successful, you probably have some type of name resolution problem and need to check your DNS settings. But if the ping to the remote server fails, then you know you have some type of remote physical network problem and need to go to the server and work through steps 1 through 3 until you find the snag.

Before we move on to determining IP address problems and how to fix them, I just want to mention some basic DOS commands that you can use to help troubleshoot your network from both a PC and a Cisco router (the commands might do the same thing, but they are implemented differently).

Packet InterNet Groper (ping)   Uses ICMP echo request and replies to test if a node IP stack is initialized and alive on the network.

traceroute   Displays the list of routers on a path to a network destination by using TTL time-outs and ICMP error messages. This command will not work from a DOS prompt.

tracert   Same command as `traceroute`, but it's a Microsoft Windows command and will not work on a Cisco router.

arp -a   Displays IP-to-MAC-address mappings on a Windows PC.

show ip arp   Same command as `arp -a`, but displays the ARP table on a Cisco router. Like the commands `traceroute` and `tracert`, they are not interchangeable through DOS and Cisco.

ipconfig /all   Used only from a DOS prompt, shows you the PC network configuration.

Once you've gone through all these steps and used the appropriate DOS commands, if necessary, what do you do if you find a problem? How do you go about fixing an IP address configuration error? Let's move on and discuss how to determine the IP address problems and how to fix them.

Determining IP Address Problems

It's common for a host, router, or other network device to be configured with the wrong IP address, subnet mask, or default gateway. Because this happens way too often, I'm going to teach you how to both determine and fix IP address configuration errors.

Once you've worked through the four basic steps of troubleshooting and determined there's a problem, you obviously then need to find and fix it. It really helps to draw out the network and IP addressing scheme. If it's already done, consider yourself lucky and go buy a lottery ticket, because although it should be done, it rarely is. And if it is, it's usually outdated or inaccurate anyway. Typically it is not done, and you'll probably just have to bite the bullet and start from scratch.

Once you have your network accurately drawn out, including the IP addressing scheme, you need to verify each host's IP address, mask, and default gateway address to determine the problem. (I'm assuming that you don't have a physical problem or that if you did, you've already fixed it.)

Let's check out the example illustrated in Figure 1.22. A user in the sales department calls and tells you that she can't get to ServerA in the marketing department. You ask her if she can get to ServerB in the marketing department, but she doesn't know because she doesn't have rights to log on to that server. What do you do?

You ask the client to go through the four troubleshooting steps that you learned about in the preceding section. Steps 1 through 3 work, but step 4 fails. By looking at the figure, can you determine the problem? Look for clues in the network drawing. First, the WAN link between the Lab_A router and the Lab_B router shows the mask as a /27. You should already know that this mask is 255.255.255.224 and then determine that all networks are using this mask. The network address is 192.168.1.0. What are our valid subnets and hosts? 256 – 224 = 32, so this makes our subnets 32, 64, 96, 128, and so on. So, by looking at the figure, you can see that subnet 32 is being used by the sales department, the WAN link is using subnet 96, and the marketing department is using subnet 64.

FIGURE 1.22   IP address problem 1

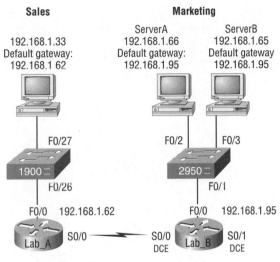

Now you've got to determine what the valid host ranges are for each subnet. From what you learned at the beginning of this chapter, you should now be able to easily determine the subnet address, broadcast addresses, and valid host ranges. The valid hosts for the Sales LAN are 33 through 62—the broadcast address is 63 because the next subnet is 64, right? For the Marketing LAN, the valid hosts are 65 through 94 (broadcast 95), and for the WAN link, 97 through 126 (broadcast 127). By looking at the figure, you can determine that the default gateway on the Lab_B router is incorrect. That address is the broadcast address of the 64 subnet, so there's no way it could be a valid host.

Did you get all that? Maybe we should try another one, just to make sure. Figure 1.23 shows a network problem. A user in the Sales LAN can't get to ServerB. You have the user run through the four basic troubleshooting steps and find that the host can communicate to the local network but not to the remote network. Find and define the IP addressing problem.

If you use the same steps used to solve the last problem, you can see first that the WAN link again provides the subnet mask to use— /29, or 255.255.255.248. You need to determine what the valid subnets, broadcast addresses, and valid host ranges are to solve this problem.

The 248 mask is a block size of 8 (256 – 248 = 8), so the subnets both start and increment in multiples of 8. By looking at the figure, you see that the Sales LAN is in the 24 subnet, the WAN is in the 40 subnet, and the Marketing LAN is in the 80 subnet. Can you see the problem yet? The valid host range for the Sales LAN is 25–30, and the configuration appears correct. The valid host range for the WAN link is 41–46, and this also appears correct. The valid host range for the 80 subnet is 81–86, with a broadcast address of 87 because the next subnet is 88. ServerB has been configured with the broadcast address of the subnet.

Okay, now that you can figure out misconfigured IP addresses on hosts, what do you do if a host doesn't have an IP address and you need to assign one? What you need to do is look at other hosts on the LAN and figure out the network, mask, and default gateway. Let's take a look at a couple of examples of how to find and apply valid IP addresses to hosts.

FIGURE 1.23   IP address problem 2

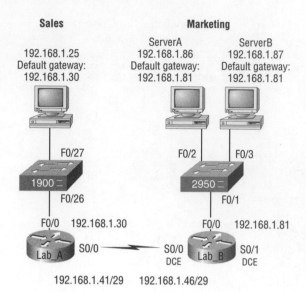

You need to assign a server and router IP addresses on a LAN. The subnet assigned on that segment is 192.168.20.24/29, and the router needs to be assigned the first usable address and the server the last valid host ID. What are the IP address, mask, and default gateway assigned to the server?

To answer this, you must know that a /29 is a 255.255.255.248 mask, which provides a block size of 8. The subnet is known as 24, the next subnet in a block of 8 is 32, so the broadcast address of the 24 subnet is 31, which makes the valid host range 25–30.

Server IP address: 192.168.20.30

Server mask: 255.255.255.248

Default gateway: 192.168.20.25 (router's IP address)

As another example, let's take a look at Figure 1.24 and solve this problem.

FIGURE 1.24   Find the valid host.

RouterA

E0: 192.168.10.33/27

HostA

Look at the router's IP address on Ethernet0. What IP address, subnet mask, and valid host range could be assigned to the host?

The IP address of the router's Ethernet0 is 192.168.10.33/27. As you already know, a /27 is a 224 mask with a block size of 32. The router's interface is in the 32 subnet. The next subnet is 64, so that makes the broadcast address of the 32 subnet 63 and the valid host range 33–62.

Host IP address: 192.168.10.34–62 (any address in the range except for 33, which is assigned to the router)

Mask: 255.255.255.224

Default gateway: 192.168.10.33

Figure 1.25 shows two routers with Ethernet configurations already assigned. What are the host addresses and subnet masks of hosts A and B?

FIGURE 1.25   Find the valid host #2

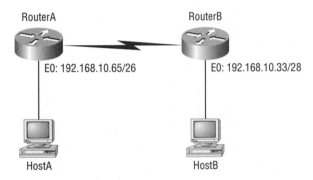

RouterA has an IP address of 192.168.10.65/26, and RouterB has an IP address of 192.168.10.33/28. What are the host configurations? RouterA Ethernet0 is in the 192.168.10.64 subnet, and RouterB Ethernet0 is in the 192.168.10.32 network.

Host A IP address: 192.168.10.66–126

Host A mask: 255.255.255.192

Host A default gateway: 192.168.10.65

Host B IP address: 192.168.10.34–46

Host B mask: 255.255.255.240

Host B default gateway: 192.168.10.33

Let's try another example. Figure 1.26 shows two routers; you need to configure the S0/0 interface on RouterA. The network assigned to the serial link is 172.16.17.0/22. What IP address can be assigned?

First, you must know that a /22 CIDR is 255.255.252.0, which makes a block size of 4 in the third octet. Since 17 is listed, the available range is 16.1 through 19.254; so, for example, the IP address S0/0 could be 172.16.18.255 since that's within the range.

FIGURE 1.26   Find the valid host address #3

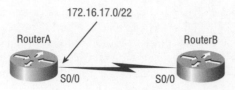

172.16.17.0/22

RouterA   RouterB

S0/0   S0/0

Here's one final example. You have one Class C network ID and you need to provide one usable subnet per city while allowing enough usable host addresses for each city specified in Figure 1.27. What is your mask?

FIGURE 1.27   Find the valid subnet mask.

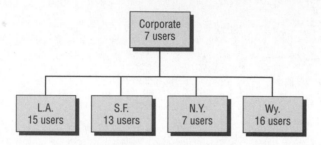

Corporate
7 users

L.A.   S.F.   N.Y.   Wy.
15 users   13 users   7 users   16 users

Actually, this is probably the easiest thing you've done all day! I count 5 subnets needed, and the Wyoming office needs 16 users (always look for the network that needs the most hosts). What block size is needed for the Wyoming office? 32. (Remember, you cannot use a block size of 16 because you always have to subtract 2!) What mask provides you with a block size of 32? 224. Bingo! This provides 8 subnets, each with 30 hosts.

Exam Essentials

Remember how to test your local stack.   You can ping 127.0.0.1 to test that the IP protocol is initialed on your system.

Understand how to test IP on your local host.   To verify that IP is communicating on your host, you need to ping your IP address. Open a DOS prompt and use the ipconfig command to find your IP address. This will verify that your host is communicating from IP to your LAN driver.

Understand how to verify that your host is communicating on the local network.   The best way to verify that your hosts is communicating on the local network is to ping your default gateway.

1.11 Differentiate between LAN/WAN operation and features

Layer 2 switching is considered hardware-based bridging because it uses specialized hardware called an *application-specific integrated circuit (ASIC)*. ASICs can run up to gigabit speeds with very low latency rates.

 Latency is the time measured from when a frame enters a port to the time it exits a port.

Bridges and switches read each frame as it passes through the network. The layer 2 device then puts the source hardware address in a filter table and keeps track of which port the frame was received on. This information (logged in the bridge's or switch's filter table) is what helps the machine determine the location of the specific sending device. Figure 1.28 shows a switch in an internetwork.

FIGURE 1.28   A switch in an internetwork

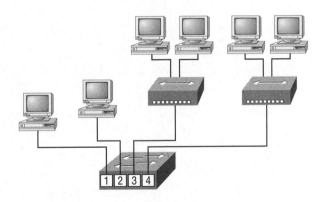

Each segment has its own collision domain.
All segments are in the same broadcast domain.

The real estate business is all about location, location, location, and it's the same for both layer 2 and layer 3 devices. Although both need to be able to negotiate the network, it's crucial to remember that they're concerned with very different parts of it. Primarily, layer 3 machines (such as routers) need to locate specific networks, whereas layer 2 machines (switches and bridges) need to eventually locate specific devices. So, networks are to routers as individual devices are to switches and bridges. And routing tables that "map" the internetwork are for routers as filter tables that "map" individual devices are for switches and bridges.

After a filter table is built on the layer 2 device, it will forward frames only to the segment where the destination hardware address is located. If the destination device is on the same segment as the frame, the layer 2 device will block the frame from going to any other segments. If the destination is on a different segment, the frame can be transmitted only to that segment. This is called *transparent bridging*.

When a switch interface receives a frame with a destination hardware address that isn't found in the device's filter table, it will forward the frame to all connected segments. If the unknown device that was sent the "mystery frame" replies to this forwarding action, the switch updates its filter table regarding that device's location. But in the event the destination address of the transmitting frame is a broadcast address, the switch will forward all broadcasts to every connected segment by default.

All devices that the broadcast is forwarded to are considered to be in the same broadcast domain. This can be a problem; layer 2 devices propagate layer 2 broadcast storms that choke performance, and the only way to stop a broadcast storm from propagating through an internetwork is with a layer 3 device—a router.

The biggest benefit of using switches instead of hubs in your internetwork is that each switch port is actually its own collision domain. (Conversely, a hub creates one large collision domain.) But even armed with a switch, you still can't break up broadcast domains. Neither switches nor bridges will do that. They'll typically simply forward all broadcasts instead.

Another benefit of LAN switching over hub-centered implementations is that each device on every segment plugged into a switch can transmit simultaneously—at least, they can as long as there is only one host on each port and a hub isn't plugged into a switch port. As you might have guessed, hubs allow only one device per network segment to communicate at a time.

Ethernet Networking

Ethernet is a contention media access method that allows all hosts on a network to share the same bandwidth of a link. Ethernet is popular because it's readily scalable, meaning that it's comparatively easy to integrate new technologies, such as Fast Ethernet and Gigabit Ethernet, into an existing network infrastructure. It's also relatively simple to implement in the first place, and with it, troubleshooting is reasonably straightforward. Ethernet uses both Data Link and Physical layer specifications, and this section of the chapter will give you both the Data Link layer and Physical layer information you need to effectively implement, troubleshoot, and maintain an Ethernet network.

Ethernet networking uses *Carrier Sense Multiple Access with Collision Detection (CSMA/CD)*, a protocol that helps devices share the bandwidth evenly without having two devices transmit at the same time on the network medium. CSMA/CD was created to overcome the problem of those collisions that occur when packets are transmitted simultaneously from different nodes. And trust me—good collision management is crucial, because when a node transmits in a CSMA/CD network, all the other nodes on the network receive and examine that transmission. Only bridges and routers can effectively prevent a transmission from propagating throughout the entire network!

So, how does the CSMA/CD protocol work? Let's start by taking a look at Figure 1.29.

FIGURE 1.29   CSMA/CD

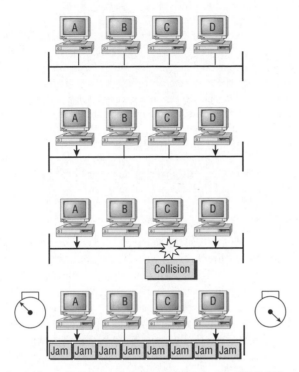

Carrier Sense Multiple Access with Collision Detection (CSMA/CD)

When a host wants to transmit over the network, it first checks for the presence of a digital signal on the wire. If all is clear (no other host is transmitting), the host will then proceed with its transmission. But it doesn't stop there. The transmitting host constantly monitors the wire to make sure that no other hosts begin transmitting. If the host detects another signal on the wire, it sends out an extended jam signal that causes all nodes on the segment to stop sending data (think busy signal). The nodes respond to that jam signal by waiting a while before attempting to transmit again. Backoff algorithms determine when the colliding stations can retransmit. If collisions keep occurring after 15 tries, the nodes attempting to transmit will then timeout. Pretty clean!

When a collision occurs on an Ethernet LAN, the following happens:

- A jam signal informs all devices that a collision occurred.

- The collision invokes a random backoff algorithm.

- Each device on the Ethernet segment stops transmitting for a short time until the timers expire.

- All hosts have equal priority to transmit after the timers have expired.

The following are the effects of having a CSMA/CD network sustaining heavy collisions:

- Delay

- Low throughput

- Congestion

Backoff on an 802.3 network is the retransmission delay that's enforced when a collision occurs. When a collision occurs, a host will resume transmission after the forced time delay has expired. After this backoff delay period has expired, all stations have equal priority to transmit data.

In the following sections, I am going to cover Ethernet in detail at both the Data Link layer (layer 2) and the Physical layer (layer 1).

Half- and Full-Duplex Ethernet

Half-duplex Ethernet is defined in the original 802.3 Ethernet; Cisco says it uses only one wire pair with a digital signal running in both directions on the wire. Certainly, the IEEE specifications discuss the process of half-duplex somewhat differently, but what Cisco is talking about is a general sense of what is happening here with Ethernet.

It also uses the CSMA/CD protocol to help prevent collisions and to permit retransmitting if a collision does occur. If a hub is attached to a switch, it must operate in half-duplex mode because the end stations must be able to detect collisions. Half-duplex Ethernet—typically 10BaseT—is only about 30 to 40 percent efficient as Cisco sees it because a large 10BaseT network will usually only give you 3 to 4Mbps, at most.

But full-duplex Ethernet uses two pairs of wires instead of one wire pair like half-duplex. And full-duplex uses a point-to-point connection between the transmitter of the transmitting device and the receiver of the receiving device. This means that with full-duplex data transfer, you get a faster data transfer than with half-duplex. And because the transmitted data is sent on a different set of wires than the received data, no collisions will occur.

The reason that you don't need to worry about collisions is because now it's like there is a freeway with multiple lanes instead of the single-lane road provided by half-duplex. Full-duplex Ethernet is supposed to offer 100 percent efficiency in both directions—for example, you can get 20Mbps with a 10Mbps Ethernet running full-duplex or 200Mbps for Fast Ethernet. But this rate is something known as an aggregate rate, which translates as "you're supposed to get" 100 percent efficiency. No guarantees, in networking as in life.

Full-duplex Ethernet can be used in three situations:

- With a connection from a switch to a host

- With a connection from a switch to a switch

- With a connection from a host to a host using a crossover cable

Full-duplex Ethernet requires a point-to-point connection when only two nodes are present. You can run full-duplex with just about any device except a hub.

Now, if it's capable of all that speed, why wouldn't it deliver? Well, when a full-duplex Ethernet port is powered on, it first connects to the remote end and then negotiates with the other end of the Fast Ethernet link. This is called an *auto-detect mechanism*. This mechanism first decides on the exchange capability, which means that it checks to see if it can run at 10 or 100Mbps. It then checks to see if it can run full-duplex, and if it can't, it will run half-duplex.

 Remember that half-duplex Ethernet shares a collision domain and provides a lower effective throughput than full-duplex Ethernet, which typically has a private collision domain and a higher effective throughput.

Last, remember these important points:

- There are no collisions in full-duplex mode.
- A dedicated switch port is required for each full-duplex node.
- The host network card and the switch port must be capable of operating in full-duplex mode.

So, what, exactly, is it that makes something a *wide area network (WAN)* instead of a local area network (LAN)? Well, there's obviously the distance thing, but these days, wireless LANs can cover some serious turf. What about bandwidth? Well, here again, some really big pipes can be had for a price in many places, so that's not it either. So, what is it then?

One of the main ways a WAN differs from a LAN is that while you generally own a LAN infrastructure, you usually lease WAN infrastructure from a service provider. To be honest, modern technologies even blur this definition, but it still fits neatly into the context of Cisco's exam objectives.

Anyway, I've already talked about the data link that you usually own (Ethernet), but now we're going to find out about the kind you usually don't own—the type most often leased from a service provider.

The key to understanding WAN technologies is to be familiar with the different WAN terms and connection types commonly used by service providers to join your networks together.

Defining WAN Terms

Before you run out and order a WAN service type from a provider, it would be a really good idea to understand the following terms that service providers typically use:

Customer premises equipment (CPE)   *Customer premises equipment (CPE)* is equipment that's owned by the subscriber and located on the subscriber's premises.

Demarcation point   The *demarcation point* is the precise spot where the service provider's responsibility ends and the CPE begins. It's generally a device in a telecommunications closet owned and installed by the telecommunications company (telco). It's your responsibility to cable (extended demarc) from this box to the CPE, which is usually a connection to a CSU/DSU or ISDN interface.

Local loop   The *local loop* connects the demarc to the closest switching office, which is called a central office.

Central office (CO) This point connects the customer's network to the provider's switching network. Good to know is that a *central office (CO)* is sometimes referred to as a *point of presence (POP)*.

Toll network The *toll network* is a trunk line inside a WAN provider's network. This network is a collection of switches and facilities owned by the ISP.

Definitely familiarize yourself with these terms because they're crucial to understanding WAN technologies.

WAN Connection Types

As you're probably aware, a WAN can use a number of different connection types, and I'm going to introduce you to each of the various types of WAN connections you'll find on the market today. Figure 1.30 shows the different WAN connection types that can be used to connect your LANs together (DTE) over a DCE network.

FIGURE 1.30 WAN connection types

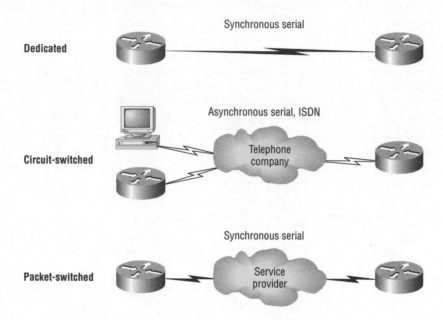

Here's a list explaining the different WAN connection types:

Leased lines These are usually referred to as a *point-to-point* or dedicated connection. A *leased line* is a preestablished WAN communications path that goes from the CPE through the DCE switch, then over to the CPE of the remote site. The CPE enables DTE networks to communicate at any time with no cumbersome setup procedures to muddle through before transmitting data. When you've got plenty of cash, this is really the way to go because it uses synchronous serial lines up to 45Mbps. HDLC and PPP encapsulations are frequently used on leased lines; I'll go over them with you in detail in a bit.

Circuit switching   When you hear the term *circuit switching*, think phone call. The big advantage is cost—you only pay for the time you actually use. No data can transfer before an end-to-end connection is established. Circuit switching uses dial-up modems or ISDN and is used for low-bandwidth data transfers. Okay—I know what you're thinking: "Modems? Did he say modems? Aren't those only in museums by now?" After all, with all the wireless technologies available, who would use a modem these days? Well, some people do have ISDN, and it still is viable (and I do suppose someone does use a modem now and then), but circuit switching can be used in some of the newer WAN technologies as well.

Packet switching   This is a WAN switching method that allows you to share bandwidth with other companies to save money. *Packet switching* can be thought of as a network that's designed to look like a leased line yet charges you more like circuit switching. But less cost isn't always better—there's definitely a downside: If you need to transfer data constantly, just forget about this option. Instead, get yourself a leased line. Packet switching will only work for you if your data transfers are the bursty type—not continuous. Frame Relay and X.25 are packet-switching technologies with speeds that can range from 56Kbps up to T3 (45Mbps).

MultiProtocol Label Switching (MPLS) uses a combination of both circuit switching and packet switching, but it's out of this book's range. Even so, after you pass your CCNA exam, it would be well worth your time to look into MPLS, so I'll talk about MPLS briefly in a minute.

WAN Support

Basically, Cisco just supports HDLC, PPP, and Frame Relay on its serial interfaces, and you can see this with the encapsulation ? command from any serial interface (your output may vary depending on the IOS version you are running):

```
Corp#config t
Corp(config)#int s0/0/0
Corp(config-if)#encapsulation ?
  atm-dxi      ATM-DXI encapsulation
  frame-relay  Frame Relay networks
  hdlc         Serial HDLC synchronous
  lapb         LAPB (X.25 Level 2)
  ppp          Point-to-Point protocol
  smds         Switched Megabit Data Service (SMDS)
  x25          X.25
```

Understand that if I had other types of interfaces on my router, I would have other encapsulation options, like ISDN or ADSL. And remember, you can't configure Ethernet or Token Ring encapsulation on a serial interface.

Next, I'm going to define the most prominently known WAN protocols used today: Frame Relay, ISDN, LAPB, LAPD, HDLC, PPP, PPPoE, Cable, DSL, MPLS, and ATM. Just so you know, the only WAN protocols you'll usually find configured on a serial interface are HDLC, PPP, and Frame Relay, but who said we're stuck with using only serial interfaces for wide area connections?

Frame Relay A packet-switched technology that made its debut in the early 1990s, *Frame Relay* is a high-performance Data Link and Physical layer specification. It's pretty much a successor to X.25, except that much of the technology in X.25 used to compensate for physical errors (noisy lines) has been eliminated. An upside to Frame Relay is that it can be more cost effective than point-to-point links, plus it typically runs at speeds of 64Kbps up to 45Mbps (T3). Another Frame Relay benefit is that it provides features for dynamic bandwidth allocation and congestion control.

ISDN *Integrated Services Digital Network (ISDN)* is a set of digital services that transmits voice and data over existing phone lines. ISDN offers a cost-effective solution for remote users who need a higher-speed connection than analog dial-up links can give them, and it's also a good choice to use as a backup link for other types of links like Frame Relay or T1 connections.

LAPB *Link Access Procedure, Balanced (LAPB)* was created to be a connection-oriented protocol at the Data Link layer for use with X.25, but it can also be used as a simple data link transport. A not-so-good characteristic of LAPB is that it tends to create a tremendous amount of overhead due to its strict time-out and windowing techniques.

LAPD *Link Access Procedure, D-Channel (LAPD)* is used with ISDN at the Data Link layer (layer 2) as a protocol for the D (signaling) channel. LAPD was derived from the Link Access Procedure, Balanced (LAPB) protocol and is designed primarily to satisfy the signaling requirements of ISDN basic access.

HDLC *High-Level Data-Link Control (HDLC)* was derived from Synchronous Data Link Control (SDLC), which was created by IBM as a Data Link connection protocol. HDLC works at the Data Link layer and creates very little overhead compared to LAPB.

It wasn't intended to encapsulate multiple Network layer protocols across the same link—the HDLC header doesn't contain any identification about the type of protocol being carried inside the HDLC encapsulation. Because of this, each vendor that uses HDLC has its own way of identifying the Network layer protocol, meaning each vendor's HDLC is proprietary with regard to its specific equipment.

PPP *Point-to-Point Protocol (PPP)* is a pretty famous, industry-standard protocol. Because all multiprotocol versions of HDLC are proprietary, PPP can be used to create point-to-point links between different vendors' equipment. It uses a Network Control Protocol field in the Data Link header to identify the Network layer protocol and allows authentication and multi-link connections to be run over asynchronous and synchronous links.

PPPoE   Point-to-Point Protocol over Ethernet encapsulates PPP frames in Ethernet frames and is usually used in conjunction with ADSL services. It gives you a lot of the familiar PPP features like authentication, encryption, and compression, but there's a downside—it has a lower maximum transmission unit (MTU) than standard Ethernet does, and if your firewall isn't solidly configured, this little attribute can really give you some grief!

Still somewhat popular in the United States, PPPoE on Ethernet's main feature is that it adds a direct connection to Ethernet interfaces while providing DSL support as well. It's often used by many hosts on a shared Ethernet interface for opening PPP sessions to various destinations via at least one bridging modem.

In a modern HFC network, typically 500 to 2,000 active data subscribers are connected to a certain cable network segment, all sharing the upstream and downstream bandwidth. (*Hybrid fibre-coaxial*, or HFC, is a telecommunications industry term for a network that incorporates both optical fiber and coaxial cable to create a broadband network.) The actual bandwidth for Internet service over a cable TV (CATV) line can be up to about 27Mbps on the download path to the subscriber, with about 2.5Mbps of bandwidth on the upload path. Typically, users get an access speed from 256Kbps to 6Mbps. This data rate varies greatly throughout the U.S.

DSL   *Digital subscriber line* is a technology used by traditional telephone companies to deliver advanced services (high-speed data and sometimes video) over twisted-pair copper telephone wires. It typically has lower data-carrying capacity than HFC networks, and data speeds can be range limited by line lengths and quality. Digital subscriber line is not a complete end-to-end solution but rather a Physical layer transmission technology like dial-up, cable, or wireless. DSL connections are deployed in the last mile of a local telephone network—the local loop. The connection is set up between a pair of modems on either end of a copper wire that is run between the CPE and the Digital Subscriber Line Access Multiplexer (DSLAM). A *DSLAM* is the device located at the provider's CO and concentrates connections from multiple DSL subscribers.

MPLS   *MultiProtocol Label Switching (MPLS)* is a data-carrying mechanism that emulates some properties of a circuit-switched network over a packet-switched network. MPLS is a switching mechanism that imposes labels (numbers) on packets and then uses those labels to forward packets. The labels are assigned on the edge of the MPLS of the network, and forwarding inside the MPLS network is done solely based on labels. Labels usually correspond to a path to layer 3 destination addresses (equal to IP destination-based routing). MPLS was designed to support forwarding of protocols other than TCP/IP. Because of this, label switching within the network is performed the same regardless of the layer 3 protocol. In larger networks, the result of MPLS labeling is that only the edge routers perform a routing lookup. All the core routers forward packets based on the labels, which makes forwarding the packets through the service provider network faster. (Most companies are replacing their Frame Relay networks with MPLS today).

ATM   Asynchronous Transfer Mode (ATM) was created for time-sensitive traffic, providing simultaneous transmission of voice, video, and data. ATM uses cells that are a fixed 53 bytes long instead of packets. It also can use isochronous clocking (external clocking) to help the data move faster. Typically, if you are running Frame Relay today, you will be running Frame Relay over ATM.

Exam Essentials

Know the differences among leased lines, circuit switching, and packet switching. A leased line is a dedicated connection, a circuit switched connection is like a phone call and can be on or off, and packet switching is essentially a connection that looks like a leased line but is priced more like a circuit-switched connection.

Understand the different WAN protocols. Pay particular attention to HDLC, Frame Relay, and PPP. HDLC is the default encapsulation on Cisco routers, PPP provides an industry-standard way of encapsulating multiple routed protocols across a link and must be used when connecting equipment from multiple vendors. Frame relay is a packet-switched technology that can offer cost advantages over leased lines but has more complex configuration options.

Review Questions

1. Which of the following allows a router to respond to an ARP request that is intended for a remote host?

    A. Gateway DP

    B. Reverse ARP (RARP)

    C. Proxy ARP

    D. Inverse ARP (IARP)

    E. Address Resolution Protocol (ARP)

2. You want to implement a mechanism that automates the IP configuration, including IP address, subnet mask, default gateway, and DNS information. Which protocol will you use to accomplish this?

    A. SMTP

    B. SNMP

    C. DHCP

    D. ARP

3. Which class of IP address provides a maximum of only 254 host addresses per network ID?

    A. Class A

    B. Class B

    C. Class C

    D. Class D

    E. Class E

4. Which of the following describe the DHCP Discover message? (Choose two.)

    A. It uses FF:FF:FF:FF:FF:FF as a layer 2 broadcast.

    B. It uses UDP as the Transport layer protocol.

    C. It uses TCP as the Transport layer protocol.

    D. It does not use a layer 2 destination address.

5. What are two charcterisitics of Telnet (choose 2)?

    A. It send data in clear text format

    B. It is a protocol designed and used only by Cisco routers

    C. It is more secure then using Secure Shell (SSH)

    D. You must purchase Telnet from Microsoft

    E. It requires the destiatnion device be confiugre to support Telnet services and connections

6. Which of the following services use UDP? (Choose three.)

    A. DHCP

    B. SMTP

    C. SNMP

    D. FTP

    E. HTTP

    F. TFTP

7. Which of the following are TCP/IP protocols used at the Application layer of the OSI model? (Choose three.)

    A. IP

    B. TCP

    C. Telnet

    D. FTP

    E. TFTP

8. When data is encapsulated, which is the correct order?

    A. Data, frame, packet, segment, bit

    B. Segment, data, packet, frame, bit

    C. Data, segment, packet, frame, bit

    D. Data, segment, frame, packet, bit

9. Which two statements about a reliable connection-oriented data transfer are true?

    A. Receiving hosts acknowledge receipt of data.

    B. When buffers are full, packets are discarded and are not retransmitted.

    C. Windowing is used to provide flow control and unacknowledged data segments.[

    D. If the transmitting host's timer expires before receipt of an acknowledgment, the transmitting host drops the virtual circuit.

10. Which of the following describe router functions? (Choose four.)

    A. Packet switching

    B. Collision prevention

    C. Packet filtering

    D. Broadcast domain enlargement

    E. Internetwork communication

    F. Broadcast forwarding

    G. Path selection

Answers to Review Questions

1. C. Proxy ARP can help machines on a subnet reach remote subnets without configuring routing or a default gateway.

2. C. Dynamic Host Configuration Protocol (DHCP) is used to provide IP information to hosts on your network. DHCP can provide a lot of information, but the most common is IP address, subnet mask, default gateway, and DNS information.

3. C. A Class C network address has only 8 bits for defining hosts: $2^8 - 2 = 254$.

4. A, B. A client that sends out a DHCP Discover message in order to receive an IP address sends out a broadcast at both layer 2 and layer 3. The layer 2 broadcast is all *F*s in hex, or FF:FF:FF:FF:FF:FF. The layer 3 broadcast is 255.255.255.255, which means all networks and all hosts. DHCP is connectionless, which means it uses User Datagram Protocol (UDP) at the Transport layer, also called the Host-to-Host layer.

5. A, E. Telnet has been around as long as networking and there is no cost to implement Telnet services on your network. However, all data is sent in a clear text format and both the sending and receiving devices must have telnet services running.

6. A, C, F. DHCP, SNMP, and TFTP use UDP. SMTP, FTP, and HTTP use TCP.

7. C, D, E. Telnet, File Transfer Protocol (FTP), and Trivial FTP (TFTP) are all Application layer protocols. IP is a Network layer protocol. Transmission Control Protocol (TCP) is a Transport layer protocol.

8. C. The encapsulation method is data, segment, packet, frame, bit.

9. A, C. When a virtual circuit is created, windowing is used for flow control and acknowledgment of data.

10. A, C, E, G. Routers provide packet switching, packet filtering, internetwork communication, and path selection.

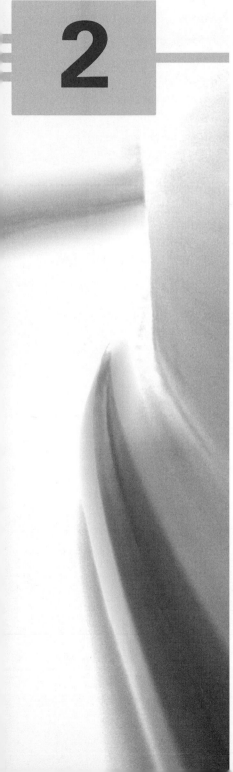

Chapter

2

Configure, verify, and troubleshoot a switch with VLANs and interswitch communications

THE CISCO CCNA EXAM OBJECTIVES COVERED IN THIS CHAPTER INCLUDE:

- 2.1 Select the appropriate media, cables, ports, and connectors to connect switches to other network devices and hosts

- 2.2 Explain the technology and media access control method for Ethernet networks

- 2.3 Explain network segmentation and basic traffic management concepts

- 2.4 Explain basic switching concepts and the operation of Cisco switches

- 2.5 Perform and verify initial switch configuration tasks, including remote access management

- 2.6 Verify network status and switch operation using basic utilities (including: ping, traceroute, Telnet, SSH, arp, ipconfig), SHOW & DEBUG commands

- 2.7 Identify, prescribe, and resolve common switched network media issues, configuration issues, auto negotiation, and switch hardware failures

- 2.8 Describe enhanced switching technologies (including VTP, RSTP, VLAN, PVSTP, 802.1q)

- 2.9 Describe how VLANs create logically separate networks and the need for routing between them

- 2.10 Configure, verify, and troubleshoot VLANs
- 2.11 Configure, verify, and troubleshoot trunking on Cisco switches
- 2.12 Configure, verify, and troubleshoot interVLAN routing
- 2.13 Configure, verify, and troubleshoot VTP
- 2.14 Configure, verify, and troubleshoot RSTP operation
- 2.15 Interpret the output of various show and debug commands to verify the operational status of a Cisco switched network
- 2.16 Implement basic switch security (including: port security, trunk access, management vlan other than vlan1, etc.)

When folks at Cisco discuss switching, they're talking about layer 2 switching unless they say otherwise. *Layer 2 switching* is the process of using the hardware address of devices on a LAN to segment a network. Since you've got the basic ideas down, I'm now going to focus on the particulars of layer 2 switching and nail down how it works.

You know that switching breaks up large collision domains into smaller ones and that a collision domain is a network segment with two or more devices sharing the same bandwidth. A hub network is a typical example of this type of technology. But since each port on a switch is actually its own collision domain, you can make a much better Ethernet LAN network just by replacing your hubs with switches!

Switches truly have changed the way networks are designed and implemented. If a pure switched design is properly implemented, it absolutely will result in a clean, cost-effective, and resilient internetwork. In this chapter, we'll survey and compare how networks were designed before and after switching technologies were introduced.

In contrast to the networks of yesterday that were based on collapsed backbones, today's network design is characterized by a flatter architecture—thanks to switches. So now what? How do we break up broadcast domains in a pure switched internetwork? By creating a virtual local area network (VLAN). A *VLAN* is a logical grouping of network users and resources connected to administratively defined ports on a switch. When you create VLANs, you're given the ability to create smaller broadcast domains within a layer 2 switched internetwork by assigning different ports on the switch to different subnetworks. A VLAN is treated like its own subnet or broadcast domain, meaning that frames broadcast onto the network are only switched between the ports logically grouped within the same VLAN.

So, does this mean we no longer need routers? Maybe yes; maybe no. It really depends on what you want or what your needs are. By default, hosts in a specific VLAN cannot communicate with hosts that are members of another VLAN, so if you want inter-VLAN communication, the answer is that you still need a router.

In this chapter, you're going to learn, in detail, exactly what a VLAN is and how VLAN memberships are used in a switched network. Also, I'm going to tell you all about how VLAN Trunk Protocol (VTP) is used to update switch databases with VLAN information and how trunking is used to send information from all VLANs across a single link. I'll wrap things up by demonstrating how you can make inter-VLAN communication happen by introducing a router into a switched network.

For up-to-the-minute updates on the CCNA objectives covered by this chapter, please see www.lammle.com and/or www.sybex.com.

2.1 Select the appropriate media, cables, ports, and connectors to connect switches to other network devices and hosts

Ethernet cabling is an important discussion, especially if you are planning on taking the Cisco exams. Three types of Ethernet cables are available:

- Straight-through cable
- Crossover cable
- Rolled cable

We will look at each in the following sections.

Straight-Through Cable

The *straight-through cable* is used to connect

- Host to switch or hub
- Router to switch or hub

Four wires are used in straight-through cable to connect Ethernet devices. It is relatively simple to create this type; Figure 2.1 shows the four wires used in a straight-through Ethernet cable.

FIGURE 2.1   Straight-through Ethernet cable

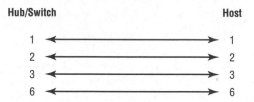

Notice that only pins 1, 2, 3, and 6 are used. Just connect 1 to 1, 2 to 2, 3 to 3, and 6 to 6, and you'll be up and networking in no time. However, remember that this would be an Ethernet-only cable and wouldn't work with voice, Token Ring, ISDN, and so on.

Crossover Cable

The *crossover cable* can be used to connect

- Switch to switch
- Hub to hub

- Host to host
- Hub to switch
- Router direct to host

The same four wires are used in this cable as in the straight-through cable; we just connect different pins together. Figure 2.2 shows how the four wires are used in a crossover Ethernet cable.

Notice that instead of connecting 1 to 1, 2 to 2, and so on, here we connect pins 1 to 3 and 2 to 6 on each side of the cable.

FIGURE 2.2   Crossover Ethernet cable

Rolled Cable

Although *rolled cable* isn't used to connect any Ethernet connections, you can use a rolled Ethernet cable to connect a host to a router console serial communication (com) port.

If you have a Cisco router or switch, you would use this cable to connect your PC running HyperTerminal to the Cisco hardware. Eight wires are used in this cable to connect serial devices, although not all eight are used to send information, just as in Ethernet networking. Figure 2.3 shows the eight wires used in a rolled cable.

These are probably the easiest cables to make because you just cut the end off on one side of a straight-through cable, turn it over, and put it back on (with a new connector, of course).

FIGURE 2.3   Rolled Ethernet cable

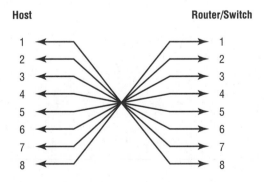

Once you have the correct cable connected from your PC to the Cisco router or switch, you can start HyperTerminal to create a console connection and configure the device. Set the configuration as follows:

1. Open HyperTerminal and enter a name for the connection. It is irrelevant what you name it, but I always just use Cisco. Then click OK.

2. Choose the communications port—either COM1 or COM2, whichever is open on your PC.

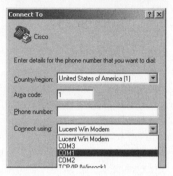

3. Now set the port settings. The default values (2400bps and no flow control hardware) will not work; you must set the port settings as shown in Figure 2.4.

FIGURE 2.4   Port settings for a rolled cable connection

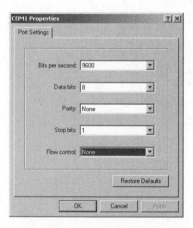

Notice that the bit rate is now set to 9600 and the flow control is set to None. At this point, you can click OK and press the Enter key and you should be connected to your Cisco device console port.

We've taken a look at the various RJ45 unshielded twisted pair (UTP) cables. Keeping this in mind, what cable is used between the switches in Figure 2.5?

FIGURE 2.5   RJ45 UTP cable question #1

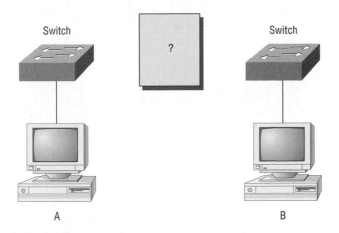

In order for host A to ping host B, you need a crossover cable to connect the two switches. But what types of cables are used in the network shown in Figure 2.6?

FIGURE 2.6   RJ45 UTP cable question #2

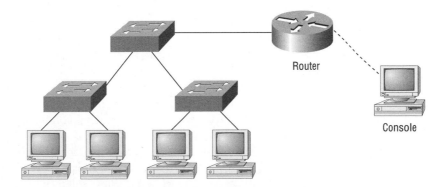

In Figure 2.6, there are a variety of cables in use. For the connection between the switches, we'd obviously use a crossover cable as you saw in Figure 2.2. The trouble is, we have a console connection that uses a rolled cable. Plus, the connection from the router to the switch is a straight-through cable, as is true for the hosts to the switches. Keep in mind that if we had a serial connection (which we don't), it would be a V.35 that we'd use to connect us to a WAN.

Exam Objectives

Remember the types of Ethernet cabling and when you would use them. The three types of cables that can be created from an Ethernet cable are straight-through (to connect a PC's or a router's Ethernet interface to a hub or switch), crossover (to connect hub to hub, hub to switch, switch to switch, or PC to PC), and rolled (for a console connection from a PC to a router or switch).

Understand how to connect a console cable from a PC to a router and start HyperTerminal. Take a rolled cable and connect it from the COM port of the host to the console port of a router. Start HyperTerminal, and set the BPS to 9600 and flow control to None.

2.2 Explain the technology and media access control method for Ethernet networks

Ethernet is a contention media access method that allows all hosts on a network to share the same bandwidth of a link. Ethernet is popular because it's readily scalable, meaning that it's comparatively easy to integrate new technologies, such as Fast Ethernet and Gigabit Ethernet, into an existing network infrastructure. It's also relatively simple to implement in the first place, and with it, troubleshooting is reasonably straightforward. Ethernet uses both Data Link and Physical layer specifications, and this section of the chapter will give you both the Data Link layer and Physical layer information you need to effectively implement, trouble-shoot, and maintain an Ethernet network.

Ethernet networking uses *Carrier Sense Multiple Access with Collision Detection (CSMA/CD)*, a protocol that helps devices share the bandwidth evenly without having two devices transmit at the same time on the network medium. CSMA/CD was created to overcome the problem of those collisions that occur when packets are transmitted simultaneously from different nodes. And trust me—good collision management is crucial, because when a node transmits in a CSMA/CD network, all the other nodes on the network receive and examine that transmission. Only bridges and routers can effectively prevent a transmission from propagating throughout the entire network!

So, how does the CSMA/CD protocol work? Let's start by taking a look at Figure 2.7.

When a host wants to transmit over the network, it first checks for the presence of a digital signal on the wire. If all is clear (no other host is transmitting), the host will then proceed with its transmission. But it doesn't stop there. The transmitting host constantly monitors the wire to make sure no other hosts begin transmitting. If the host detects another signal on the wire, it sends out an extended jam signal that causes all nodes on the segment to stop sending data (think busy signal). The nodes respond to that jam signal by waiting a while before attempting to transmit again. Backoff algorithms determine when the colliding stations can retransmit. If collisions keep occurring after 15 tries, the nodes attempting to transmit will then timeout. Pretty clean!

FIGURE 2.7   CSMA/CD

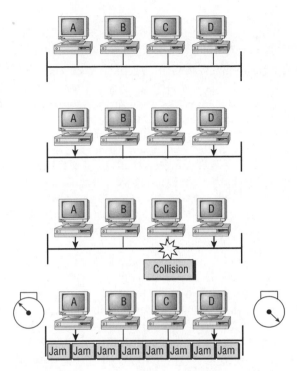

Carrier Sense Multiple Access with Collision Detection (CSMA/CD)

When a collision occurs on an Ethernet LAN, the following happens:

- A jam signal informs all devices that a collision occurred.
- The collision invokes a random backoff algorithm.
- Each device on the Ethernet segment stops transmitting for a short time until the timers expire.
- All hosts have equal priority to transmit after the timers have expired.

The following are the effects of having a CSMA/CD network sustaining heavy collisions:

- Delay
- Low throughput
- Congestion

Backoff on an 802.3 network is the retransmission delay that's enforced when a collision occurs. When a collision occurs, a host will resume transmission after the forced time delay has expired. After this backoff delay period has expired, all stations have equal priority to transmit data.

In the following sections, I am going to cover Ethernet in detail at both the Data Link layer (layer 2) and the Physical layer (layer 1).

Half- and Full-Duplex Ethernet

Half-duplex Ethernet is defined in the original 802.3 Ethernet; Cisco says it uses only one wire pair with a digital signal running in both directions on the wire. Certainly, the IEEE specifications discuss the process of half-duplex somewhat differently, but what Cisco is talking about is a general sense of what is happening here with Ethernet.

It also uses the CSMA/CD protocol to help prevent collisions and to permit retransmitting if a collision does occur. If a hub is attached to a switch, it must operate in half-duplex mode because the end stations must be able to detect collisions. Half-duplex Ethernet—typically 10BaseT—is only about 30 to 40 percent efficient as Cisco sees it because a large 10BaseT network will usually only give you 3 to 4Mbps, at most.

But *full-duplex Ethernet* uses two pairs of wires instead of one wire pair like half-duplex. And full-duplex uses a point-to-point connection between the transmitter of the transmitting device and the receiver of the receiving device. This means that with full-duplex data transfer, you get a faster data transfer compared to half-duplex. And because the transmitted data is sent on a different set of wires than the received data, no collisions will occur.

The reason you don't need to worry about collisions is that now it's like there is a freeway with multiple lanes instead of the single-lane road provided by half-duplex. Full-duplex Ethernet is supposed to offer 100 percent efficiency in both directions—for example, you can get 20Mbps with a 10Mbps Ethernet running full-duplex or 200Mbps for Fast Ethernet. But this rate is something known as an *aggregate rate*, which translates as "you're supposed to get" 100 percent efficiency. No guarantees, in networking as in life.

Full-duplex Ethernet can be used in three situations:

- With a connection from a switch to a host

- With a connection from a switch to a switch

- With a connection from a host to a host using a crossover cable

Full-duplex Ethernet requires a point-to-point connection when only two nodes are present. You can run full-duplex with just about any device except a hub.

Now, if it's capable of all that speed, why wouldn't it deliver? Well, when a full-duplex Ethernet port is powered on, it first connects to the remote end and then negotiates with the other end of the Fast Ethernet link. This is called an *auto-detect mechanism*. This mechanism first decides on the exchange capability, which means that it checks to see if it can run at 10 or 100Mbps. It then checks to see if it can run full-duplex, and if it can't, it will run half-duplex.

Remember that half-duplex Ethernet shares a collision domain and provides a lower effective throughput than full-duplex Ethernet, which typically has a private collision domain and a higher effective throughput.

Last, remember these important points:

- There are no collisions in full-duplex mode.
- A dedicated switch port is required for each full-duplex node.
- The host network card and the switch port must be capable of operating in full-duplex mode.

Now let's take a look at how Ethernet works at the Data Link layer.

Ethernet at the Data Link Layer

Ethernet at the Data Link layer is responsible for Ethernet addressing, commonly referred to as hardware addressing or MAC addressing. Ethernet is also responsible for framing packets received from the Network layer and preparing them for transmission on the local network through the Ethernet contention media access method.

Ethernet Addressing

Here's where we get into how Ethernet addressing works. It uses the *Media Access Control (MAC) address* burned into each and every Ethernet network interface card (NIC). The MAC, or hardware, address is a 48-bit (6-byte) address written in a hexadecimal format.

Figure 2.8 shows the 48-bit MAC addresses and how the bits are divided.

FIGURE 2.8　　Ethernet addressing using MAC addresses

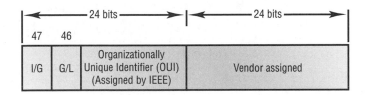

The *organizationally unique identifier (OUI)* is assigned by the IEEE to an organization. It's composed of 24 bits, or 3 bytes. The organization, in turn, assigns a globally administered address (24 bits, or 3 bytes) that is unique (supposedly, again—no guarantees) to each and every adapter it manufactures. Look closely at the figure. The high-order bit is the Individual/Group (I/G) bit. When it has a value of 0, we can assume that the address is the MAC address of a device and may well appear in the source portion of the MAC header. When it is a 1, we can assume that the address represents either a broadcast or multicast address in Ethernet or a broadcast or functional address in TR and FDDI (who really knows about FDDI?).

The next bit is the global/local bit, or just G/L bit (also known as U/L, where U means *universal*).When set to 0, this bit represents a globally administered address (as by the IEEE). When the bit is a 1, it represents a locally governed and administered address (as in what DECnet used to do). The low-order 24 bits of an Ethernet address represent a locally administered or manufacturer-assigned code. This portion commonly starts with 24 0s for the first card made and continues in order until there are twenty-four 1s for the last (16,777,216th) card made. You'll find that many manufacturers use these same six hex digits as the last six characters of their serial number on the same card.

Ethernet Frames

The Data Link layer is responsible for combining bits into bytes and bytes into frames. Frames are used at the Data Link layer to encapsulate packets handed down from the Network layer for transmission on a type of media access.

The function of Ethernet stations is to pass data frames between each other using a group of bits known as a *MAC frame format*. This provides error detection from a cyclic redundancy check (CRC). But remember—this is error detection, not error correction. The 802.3 frames and Ethernet frame are shown in Figure 2.9.

 Encapsulating a frame within a different type of frame is called *tunneling*.

FIGURE 2.9   802.3 and Ethernet frame formats

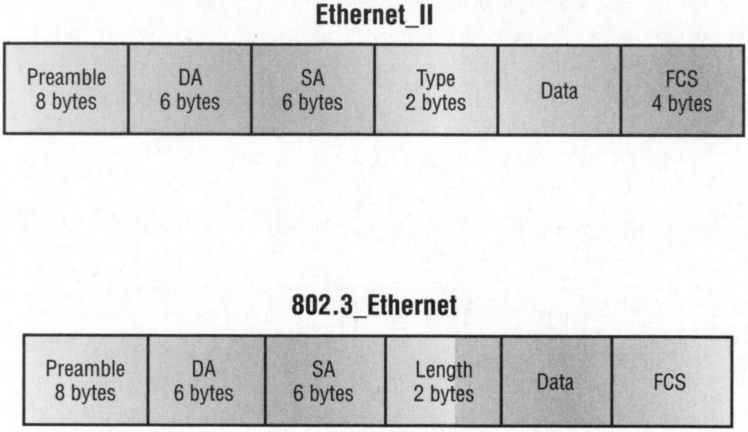

Ethernet_II

Preamble 8 bytes	DA 6 bytes	SA 6 bytes	Type 2 bytes	Data	FCS 4 bytes

802.3_Ethernet

Preamble 8 bytes	DA 6 bytes	SA 6 bytes	Length 2 bytes	Data	FCS

Following are the details of the different fields in the 802.3 and Ethernet frame types:

Preamble   An alternating 1,0 pattern provides a 5MHz clock at the start of each packet, which allows the receiving devices to lock the incoming bit stream.

Start Frame Delimiter (SFD)/Synch   The preamble is seven octets, and the SFD is one octet (synch). The SFD is 10101011, where the last pair of 1s allows the receiver to come into the alternating 1,0 pattern somewhere in the middle and still sync up and detect the beginning of the data.

Destination Address (DA)   This transmits a 48-bit value using the least significant bit (LSB) first. The DA is used by receiving stations to determine whether an incoming packet is addressed to a particular node. The destination address can be an individual address or a broadcast or multicast MAC address. Remember that a broadcast is all 1s (or Fs in hex) and is sent to all devices but a multicast is sent only to a similar subset of nodes on a network.

Source Address (SA)   The SA is a 48-bit MAC address used to identify the transmitting device, and it uses the LSB first. Broadcast and multicast address formats are illegal within the SA field.

Length or Type   802.3 uses a Length field, but the Ethernet frame uses a Type field to identify the Network layer protocol. 802.3 cannot identify the upper-layer protocol and must be used with a proprietary LAN—IPX, for example.

Data   This is a packet sent down to the Data Link layer from the Network layer. The size can vary from 64 to 1500 bytes.

Frame Check Sequence (FCS)   FCS is a field at the end of the frame that's used to store the CRC.

Let's pause here for a minute and take a look at some frames caught on our trusty OmniPeek network analyzer. You can see that the frame below has only three fields: Destination, Source, and Type (shown as Protocol Type on this analyzer):

```
Destination:   00:60:f5:00:1f:27
Source:        00:60:f5:00:1f:2c
Protocol Type: 08-00 IP
```

This is an Ethernet_II frame. Notice that the type field is IP, or 08-00 (mostly just referred to as 0x800) in hexadecimal.

The next frame has the same fields, so it must be an Ethernet_II frame too:

```
Destination:   ff:ff:ff:ff:ff:ff Ethernet Broadcast
Source:        02:07:01:22:de:a4
Protocol Type: 08-00 IP
```

Did you notice that this frame was a broadcast? You can tell because the destination hardware address is all 1s in binary, or all *F*s in hexadecimal.

Let's take a look at one more Ethernet_II frame. You can see that the Ethernet frame is the same Ethernet_II frame we use with the IPv4 routed protocol, but the type field has 0x86dd when we are carrying IPv6 data, and when we have IPv4 data, we use 0x0800 in the protocol field:

```
Destination: IPv6-Neighbor-Discovery_00:01:00:03 (33:33:00:01:00:03)
Source: Aopen_3e:7f:dd (00:01:80:3e:7f:dd)
Type: IPv6 (0x86dd)
```

This is the beauty of the Ethernet_II frame. Because of the protocol field, we can run any Network layer routed protocol, and it will carry the data because it can identify the Network layer protocol.

Ethernet at the Physical Layer

Ethernet was first implemented by a group called *DIX* (Digital, Intel, and Xerox). They created and implemented the first Ethernet LAN specification, which the IEEE used to create the

IEEE 802.3 Committee. This was a 10Mbps network that ran on coax and then eventually twisted-pair and fiber physical media.

The IEEE extended the 802.3 Committee to two new committees known as 802.3u (Fast Ethernet) and 802.3ab (Gigabit Ethernet on category 5) and then finally 802.3ae (10Gbps over fiber and coax).

Figure 2.10 shows the IEEE 802.3 and original Ethernet Physical layer specifications.

FIGURE 2.10   Ethernet Physical layer specifications

Data Link (MAC layer)	Ethernet	802.3						
Physical		10Base2	10Base5	10BaseT	10BaseF	100BaseTX	100BaseFX	100BaseT4

When designing your LAN, it's really important to understand the different types of Ethernet media available to you. Sure, it would be great to run Gigabit Ethernet to each desktop and 10Gbps between switches, and although this might happen one day, justifying the cost of that network today would be pretty difficult. But if you mix and match the different types of Ethernet media methods currently available, you can come up with a cost-effective network solution that works great.

The EIA/TIA (Electronic Industries Association and the newer Telecommunications Industry Alliance) is the standards body that creates the Physical layer specifications for Ethernet. The EIA/TIA specifies that Ethernet use a *registered jack (RJ) connector* with a 4 5 wiring sequence on *unshielded twisted-pair (UTP)* cabling (RJ45). However, the industry is moving toward calling this just an 8-pin modular connector.

Each Ethernet cable type that is specified by the EIA/TIA has inherent attenuation, which is defined as the loss of signal strength as it travels the length of a cable and is measured in decibels (dB). The cabling used in corporate and home markets is measured in categories. A higher-quality cable will have a higher-rated category and lower attenuation. For example, category 5 is better than category 3 because category 5 cables have more wire twists per foot and therefore less crosstalk. Crosstalk is the unwanted signal interference from adjacent pairs in the cable.

Here are the original IEEE 802.3 standards:

10Base2   10Mbps, baseband technology, up to 185 meters in length. Known as *thinnet* and can support up to 30 workstations on a single segment. Uses a physical and logical bus with AUI connectors. The 10 means 10Mbps, *Base* means baseband technology (which is a signaling method for communication on the network), and the 2 means almost 200 meters. 10Base2 Ethernet cards use BNC (British Naval Connector, Bayonet Neill Concelman, or Bayonet Nut Connector) and T-connectors to connect to a network.

10Base5   10Mbps, baseband technology, up to 500 meters in length. Known as *thicknet*. Uses a physical and logical bus with AUI connectors. Up to 2,500 meters with repeaters and 1,024 users for all segments.

10BaseT   10Mbps using category 3 UTP wiring. Unlike with the 10Base2 and 10Base5 networks, each device must connect into a hub or switch, and you can have only one host per segment or wire. Uses an RJ45 connector (8-pin modular connector) with a physical star topology and a logical bus.

Each of the 802.3 standards defines an Attachment Unit Interface (AUI), which allows a one-bit-at-a-time transfer to the Physical layer from the Data Link media access method. This allows the MAC to remain constant but means that the Physical layer can support any existing and new technologies. The original AUI interface was a 15-pin connector, which allowed a transceiver (transmitter/receiver) that provided a 15-pin-to-twisted-pair conversion.

The thing is, the AUI interface cannot support 100Mbps Ethernet because of the high frequencies involved. So, 100BaseT needed a new interface, and the 802.3u specifications created one called the Media Independent Interface (MII), which provides 100Mbps throughput. The MII uses a *nibble*, defined as 4 bits. Gigabit Ethernet uses a Gigabit Media Independent Interface (GMII) and transmits 8 bits at a time.

802.3u (Fast Ethernet) is compatible with 802.3 Ethernet because they share the same physical characteristics. Fast Ethernet and Ethernet use the same maximum transmission unit (MTU), use the same MAC mechanisms, and preserve the frame format that is used by 10BaseT Ethernet. Basically, Fast Ethernet is just based on an extension to the IEEE 802.3 specification, except that it offers a speed increase of 10 times that of 10BaseT.

Here are the expanded IEEE Ethernet 802.3 standards:

100BaseTX (IEEE 802.3u)   EIA/TIA category 5, 6, or 7 UTP two-pair wiring. One user per segment; up to 100 meters long. It uses an RJ45 connector with a physical star topology and a logical bus.

100BaseFX (IEEE 802.3u)   Uses fiber cabling 62.5/125-micron multimode fiber. Point-to-point topology; up to 412 meters long. It uses an ST or SC connector, which are media-interface connectors.

1000BaseCX (IEEE 802.3z)   Copper twisted-pair called *twinax* (a balanced coaxial pair) that can only run up to 25 meters.

1000BaseT (IEEE 802.3ab)   Category 5, four-pair UTP wiring up to 100 meters long.

1000BaseSX (IEEE 802.3z)   MMF using 62.5- and 50-micron core; uses an 850 nanometer laser and can go up to 220 meters with 62.5 micron, 550 meters with 50 micron.

1000BaseLX (IEEE 802.3z)   Single-mode fiber that uses a 9-micron core and 1300 nanometer laser and can go from 3 kilometers up to 10 kilometers.

 If you want to implement a network medium that is not susceptible to electromagnetic interference (EMI), fiber-optic cable provides a more secure, long-distance cable that is not susceptible to EMI at high speeds.

Exam Objectives

Remember the length and expression of a hardware address.   A hardware address, also called a MAC address, is 48 bits long, expressed in hexadecimal.

Understand half-duplex technology.   Half-duplex only uses one wire pair at a time to both transmit and receive. Hubs can only run half-duplex.

Understand full-duplex technology   Full-duplex devices use both wire pairs, so they can both transmit and receive at the same time. Hubs cannot run full-duplex. You must have a switch to run full-duplex on your PC.

Understand Ethernet Addressing   Ethernet uses hardware addresses, also called MAC addresses or burned in addresses. They are 6-bytes, represented in hexadecimal.

2.3 Explain network segmentation and basic traffic management concepts

There are a number of interchangeable terms we can use for "LAN," depending on the context. They include:

- Broadcast domain (in the context of layer 2 vs. layer 1 segmentation)
- Subnet or network (in the context of IP networking)
- Data Link (layer 2 in the OSI model)
- VLAN (in the context of creating broadcast domains in switched Ethernet environments)

As was mentioned, these terms are roughly equivalent. They are used to describe the simple LAN in different contexts. Why discuss a simple LAN? Well, it is the basis of every internetwork. An internetwork is simply a collection of connected LANs. An individual LAN is created using a variety of devices and techniques, such as. These devices connect the hosts on the single LAN to each other, and connect the LAN to the other LANs forming the internetwork.

Networks and networking have grown exponentially over the last 15 years—understandably so. They've had to evolve at light speed just to keep up with huge increases in basic mission-critical user needs like sharing data and printers, as well as more advanced demands like video conferencing. Unless everyone who needs to share network resources is located in the same office area (an increasingly uncommon situation), the challenge is to connect the relevant and sometimes many networks together so that all users can share the networks' wealth.

It's likely that at some point, you'll have to break up one large network into a number of smaller ones because user response has dwindled to a trickle as networks have grown and grown and LAN traffic congestion reached overwhelming proportions. Congestion is a really big problem. Some possible causes of LAN traffic congestion are:

- Too many hosts in a broadcast domain
- Broadcast storms

- Multicasting
- Low bandwidth

You can help solve the congestion issue by breaking up a larger network into a number of smaller (otherwise known as *network segmentation)*. Network segmentation is accomplished using *routers, switches,* and *bridges.*

Routers

Routers are used to connect networks together and route packets of data from one network to another. Cisco became the de facto standard of routers because of their high-quality router products, great selection, and fantastic service. Routers, by default, break up a *broadcast domain,* which is the set of all devices on a network segment that hear all broadcasts sent on that segment. Breaking up a broadcast domain is important because when a host or server sends a network broadcast, every device on the network must read and process that broadcast—unless you've got a router. When the router's interface receives this broadcast, it can respond by basically saying "Thanks, but no thanks," and discard the broadcast without forwarding it on to other networks. Even though routers are known for breaking up broadcast domains by default, it's important to remember that they also break up collision domains as well.

Two advantages of using routers in your network:

They don't forward broadcasts by default

They can filter the network based on layer-3 information (i.e., IP address)

Switches

Conversely, switches aren't used to create internetworks; they're employed to add functionality to a LAN. The main purpose of a switch is to make a LAN work better—to optimize its performance—providing more bandwidth for the LAN's users. And switches don't forward packets to other networks like routers do. Instead, they only "switch" frames from one port to another within the switched network.

By default, switches break up *collision domains.* This is an Ethernet term used to describe a network scenario wherein one particular device sends a packet on a network segment, forcing every other device on that same segment to pay attention to it. At the same time, a different device tries to transmit, leading to a collision, after which both devices must retransmit, one at a time. Not good—very inefficient! This situation is typically found in a hub environment where each host segment connects to a hub that represents only one collision domain and only one broadcast domain. By contrast, each and every port on a switch represents its own collision domain.

 Switches create separate collision domains, but a single broadcast domain. Routers separate broadcast domains.

Bridges

The term *bridging* was introduced before routers and hubs were implemented, so it's pretty common to hear people referring to bridges as "switches." That's because bridges and switches basically do the same thing—break up collision domains on a LAN. So, what this means is that a switch is basically just a multiple port bridge with more brainpower, right? Well, pretty much, but there are differences. Switches do provide this function, but they do so with greatly enhanced management ability and features. Plus, most of the time, bridges only had two or four ports. Yes, you could get your hands on a bridge with up to 16 ports, but that's nothing compared to the hundreds available on some switches!

> You would use a bridge in a network to reduce collisions within broadcast domains and to increase the number of collision domains in your network, which provides more bandwidth for users.

Exam Objectives

Understand the different terms used to describe a LAN   A LAN is basically the same thing as a VLAN, subnet or network, broadcast domain, or data link. These terms all describe roughly the same concept in a different context.

Understand which devices create a LAN and which separate and connect LANs.   Switches and bridges are used to create LANs. While they do separate collision domains, they do not create separate LANs (collision domain and LAN are not the same concept). Routers are used to separate LANs and connect LANs (broadcast domains).

2.4 Explain basic switching concepts and the operation of Cisco switches

Unlike bridges, which use software to create and manage a filter table, switches use application-specific integrated circuits (ASICs) to build and maintain their filter tables. But it's still okay to think of a layer 2 switch as a multiport bridge because their basic reason for being is the same: to break up collision domains.

Layer 2 switches and bridges are faster than routers because they don't take up time looking at the Network layer header information. Instead, they look at the frame's hardware addresses before deciding to either forward, flood, or drop the frame.

Switches create private, dedicated collision domains and provide independent bandwidth on each port, unlike hubs. Figure 2.11 shows five hosts connected to a switch—all running 10Mbps half-duplex to the server. Unlike with a hub, each host has 10Mbps dedicated communication to the server.

FIGURE 2.11   Switches create private domains.

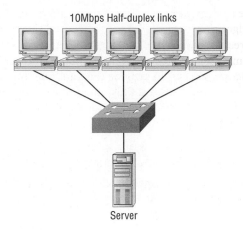

Layer 2 switching provides the following:

- Hardware-based bridging (ASIC)
- Wire speed
- Low latency
- Low cost

What makes layer 2 switching so efficient is that no modification to the data packet takes place. The device only reads the frame encapsulating the packet, which makes the switching process considerably faster and less error-prone than routing processes are.

And if you use layer 2 switching for both workgroup connectivity and network segmentation (breaking up collision domains), you can create a flatter network design with more network segments than you can with traditional routed networks.

Plus, layer 2 switching increases bandwidth for each user because, again, each connection (interface) into the switch is its own collision domain. This feature makes it possible for you to connect multiple devices to each interface.

In the following sections, I will dive deeper into the layer 2 switching technology.

Limitations of Layer 2 Switching

Since we commonly stick layer 2 switching into the same category as bridged networks, we also tend to think it has the same hang-ups and issues that bridged networks do. Keep in mind that bridges are good and helpful things if we design the network correctly, keeping their features as well as their limitations in mind. And to design well with bridges, these are the two most important considerations:

- We absolutely must break up the collision domains correctly.
- The right way to create a functional bridged network is to make sure that its users spend 80 percent of their time on the local segment.

Bridged networks break up collision domains, but remember, that network is still one large broadcast domain. Neither layer 2 switches nor bridges break up broadcast domains by default—something that not only limits your network's size and growth potential but also can reduce its overall performance.

Broadcasts and multicasts, along with the slow convergence time of spanning trees, can give you some major grief as your network grows. These are the big reasons that layer 2 switches and bridges cannot completely replace routers (layer 3 devices) in the internetwork.

Bridging vs. LAN Switching

It's true—layer 2 switches really are pretty much just bridges that give us a lot more ports, but there are some important differences you should always keep in mind:

- Bridges are software based, while switches are hardware based because they use ASIC chips to help make filtering decisions.

- A switch can be viewed as a multiport bridge.

- There can be only one spanning-tree instance per bridge, while switches can have many. (I'm going to tell you all about spanning trees in a bit.)

- Switches have a higher number of ports than most bridges.

- Both bridges and switches forward layer 2 broadcasts.

- Bridges and switches learn MAC addresses by examining the source address of each frame received.

- Both bridges and switches make forwarding decisions based on layer 2 addresses.

Three Switch Functions at Layer 2

There are three distinct functions of layer 2 switching (you need to remember these!): *address learning*, *forward/filter decisions*, and *loop avoidance*.

Address learning   Layer 2 switches and bridges remember the source hardware address of each frame received on an interface, and they enter this information into a MAC database called a *forward/filter table*.

Forward/filter decisions   When a frame is received on an interface, the switch looks at the destination hardware address and finds the exit interface in the MAC database. The frame is only forwarded out the specified destination port.

Loop avoidance   If multiple connections between switches are created for redundancy purposes, network loops can occur. Spanning Tree Protocol (STP) is used to stop network loops while still permitting redundancy.

I'm going to talk about address learning, forward/filtering decisions, and loop avoidance in detail in the next sections.

Address Learning

When a switch is first powered on, the MAC forward/filter table is empty, as shown in Figure 2.12.

FIGURE 2.12   Empty forward/filter table on a switch

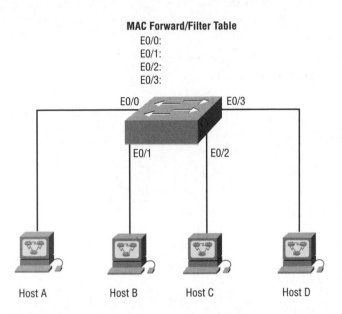

When a device transmits and an interface receives a frame, the switch places the frame's source address in the MAC forward/filter table, allowing it to remember which interface the sending device is located on. The switch then has no choice but to flood the network with this frame out of every port except the source port because it has no idea where the destination device is actually located.

If a device answers this flooded frame and sends a frame back, then the switch will take the source address from that frame and place that MAC address in its database as well, associating this address with the interface that received the frame. Since the switch now has both of the relevant MAC addresses in its filtering table, the two devices can now make a point-to-point connection. The switch doesn't need to flood the frame as it did the first time because now the frames can and will be forwarded only between the two devices. This is exactly the thing that makes layer 2 switches better than hubs. In a hub network, all frames are forwarded out all ports every time—no matter what. Figure 2.13 shows the processes involved in building a MAC database.

In this figure, you can see four hosts attached to a switch. When the switch is powered on, it has nothing in its MAC address forward/filter table, just as in Figure 8.5. But when the hosts start communicating, the switch places the source hardware address of each frame in the table along with the port that the frame's address corresponds to.

FIGURE 2.13   How switches learn hosts' locations

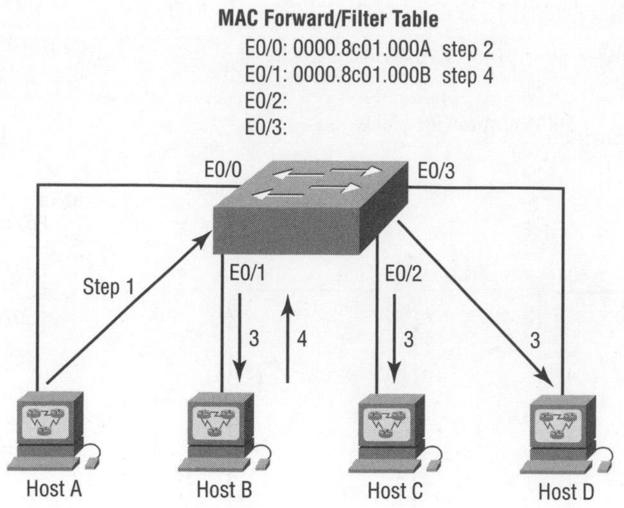

Let me give you an example of how a forward/filter table is populated:

1. Host A sends a frame to Host B. Host A's MAC address is 0000.8c01.000A; Host B's MAC address is 0000.8c01.000B.

2. The switch receives the frame on the E0/0 interface and places the source address in the MAC address table.

3. Since the destination address is not in the MAC database, the frame is forwarded out all interfaces—except the source port.

4. Host B receives the frame and responds to Host A. The switch receives this frame on interface E0/1 and places the source hardware address in the MAC database.

5. Host A and Host B can now make a point-to-point connection and only the two devices will receive the frames. Hosts C and D will not see the frames, nor are their MAC addresses found in the database because they haven't yet sent a frame to the switch.

If Host A and Host B don't communicate to the switch again within a certain amount of time, the switch will flush their entries from the database to keep it as current as possible.

Forward/Filter Decisions

When a frame arrives at a switch interface, the destination hardware address is compared to the forward/filter MAC database. If the destination hardware address is known and listed in the database, the frame is only sent out the correct exit interface. The switch doesn't transmit the frame out any interface except for the destination interface. This preserves bandwidth on the other network segments and is called *frame filtering*.

But if the destination hardware address is not listed in the MAC database, then the frame is flooded out all active interfaces except the interface the frame was received on. If a device answers the flooded frame, the MAC database is updated with the device's location (interface).

If a host or server sends a broadcast on the LAN, the switch will flood the frame out all active ports except the source port by default. Remember, the switch creates smaller collision domains, but it's still one large broadcast domain by default.

In Figure 2.14, Host A sends a data frame to Host D. What will the switch do when it receives the frame from Host A?

FIGURE 2.14   Forward/filter table

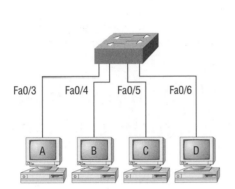

```
Switch#sh mac address-table
Vlan    Mac Address        Ports
----    -----------        -----
   1    0005.dccb.d74b     Fa0/4
   1    000a.f467.9e80     Fa0/5
   1    000a.f467.9e8b     Fa0/6
```

Fa0/3   Fa0/4   Fa0/5   Fa0/6

A   B   C   D

Since Host A's MAC address is not in the forward/filter table, the switch will add the source address and port to the MAC address table and then forward the frame to Host D. If Host D's MAC address was not in the forward/filter table, the switch would have flooded the frame out all ports except for port Fa0/3.

Now let's take a look at the output of a show mac address-table:

```
Switch#sh mac address-table
Vlan    Mac Address        Type        Ports
----    -----------        --------    -----
   1    0005.dccb.d74b     DYNAMIC     Fa0/1
   1    000a.f467.9e80     DYNAMIC     Fa0/3
   1    000a.f467.9e8b     DYNAMIC     Fa0/4
   1    000a.f467.9e8c     DYNAMIC     Fa0/3
   1    0010.7b7f.c2b0     DYNAMIC     Fa0/3
   1    0030.80dc.460b     DYNAMIC     Fa0/3
   1    0030.9492.a5dd     DYNAMIC     Fa0/1
   1    00d0.58ad.05f4     DYNAMIC     Fa0/1
```

Suppose the preceding switch received a frame with the following MAC addresses:

Source MAC: **0005.dccb.d74b**

Destination MAC: **000a.f467.9e8c**

How will the switch handle this frame? Answer: The destination MAC address will be found in the MAC address table and the frame will be forwarded out Fa0/3 only. Remember that if the destination MAC address is not found in the forward/filter table, it will forward the frame out all ports of the switch looking for the destination device.

Exam Objectives

Remember the three switch functions.   Address learning, forward/filter decisions, and loop avoidance are the functions of a switch.

Remember the command `show mac address-table`.   The command `show mac address-table` will show you the forward/filter table used on the LAN switch.

2.5 Perform and verify initial switch configuration tasks, including remote access management

Cisco Catalyst switches come in many flavors—some run 10Mbps, and some jam all the way up to 10Gbps switched ports with a combination of twisted-pair and fiber. These newer switches (specifically the 2960 and 3560's) have more intelligence, so they can give you data fast—video and voice services, too.

It's time to get down to it—I'm going to show you how to start up and configure a Cisco Catalyst switch using the command-line interface (CLI). After you get the basic commands down, I'll show you how to configure virtual LANs (VLANs) plus Inter-Switch Link (ISL), 802.1q routing, and Cisco's Virtual Trunk Protocol (VTP).

Here's a list of the basic tasks we'll be covering in this section and the rest of this chapter:

- Administrative functions
- Configuring the IP address and subnet mask
- Setting the IP default gateway
- Setting port security
- Setting PortFast
- Enabling BPDUGuard and BPDUFilter
- Enabling UplinkFast
- Enabling BackboneFast
- Enabling RSTP (802.1w)
- Enabling EtherChannel
- Configuring an STP root switch
- Using the CNA to configure a switch

You can learn all about the Cisco family of Catalyst switches at
www.cisco.com/en/US/products/hw/switches/index.html.

Catalyst Switch Configuration

Figure 2.15 shows the switched network I'll be working on to show you Cisco's Catalyst
switch configuraitons.

FIGURE 2.15   Our switched network

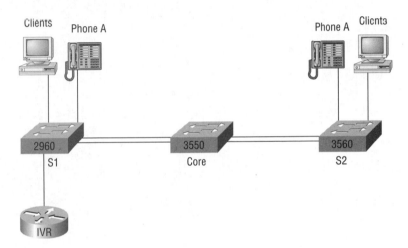

I'm going to use a new 3560, a 2960, and a 3550 switch. But before we actually get into
configuring one of the Catalyst switches, I've got to fill you in regarding the bootup process
of these switches. Figure 2.16 shows the detail of a typical Cisco Catalyst switch, and I need
to tell you about the different interfaces and features of this product.

FIGURE 2.16   A Cisco Catalyst switch

The first thing I want you to know is that the console port for the Catalyst switches are typically located on the back of the switch. But on a smaller switch, like the 3560 shown in the
figure, the console is right in the front to make it easier to use. (The eight-port 2960 looks

exactly the same.) If the POST completes successfully, the system LED turns green; if the POST fails, it will turn amber. And seeing the amber glow is a very bad thing—typically fatal. So, you may just want to keep a spare switch around—especially in case it happens to be a production switch that's croaked! The bottom button is used to show you which lights are providing Power over Ethernet (PoE). You can see this by pressing the Mode button. The PoE is a very nice feature of these switches. It allows me to power my access point and phone by just connecting them into the switch with an Ethernet cable! Sweet.

After a switch boots up, you can use the Express Setup HTTP screen. Figure 2.17 shows the screen you'll get when you connect to a new switch and use 10.0.0.1 in the HTTP field of your browser. Oh, and obviously your host needs to be in the same subnet.

FIGURE 2.17   Express Setup HTTP screen

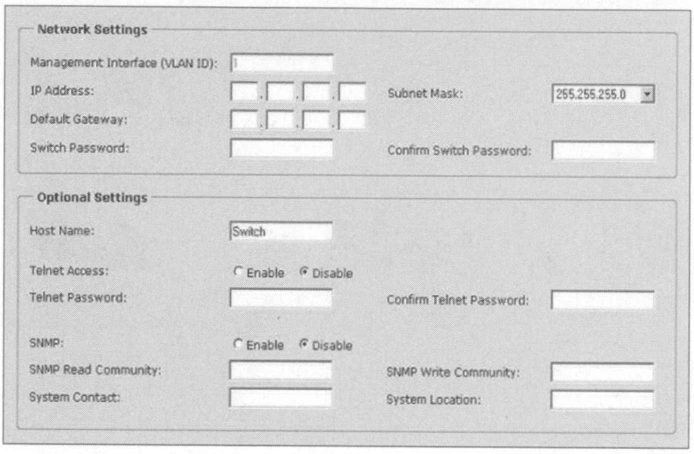

The screen shows us that we can set some basic functions. To me, it's easier to configure the information from the CLI, which I'll show you next, but this is actually just one of your options. You can configure the IP address, mask, and default gateway of the switch, plus the passwords. You can also configure the management VLAN, but I'm going to hold off on that for now and show you how to do that in the next chapter. Moving on, optionally, you can configure the hostname, system contact, and location and set up Telnet access. And last, the Express Setup HTTP screen provides you with some simple help on setting the switch up with SNMP so that your Network Management System (NMS) can find it.

Now if we connect our switches to each other, as shown in Figure 2.15, remember that first we'll need a crossover cable between the switches. My 2960 and 3560 switches autodetect the connection type, so I was able to use straight-through cables. But a 2950 or 3550 switch won't auto-detect the cable type. Different switches have different needs and abilities, so just keep this in mind when connecting your various switches together.

When you first connect the switch ports to each other, the link lights are amber and then turn green indicating normal operation. This is spanning-tree converging, and as you already know, this process takes around 50 seconds with no extensions enabled. But if you connect into a switch port and the switch port LED is alternating green and amber, this means the port is experiencing errors. If this happens, check the host NIC or the cabling.

Okay—let's start our configuration by connecting into a switch and setting the administrative functions. We'll also assign an IP address to theswitch, but this isn't really necessary to make our network function. The only reason we're going to do that is so we can manage/administer it. Let's use a simple IP scheme like 192.168.10.16/28. This mask should be familiar to you!

Check out the following output:

```
Switch>en
Switch#config t
Enter configuration commands, one per line.  End with CNTL/Z.
Switch(config)#hostname S1
S1(config)#enable secret todd
S1(config)#int f0/1
S1(config-if)#description 1st Connection to Core Switch
S1(config-if)#int f0/2
S1(config-if)#description 2nd Connection to Core Switch
S1(config-if)#int f0/3
S1(config-if)#description Connection to HostA
S1(config-if)#int f0/4
S1(config-if)#description Connection to PhoneA
S1(config-if)#int f0/8
S1(config-if)#description Connection to IVR
S1(config-if)#line console 0
S1(config-line)#password console
S1(config-line)#login
S1(config-line)#exit
S1(config)#line vty 0 ?
  <1-15>  Last Line number
  <cr>
S1(config)#line vty 0 15
S1(config-line)#password telnet
S1(config-line)#login
S1(config-line)#int vlan 1
S1(config-if)#ip address 192.168.10.17 255.255.255.240
S1(config-if)#no shut
S1(config-if)#exit
S1(config)#banner motd # This is the S1 switch #
S1(config)#exit
S1(config)#ip default-gateway 192.168.10.30
S1#copy run start
Destination filename [startup-config]? [enter]
Building configuration...
[OK]
S1#
```

The first thing to notice about this is that there's no IP address configured on the switch's interfaces. Since all ports on a switch are enabled by default, there's not so much to configure. The IP address is configured under a logical interface, called a management domain or VLAN. You would typically use the default VLAN 1 to manage a switched network just as we're doing here.

The rest of the configuration is basically the same as the process you go through for router configuration. Remember, no IP addresses on switch interfaces, no routing protocols, and so on. We're performing layer 2 switching at this point, not routing! Also, note that there is no aux port on Cisco switches.

Exam Objectives

Remember how to set an IP address on a switch.   To configure an IP address on a switch, an address is never configured on a switch port, but rather what is called the management VLAN. By default this is VLAN 1. Here is an example on how to set an IP address on a switch using the default VLAN:

```
Switch(config-line)#int vlan 1
Switch(config-if)#ip address 192.168.10.17 255.255.255.240
Switch(config-if)#no shut
```

Remember how to configure a switch for remote management.   To allow hosts from outside the management VLAN to access the switch for administrative purposes you need to set a default gateway on the switch. Here is how you would do that:

```
Switch(config)#ip default-gateway 192.168.10.30
```

2.6 Verify network status and switch operation using basic utilities (including: ping, traceroute, Telnet, SSH, arp, ipconfig), SHOW & DEBUG commands

Before we move on to determining IP address problems and how to fix them, I just want to mention some basic DOS commands that you can use to help troubleshoot your network from both a PC and a Cisco router (the commands might do the same thing, but they are implemented differently).

Packet InterNet Groper (ping)   Uses ICMP echo request and replies to test if a node IP stack is initialized and alive on the network.

traceroute   Displays the list of routers on a path to a network destination by using TTL time-outs and ICMP error messages. This command will not work from a DOS prompt.

tracert   Same command as `traceroute`, but it's a Microsoft Windows command and will not work on a Cisco router.

arp -a   Displays IP-to-MAC-address mappings on a Windows PC.

show ip arp   Same command as `arp -a`, but displays the ARP table on a Cisco router. Like the commands `traceroute` and `tracert`, they are not interchangeable through DOS and Cisco.

ipconfig /all   Used only from a DOS prompt, shows you the PC network configuration.

Once you've gone through all these steps and used the appropriate DOS commands, if necessary, what do you do if you find a problem? How do you go about fixing an IP address configuration error? Let's move on and discuss how to determine the IP address problems and how to fix them.

Checking Network Connectivity

You can use the `ping` and `traceroute` commands to test connectivity to remote devices, and both of them can be used with many protocols, not just IP.

Using the *Ping* Command

So far, you've seen many examples of pinging devices to test IP connectivity and name resolution using the DNS server. To see all the different protocols that you can use with `ping`, use the `ping ?` command like this:

```
Todd2509#ping ?
  WORD       Ping destination address or hostname
  apollo     Apollo echo
  appletalk  Appletalk echo
  clns       CLNS echo
  decnet     DECnet echo
  ip         IP echo
  ipx        Novell/IPX echo
  srb        srb echo
  tag        Tag encapsulated IP echo
  vines      Vines echo
  xns        XNS echo
  <cr>
```

The ping output displays the minimum, average, and maximum times it takes for a Ping packet to find a specified system and return. Here's another example:

```
Todd2509#ping todd2509
Translating "todd2509"...domain server (192.168.0.70)[OK]
Type escape sequence to abort.
Sending 5, 100-byte ICMP Echos to 192.168.0.121, timeout
  is 2 seconds:
!!!!!
Success rate is 100 percent (5/5), round-trip min/avg/max
  = 32/32/32 ms
Todd2509#
```

You can see that the DNS server was used to resolve the name, and the device was pinged in 32ms (milliseconds).

The ping command can be used in user and privileged mode, but not configuration mode.

Using the *Traceroute* Command

Traceroute (the traceroute command, or trace for short) shows the path a packet takes to get to a remote device. To see the protocols that you can use with traceroute, use the traceroute ? command, do this:

```
Todd2509#traceroute ?
  WORD      Trace route to destination address or
            hostname
  appletalk AppleTalk Trace
  clns      ISO CLNS Trace
  ip        IP Trace
  ipx       IPX Trace
  oldvines  Vines Trace (Cisco)
  vines     Vines Trace (Banyan)
  <cr>
```

The trace command shows the hop or hops that a packet traverses on its way to a remote device. Here's an example:

```
Todd2509#trace 2501b
Type escape sequence to abort.
Tracing the route to 2501b.lammle.com (172.16.10.2)
```

```
  1 2501b.lammle.com (172.16.10.2) 16 msec *  16 msec
Todd2509#
```

You can see that the packet went through only one hop to find the destination.

Do not get confused on the exam. You can't use the `tracert` command—it's a Windows command. For a router, use the `traceroute` command!

Verifying Cisco Catalyst Switches

The first thing I like to do with any router or switch is to run through the configurations with a show running-config command. Why? Because doing this gives me a really great headshot of each device. However, it's time-consuming, and showing you all the configs would take up a whole bunch of pages in this book. Besides, we can run other commands that will still stock us with really good information.

For example, to verify the IP address set on a switch, we can use the `show interface` command. Here is the output:

```
S1#sh int vlan 1
Vlan1 is up, line protocol is up
  Hardware is EtherSVI, address is 001b.2b55.7540 (bia 001b.2b55.7540)
  Internet address is 192.168.10.17/28
  MTU 1500 bytes, BW 1000000 Kbit, DLY 10 usec,
     reliability 255/255, txload 1/255, rxload 1/255
  Encapsulation ARPA, loopback not set, reliability 255/255, txload 1/255,
rxload 1/255
  [output cut]
```

Remember that IP addresses aren't needed on a switch. The only reason we would set an IP address, mask, and default gateway is for management purposes.

show mac address-table

I'm sure you remember being shown this command earlier in the chapter. Using it displays the forward filter table, also called a content addressable memory (CAM) table. Here's the output from the S1 switch:

```
S1#sh mac address-table
        Mac Address Table
-------------------------------------------
```

```
Vlan    Mac Address      Type       Ports
----    -----------      --------   -----
 All    0100.0ccc.cccc   STATIC     CPU
 All    ffff.ffff.ffff   STATIC     CPU
[output cut]
   1    0002.1762.b235   DYNAMIC    Po1
   1    0009.b79f.c080   DYNAMIC    Po1
   1    000d.29bd.4b87   DYNAMIC    Po1
   1    000d.29bd.4b88   DYNAMIC    Po1
   1    0016.4662.52b4   DYNAMIC    Fa0/4
   1    0016.4677.5eab   DYNAMIC    Po1
   1    001a.2f52.49d8   DYNAMIC    Po1
   1    001a.2fe7.4170   DYNAMIC    Fa0/8
   1    001a.e2ce.ff40   DYNAMIC    Po1
   1    0050.0f02.642a   DYNAMIC    Fa0/3
Total Mac Addresses for this criterion: 31
S1#
```

The switches use what are called *base MAC addresses* that are assigned to the CPU, and the 2960s use 20. From the preceding output, you can see that we have five MAC addresses dynamically assigned to EtherChannel port 1. Ports Fa0/3, Fa0/8, and Fa0/4 only have one MAC address assigned, and all ports are assigned to VLAN 1.

Let's take a look at the S2 switch CAM and see what we can find. Keep in mind that the S2 switch doesn't have EtherChannel configured as the S1 switch does, so STP will shut down one of the redundant links to the Core switch:

```
S2#sh mac address-table
         Mac Address Table
-------------------------------------------

Vlan    Mac Address      Type       Ports
----    -----------      --------   -----
 All    0008.205a.85c0   STATIC     CPU
 All    0100.0ccc.cccc   STATIC     CPU
 All    0100.0ccc.cccd   STATIC     CPU
 All    0100.0cdd.dddd   STATIC     CPU
[output cut]
   1    0002.1762.b235   DYNAMIC    Fa0/3
   1    000d.29bd.4b80   DYNAMIC    Fa0/1
   1    000d.29bd.4b85   DYNAMIC    Fa0/1
   1    0016.4662.52b4   DYNAMIC    Fa0/1
   1    0016.4677.5eab   DYNAMIC    Fa0/4
```

```
     1    001b.2b55.7540    DYNAMIC    Fa0/1
Total Mac Addresses for this criterion: 26
S2#
```

We can see in the preceding output that we have four MAC addresses assigned to Fa0/1. And of course, we can also see that we have one connection for each host on ports 3 and 4. But where's port 2? Since port 2 is a redundant link, STP placed Fa0/2 into blocking mode. I'll get into more about this again in a minute.

You can set a static MAC address in the MAC address table, but like setting static MAC port security, it's a ton of work. But in case you want to do it, here's how it's done:

```
S1#config t
S1(config)#mac-address-table static aaaa.bbbb.cccc vlan 1 int fa0/5
S1(config)#do show mac address-table
          Mac Address Table
-------------------------------------------

Vlan    Mac Address      Type       Ports
----    -----------      --------   -----
 All    0100.0ccc.cccc   STATIC     CPU
[output cut]
  1     0002.1762.b235   DYNAMIC    Po1
  1     0009.b79f.c080   DYNAMIC    Po1
  1     000d.29bd.4b87   DYNAMIC    Po1
  1     000d.29bd.4b88   DYNAMIC    Po1
  1     0016.4662.52b4   DYNAMIC    Fa0/4
  1     0016.4677.5eab   DYNAMIC    Po1
  1     001a.2f52.49d8   DYNAMIC    Po1
  1     001a.2fe7.4170   DYNAMIC    Fa0/8
  1     001a.e2ce.ff40   DYNAMIC    Po1
  1     0050.0f02.642a   DYNAMIC    Fa0/3
  1     aaaa.bbbb.cccc   STATIC     Fa0/5
Total Mac Addresses for this criterion: 31
S1(config)#
```

You can see that a static MAC address is now assigned permanently to interface Fa0/5 and that it's also assigned to VLAN 1 only.

show spanning-tree

By this time you know that the show spanning-tree command is important. With it, you can see who the root bridge is and what our priorities are set to for each VLAN.

Understand that Cisco switches run what is called *Per-VLAN Spanning Tree* (PVST), which basically means that each VLAN runs its own instance of the STP protocol. If we typed **show spanning-tree**, we'd receive information for each VLAN, starting with VLAN 1. So, say we've got multiple VLANs and we want to see what's up with VLAN 2—we'd use the command **show spanning-tree vlan 2**.

Here is an output from the **show spanning-tree** command from switch S1. Since we are only using VLAN 1, we don't need to add the VLAN number to the command:

```
S1#sh spanning-tree
VLAN0001
  Spanning tree enabled protocol ieee
  Root ID    Priority    32769
             Address     000d.29bd.4b80
             Cost        3012
             Port        56 (Port-channel1)
             Hello Time   2 sec  Max Age 20 sec  Forward Delay 15 sec

  Bridge ID  Priority    49153  (priority 49152 sys-id-ext 1)
             Address     001b.2b55.7500
             Hello Time   2 sec  Max Age 20 sec  Forward Delay 15 sec
             Aging Time  15
  Uplinkfast enabled

Interface        Role Sts Cost      Prio.Nbr Type
---------------- ---- --- --------- -------- ----------
Fa0/3            Desg FWD 3100      128.3    Edge Shr
Fa0/4            Desg FWD 3019      128.4    Edge P2p
Fa0/8            Desg FWD 3019      128.8    P2p
Po1              Root FWD 3012      128.56   P2p
```

Since we only have VLAN 1 configured, there's no more output for this command, but if we had more, we would get another page for each VLAN configured on the switch. The default priority is 32768, but there's something called the system ID extension (sys-id-ext), which is the VLAN identifier. The Bridge ID priority is incremented by the number of that VLAN. And since we only have VLAN 1, we increment by one to 32769. But understand, by default, BackboneFast raises the default priority to 49152 to prevent that bridge from becoming the root.

Exam Objectives

Understand when you would use the *ping* command.   Packet Internet Groper (Ping) uses ICMP echo request and ICMP echo replies to verify an active IP address on a network.

Understand the main purpose of the spanning tree protocol in a switched LAN.   The main purpose of STP is to prevent switching loops in a network with redundant switched paths.

Remember the command `show spanning-tree`.   You must be familiar with the command `show spanning-tree` and how to determine which switch is the root bridge.

2.7 Identify, prescribe, and resolve common switched network media issues, configuration issues, auto negotiation, and switch hardware failures

A network port, also called an *RJ-45 port*, connects a computer to a network or VLAN. The connection speed depends on the type of network port. Standard Ethernet can transmit up to 10Mbps; however, it is very common to have Fast Ethernet which can transmit up to 100 Mbps. Gigabit Ethernet ports can transmit up to 1000 Mbps. The maximum length of network cable is 328 feet (100 meters).

Twisted-pair is a type of copper cabling that started in telephone communications and now is used in both telephony and most Ethernet networks. A pair of wires forms a circuit that can transmit data. The pair is twisted to provide protection against crosstalk, which is the noise generated by adjacent pairs of wires in the cable.

Common issues with cabling on a switched network include basic switch configuration issues, negotiating both the speed and duplex of a link from a PC to a switch, and the uncommon switch hardware failures.

The most common switch configuration error is not having a port configured into the correct switch membership. By using the `show running-config` command or `show vlan` command, you can easily see the port memberships. Always check your VLAN memberships when troubleshooting a command switch issue.

At times, you may find a host is not communicating to a switch because of mismatched speed or duplex issues. This is not as much a problem as it has been in the past because of the better hardware being produced, but it still may show up from time to time. The default on a switch and host is to use 100Mbps full-duplex. If your host or switch port does not support this configuration, you can configure the switch port with the `duplex` and `speed` command.

The port LED will be green when everything is OK, however, it will be amber if the port is blocked by STP, and it will turn from green to amber when the port experiences errors.

Switches are made pretty resilient today; however, if you boot a switch and the POST completes successfully, the system LED turns green; if the POST fails, it will turn amber. And seeing the amber glow is a very bad thing—typically fatal.

Exam Objectives

Remember how the system LED responds when the post test runs.   If you boot a switch and the POST completes successfully, the system LED turns green; if the POST fails, it will turn amber.

Remember how the system LED responds if there are errors on a switch port   A switch port will turn from green to amber when the port experiences errors.

2.8 Describe enhanced switching technologies (including: VTP, RSTP, VLAN, PVSTP, 802.1q)

The basic goals of *VLAN Trunking Protocol (VTP)* are to manage all configured VLANs across a switched internetwork and to maintain consistency throughout that network. VTP allows you to add, delete, and rename VLANs—information that is then propagated to all other switches in the VTP domain.

Here's a list of some of the cool features VTP has to offer:

- Consistent VLAN configuration across all switches in the network

- VLAN trunking over mixed networks, such as Ethernet to ATM LANE or even FDDI

- Accurate tracking and monitoring of VLANs

- Dynamic reporting of added VLANs to all switches in the VTP domain

- Plug and Play VLAN adding

Very nice, but before you can get VTP to manage your VLANs across the network, you have to create a VTP server. All servers that need to share VLAN information must use the same domain name, and a switch can be in only one domain at a time. ,So, basically, this means that a switch can only share VTP domain information with other switches if they're configured into the same VTP domain. You can use a VTP domain if you have more than one switch connected in a network, but if you've got all your switches in only one VLAN, you just don't need to use VTP. Do keep in mind that VTP information is sent between switches only via a trunk port.

Switches advertise VTP management domain information as well as a configuration revision number and all known VLANs with any specific parameters. But there's also something called *VTP transparent mode.* In it, you can configure switches to forward VTP information through trunk ports but not to accept information updates or update their VTP databases.

If you've got sneaky users adding switches to your VTP domain behind your back, you can include passwords, but don't forget—every switch must be set up with the same password. And as you can imagine, this little snag can be a real hassle administratively!

Switches detect any added VLANs within a VTP advertisement, then prepare to send information on their trunk ports with the newly defined VLAN in tow. Updates are sent out as revision numbers that consist of the notification plus 1. Anytime a switch sees a higher revision number, it knows the information it's getting is more current, so it will overwrite the existing database with the latest information.

You should know these three requirements for VTP to communicate VLAN information between switches:

- The VTP management domain name of both switches must be set the same.
- One of the switches has to be configured as a VTP server.
- No router is necessary.

Now that you've got that down, we're going to delve deeper in the world of VTP with VTP modes and VTP pruning.

VTP Modes of Operation

Figure 2.18 shows you all three different modes of operation within a VTP domain:

Server   This is the default mode for all Catalyst switches. You need at least one server in your VTP domain to propagate VLAN information throughout that domain. Also important: The switch must be in server mode to be able to create, add, and delete VLANs in a VTP domain. VTP information has to be changed in server mode, and any change made to a switch in server mode will be advertised to the entire VTP domain. In VTP server mode, VLAN configurations are saved in NVRAM.

Client   In client mode, switches receive information from VTP servers, but they also send and receive updates, so in this way, they behave like VTP servers. The difference is that they can't create, change, or delete VLANs. Plus, none of the ports on a client switch can be added to a new VLAN before the VTP server notifies the client switch of the new VLAN. Also good to know is that VLAN information sent from a VTP server isn't stored in NVRAM, which is important because it means that if the switch is reset or reloaded, the VLAN information will be deleted. Here's a hint: If you want a switch to become a server, first make it a client so it receives all the correct VLAN information, then change it to a server—so much easier!

So basically, a switch in VTP client mode will forward VTP summary advertisements and process them. This switch will learn about but won't save the VTP configuration in the running configuration, and it won't save it in NVRAM. Switches that are in VTP client mode will only learn about and pass along VTP information—that's it!

Transparent   Switches in transparent mode don't participate in the VTP domain or share its VLAN database, but they'll still forward VTP advertisements through any configured trunk links. They can create, modify, and delete VLANs because they keep their own database—one they keep secret from the other switches. Despite being kept in NVRAM, the VLAN database in transparent mode is actually only locally significant. The whole purpose of transparent mode is to allow remote switches to receive the VLAN database from a VTP server-configured switch through a switch that is not participating in the same VLAN assignments.

VTP only learns about normal-range VLANs, with VLAN IDs 1 to 1005; VLANs with IDs greater than 1005 are called extended-range VLANs and they're not stored in the VLAN database. The switch must be in VTP transparent mode when you create VLAN IDs from 1006 to 4094, so it would be pretty rare that you'd ever use these VLANs. One other thing: VLAN IDs 1 and 1002 to 1005 are automatically created on all switches and can't be removed.

FIGURE 2.18   VTP modes

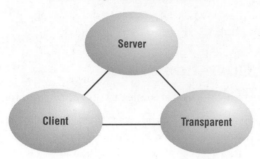

Server configuration: Saved in NVRAM

Client configuration: Not saved in NVRAM   Transparent configuration: Saved in NVRAM

Rapid Spanning-Tree Protocol (RSTP) 802.1w

How would you like to have a good STP configuration running on your switched network (regardless of the brand of switches) and have all the features we just discussed built in and enabled on every switch? Absolutely—yes! Well then, welcome to the world of Rapid Spanning-Tree Protocol (RSTP).

Cisco created PortFast, UplinkFast, and BackboneFast to "fix" the holes and liabilities the IEEE 802.1d standard presented. The drawbacks to these enhancements are only that they are Cisco proprietary and need additional configuration. But the new 802.1w standard (RSTP) addresses all these "issues" in one tight package—just turn on RSTP and you're good to go. Importantly, you must make sure that all the switches in your network are running the 802.1w protocol for 802.1w to work properly!

It might come as a surprise, but RSTP actually can interoperate with legacy STP protocols. Just know that the inherently fast convergence ability of 802.1w is lost when it interacts with legacy bridges.

PVST

Understand that Cisco switches run what is called Per-VLAN Spanning-Tree (PVST), which basically means that each VLAN runs its own instance of the STP protocol. If we typed **show spanning-tree,** we'd receive information for each VLAN, starting with VLAN 1. So, say we've got multiple VLANs, and we want to see what's up with VLAN 2—we'd use the command **show spanning-tree vlan 2.**

IEEE 802.1Q

Created by the IEEE as a standard method of frame tagging, IEEE 802.1Q actually inserts a field into the frame to identify the VLAN. If you're trunking between a Cisco switched link and a different brand of switch, you've got to use 802.1Q for the trunk to work.

It works like this: You first designate each port that is going to be a trunk with 802.1Q encapsulation. The ports must be assigned a specific VLAN ID, which makes them the native VLAN, in order for them to communicate. The ports that populate the same trunk create a group with this native VLAN, and each port gets tagged with an identification number reflecting that, again, the default is VLAN 1. The native VLAN allows the trunks to carry information that was received without any VLAN identification or frame tag.

The 2960s support only the IEEE 802.1Q trunking protocol, but the 3560s will support both the ISL and IEEE methods.

The basic purpose of ISL and 802.1Q frame-tagging methods is to provide interswitch VLAN communication. Also, remember that any ISL or 802.1Q frame tagging is removed if a frame is forwarded out an access link—tagging is used across trunk links only!

Exam Objectives

Understand the Rapid Spanning-Tree Protocol.   The 802.1w STP standard (RSTP) addresses all the problems found in the 802.1d STP protocol and is not Cisco proprietary. This is not enabled on any Cisco switch by default, and if you enable this protocol, you should enable it on all your switches for the fastest convergence times.

Understand the purpose and configuration of VTP.   VTP provides propagation of the VLAN database throughout your switched network. All switches must be in the same VTP domain.

Be able to define PVST.   Per-VLAN Spanning-Tree; each VLAN runs its own instance of the STP protocol.

2.9 Describe how VLANs create logically separate networks and the need for routing between them

Figure 2.19 shows how layer 2 switched networks are typically designed—as flat networks. With this configuration, every broadcast packet transmitted is seen by every device on the network regardless of whether the device needs to receive that data or not.

By default, routers allow broadcasts to occur only within the originating network, while switches forward broadcasts to all segments. Oh, and by the way, the reason it's called a *flat network* is because it's one *broadcast domain*, not because the actual design is physically flat. In Figure 2.19 we see Host A sending out a broadcast and all ports on all switches forwarding it—all except the port that originally received it.

FIGURE 2.19   Flat network structure

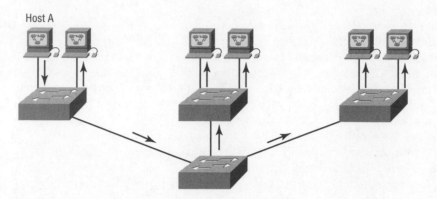

Now check out Figure 2.20. It depicts a switched network and shows Host A sending a frame with Host D as its destination. What's important is that, as you can see, that frame is only forwarded out the port where Host D is located. This is a huge improvement over the old hub networks, unless having one *collision domain* by default is what you really want. (Probably not!)

FIGURE 2.20   The benefit of a switched network

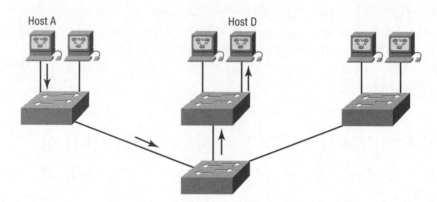

Now you already know that the largest benefit you gain by having a layer 2 switched network is that it creates individual collision domain segments for each device plugged into each port on the switch. This scenario frees us from the Ethernet distance constraints, so now larger networks can be built. But often, each new advance comes with new issues. For instance, the larger the number of users and devices, the more broadcasts and packets each switch must handle.

And here's another issue: security! This one's real trouble because within the typical layer 2 switched internetwork, all users can see all devices by default. And you can't stop devices from broadcasting, plus you can't stop users from trying to respond to broadcasts. This means your security options are dismally limited to placing passwords on your servers and other devices.

But wait—there's hope! That is, if you create a *virtual LAN (VLAN)*. You can solve many of the problems associated with layer 2 switching with VLANs, as you'll soon see.

Here's a short list of ways VLANs simplify network management:

- Network adds, moves, and changes are achieved with ease by just configuring a port into the appropriate VLAN.
- A group of users that need an unusually high level of security can be put into its own VLAN so that users outside of the VLAN can't communicate with them.
- As a logical grouping of users by function, VLANs can be considered independent from their physical or geographic locations.
- VLANs greatly enhance network security.
- VLANs increase the number of broadcast domains while decreasing their size.

Coming up, I'm going to tell you all about switching characteristics and thoroughly describe how switches provide us with better network services than hubs can in our networks today.

Broadcast Control

Broadcasts occur in every protocol, but how often they occur depends upon three things:

- The type of protocol
- The application(s) running on the internetwork
- How these services are used

Some older applications have been rewritten to reduce their bandwidth appetites, but there's a new generation of applications that are incredibly bandwidth greedy that will consume any and all they can find. These bandwidth gluttons are multimedia applications that use both broadcasts and multicasts extensively. And faulty equipment, inadequate segmentation, and poorly designed firewalls seriously compound the problems that these broadcast-intensive applications create. All of this has added a major new dimension to network design and presents a bunch of new challenges for an administrator. Positively making sure your network is properly segmented so that you can quickly isolate a single segment's problems to prevent them from propagating throughout your entire internetwork is imperative! And the most effective way to do that is through strategic switching and routing.

Since switches have become more affordable lately, a lot of companies are replacing their flat hub networks with pure switched network and VLAN environments. All devices within a VLAN are members of the same broadcast domain and receive all broadcasts. By default, these broadcasts are filtered from all ports on a switch that aren't members of the same VLAN. This is great because you get all the benefits you would with a switched design without getting hit with all the problems you'd have if all your users were in the same broadcast domain—sweet!

Security

Okay, I know. There's always a catch, though right? Time to get back to those security issues. A flat internetwork's security used to be tackled by connecting hubs and switches with routers. So, it was basically the router's job to maintain security. This arrangement was pretty ineffective for several reasons. First, anyone connecting to the physical network could access the network resources located on that particular physical LAN. Second, all anyone had to do to observe any and all traffic happening in that network was to simply plug a network analyzer into the hub. And similar to that last ugly fact, users could join a workgroup by just plugging their workstations into the existing hub. That's about as secure as an open barrel of honey in a bear enclosure!

But that's exactly what makes VLANs so cool. If you build them and create multiple broadcast groups, you have total control over each port and user! So, the days when anyone could just plug their workstation into any switch port and gain access to network resources are history because now you get to control each port, plus whatever resources that port can access. What's more, with the new 2960/3560 switches, this actually happens automatically!

And it doesn't end there, my friends, because VLANs can be created in accordance with the network resources a given user requires, plus switches can be configured to inform a network management station of any unauthorized access to network resources. And if you need inter-VLAN communication, you can implement restrictions on a router to make that happen. You can also place restrictions on hardware addresses, protocols, and applications. *Now* we're talking security—the honey barrel is now sealed, shrouded in razor wire, and made of solid titanium!

Flexibility and Scalability

If you were paying attention to what you've read so far, you know that layer 2 switches only read frames for filtering—they don't look at the Network layer protocol. And by default, switches forward all broadcasts. But if you create and implement VLANs, you're essentially creating smaller broadcast domains at layer 2.

What this means is that broadcasts sent out from a node in one VLAN won't be forwarded to ports configured to belong to a different VLAN. So, by assigning switch ports or users to VLAN groups on a switch or group of connected switches, you gain the flexibility to add only the users you want into that broadcast domain regardless of their physical location. This setup can also work to block broadcast storms caused by a faulty NIC as well as prevent an intermediate device from propagating broadcast storms throughout the entire internetwork. Those evils can still happen on the VLAN where the problem originated, but the device with the disease will be quarantined to that one ailing VLAN.

Another advantage is that when a VLAN gets too big, you can create more VLANs to keep the broadcasts from consuming too much bandwidth—the fewer users in a VLAN, the fewer users affected by broadcasts. This is all well and good, but you seriously need to keep network services in mind and understand how the users connect to these services when you create your VLAN. It's a good move to try to keep all services, except for the email and Internet access that everyone needs, local to all users whenever possible.

To understand how a VLAN looks to a switch, it's helpful to begin by first looking at a traditional network. Figure 2.21 shows how a network was created by using hubs to connect physical LANs to a router.

FIGURE 2.21   Physical LANs connected to a router

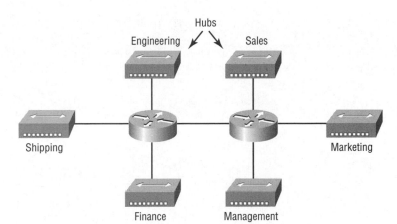

Here, you can see that each network is attached with a hub port to the router (each segment also has its own logical network number even though this isn't obvious from looking at the figure). Each node attached to a particular physical network has to match that network's number in order to be able to communicate on the internetwork. Notice that each department has its own LAN, so if you needed to add new users to, let's say, Sales, you would just plug them into the Sales LAN and they would automatically be part of the Sales collision and broadcast domain. This design really did work well for many years.

But there was one major flaw: What happens if the hub for Sales is full and we need to add another user to the Sales LAN? Or, what do we do if there's no more physical space where the Sales team is located for this new employee? Well, let's say there just happens to be plenty of room in the Finance section of the building. That new Sales team member will just have to sit on the same side of the building as the Finance people, and we'll just plug the poor soul into the hub for Finance.

Doing this obviously makes the new user part of the Finance LAN, which is very bad for many reasons. First and foremost, we now have a major security issue. Because the new Sales employee is a member of the Finance broadcast domain, the newbie can see all the same servers and access all network services that the Finance folks can. Second, for this user to access the Sales network services that they need to get their job done, they would have to go through the router to log in to the Sales server—not exactly efficient!

Now let's look at what a switch accomplishes for us. Figure 2.22 demonstrates how switches come to the rescue by removing the physical boundary to solve our problem. It also shows how six VLANs (numbered 2 through 7) are used to create a broadcast domain for each department. Each switch port is then administratively assigned a VLAN membership, depending on the host and which broadcast domain it's placed in.

FIGURE 2.22   Switches removing the physical boundary

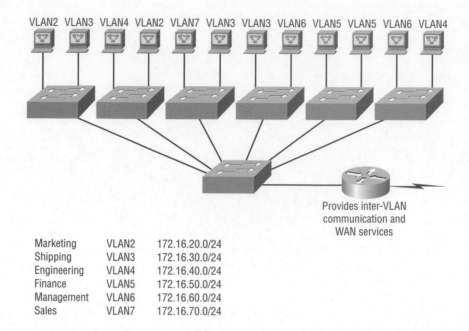

Marketing	VLAN2	172.16.20.0/24
Shipping	VLAN3	172.16.30.0/24
Engineering	VLAN4	172.16.40.0/24
Finance	VLAN5	172.16.50.0/24
Management	VLAN6	172.16.60.0/24
Sales	VLAN7	172.16.70.0/24

So now, if we needed to add another user to the Sales VLAN (VLAN 7), we could just assign the port to VLAN 7 regardless of where the new Sales team member is physically located—nice! This illustrates one of the sweetest advantages to designing your network with VLANs over the old collapsed backbone design. Now, cleanly and simply, each host that needs to be in the Sales VLAN is merely assigned to VLAN 7. And by using the new switches with the predefined macros, we can just use CNA and Smartports to configure the port to be a Desktop connection and voilà! The port configuration is simply completed for us.

Notice that I started assigning VLANs with VLAN number 2. The number is irrelevant, but you might be wondering what happened to VLAN 1? Well that VLAN is an administrative VLAN, and even though it can be used for a workgroup, Cisco recommends that you use it for administrative purposes only. You can't delete or change the name of VLAN 1, and by default, all ports on a switch are members of VLAN 1 until you change them.

Since each VLAN is considered a broadcast domain, it's got to also have its own subnet number (refer again to Figure 2.22). And if you're also using IPv6, then each VLAN must also be assigned its own IPv6 network number. So you don't get confused, just keep thinking of VLANs as separate subnets or networks.

Now let's get back to that "because of switches, we don't need routers anymore" misconception. Looking at Figure 2.22, notice that there are seven VLANs, or broadcast domains, counting VLAN 1. The nodes within each VLAN can communicate with each other but not with anything in a different VLAN because the nodes in any given VLAN "think" that they're actually in a collapsed backbone, as illustrated in Figure 9.21.

So, what handy little tool do we need to enable the hosts in Figure 9.23 to communicate to a node or host on a different VLAN? You guessed it—a router! Those nodes positively need to go through a router, or some other layer 3 device, just as when they're configured for inter-network communication (as shown in Figure 9.21). It works the same way it would if we were trying to connect different physical networks. Communication between VLANs must go through a layer 3 device. So, don't expect mass router extinction anytime soon!

Exam Objectives

Remember that hosts in a VLAN can only communicate with hosts in the same VLAN.   If you have multiple VLANs and need inter-VLAN communication, you must configure a router or buy a more expensive layer 3 switch to provide the routing on the backplane of the switch.

Remember how to create a Cisco "router on a stick" to provide inter-VLAN communication. You can use a Cisco FastEthernet of Gigabit Ethernet interface to provide inter-VLAN routing. The switch port connected to the router must be a trunk port, then you must create virtual inter-faces (subinterfaces) on the router port for each VLAN connecting. The hosts in each VLAN will use this subinterface address as their default gateway address.

2.10 Configure, verify, and troubleshoot VLANs

It may come as a surprise to you, but configuring VLANs is actually pretty easy. Figuring out which users you want in each VLAN is not; it's extremely time-consuming. But once you've decided on the number of VLANs you want to create and established which users you want to belong to each one, it's time to bring your first VLAN into the world.

To configure VLANs on a Cisco Catalyst switch, use the global config `vlan` command. In the following example, I'm going to demonstrate how to configure VLANs on the S1 switch by creating three VLANs for three different departments—again, remember that VLAN 1 is the native and administrative VLAN by default:

```
S1#config t
S1(config)#vlan ?
  WORD      ISL VLAN IDs 1-4094
  internal  internal VLAN
S1(config)#vlan 2
S1(config-vlan)#name Sales
S1(config-vlan)#vlan 3
S1(config-vlan)#name Marketing
S1(config-vlan)#vlan 4
S1(config-vlan)#name Accounting
S1(config-vlan)#^Z
S1#
```

From the preceding, you can see that you can create VLANs from 2 to 4094. This is only mostly true. As I said, VLANs can really only be created up to 1005, and you can't use, change, rename, or delete VLANs 1 and 1002 through 1005 because they're reserved. The VLAN numbers above that are called extended VLANs and won't be saved in the database unless your switch is set to VTP transparent mode. You won't see these VLAN numbers used too often in production. Here's an example of setting my S1 switch to VLAN 4000 when my switch is set to VTP server mode (the default VTP mode):

```
S1#config t
S1(config)#vlan 4000
S1(config-vlan)#^Z
% Failed to create VLANs 4000
Extended VLAN(s) not allowed in current VTP mode.
%Failed to commit extended VLAN(s) changes.
```

After you create the VLANs that you want, you can use the show vlan command to check them out. But notice that, by default, all ports on the switch are in VLAN 1. To change the VLAN associated with a port, you need to go to each interface and tell it which VLAN to be a part of.

Remember that a created VLAN is unused until it is assigned to a switch port or ports and that all ports are always assigned in VLAN 1 unless set otherwise.

Once the VLANs are created, verify your configuration with the show vlan command (sh vlan for short):

```
S1#sh vlan
```

VLAN	Name	Status	Ports
1	default	active	Fa0/3, Fa0/4, Fa0/5, Fa0/6
			Fa0/7, Fa0/8, Gi0/1
2	Sales	active	
3	Marketing	active	
4	Accounting	active	

[output cut]

This may seem repetitive, but it's important, and I want you to remember it: You can't change, delete, or rename VLAN 1 because it's the default VLAN and you just can't change that—period. It's the native VLAN of all switches by default, and Cisco recommends that you use it as your administrative VLAN. Basically, any packets that aren't specifically assigned to a different VLAN will be sent down to the native VLAN.

In the preceding S1 output, you can see that ports Fa0/3 through Fa0/8 and the Gi0/1 uplink are all in VLAN 1, but where are ports 1 and 2? Ports one and two are trunked. Any port that is a trunk port won't show up in the VLAN database. You have to use the show interface trunk command to see your trunked ports.

Assigning Switch Ports to VLANs

You configure a port to belong to a VLAN by assigning a membership mode that specifies the kind of traffic the port carries, plus the number of VLANs to which it can belong. You can configure each port on a switch to be in a specific VLAN (access port) by using the interface switchport command. You can also configure multiple ports at the same time with the interface range command.

Remember that you can configure either static memberships or dynamic memberships on a port. For this book's purpose, I'm only going to cover the static flavor. In the following example, I'll configure interface fa0/3 to VLAN 3. This is the connection from the S1 switch to the HostA device:

```
S1#config t S1(config)#int fa0/3
S1(config-if)#switchport ?
    access        Set access mode characteristics of the interface
    backup        Set backup for the interface
    block         Disable forwarding of unknown uni/multi cast addresses
    host          Set port host
    mode          Set trunking mode of the interface
    nonegotiate   Device will not engage in negotiation protocol on this
                  interface
    port-security Security related command
    priority      Set appliance 802.1p priority
    protected     Configure an interface to be a protected port
    trunk         Set trunking characteristics of the interface
    voice         Voice appliance attributes
```

Well now, what do we have here? There's some new stuff showing up in the preceding output. We can see various commands—some that I've already covered, but no worries; I'm going to cover the access, mode, nonegotiate, trunk, and voice commands very soon in this chapter. Let's start with setting an access port on S1, which is probably the most widely used type of port on production switches that has VLANs configured:

```
S1(config-if)#switchport mode ?
  access  Set trunking mode to ACCESS unconditionally
  dynamic  Set trunking mode to dynamically negotiate access or
trunk mode
  trunk   Set trunking mode to TRUNK unconditionally

S1(config-if)#switchport mode access
S1(config-if)#switchport access vlan 3
```

By starting with the `switchport mode access` command, you're telling the switch that this is a layer 2 port. You can then assign a VLAN to the port with the `switchport access` command. Remember, you can choose many ports to configure at the same time if you use the `interface range` command. The `dynamic` and `trunk` commands are used for trunk ports exclusively.

That's it. Well, sort of. If you plugged devices into each VLAN port, they can only talk to other devices in the same VLAN. We want to enable inter-VLAN communication, and we're going to do that, but first you need to learn a bit more about trunking.

Exam Objectives

Remember to check a switch port's VLAN assignment when plugging in a new host.   If you plug a new host into a switch, then you must verify the VLAN membership of that port. If the membership is different from what is needed for that host, the host will not be able to reach the needed network services, such as a workgroup server.

Remember how to set a switch port to a VLAN membership.   By default, all switch ports are members of VLAN 1. In order to change the membership, you must change the port. Here is an example of changing a switch port to VLAN 3:

```
Switch(config)#int f0/1
Switch(config-if)#switchport access vlan 3
```

2.11 Configure, verify, and troubleshoot trunking on Cisco switches

The 2960 switch only runs the IEEE 802.1Q encapsulation method. To configure trunking on a Fast Ethernet port, use the interface command `trunk [parameter]`. It's a tad different on the 3560 switch, and I'll show you that in the next section.

The following switch output shows the trunk configuration on interface fa0/8 as set to trunk on:

```
S1#config t
S1(config)#int fa0/8
S1(config-if)#switchport mode trunk
```

The following list describes the different options available when configuring a switch interface:

switchport mode access   I discussed this in the previous section, but this puts the interface (access port) into permanent nontrunking mode and negotiates to convert the link into a nontrunk link. The interface becomes a nontrunk interface regardless of whether the neighboring interface is a trunk interface. The port would be a dedicated layer 2 port.

switchport mode dynamic auto   This mode makes the interface able to convert the link to a trunk link. The interface becomes a trunk interface if the neighboring interface is set to trunk or desirable mode. This is now the default switchport mode for all Ethernet interfaces on all new Cisco switches.

switchport mode dynamic desirable   This one makes the interface actively attempt to convert the link to a trunk link. The interface becomes a trunk interface if the neighboring interface is set to trunk, desirable, or auto mode. I used to see this mode as the default on some older switches, but not any longer. The default is dynamic auto now.

switchport mode trunk   Puts the interface into permanent trunking mode and negotiates to convert the neighboring link into a trunk link. The interface becomes a trunk interface even if the neighboring interface isn't a trunk interface.

switchport nonegotiate   Prevents the interface from generating DTP frames. You can use this command only when the interface switchport mode is access or trunk. You must manually configure the neighboring interface as a trunk interface to establish a trunk link.

Dynamic Trunking Protocol (DTP) is used for negotiating trunking on a link between two devices, as well as negotiating the encapsulation type of either 802.1Q or ISL. I use the nonegotiate command when I want dedicated trunk ports no questions asked.

To disable trunking on an interface, use the switchport mode access command, which sets the port back to a dedicated layer 2 switch port.

Trunking with the Cisco Catalyst 3560 Switch

Okay, let's take a look at one more switch—the Cisco Catalyst 3560. The configuration is pretty much the same as it is for a 2960, with the exception that the 3560 can provide layer 3 services and the 2960 can't. Plus, the 3560 can run both the ISL and the IEEE 802.1Q trunking encapsulation methods—the 2960 can only run 802.1Q. With all this in mind, let's take a quick look at the VLAN encapsulation difference regarding the 3560 switch.

The 3560 has the encapsulation command, which the 2960 switch doesn't:

```
Core(config-if)#switchport trunk encapsulation ?
  dot1q      Interface uses only 802.1q trunking encapsulation
 when trunking
  isl        Interface uses only ISL trunking encapsulation
 when trunking
  negotiate  Device will negotiate trunking encapsulation with peer on
             interface
Core(config-if)#switchport trunk encapsulation dot1q
Core(config-if)#switchport mode trunk
```

As you can see, we've got the option to add either the IEEE 802.1Q (dot1q) encapsulation or the ISL encapsulation to the 3560 switch. After you set the encapsulation, you still have to set the interface mode to trunk. Honestly, it's pretty rare that you'd continue to use the ISL encapsulation method. Cisco is moving away from ISL—its new routers don't even support it.

Defining the Allowed VLANs on a Trunk

As I've mentioned, trunk ports send and receive information from all VLANs by default, and if a frame is untagged, it's sent to the management VLAN. This applies to the extended range VLANs as well.

But we can remove VLANs from the allowed list to prevent traffic from certain VLANs from traversing a trunked link. Here's how you'd do that:

```
S1#config t
S1(config)#int f0/1
S1(config-if)#switchport trunk allowed vlan ?
  WORD    VLAN IDs of the allowed VLANs when this port is in
trunking mode
  add     add VLANs to the current list
  all     all VLANs
  except  all VLANs except the following
  none    no VLANs
  remove  remove VLANs from the current list
S1(config-if)#switchport trunk allowed vlan remove ?
  WORD    VLAN IDs of disallowed VLANS when this port is in trunking mode
S1(config-if)#switchport trunk allowed vlan remove 4
```

The preceding command stopped the trunk link configured on S1 port f0/1, causing it to drop all traffic sent and received for VLAN 4. You can try to remove VLAN 1 on a trunk link, but it will still send and receive management like CDP, PAgP, LACP, DTP, and VTP, so what's the point?

To remove a range of VLANs, just use a hyphen:

```
S1(config-if)#switchport trunk allowed vlan remove 4-8
```

If by chance someone has removed some VLANs from a trunk link and you want to set the trunk back to default, just use this command:

```
S1(config-if)#switchport trunk allowed vlan all
```

Or this command to accomplish the same thing:

```
S1(config-if)#no switchport trunk allowed vlan
```

Next, I want to show you how to configure pruning for VLANs before we start routing between VLANs.

Changing or Modifying the Trunk Native VLAN

You really don't want to change the trunk port native VLAN from VLAN 1, but you can, and some people do it for security reasons. To change the native VLAN, use the following command:

```
S1#config t
S1(config)#int f0/1
S1(config-if)#switchport trunk ?
  allowed  Set allowed VLAN characteristics when interface is
in trunking mode
  native   Set trunking native characteristics when interface
is in trunking mode
  pruning  Set pruning VLAN characteristics when interface is
in trunking mode
S1(config-if)#switchport trunk native ?
  vlan  Set native VLAN when interface is in trunking mode
S1(config-if)#switchport trunk native vlan ?
  <1-4094>  VLAN ID of the native VLAN when this port is in
 trunking mode
S1(config-if)#switchport trunk native vlan 40
S1(config-if)#^Z
```

So, we've changed our native VLAN on our trunk link to 40, and by using the show running-config command, we can see the configuration under the trunk link:

```
!
interface FastEthernet0/1
 switchport trunk native vlan 40
 switchport trunk allowed vlan 1-3,9-4094
 switchport trunk pruning vlan 3,4
!
```

Hold on there partner! You didn't think it would be this easy and would just start working, did you? Sure you didn't. Here's the rub: If all switches don't have the same native VLAN configured on the trunk links, then we'll start to receive this error:

```
19:23:29: %CDP-4-NATIVE_VLAN_MISMATCH: Native VLAN mismatch
discovered on FastEthernet0/1 (40), with Core FastEthernet0/7 (1).
19:24:29: %CDP-4-NATIVE_VLAN_MISMATCH: Native VLAN mismatch
discovered on FastEthernet0/1 (40), with Core FastEthernet0/7 (1).
```

Actually, this is a good, noncryptic error, so either we go to the other end of our trunk link(s) and change the native VLAN or we set the native VLAN back to the default. Here's how we'd do that:

```
S1(config-if)#no switchport trunk native vlan
```

Now our trunk link is using the default VLAN 1 as the native VLAN. Just remember that all switches must use the same native VLAN or you'll have some serious problems.

Exam Objectives

Remember how to configure a trunk port on a 2960 switch.   The 2960 switch runs only the 802.1q trunking method, so the command to trunk a port is simple:

```
Switch(config-if)#switchport mode trunk
```

Remember how to configure a trunk port on a 3560 switch.   The 3560 switch can use both the ISL and 802.1q frame-tagging methods, so you must set the encapsulation first. Here is an example of trunking a port on a 3560 switch using the 802.1q method:

```
Switch(config-if)#switchport trunk encapsulation dot1q
Switch(config-if)#switchport mode trunk
```

2.12 Configure, verify, and troubleshoot interVLAN routing

By default, only hosts that are members of the same VLAN can communicate. To change this and allow inter-VLAN communication, you need a router or a layer 3 switch. I'm going to start with the router approach.

To support ISL or 802.1Q routing on a Fast Ethernet interface, the router's interface is divided into logical interfaces—one for each VLAN. These are called *subinterfaces*. From a Fast Ethernet or Gigabit interface, you can set the interface to trunk with the `encapsulation` command:

```
ISR#config t
ISR(config)#int f0/0.1
ISR(config-subif)#encapsulation ?
  dot1Q  IEEE 802.1Q Virtual LAN
ISR(config-subif)#encapsulation dot1Q ?
  <1-4094>  IEEE 802.1Q VLAN ID
```

Notice that my 2811 router (named ISR) only supports 802.1Q. We'd need an older-model router to run the ISL encapsulation, but why bother?

The subinterface number is only locally significant, so it doesn't matter which subinterface numbers are configured on the router. Most of the time, I'll configure a subinterface with the same number as the VLAN I want to route. It's easy to remember that way, since the subinterface number is used only for administrative purposes.

It's really important that you understand that each VLAN is a separate subnet. True, I know—they don't *have* to be. But it really is a good idea to configure your VLANs as separate subnets, so just do that.

Now, I need to make sure you're fully prepared to configure inter-VLAN routing, as well as determine the port IP addresses of hosts connected in a switched VLAN environment. And as always, it's also a good idea to be able to fix any problems that may arise. To set you up for success, let me give you few examples.

First, start by looking at Figure 2.23, and read the router and switch configuration within it. By this point in the book, you should be able to determine the IP address, masks, and default gateways of each of the hosts in the VLANs.

FIGURE 2.23   Configuring Inter-VLAN example 1

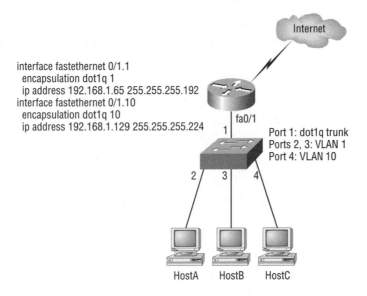

The next step after that is to figure out which subnets are being used. By looking at the router configuration in the figure, you can see that we're using 192.168.1.64/26 with VLAN 1 and 192.168.1.128/27 with VLAN 10. And by looking at the switch configuration, you can see that ports 2 and 3 are in VLAN 1 and port 4 is in VLAN 10. This means that HostA and HostB are in VLAN 1, and HostC is in VLAN 10.

Here's what the hosts' IP addresses should be:

HostA: 192.168.1.66, 255.255.255.192, default gateway 192.168.1.65

HostB: 192.168.1.67, 255.255.255.192, default gateway 192.168.1.65

HostC: 192.168.1.130, 255.255.255.224, default gateway 192.168.1.129

The hosts could be any address in the range—I just choose the first available IP address after the default gateway address. That wasn't so hard, was it?

Now, again using Figure 2.24, let's go through the commands necessary to configure switch port 1 to establish a link with the router and provide inter-VLAN communication using the IEEE version for encapsulation. Keep in mind that the commands can vary slightly depending on what type of switch you're dealing with.

For a 2960 switch, use the following:

```
2960#config t
2960(config)#interface fa0/1
2960(config-if)#switchport mode trunk
```

As you already know, the 2960 switch can only run the 802.1Q encapsulation, so there's no need to specify it. You can't anyway! For a 3560, it's basically the same, but since it can run ISL and 802.1Q, you have to specify the trunking protocol you're going to use.

Remember that when you create a trunked link, all VLANs are allowed to pass data by default.

Let's take a look at Figure 2.24 and see what we can learn from it. This figure shows three VLANs, with two hosts in each of them.

The router in Figure 2.24 is connected to the fa0/1 switch port, and VLAN 2 is configured on port f0/6. Looking at the diagram, these are the things that Cisco expects you to know:

- The router is connected to the switch using subinterfaces.
- The switch port connecting to the router is a trunk port.
- The switch ports connecting to the clients and the hub are access ports, not trunk ports.

FIGURE 2.24   Inter-VLAN example 2

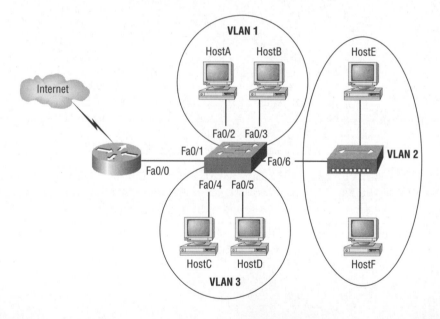

The configuration of the switch would look something like this:

```
2960#config t
2960(config)#int f0/1
2960(config-if)#switchport mode trunk
2960(config-if)#int f0/2
2960(config-if)#switchport access vlan 1
2960(config-if)#int f0/3
2960(config-if)#switchport access vlan 1
2960(config-if)#int f0/4
2960(config-if)#switchport access vlan 3
2960(config-if)#int f0/5
2960(config-if)#switchport access vlan 3
2960(config-if)#int f0/6
2960(config-if)#switchport access vlan 2
```

Before we configure the router, we need to design our logical network:

VLAN 1: 192.168.10.16/28

VLAN 2: 192.168.10.32/28

VLAN 3: 192.168.10.48/28

The configuration of the router would then look like this:

```
ISR#config t
ISR(config)#int f0/0
ISR(config-if)#no ip address
ISR(config-if)#no shutdown
ISR(config-if)#int f0/0.1
ISR(config-subif)#encapsulation dot1q 1
ISR(config-subif)#ip address 192.168.10.17 255.255.255.240
ISR(config-subif)#int f0/0.2
ISR(config-subif)#encapsulation dot1q 2
ISR(config-subif)#ip address 192.168.10.33 255.255.255.240
ISR(config-subif)#int f0/0.3
ISR(config-subif)#encapsulation dot1q 3
ISR(config-subif)#ip address 192.168.10.49 255.255.255.240
```

The hosts in each VLAN would be assigned an address from their subnet range, and the default gateway would be the IP address assigned to the router's subinterface in that VLAN.

Now, let's take a look at another figure and see if you can determine the switch and router configurations without looking at the answer—no cheating! Figure 2.25 shows a router connected to a 2960 switch with two VLANs. One host in each VLAN is assigned an IP address. What are your router and switch configurations based on these IP addresses?

FIGURE 2.25 Inter-VLAN example 3

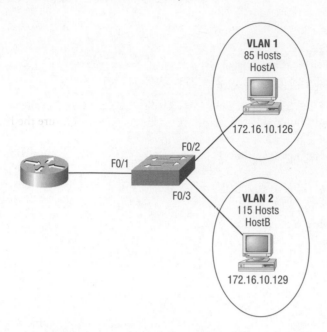

Since the hosts don't list a subnet mask, you have to look for the number of hosts used in each VLAN to figure out the block size. VLAN 1 has 85 hosts and VLAN 2 has 115 hosts. Each of these will fit in a block size of 128, which is a /25 mask, or 255.255.255.128.

You should know by now that the subnets are 0 and 128; the 0 subnet (VLAN 1) has a host range of 1–126, and the 128 subnet (VLAN 2) has a range of 129–254. You can almost be fooled since HostA has an IP address of 126, which makes it *almost* seem that HostA and B are in the same subnet. But they're not, and you're way too smart by now to be fooled by this one!

Here is the switch configuration:

```
2960#config t
2960(config)#int f0/1
2960(config-if)#switchport mode trunk
2960(config-if)#int f0/2
2960(config-if)#switchport access vlan 1
2960(config-if)#int f0/3
2960(config-if)#switchport access vlan 2
```

Here is the router configuration:

```
ISR#config t
ISR(config)#int f0/0
ISR(config-if)#no ip address
ISR(config-if)#no shutdown
```

```
ISR(config-if)#int f0/0.1
ISR(config-subif)#encapsulation dot1q 1
ISR(config-subif)#ip address 172.16.10.1 255.255.255.128
ISR(config-subif)#int f0/0.2
ISR(config-subif)#encapsulation dot1q 2
ISR(config-subif)#ip address 172.16.10.254 255.255.255.128
```

I used the first address in the host range for VLAN 1 and the last address in the range for VLAN 2, but any address in the range would work. You just have to configure the host's default gateway to whatever you make the router's address.

Now, before we go on to the next example, I need to make sure that you know how to set the IP address on the switch. Since VLAN 1 is typically the administrative VLAN, we'll use an IP address from that pool of addresses. Here's how to set the IP address of the switch (I'm not nagging, but you really should already know this!):

```
2960#config t
2960(config)#int vlan 1
2960(config-if)#ip address 172.16.10.2 255.255.255.128
2960(config-if)#no shutdown
```

Yes, you have to do a `no shutdown` on the VLAN interface.

One more example, and then we'll move on to VTP—another important subject that you definitely don't want to miss! In Figure 2.26 there are two VLANs. By looking at the router configuration, what's the IP address, mask, and default gateway of HostA? Use the last IP address in the range for HostA's address:

If you really look carefully at the router configuration (the hostname in this figure is just Router), there is a simple and quick answer. Both subnets are using a /28, or 255.255.255.240 mask, which is a block size of 16. The router's address for VLAN 1 is in subnet 128. The next subnet is 144, so the broadcast address of VLAN 1 is 143 and the valid host range is 129–142. So, the host address would be this:

IP Address: 192.168.10.142

Mask: 255.255.255.240

Default Gateway: 192.168.10.129

Exam Objectives

Remember that hosts in a VLAN can only communicate with hosts in the same VLAN. If you have multiple VLANs and need inter-VLAN communication, you must configure a router or buy a more expensive layer 3 switch to provide the routing on the backplane of the switch.

Remember how to create a Cisco "router on a stick" to provide inter-VLAN communication. You can use a Cisco FastEthernet of Gigabit Ethernet interface to provide inter-VLAN routing. The switch port connected to the router must be a trunk port, then you must create virtual interfaces (subinterfaces) on the router port for each VLAN connecting. The hosts in each VLAN will use this subinterface address as their default gateway address.

FIGURE 2.26 Inter-VLAN example 4

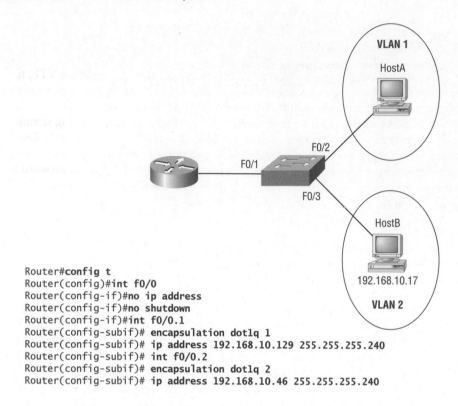

```
Router#config t
Router(config)#int f0/0
Router(config-if)#no ip address
Router(config-if)#no shutdown
Router(config-if)#int f0/0.1
Router(config-subif)# encapsulation dot1q 1
Router(config-subif)# ip address 192.168.10.129 255.255.255.240
Router(config-subif)# int f0/0.2
Router(config-subif)# encapsulation dot1q 2
Router(config-subif)# ip address 192.168.10.46 255.255.255.240
```

Remember how to create a subinterface on a router port. By creating a subinterface on a router, you can use one router port to allow inter-VLAN communication. You must create a subinterface for each VLAN. Here is an example on how to create a subinterface on a router port for VLAN 2:

Router#**config t**

Rotuer(config)#**int f0/0.1**

Router(config-subif)#**encapsulation dot1Q 2**

Remember how to configure a trunk port on a 2960 switch. The 2960 switch only runs the 802.1q trunking method, so the command to trunk a port is simple:

Switch(config-if)#**switchport mode trunk**

2.13 Configure, verify, and troubleshoot VTP

All Cisco switches are configured to be VTP servers by default. To configure VTP, first you have to configure the domain name you want to use. And of course, once you configure the VTP information on a switch, you need to verify it.

When you create the VTP domain, you have a bunch of options, including setting the domain name, password, operating mode, and pruning capabilities of the switch. Use the vtp global configuration mode command to set all this information. In the following example, I'll set the S1 switch to vtp server, the VTP domain to Lammle, and the VTP password to todd:

```
S1#config t
S1#(config)#vtp mode server
Device mode already VTP SERVER.
S1(config)#vtp domain Lammle
Changing VTP domain name from null to Lammle
S1(config)#vtp password todd
Setting device VLAN database password to todd
S1(config)#do show vtp password
VTP Password: todd
S1(config)#do show vtp status
VTP Version                    : 2
Configuration Revision         : 0
Maximum VLANs supported locally : 255
Number of existing VLANs       : 8
VTP Operating Mode             : Server
VTP Domain Name                : Lammle
VTP Pruning Mode               : Disabled
VTP V2 Mode                    : Disabled
VTP Traps Generation           : Disabled
MD5 digest                     : 0x15 0x54 0x88 0xF2 0x50 0xD9 0x03 0x07
Configuration last modified by 192.168.24.6 at 3-14-93 15:47:32
Local updater ID is 192.168.24.6 on interface Vl1 (lowest numbered VLAN
interface found)
```

Please make sure that you remember that all switches are set to VTP server mode by default, and if you want to change any VLAN information on a switch, you absolutely must be in VTP server mode. After you configure the VTP information, you can verify it with the show vtp command as shown in the preceding output. The preceding switch output shows the VTP domain, the VTP password, and the switch's mode.

Before we move onward to configuring the Core and the S2 switch with VTP information, take a minute to reflect on the fact that the show vtp status output shows that the maximum number of VLANs supported locally is only 255. Since you can create more than 1,000 VLANs on a switch, this seems like it would definitely be a problem if you have more then 255 switches and you're using VTP. And, well, yes, it is problem—if you are trying to configure the 256th VLAN on a switch, you'll get a nice little error message stating that there are not enough hardware resources available, and then it will shut down the VLAN and the 256th VLAN will show up in suspended state in the output of the show vlan command. Not so good!

Let's go to the Core and S2 switches and set them into the Lammle VTP domain. It is very important to remember that the VTP domain name is case sensitive! VTP is not forgiving—one teeny small mistake and it just won't work.

```
Core#config t
Core(config)#vtp mode client
Setting device to VTP CLIENT mode.
Core(config)#vtp domain Lammle
Changing VTP domain name from null to Lammle
Core(config)#vtp password todd
Setting device VLAN database password to todd
Core(config)#do show vtp status
VTP Version                        : 2
Configuration Revision             : 0
Maximum VLANs supported locally : 1005
Number of existing VLANs           : 5
VTP Operating Mode                 : Server
VTP Domain Name                    : Lammle
VTP Pruning Mode                   : Disabled
VTP V2 Mode                        : Disabled
VTP Traps Generation               : Disabled
MD5 digest                         : 0x2A 0x6B 0x22 0x17 0x04 0x4F 0xB8 0xC2
Configuration last modified by 192.168.10.19 at 3-1-93 03:13:16
Local updater ID is 192.168.24.7 on interface Vl1 (first interface found)
S2#config t
S2(config)#vtp mode client
Setting device to VTP CLIENT mode.
S2(config)#vtp domain Lammle
Changing VTP domain name from null to Lammle
S2(config)#vtp password todd
Setting device VLAN database password to todd
S2(config)#do show vtp status
VTP Version                        : 2
Configuration Revision             : 0
```

```
Maximum VLANs supported locally : 1005
Number of existing VLANs        : 5
VTP Operating Mode              : Client
VTP Domain Name                 : Lammle
VTP Pruning Mode                : Disabled
VTP V2 Mode                     : Disabled
VTP Traps Generation            : Disabled
MD5 digest                      : 0x02 0x11 0x18 0x4B 0x36 0xC5 0xF4 0x1F
Configuration last modified by 0.0.0.0 at 0-0-00 00:00:00
```

Nice—now that all our switches are set to the same VTP domain and password, the VLANs I created earlier on the S1 switch should be advertised to the Core and S2 VTP client switches. Let's take a look using the show vlan brief command on the Core and S2 switch:

```
Core#sh vlan brief
VLAN Name                 Status     Ports
---- ------------------   ---------  ---------------------
1    default              active     Fa0/1,Fa0/2,Fa0/3,Fa0/4
                                     Fa0/9,Fa0/10,Fa0/11,Fa0/12
                                     Fa0/13,Fa0/14,Fa0/15,
                                     Fa0/16, Fa0/17, Fa0/18, Fa0/19,
                                     Fa0/20,Fa0/21, Fa0/22, Fa0/23,
                                     Fa0/24, Gi0/1, Gi0/2
2    Sales                active
3    Marketing            active
4    Accounting           active
[output cut]


S2#sh vlan bri
VLAN Name                    Status     Ports
---- -----------------------  ---------  ---------------------
1    default                 active     Fa0/3, Fa0/4, Fa0/5, Fa0/6
                                        Fa0/7, Fa0/8, Gi0/1
2    Sales                   active
3    Marketing               active
4    Accounting              active
[output cut]
```

The VLAN database that I created on the S1 (2960) switch earlier in this chapter was uploaded to the Core and S2 switch via VTP advertisements. VTP is a great way to keep VLAN naming consistent across the switched network. We can now assign VLANs to the ports on the Core and S1 switches, and they'll communicate with the hosts in the same VLANs on the S1 switch across the trunked ports between switches.

It's imperative that you can assign a VTP domain name, set the switch to VTP server mode, and create a VLAN!

Troubleshooting VTP

You connect your switches with crossover cables, the lights go green on both ends, and you're up and running! Yeah—in a perfect world, right? Don't you wish it was that easy? Well, actually, it pretty much is—without VLANs, of course. But if you're using VLANs—and you definitely should be—then you need to use VTP if you have multiple VLANs configured in your switched network.

But here there be monsters: If VTP is not configured correctly, it (surprise!) will not work, so you absolutely must be capable of troubleshooting VTP. Let's take a look at a couple of configurations and solve the problems. Study the output from the two following switches:

```
SwitchA#sh vtp status
VTP Version                      : 2
Configuration Revision           : 0
Maximum VLANs supported locally  : 64
Number of existing VLANs         : 7
VTP Operating Mode               : Server
VTP Domain Name                  : RouterSim
VTP Pruning Mode                 : Disabled
VTP V2 Mode                      : Disabled
VTP Traps Generation             : Disabled

SwitchB#sh vtp status
VTP Version                      : 2
Configuration Revision           : 1
Maximum VLANs supported locally  : 64
Number of existing VLANs         : 7
VTP Operating Mode               : Server
VTP Domain Name                  : GlobalNet
VTP Pruning Mode                 : Disabled
VTP V2 Mode                      : Disabled
VTP Traps Generation             : Disabled
```

So, what's happening with these two switches? Why won't they share VLAN information? At first glance, it seems that both servers are in VTP server mode, but that's not the problem. Servers in VTP server mode will share VLAN information using VTP. The problem is that they're in two different VTP *domains*. SwitchA is in VTP domain RouterSim and SwitchB is in VTP domain GlobalNet. They will never share VTP information because the VTP domain names are configured differently.

Now that you know how to look for common VTP domain configuration errors in your switches, let's take a look at another switch configuration:

```
SwitchC#sh vtp status
VTP Version                    : 2
Configuration Revision         : 1
Maximum VLANs supported locally : 64
Number of existing VLANs       : 7
VTP Operating Mode             : Client
VTP Domain Name                : Todd
VTP Pruning Mode               : Disabled
VTP V2 Mode                    : Disabled
VTP Traps Generation           : Disabled
```

There you are just trying to create a new VLAN on SwitchC, and what do you get for your trouble? A loathsome error! Why can't you create a VLAN on SwitchC? Well, the VTP domain name isn't the important thing in this example. What is critical here is the VTP *mode*. The VTP mode is client, and a VTP client cannot create, delete, add, or change VLANs, remember? VTP clients only keep the VTP database in RAM, and that's not saved to NVRAM. So, in order to create a VLAN on this switch, you've got to make the switch a VTP server first.

Here's what will happen when you have the preceding VTP configuration:

```
SwitchC(config)#vlan 50
VTP VLAN configuration not allowed when device is in CLIENT mode.
```

So, to fix this problem, here's what you need to do:

```
SwitchC(config)#vtp mode server
Setting device to VTP SERVER mode
SwitchC(config)#vlan 50
SwitchC(config-vlan)#
```

Wait, we're not done. Now take a look at the output from these two switches and determine why SwitchB is not receiving VLAN information from SwitchA:

```
SwitchA#sh vtp status
VTP Version                    : 2
Configuration Revision         : 4
Maximum VLANs supported locally : 64
Number of existing VLANs       : 7
VTP Operating Mode             : Server
VTP Domain Name                : GlobalNet
```

```
VTP Pruning Mode              : Disabled
VTP V2 Mode                   : Disabled
VTP Traps Generation          : Disabled

SwitchB#sh vtp status
VTP Version                   : 2
Configuration Revision        : 14
Maximum VLANs supported locally : 64
Number of existing VLANs      : 7
VTP Operating Mode            : Server
VTP Domain Name               : GlobalNet
VTP Pruning Mode              : Disabled
VTP V2 Mode                   : Disabled
VTP Traps Generation          : Disabled
```

You may be tempted to say it's because they're both VTP servers, but that is not the problem. All your switches can be servers and they can still share VLAN information. As a matter of fact, Cisco actually suggests that all switches stay VTP servers and that you just make sure the switch you want to advertise VTP VLAN information has the highest revision number. If all switches are VTP servers, then all of the switches will save the VLAN database. But SwitchB isn't receiving VLAN information from SwitchA because SwitchB has a higher revision number than SwitchA. It's very important that you can recognize this problem.

There are a couple ways to go about resolving this issue. The first thing you could do is to change the VTP domain name on SwitchB to another name, then set it back to GlobalNet, which will reset the revision number to zero (0) on SwitchB. The second approach would be to create or delete VLANs on SwitchA until the revision number passes the revision number on SwitchB. I didn't say the second way was better; I just said it's another way to fix it!

Exam Objectives

Understand the purpose and configuration of VTP.   VTP provides propagation of the VLAN database throughout your switched network. All switches must be in the same VTP domain.

Remember the command to verify VTP.   Unfortunately, there are not a lot of ways to verify your VTP configuration. The best way is by using the command show vtp status. This shows you your domain name, password, and revision number.

2.14 Configure, verify, and troubleshoot RSTP operation

Configuring RSTP actually is as easy as configuring any of our other 802.1d extensions. Considering how much better it is than 802.1d, you'd think the configuration would be more complex, but we're in luck—it's not. So, let's turn it on in the Core switch now and see what happens:

```
Core#config t
Core(config)#spanning-tree mode ?
  mst        Multiple spanning tree mode
  pvst       Per-Vlan spanning tree mode
  rapid-pvst Per-Vlan rapid spanning tree mode
Core(config)#spanning-tree mode rapid-pvst
Core(config)#
1d02h: %LINEPROTO-5-UPDOWN: Line protocol on Interface Vlan1,
 changed state to down
1d02h: %LINEPROTO-5-UPDOWN: Line protocol on Interface Vlan1,
 changed state to up
```

Sweet! The Core switch is now running the 802.1w STP. Let's verify that:

```
Core(config)#do show spanning-tree
VLAN0001
  Spanning tree enabled protocol rstp
  Root ID    Priority    32769
             Address     000d.29bd.4b80
             This bridge is the root
             Hello Time   2 sec  Max Age 20 sec  Forward Delay 15 sec

  Bridge ID  Priority    32769  (priority 32768 sys-id-ext 1)
             Address     000d.29bd.4b80
             Hello Time   2 sec  Max Age 20 sec  Forward Delay 15 sec
             Aging Time 300

Interface        Role Sts Cost      Prio.Nbr Type
---------------- ---- --- --------- -------- ------------
Fa0/5            Desg FWD 19        128.5    P2p Peer(STP)
Fa0/6            Desg FWD 19        128.6    P2p Peer(STP)
Fa0/7            Desg FWD 19        128.7    P2p Peer(STP)
Fa0/8            Desg FWD 19        128.8    P2p Peer(STP)
```

Interesting . . . it looks like nothing really happened. I can see on my two other switches that all ports have converged. Once everything was up, everything looked the same. 802.1d and 802.1w seem to be cohabiting with no problem.

But, if we were to look under the hood more closely, we'd see that the 802.1w switch has changed from 802.1w BPDUs to 802.1d BPDUs on the ports connecting to the other switches running 802.1d (which is all of them).

The S1 and S2 switches believe that the Core switch is actually running 802.1d because the Core reverted to 802.1d BPDUs just for them. And even though the S1 and S2 switches receive the 802.1w BPDUs, they don't understand them, so they simply drop them. However, the Core does receive the 802.1d BPDUs and accepts them from the S1 and S2 switches, now knowing which ports to run 802.1d on. In other words, turning 802.1w on for just one switch didn't really help our network at all!

One small annoying issue is that once the Core switch knows to send 802.1d BPDUs out the ports connected to S1 and S2, it won't change this automatically if the S1 and S2 switches were later configured with 802.1w—we'd still need to reboot the Core switch to stop the 802.1d BPDUs.

Exam Objectives

Remember how to enable RSVP.   To enable RSVP, use the following command:

```
Router(config)#spanning-tree mode rapid-pvst
```

Remember to reboot the switch when changing to RSVP.   If you have a switch in your network that is not running 802.1w, then you need to reboot your switches when enabling RSTP to stop the 802.1d BPDU's from being sent out the switch port.

2.15 Interpret the output of various show and debug commands to verify the operational status of a Cisco switched network

For information on this objective, please review objective 2.6.

2.16 Implement basic switch security (including: port security, trunk access, management vlan other than vlan1, etc.)

So, just how do you stop someone from simply plugging a host into one of your switch ports— or worse, adding a hub, switch, or access point into the Ethernet jack in their office? By default, MAC addresses will just dynamically appear in your MAC forward/filter database. You can stop them in their tracks by using port security. Here are your options:

```
Switch#config t
Switch(config)#int f0/1
Switch(config-if)#switchport port-security ?
  aging          Port-security aging commands
  mac-address    Secure mac address
  maximum        Max secure addresses
  violation      Security violation mode
  <cr>
```

You can see clearly in the preceding output that the `switchport port-security` command can be used with four options. Personally, I like the `port-security` command because it allows me to easily control users on my network. You can use the `switchport port-security mac-address` *mac-address* command to assign individual MAC addresses to each switch port, but if you choose to go there, you'd better have a lot of time on your hands!

If you want to set up a switch port to allow only one host per port, and to shut down the port if this rule is violated, use the following commands:

```
Switch#config t
Switch(config)#int f0/1
Switch(config-if)#switchport port-security maximum 1
Switch(config-if)#switchport port-security violation shutdown
```

These commands are probably the most popular because they prevent users from connecting to a switch or access point that's in their office. The `maximum` setting of 1 means that only one MAC address can be used on that port; if the user tries to add another host on that segment, the switch port will shut down. If that happens, you'd have to manually go into the switch and enable the port with a `no shutdown` command.

Probably one of my favorite commands is the `sticky` command. Not only does it perform a cool function; it's got a cool name! You can find this command under the `mac-address` command:

```
Switch(config-if)#switchport port-security mac-address sticky
Switch(config-if)#switchport port-security maximum 2
Switch(config-if)#switchport port-security violation shutdown
```

Basically, what this does is provide static MAC address security without having to type in everyone's MAC address on the network. As I said—cool!

In the preceding example, the first two MAC addresses into the port "stick" as static addresses and will stay that way for however long you set the aging command for. Why did I set it to 2? Well, I needed one for the PC/data and one for telephony/phone.

Configuring Trunk Ports

The 2960 switch only runs the IEEE 802.1Q encapsulation method. To configure trunking on a Fast Ethernet port, use the interface command trunk [*parameter*]. It's a tad different on the 3560 switch, and I'll show you that in the next section.

The following switch output shows the trunk configuration on interface fa0/8 as set to trunk on:

```
S1#config t
S1(config)#int fa0/8
S1(config-if)#switchport mode trunk
```

The following list describes the different options available when configuring a switch interface:

switchport mode access   I discussed this in the previous section, but this puts the interface (access port) into permanent nontrunking mode and negotiates to convert the link into a nontrunk link. The interface becomes a nontrunk interface regardless of whether the neighboring interface is a trunk interface. The port would be a dedicated layer 2 port.

switchport mode dynamic auto   This mode makes the interface able to convert the link to a trunk link. The interface becomes a trunk interface if the neighboring interface is set to trunk or desirable mode. This is now the default switchport mode for all Ethernet interfaces on all new Cisco switches.

switchport mode dynamic desirable   This one makes the interface actively attempt to convert the link to a trunk link. The interface becomes a trunk interface if the neighboring interface is set to trunk, desirable, or auto mode. I used to see this mode as the default on some older switches, but not any longer. The default is dynamic auto now.

switchport mode trunk   Puts the interface into permanent trunking mode and negotiates to convert the neighboring link into a trunk link. The interface becomes a trunk interface even if the neighboring interface isn't a trunk interface.

switchport nonegotiate   Prevents the interface from generating DTP frames. You can use this command only when the interface switchport mode is access or trunk. You must manually configure the neighboring interface as a trunk interface to establish a trunk link.

Dynamic Trunking Protocol (DTP) is used for negotiating trunking on a link between two devices, as well as negotiating the encapsulation type of either 802.1Q or ISL. I use the nonegotiate command when I want dedicated trunk ports no questions asked.

To disable trunking on an interface, use the switchport mode access command, which sets the port back to a dedicated layer 2 switch port.

Trunking with the Cisco Catalyst 3560 Switch

Okay, let's take a look at one more switch—the Cisco Catalyst 3560. The configuration is pretty much the same as it is for a 2960, with the exception that the 3560 can provide layer 3 services and the 2960 can't. Plus, the 3560 can run both the ISL and the IEEE 802.1Q trunking encapsulation methods—the 2960 can only run 802.1Q. With all this in mind, let's take a quick look at the VLAN encapsulation difference regarding the 3560 switch.

The 3560 has the encapsulation command, which the 2960 switch doesn't:

```
Core(config-if)#switchport trunk encapsulation ?
  dot1q     Interface uses only 802.1q trunking encapsulation
 when trunking
  isl       Interface uses only ISL trunking encapsulation
 when trunking
  negotiate Device will negotiate trunking encapsulation with peer on
            interface
Core(config-if)#switchport trunk encapsulation dot1q
Core(config-if)#switchport mode trunk
```

As you can see, we've got the option to add either the IEEE 802.1Q (dot1q) encapsulation or the ISL encapsulation to the 3560 switch. After you set the encapsulation, you still have to set the interface mode to trunk. Honestly, it's pretty rare that you'd continue to use the ISL encapsulation method. Cisco is moving away from ISL—its new routers don't even support it.

Defining the Allowed VLANs on a Trunk

As I've mentioned, trunk ports send and receive information from all VLANs by default, and if a frame is untagged, it's sent to the management VLAN. This applies to the extended range VLANs as well.

But we can remove VLANs from the allowed list to prevent traffic from certain VLANs from traversing a trunked link. Here's how you'd do that:

```
S1#config t
S1(config)#int f0/1
S1(config-if)#switchport trunk allowed vlan ?
  WORD    VLAN IDs of the allowed VLANs when this port is in
 trunking mode
  add     add VLANs to the current list
  all     all VLANs
  except  all VLANs except the following
  none    no VLANs
  remove  remove VLANs from the current list
S1(config-if)#switchport trunk allowed vlan remove ?
  WORD    VLAN IDs of disallowed VLANS when this port is in trunking mode
S1(config-if)#switchport trunk allowed vlan remove 4
```

The preceding command stopped the trunk link configured on S1 port f0/1, causing it to drop all traffic sent and received for VLAN 4. You can try to remove VLAN 1 on a trunk link, but it will still send and receive management like CDP, PAgP, LACP, DTP, and VTP, so what's the point?

To remove a range of VLANs, just use a hyphen:

```
S1(config-if)#switchport trunk allowed vlan remove 4-8
```

If by chance someone has removed some VLANs from a trunk link and you want to set the trunk back to default, just use this command:

```
S1(config-if)#switchport trunk allowed vlan all
```

Or this command to accomplish the same thing:

```
S1(config-if)#no switchport trunk allowed vlan
```

Next, I want to show you how to configure pruning for VLANs before we start routing between VLANs.

Changing or Modifying the Trunk Native VLAN

You really don't want to change the trunk port native VLAN from VLAN 1, but you can, and some people do it for security reasons. To change the native VLAN, use the following command:

```
S1#config t
S1(config)#int f0/1
S1(config-if)#switchport trunk ?
  allowed  Set allowed VLAN characteristics when interface is
in trunking mode
  native   Set trunking native characteristics when interface
is in trunking mode
  pruning  Set pruning VLAN characteristics when interface is
in trunking mode
S1(config-if)#switchport trunk native ?
  vlan  Set native VLAN when interface is in trunking mode
S1(config-if)#switchport trunk native vlan ?
  <1-4094>  VLAN ID of the native VLAN when this port is in
 trunking mode
S1(config-if)#switchport trunk native vlan 40
S1(config-if)#^Z
```

So we've changed our native VLAN on our trunk link to 40, and by using the show running-config command, I can see the configuration under the trunk link:

```
!
interface FastEthernet0/1
```

```
 switchport trunk native vlan 40
 switchport trunk allowed vlan 1-3,9-4094
 switchport trunk pruning vlan 3,4
!
```

Hold on there, partner! You didn't think it would be this easy and would just start working, did you? Sure you didn't. Here's the rub: If all switches don't have the same native VLAN configured on the trunk links, then we'll start to receive this error:

```
19:23:29: %CDP-4-NATIVE_VLAN_MISMATCH: Native VLAN mismatch
discovered on FastEthernet0/1 (40), with Core FastEthernet0/7 (1).
19:24:29: %CDP-4-NATIVE_VLAN_MISMATCH: Native VLAN mismatch
discovered on FastEthernet0/1 (40), with Core FastEthernet0/7 (1).
```

Actually, this is a good, noncryptic error, so either we go to the other end of our trunk link(s) and change the native VLAN or we set the native VLAN back to the default. Here's how we'd do that:

```
S1(config-if)#no switchport trunk native vlan
```

Now our trunk link is using the default VLAN 1 as the native VLAN. Just remember that all switches must use the same native VLAN or you'll have some serious problems. Now, let's mix it up by connecting a router into our switched network and configuring inter-VLAN communication.

Port Security

As I said earlier in the chapter, it's usually not a good thing to have your switches available for anyone to just plug into and play around with. I mean, you demand wireless security, so why wouldn't you want switch security just as much?

The answer is, you do, and by using port security, you can limit the number of MAC addresses that can be assigned dynamically to a port, set a static MAC address, and—here's my favorite part—set penalties for users who abuse your policy. Personally, I like to have the port shut down when the security policy is violated and then make the abusers bring me a memo from their boss explaining to me why they violated the security policy before I'll enable their port again. That usually really helps them remember to behave!

A secured switch port can associate anywhere from 1 to 8,192 MAC addresses, but the '50 series can support only 192, which seems like enough to me. You can choose to allow the switch to learn these values dynamically, or you can set a static address for each port using the `switchport port-security mac-address` *mac-address* command.

So, let's set port security on our S1 switch now. Ports fa0/3 and fa0/4 have only one device connected in our lab. By using port security, we can know for certain that no other device can connect once our host in port fa0/2 and the phone in fa0/3 are connected. Here's how we'll do that:

```
S1#config t
Enter configuration commands, one per line.  End with CNTL/Z.
```

```
S1(config)#int range fa0/3 - 4
S1(config-if-range)#switchport port-security maximum ?
  <1-8192>  Maximum addresses
S1(config-if-range)#switchport port-security maximum 1
S1(config-if-range)#switchport port-security mac-address sticky
S1(config-if-range)#switchport port-security violation ?
  protect   Security violation protect mode
  restrict  Security violation restrict mode
  shutdown  Security violation shutdown mode
S1(config-if-range)#switchport port-security violation shutdown
S1(config-if-range)#exit
```

The preceding command set port security on port fa0/3 and fa0/4 to allow a maximum association of one MAC address, and only the first MAC address associated to the port will be able to send frames through the switch. If a second device with a different MAC address were to try and send a frame into the switch, the port would be shut down because of our violation command. I use the sticky command because I am way too lazy to type in all the MAC addresses of each device by hand!

There are two other modes you can use instead of just shutting down the port. The protect mode means that another host can connect, but its frames will just be dropped. Restrict mode is also pretty cool—it alerts you via SNMP that a violation has occurred on a port. You can then call the abuser and tell them they're so busted—you can see them, you know what they did, and they're in big-time trouble!

In our connection between switches we have redundant links, so it's best to let STP run on those links (for now). But on our R1 and R2 switches, we also have hosts connected to port fa0/3 and fa0/4 (not the Core). So let's turn STP off on those ports.

Exam Objectives

Remember how to set port security on a switch port.   If you want to set up a switch port to allow only one host per port, and to shut down the port if this rule is violated, use the following commands:

```
Switch#config t
Switch(config)#int f0/1
Switch(config-if)#switchport port-security maximum 1
Switch(config-if)#switchport port-security violation shutdown
```

Remember how to configure a trunk port on a 2960 switch.   The 2960 switch only runs the 802.1q trunking method, so the command to trunk a port is simple:

```
Switch(config-if)#switchport mode trunk
```

Review Questions

1. You need to configure a Catalyst switch so that it can be managed remotely. Which of the following would you use to accomplish this task?

    A. Switch(configs)#int fa0/1

    B. Switch(configs-if)#ip address 192.168.10.252 255.255.255.0

    C. Switch(configs-if)#no shut

    D. Switch(configs)#int vlan 1

    E. Switch(configs-if)#ip address 192.168.10.252 255.255.255.0

    F. Switch(configs-if)#ip default-gateway 192.168.10.254 255.255.255.0

    G. Switch(configs)#ip default-gateway 192.168.10.254

    H. Switch(configs)#int vlan 1

    I. Switch(configs-if)#ip address 192.168.10.252 255.255.255.0

    J. Switch(configs-if)#no shut

    K. Switch(configs)#ip default-network 192.168.10.254

    L. Switch(configs)#int vlan 1

    M. Switch(configs-if)#ip address 192.168.10.252 255.255.255.0

    N. Switch(configs-if)#no shut

2. What does a switch do when a frame is received on an interface and the destination hardware address is unknown or not in the filter table?

    A. Forwards the switch to the first available link

    B. Drops the frame

    C. Floods the network with the frame looking for the device

    D. Sends back a message to the originating station asking for a name resolution

3. If a switch receives a frame and the source MAC address is not in the MAC address table but the destination address is, what will the switch do with the frame?

    A. Discard it and send an error message back to the originating host

    B. Flood the network with the frame

    C. Add the source address and port to the MAC address table and forward the frame out the destination port

    D. Add the destination to the MAC address table and then forward the frame

4. You want to run the new 802.1w on your switches. Which of the following would enable this protocol?

   A. `Switch(config)#spanning-tree mode rapid-pvst`

   B. `Switch#spanning-tree mode rapid-pvst`

   C. `Switch(config)#spanning-tree mode 802.1w`

   D. `Switch#spanning-tree mode 802.1w`

5. In which circumstance are multiple copies of the same unicast frame likely to be transmitted in a switched LAN?

   A. During high-traffic periods

   B. After broken links are reestablished

   C. When upper-layer protocols require high reliability

   D. In an improperly implemented redundant topology

6. Which command was used to produce the following output:

Vlan	Mac Address	Type	Ports
1	0005.dccb.d74b	DYNAMIC	Fa0/1
1	000a.f467.9e80	DYNAMIC	Fa0/3
1	000a.f467.9e8b	DYNAMIC	Fa0/4
1	000a.f467.9e8c	DYNAMIC	Fa0/3
1	0010.7b7f.c2b0	DYNAMIC	Fa0/3
1	0030.80dc.460b	DYNAMIC	Fa0/3

   A. `show vlan`

   B. `show ip route`

   C. `show mac address-table`

   D. D. `show mac address-filter`

7. If you want to disable STP on a port connected to a server, which command would you use?

   A. `disable spanning-tree`

   B. `spanning-tree off`

   C. `spanning-tree security`

   D. `spanning-tree portfast`

8. Refer to the graphic. Why does the switch have two MAC addresses assigned to the FastEthernet 0/1 port in the switch address table?

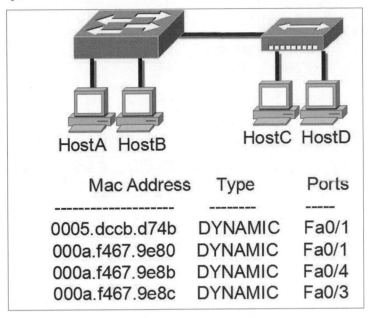

Mac Address	Type	Ports
0005.dccb.d74b	DYNAMIC	Fa0/1
000a.f467.9e80	DYNAMIC	Fa0/1
000a.f467.9e8b	DYNAMIC	Fa0/4
000a.f467.9e8c	DYNAMIC	Fa0/3

A. Data from HostC and HostD have been received by the switch port FastEthernet 0/1.

B. Data from two of the devices connected to the switch have been forwarded out to HostD.

C. HostC and HostD had their NIC replaced.

D. HostC and HostD are on different VLANs.

9. Layer 2 switching provides which of the following? (Choose four.)

A. Hardware-based bridging (ASIC)

B. B. Wire speed

C. C. Low latency

D. D. Low cost

E. E. Routing

F. WAN services

10. You type **show mac address-table** and receive the following output:

```
Switch#sh mac address-table
Vlan    Mac Address      Type       Ports
----    -----------      --------   -----
   1    0005.dccb.d74b   DYNAMIC    Fa0/1
   1    000a.f467.9e80   DYNAMIC    Fa0/3
   1    000a.f467.9e8b   DYNAMIC    Fa0/4
   1    000a.f467.9e8c   DYNAMIC    Fa0/3
   1    0010.7b7f.c2b0   DYNAMIC    Fa0/3
   1    0030.80dc.460b   DYNAMIC    Fa0/3
```

Suppose that the above switch received a frame with the following MAC addresses:

- Source MAC: 0005.dccb.d74b
- Destination MAC: 000a.f467.9e8c

What will it do?

A. It will discard the frame.

B. It will forward the frame out port Fa0/3 only.

C. It will forward it out Fa0/1 only.

D. It will send it out all ports except Fa0/1.

Answers to Review Questions

1. Answer:C. Explanation:To manage a switch remotely, you must set an IP address under the management VLAN, which is, by default, `interface vlan 1`. Then, from global configuration mode, you set the default gateway with the `ip default-gateway` command.

2. Answer:C. Explanation:Switches flood all frames that have an unknown destination address. If a device answers the frame, the switch will update the MAC address table to reflect the location of the device.

3. Answer:C. Explanation:Since the source MAC address is not in the MAC address table, the switch will add the source address and the port it is connected to into the MAC address table and then forward the frame to the outgoing port.

4. Answer:A. Explanation:802.1w is the also called Rapid Spanning-Tree Protocol. It is not enabled by default on Cisco switches, but it is a better STP to run since it has all the fixes that the Cisco extensions provide with 802.1d.

5. Answer:D. Explanation:If the Spanning-Tree Protocol is not running on your switches and you connect them together with redundant links, you will have broadcast storms and multiple frame copies

6. Answer:C. Explanation:The command `show mac address-table` will display the forward/ filter table, also called a CAM table on a switch.

7. Answer:D. Explanation:If you have a server or other devices connected into your switch that you're totally sure won't create a switching loop if STP is disabled, you can use something called `portfast` on these ports. Using it means that the port won't spend the usual 50 seconds to come up while STP is converging.

8. Answer:A. Explanation:A switch can have multiple MAC addresses associated with a port. In the graphic, a hub is connected to port Fa0/1, which has two hosts connected.

9. Answer:A, B, C, D. Explanation:Switches, unlike bridges, are hardware based. Cisco says its switches are wire speed and provide low latency, and I guess they are low cost compared to their prices in the 1990s.

10. Answer:B. Explanation:Since the destination MAC address is in the MAC address table (forward/filter table), it will send it out port Fa0/3 only.

Chapter

3

Implement an IP addressing scheme and IP Services to meet network requirements in a medium-size Enterprise branch office network.

THE CISCO CCNA EXAM OBJECTIVES COVERED IN THIS CHAPTER INCLUDE:

- 3.1 Describe the operation and benefits of using private and public IP addressing

- 3.2 Explain the operation and benefits of using DHCP and DNS

- 3.3 Configure, verify, and troubleshoot DHCP and DNS operation on a router (including CLI/SDM)

- 3.4 Implement static and dynamic addressing services for hosts in a LAN environment

- 3.5 Calculate and apply an addressing scheme, including VLSM IP addressing design, to a network

- 3.6 Determine the appropriate classless addressing scheme using VLSM and summarization to satisfy addressing requirements in a LAN/WAN environment

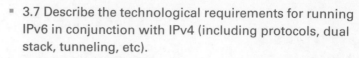

- 3.7 Describe the technological requirements for running IPv6 in conjunction with IPv4 (including protocols, dual stack, tunneling, etc).

- 3.8 Describe IPv6 addresses

- 3.9 Identify and correct common problems associated with IP addressing and host configurations

We'll start with addressing an IP network. You're going to have to really apply yourself, because this takes time and practice in order to nail it. So be patient. Do whatever it takes to get this stuff dialed in. I highly recommend that you also read Chapters 2 and 3 in my *CCNA Study Guide*, 6th edition.

After our discussion of IP subnetting, I'm going to tell you all about Variable Length Subnet Masks (VLSMs), as well as show you how to design and implement a network using VLSM networks.

Once you have mastered VLSM design and implementation, I'll show you how to summarize classful boundaries.

I also hope you're ready to learn about the nuts and bolts of Internet Protocol version 6 (IPv6), because you're going to get the rub on it in this chapter!

People refer to IPv6 as "the next-generation Internet protocol," and it was originally created as the answer to IPv4's inevitable, looming address-exhaustion crisis. Though you've probably heard a thing or two about IPv6 already, it has been improved even further in the quest to bring us the flexibility, efficiency, capability, and optimized functionality that can truly meet our ever-increasing needs. The capacity of its predecessor, IPv4, pales in comparison—and that's the reason it will eventually fade into history completely.

For up-to-the-minute updates on the CCNA objectives covered by this chapter, please see www.lammle.com and/or www.sybex.com.

3.1 Describe the operation and benefits of using private and public IP addressing

One of the most important topics in any discussion of TCP/IP is IP addressing. An *IP address* is a numeric identifier assigned to each machine on an IP network. It designates the specific location of a device on the network.

An IP address is a software address, not a hardware address—the latter is hard-coded on a network interface card (NIC) and used for finding hosts on a local network. IP addressing was designed to allow hosts on one network to communicate with a host on a different network regardless of the type of LANs the hosts are participating in.

Before we get into the more complicated aspects of IP addressing, you need to understand some of the basics. First, I'm going to explain some of the fundamentals of IP addressing and its terminology. Then you'll learn about the hierarchical IP addressing scheme and private IP addresses.

IP Terminology

Throughout this chapter, you'll learn several important terms vital to your understanding of the Internet Protocol. Here are a few to get you started:

Bit   A *bit* is one digit, either a 1 or a 0.

Byte   A *byte* is 7 or 8 bits, depending on whether parity is used. For the rest of this chapter, always assume a byte is 8 bits.

Octet   An octet, made up of 8 bits, is just an ordinary 8-bit binary number. In this chapter, the terms *byte* and *octet* are completely interchangeable.

Network address   This is the designation used in routing to send packets to a remote network—for example, 10.0.0.0, 172.16.0.0, and 192.168.10.0.

Broadcast address   The address used by applications and hosts to send information to all nodes on a network is called the *broadcast address*. Examples include 255.255.255.255, which is all networks, all nodes; 172.16.255.255, which is all subnets and hosts on network 172.16.0.0; and 10.255.255.255, which broadcasts to all subnets and hosts on network 10.0.0.0.

Class A Addresses

The designers of the IP address scheme said that the first bit of the first byte in a Class A network address must always be off, or 0. This means a Class A address must be between 0 and 127 inclusive.

Consider the following network address:

0xxxxxxx

If we turn the other 7 bits all off and then turn them all on, we'll find the Class A range of network addresses:

00000000 = 0
01111111 = 127

So, a Class A network is defined in the first octet between 0 and 127, and it can't be less or more. (I'll talk about illegal addresses in a minute.)

In a Class A network address, the first byte is assigned to the network address, and the three remaining bytes are used for the node addresses. The Class A format is:

network.node.node.node

For example, in the IP address 49.22.102.70, the 49 is the network address, and 22.102.70 is the node address. Every machine on this particular network would have the distinctive network address of 49.

Class A network addresses are 1 byte long, with the first bit of that byte reserved and the seven remaining bits available for manipulation (addressing). As a result, the maximum number of Class A networks that can be created is 128. Why? Because each of the seven bit positions can either be a 0 or a 1, thus 2^7 or 128.

To complicate matters further, the network address of all 0s (0000 0000) is reserved to designate the default route. Additionally, the address 127, which is reserved for diagnostics, can't be used either, which means that you can really only use the numbers 1 to 126 to designate Class A network addresses. This means the actual number of usable Class A network addresses is 128 minus 2, or 126.

Each Class A address has three bytes (24-bit positions) for the node address of a machine. This means there are 2^{24}—or 16,777,216—unique combinations and, therefore, precisely that many possible unique node addresses for each Class A network. Because node addresses with the two patterns of all 0s and all 1s are reserved, the actual maximum usable number of nodes for a Class A network is 2^{24} minus 2, which equals 16,777,214. Either way, that's a huge number of hosts on a network segment!

Class B Addresses

In a Class B network, the RFCs state that the first bit of the first byte must always be turned on, but the second bit must always be turned off. If you turn the other 6 bits all off and then all on, you will find the range for a Class B network:

10000000 = 128
10111111 = 191

As you can see, this means that a Class B network is defined when the first byte is configured from 128 to 191.

In a Class B network address, the first 2 bytes are assigned to the network address, and the remaining 2 bytes are used for node addresses. The format is:

network.network.node.node

For example, in the IP address 172.16.30.56, the network address is 172.16, and the node address is 30.56.

With a network address being 2 bytes (8 bits each), there would be 2^{16} unique combinations. But the Internet Protocol designers decided that all Class B network addresses should start with the binary digit 1, then 0. This leaves 14 bit positions to manipulate, and therefore 16,384 (that is, 2^{14}) unique Class B network addresses.

A Class B address uses two bytes for node addresses. This is 2^{16} minus the two reserved patterns (all 0s and all 1s), for a total of 65,534 possible node addresses for each Class B network.

Class C Addresses

For Class C networks, the RFCs define the first two bits of the first octet always turned on, but the third bit can never be on. Following the same process as the previous classes, convert from binary to decimal to find the range. Here's the range for a Class C network:

11000000 = 192
11011111 = 223

So, if you see an IP address that starts at 192 and goes to 223, you'll know it is a Class C IP address.

The first 3 bytes of a Class C network address are dedicated to the network portion of the address, with only one measly byte remaining for the node address. The format is

network.network.network.node

Using the example IP address 192.168.100.102, the network address is 192.168.100, and the node address is 102.

In a Class C network address, the first three bit positions are always the binary 110. The calculation is such: 3 bytes, or 24 bits, minus 3 reserved positions, leaves 21 positions. Hence, there are 2^{21}, or 2,097,152, possible Class C networks.

Each unique Class C network has 1 byte to use for node addresses. This leads to 2^8 or 256, minus the two reserved patterns of all 0s and all 1s, for a total of 254 node addresses for each Class C network.

Network Addresses: Special Purpose

Some IP addresses are reserved for special purposes, so network administrators can't ever assign these addresses to nodes. Table 3.1 lists the members of this exclusive little club and why they're included in it.

TABLE 3.1 Reserved IP Addresses

Address	Function
Network address of all 0s	Interpreted to mean "this network or segment."
Network address of all 1s	Interpreted to mean "all networks."
Network 127.0.0.0	Reserved for loopback tests. Designates the local node and allows that node to send a test packet to itself without generating network traffic.
Node address of all 0s	Interpreted to mean "network address." or any host on specified network.
Node address of all 1s	Interpreted to mean "all nodes" on the specified network; for example, 128.2.255.255 means "all nodes" on network 128.2 (Class B address).
Entire IP address set to all 0s	Used by Cisco routers to designate the default route. Could also mean "any network."
Entire IP address set to all 1s (same as 255.255.255.255)	Broadcast to all nodes on the current network; sometimes called an "all 1s broadcast" or limited broadcast.

Private IP Addresses

The people who created the IP addressing scheme also created what we call *private IP addresses*. These addresses can be used on a private network, but they're not routable through the Internet. This is designed for the purpose of creating a measure of much-needed security, but it also conveniently saves valuable IP address space.

If every host on every network had to have real routable IP addresses, we would have run out of IP addresses to hand out years ago. But by using private IP addresses, ISPs, corporations, and home users only need a relatively tiny group of bona fide IP addresses to connect their networks to the Internet. This is economical because they can use private IP addresses on their inside networks and get along just fine.

To accomplish this task, the ISP and the corporation—the end user, no matter who they are—need to use something called *Network Address Translation (NAT)*, which basically takes a private IP address and converts it for use on the Internet. Many people can use the same real IP address to transmit out onto the Internet. Doing things this way saves megatons of address space—good for us all!

So, What Private IP Address Should I Use?

That's a really great question: Should you use Class A, Class B, or even Class C private addressing when setting up your network? Let's take Acme Corporation in SF as an example. This company is moving into a new building and needs a whole new network (what a treat this is!). It has 14 departments, with about 70 users in each. You could probably squeeze one or two Class C addresses to use, or maybe you could use a Class B, or even a Class A just for fun.

The rule of thumb in the consulting world is, when you're setting up a corporate network—regardless of how small it is—you should use a Class A network address because it gives you the most flexibility and growth options. For example, if you used the 10.0.0.0 network address with a /24 mask, then you'd have 65,536 networks, each with 254 hosts. Lots of room for growth with that network!

But if you're setting up a home network, you'd opt for a Class C address because it is the easiest for people to understand and configure. Using the default Class C mask gives you one network with 254 hosts—plenty for a home network.

With the Acme Corporation, a nice 10.1.*x*.0 with a /24 mask (the *x* is the subnet for each department) makes this easy to design, install, and troubleshoot.

The reserved private addresses are listed in Table 3.2.

TABLE 3.2   Reserved IP Address Space

Address Class	Reserved Address Space
Class A	10.0.0.0 through 10.255.255.255
Class B	172.16.0.0 through 172.31.255.255
Class C	192.168.0.0 through 192.168.255.255

Exam Objectives

Understand the three different classes of IP address, and the associated network sizes.   Know the ranges for class A, B, and C addresses, and the rules for finding the associated network and node bits. Also, know the sizes of a class A, B, and C network.

Understand private IP addresses and NAT.   Private IP addresses are just like any other IP address, with the exception that they are not routable on the public Internet. Know the ranges for them and how they are used with NAT to connect to the Internet.

3.2 Explain the operation and benefits of using DHCP and DNS

Domain Name Service (DNS) resolves hostnames—specifically, Internet names, such as www.lammle.com. You don't have to use DNS; you can just type in the IP address of any device you want to communicate with. An IP address identifies hosts on a network and the Internet as well. However, DNS was designed to make our lives easier. Think about this: What would happen if you wanted to move your web page to a different service provider? The IP address would change, and no one would know what the new one was. DNS allows you to use a domain name to specify an IP address. You can change the IP address as often as you want, and no one will know the difference.

DNS is used to resolve a *fully qualified domain name (FQDN)*—for example, www.lammle .com or todd.lammle.com. An FQDN is a hierarchy that can logically locate a system based on its domain identifier.

If you want to resolve the name *todd*, you either must type in the FQDN of todd.lammle .com or have a device such as a PC or router add the suffix for you. For example, on a Cisco router, you can use the command ip domain-name lammle.com to append each request with the lammle.com domain. If you don't do that, you'll have to type in the FQDN to get DNS to resolve the name.

> An important thing to remember about DNS is that if you can ping a device with an IP address but cannot use its FQDN, then you might have some type of DNS configuration failure.

Dynamic Host Configuration Protocol (DHCP)/Bootstrap Protocol (BOOTP)

Dynamic Host Configuration Protocol (DHCP) assigns IP addresses to hosts. It allows easier administration and works well in small to even very large network environments. All types of hardware can be used as a DHCP server, including a Cisco router.

DHCP differs from BOOTP in that BOOTP assigns an IP address to a host but the host's hardware address must be entered manually in a BOOTP table. You can think of DHCP as a dynamic BOOTP. But remember that BOOTP is also used to send an operating system that a host can boot from. DHCP can't do that.

But there is a lot of information a DHCP server can provide to a host when the host is requesting an IP address from the DHCP server. Here's a list of the information a DHCP server can provide:

- IP address
- Subnet mask
- Domain name
- Default gateway (routers)
- DNS
- WINS information

A DHCP server can give us even more information than this, but the items in the list are the most common.

A client that sends out a DHCP Discover message in order to receive an IP address sends out a broadcast at both layer 2 and layer 3. The layer 2 broadcast is all *F*s in hex, which looks like this: FF:FF:FF:FF:FF:FF. The layer 3 broadcast is 255.255.255.255, which means all networks and all hosts. DHCP is connectionless, which means that it uses User Datagram Protocol (UDP) at the Transport layer, also known as the Host-to-Host layer, which we'll talk about next.

In case you don't believe me, here's an example of output from my trusty OmniPeek analyzer:

```
Ethernet II, Src: 192.168.0.3 (00:0b:db:99:d3:5e), Dst: Broadcast
➡(ff:ff:ff:ff:ff:ff)
Internet Protocol, Src: 0.0.0.0 (0.0.0.0), Dst: 255.255.255.255
➡(255.255.255.255)
```

The Data Link and Network layers are both sending out "all hands" broadcasts saying, "Help—I don't know my IP address!"

Understand that a DHCP client/server communication uses both broadcasts and unicasts. Figure 3.1 shows this process.

- Step 1: The DHCP client sends a broadcast packet called a *DHCPDiscover* packet. This allow the host to discover where the DHCP servers are (yes, there can be more then one).

- Step 2: The DHCP servers that receive that DHCPDiscover packet will respond with a DHCPOffer packet. This packet contains an IP address, the time the host can keep the address (the "lease"), a default gateway, and any other information you configured on the DHCP server.

- Step 3: When (if?) the host receives the DHCPOffer packets from multiple DHCP servers, the first DHCPOffer packet received is the one accepted. The host accepts this offer by broadcasting a *DHCPRequest* packet.

FIGURE 3.1 DHCP broadcasts and unicasts

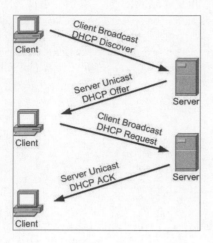

- Step 4: All DHCP servers that sent DHCPOffer packets will receive the DHCPRequest packet. If the IP address they offered the client is not accepted by the DHCPRequest the server(s) sent the client, that IP address will be placed back in the DHCP address pool. The DHCP server who had an IP address accepted sends a unicast DHCPAck (for "acknowledgement") back to the host.

In the next section, I'll show you have to configure DHCP and DNS services on a Cisco router.

Exam Objectives

Understand the purpose of DNS. The Domain Name Service is used to resolve a *fully qualified domain name (FQDN)*—for example, www.lammle.com or todd.lammle.com from an IP address. An FQDN is a hierarchy that can logically locate a system based on its domain identifier.

Understand the purpose of DHCP. *The Dynamic Host Configuration Protocol (DHCP)* assigns IP addresses to hosts. But there is a lot of information a DHCP server can provide to a host other than an IP address, such as the subnet mask, default gateway, and DNS server.

Understand the way broadcast and unicasts work with DHCP *The Dynamic Host Configuration Protocol (DHCP)* assigns IP addresses to hosts. But there is a lot of information a DHCP server can provide to a host other than an IP address, such as the subnet mask, default gateway, and DNS server.

3.3 Configure, verify, and troubleshoot DHCP and DNS operation on a router (including CLI/SDM)

Instead of using a server to provide IP addresses to clients, you can configure a router with a DHCP scope that will hand out IP addresses to hosts on a connected interface. Here is an example:

```
R2#config t
R2(config)#ip dhcp pool Admin
R2(dhcp-config)#network 10.1.8.0 255.255.255.0
R2(dhcp-config)#default-router 10.1.8.1
R2(dhcp-config)#exit
R2(config)#ip dhcp excluded-address 10.1.8.1
R2(config)#
```

Creating DHCP pools on a router is actually a pretty simple process. To do so, you just create the pool name, add the network/subnet and the default gateway, and exclude any addresses you don't want handed out (like the default gateway address). And you'd usually add a DNS server as well. Note that the excluded addresses are set from global configuration mode. But wait, we're not done. Even though we created the pool, which hosts can use this pool? Now this is where the interface configuration comes in. Notice the default-router address in the pool configuration? Any DHCP client connected off of interface fastethernet 0/0 will grab a DHCP address from the pool. Here is the finished configuration:

```
R2(config)#interface fa0/0
R2(config-if)#ip address 10.1.8.1 255.255.255.0
```

Configuring a pool from SDM is actually just as easy, if not easier, than doing so from the CLI. After you open SDM, look down at the bottom left portion of the wizard page and click the Additional Tasks button. From there, just click the Router Properties icon.

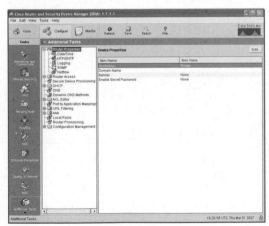

Here, you can set the hostname, MOTD banner, and enable secret password. Last, I clicked on the DHCP folder, then the DHCP pool icon. I then clicked Add and created a DHCP pool on my router.

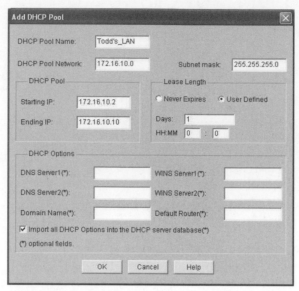

Now, let's take a look at the configuration on the router:

```
Todd#sh run
Building configuration...
[output cut]
hostname Todd
!
ip domain name lammle.com
[output cut]
ip dhcp excluded-address 172.16.10.1
ip dhcp excluded-address 172.16.10.11 172.16.10.254
!
ip dhcp pool Todd's_LAN
   import all
   network 172.16.10.0 255.255.255.0
!
```

Using DNS to Resolve Names

If you have a lot of devices and don't want to create a host table in each device, you can use a DNS server to resolve hostnames.

Any time a Cisco device receives a command it doesn't understand, it will try to resolve it through DNS by default. Watch what happens when I type the special command todd at a Cisco router prompt:

```
Corp#todd
Translating "todd"...domain server (255.255.255.255)
Translating "todd"...domain server (255.255.255.255)
Translating "todd"...domain server (255.255.255.255)
% Unknown command or computer name, or unable to find
  computer address
Corp#
```

It doesn't know my name or what command I am trying to type, so it tries to resolve this through DNS. This is really annoying for two reasons: first, because it doesn't know my name, and second, because I need to hang out and wait for the name lookup to time out. You can get around this and prevent a time-consuming DNS lookup by using the no ip domain-lookup command on your router from global configuration mode.

If you have a DNS server on your network, you need to add a few commands to make DNS name resolution work:

- The first command is **ip domain-lookup**, which is turned on by default. It needs to be entered only if you previously turned it off (with the **no ip domain-lookup** command). The command can be used without the hyphen as well (**ip domain lookup**).

- The second command is **ip name-server**. This sets the IP address of the DNS server. You can enter the IP addresses of up to six servers.

- The last command is **ip domain-name**. Although this command is optional, it really should be set. It appends the domain name to the hostname you type in. Since DNS uses a FQDN system, you must have a full DNS name, in the form **domain.com**.

Here's an example of using these three commands:

```
Corp#config t
Corp(config)#ip domain-lookup
Corp(config)#ip name-server ?
  A.B.C.D  Domain server IP address (maximum of 6)
Corp(config)#ip name-server 192.168.0.70
Corp(config)#ip domain-name lammle.com
Corp(config)#^Z
Corp#
```

After the DNS configurations are set, you can test the DNS server by using a hostname to ping or telnet a device like this:

```
Corp#ping R1
Translating "R1"...domain server (192.168.0.70) [OK]
```

```
Type escape sequence to abort.
Sending 5, 100-byte ICMP Echos to 10.2.2.2, timeout is
  2 seconds:
!!!!!
Success rate is 100 percent (5/5), round-trip min/avg/max
  = 28/31/32 ms
```

Notice that the router uses the DNS server to resolve the name.

Exam Objectives

Remember how to configure a DHCP pool on a router.   From global config mode, use the command ip dhcp pool_name network_address mask. Now from the DHCP pool prompt, you use the network command to add the subnet address. This creates the pool of addresses that can be assigned to hosts. Adding the default gateway is just as important, and the command is default-router a.b.c.d.

Remember how to configure a router to perform DNS lookups.   The command ip domain-lookup is used to enable DNS lookups on the router. The command ip name-server allows you to specify the IP address of the DNS server, up to 6, and finally the command ip domain-name is used to set the DNS hierarchical name

3.4 Implement static and dynamic addressing services for hosts in a LAN environment

Interface configuration is one of the most important router configurations because without interfaces, a router is pretty much a completely useless object. Plus, interface configurations must be totally precise to enable communication with other devices. Network layer addresses, media type, bandwidth, and other administrator commands are all used to configure an interface.

Different routers use different methods to choose the interfaces used on them. For instance, the following command shows a Cisco 2522 router with 10 serial interfaces, labeled 0 through 9:

```
Router(config)#int serial ?
 <0-9> Serial interface number
```

Now it's time to choose the interface you want to configure. Once you do that, you will be in interface configuration for that specific interface. The following command would be used to choose serial port 5, for example:

```
Router(config)#int serial 5
Router(config)-if)#
```

The 2522 router has one Ethernet 10BaseT port, and typing **interface ethernet 0** can configure that interface, as seen here:

```
Router(config)#int ethernet ?
 <0-0> Ethernet interface number
Router(config)#int ethernet 0
Router(config-if)#
```

The above router is a fixed-configuration router. This means that when you buy that model, you're stuck with that physical configuration—a huge reason why I don't use them much. I certainly never would use them in a production setting anymore.

To configure an interface, we always used the interface *type number* sequence, but with the 2600 and 2800 series routers (actually, any ISR router for that matter), there's a physical slot in the router, with a port number on the module plugged into that slot. So on a modular router, the configuration would be interface *type slot/port*, as seen here:

```
Router(config)#int fastethernet ?
 <0-1> FastEthernet interface number
Router(config)#int fastethernet 0
% Incomplete command.
Router(config)#int fastethernet 0?
/
Router(config)#int fastethernet 0/?
 <0-1> FastEthernet interface number
```

Make note of the fact that you can't just type **int fastethernet 0**. You must type the full command: *type slot/port*, or **int fastethernet 0/0** (or **int fa 0/0**).

For the ISR series, it's basically the same, only you get even more options. For example, the built-in FastEthernet interfaces work with the same configuration we used with the 2600 series:

```
Todd(config)#int fastEthernet 0/?
  <0-1>  FastEthernet interface number
Todd(config)#int fastEthernet 0/0
Todd(config-if)#
```

But the rest of the modules are different—they use three numbers instead of two. The first 0 is the router itself, and then you choose the slot, and then the port. Here's an example of a serial interface on my 2811:

```
Todd(config)#interface serial ?
  <0-2>  Serial interface number
Todd(config)#interface serial 0/0/?
  <0-1>  Serial interface number
Todd(config)#interface serial 0/0/0
Todd(config-if)#
```

This can look a little dicey, I know, but I promise it's really not that hard! It helps to remember that you should always view a running-config output first so that you know what interfaces you have to deal with. Here's my 2801 output:

```
Todd(config-if)#do show run
Building configuration...
[output cut]
!
interface FastEthernet0/0
 no ip address
 shutdown
 duplex auto
 speed auto
!
interface FastEthernet0/1
 no ip address
 shutdown
 duplex auto
 speed auto
!
interface Serial0/0/0
 no ip address
 shutdown
 no fair-queue
!
interface Serial0/0/1
 no ip address
 shutdown
!
interface Serial0/1/0
 no ip address
 shutdown
!
interface Serial0/2/0
 no ip address
 shutdown
 clock rate 2000000
!
 [output cut]
```

For the sake of brevity, I didn't include my complete running-config, but I've displayed all you need. You can see the two built-in Fast Ethernet interfaces, the two serial interfaces in slot 0 (0/0/0 and 0/0/1), the serial interface in slot 1 (0/1/0), and the serial interface in slot 2 (0/2/0). Once you see the interfaces like this, it makes it a lot easier for you to understand how the modules are inserted into the router.

Just understand that if you type **interface e0** on a 2500, **interface fastethernet 0/0** on a 2600, or **interface serial 0/1/0** on a 2800, all you're doing is choosing an interface to configure, and basically, they're all configured the same way after that.

I'm going to continue with our router interface discussion in the next sections, and I'll include how to bring up the interface and set an IP address on a router interface.

Bringing Up an Interface

You can disable an interface with the interface command shutdown and enable it with the no shutdown command.

If an interface is shut down, it'll display administratively down when you use the show interfaces command (sh int for short):

```
Todd#sh int f0/1
FastEthernet0/1 is administratively down, line protocol is down
[output cut]
```

Another way to check an interface's status is to use the show running-config command. All interfaces are shut down by default. You can bring up the interface with the no shutdown command (no shut for short):

```
Todd#config t
Todd(config)#int f0/1
Todd(config-if)#no shutdown
Todd(config-if)#
*Feb 28 22:45:08.455: %LINK-3-UPDOWN: Interface FastEthernet0/1,
    changed state to up
Todd(config-if)#do show int f0/1
FastEthernet0/1 is up, line protocol is up
[output cut]
```

Configuring an IP Address on an Interface

Even though you don't have to use IP on your routers, it's most often what people actually do use. To configure IP addresses on an interface, use the ip address command from interface configuration mode:

```
Todd(config)#int f0/1
Todd(config-if)#ip address 172.16.10.2 255.255.255.0
```

Don't forget to enable the interface with the no shutdown command. Remember to look at the command show interface *int* to see if the interface is administratively shut down or not. show running-config will also give you this information.

 The ip address *address mask* command starts the IP processing on the interface.

If you want to add a second subnet address to an interface, you have to use the secondary parameter. If you type another IP address and press Enter, it will replace the existing IP address and mask. This is definitely a most excellent feature of the Cisco IOS.

So, let's try it. To add a secondary IP address, just use the secondary parameter:

```
Todd(config-if)#ip address 172.16.20.2 255.255.255.0 ?
  secondary  Make this IP address a secondary address
  <cr>
Todd(config-if)#ip address 172.16.20.2 255.255.255.0 secondary
Todd(config-if)#^Z
Todd(config-if)#do sh run
Building configuration...
[output cut]

interface FastEthernet0/1
 ip address 172.16.20.2 255.255.255.0 secondary
 ip address 172.16.10.2 255.255.255.0
 duplex auto
 speed auto
!
```

I really wouldn't recommend having multiple IP addresses on an interface because it's ugly and inefficient, but I showed you this anyway just in case you someday find yourself dealing with an MIS manager who's in love with really bad network design and makes you administer it!

If you want to create a pool of addresses on a router using the CLI, here is how you do that:

```
R2#config t
R2(config)#ip dhcp pool Todd
R2(dhcp-config)#network 10.1.8.0 255.255.255.0
R2(dhcp-config)#default-router 10.1.8.1
R2(dhcp-config)#exit
R2(config)#ip dhcp excluded-address 10.1.8.1
R2(config)#
```

Creating DHCP pools on a router is actually a pretty simple process. To do so, you just create the pool name, add the network/subnet and the default gateway, and exclude any addresses you don't want handed out (like the default gateway address). And you'd usually add a DNS server as well.

Exam Objectives

Remember how to add an IP address to an interface.   To configure IP addresses on an interface, use the `ip address` command from interface configuration mode. Here is an example:

```
Todd(config)#int f0/1
Todd(config-if)#ip address 172.16.10.2 255.255.255.0
```

Remember how to configure a DHCP pool on a router.   I provided this information from objective 3.3, but it is important. From global config mode, use the command `ip dhcp pool_name network_address mask`. Now from the DHCP pool prompt, you use the `network` command to add the subnet address. This creates the pool of addresses that can be assigned to hosts. Adding the default gateway is just as important, and the command is `default-router a.b.c.d`.

3.5 Calculate and apply an addressing scheme, including VLSM IP addressing design, to a network

I'm going to show you a simple way to take one network and create many networks using subnet masks of different lengths on different types of network designs. This is called VLSM networking, and it does bring up another subject: classful and classless networking.

Neither RIPv1 nor IGRP routing protocols have a field for subnet information, so the subnet information gets dropped. What this means is that if a router running RIP has a subnet mask of a certain value, it assumes that *all* interfaces within the classful address space have the same subnet mask. This is called classful routing, and RIP and IGRP are both considered classful routing protocols. If you mix and match subnet mask lengths in a network running RIP or IGRP, that network just won't work!

Classless routing protocols, however, do support the advertisement of subnet information. Therefore, you can use VLSM with routing protocols such as RIPv2, EIGRP, and OSPF. The benefit of this type of network is that you save a bunch of IP address space with it.

As the name suggests, with VLSMs we can have different subnet masks for different router interfaces. Look at Figure 3.2 to see an example of why classful network designs are inefficient.

Looking at this figure, you'll notice that we have two routers, each with two LANs and connected together with a WAN serial link. In a typical classful network design (RIP or IGRP routing protocols), you could subnet a network like this:

192.168.10.0 = Network

255.255.255.240 (/28) = Mask

Our subnets would be (you know this part, right?) 0, 16, 32, 48, 64, 80, and so on. This allows us to assign 16 subnets to our internetwork. But how many hosts would be available on each network? Well, as you probably know by now, each subnet provides only 14 hosts. This means that each LAN has 14 valid hosts available—one LAN doesn't even have enough addresses needed for all the hosts! But the point-to-point WAN link also has 14 valid hosts. It's too bad we can't just nick some valid hosts from that WAN link and give them to our LANs!

FIGURE 3.2   Typical classful network

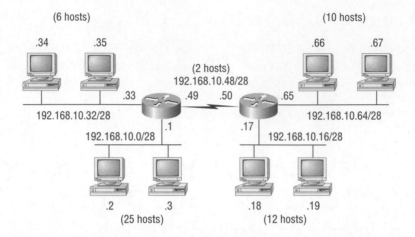

All hosts and router interfaces have the same subnet mask—again, this is called classful routing. And if we want this network to be more efficient, we definitely need to add different masks to each router interface.

But there's still another problem—the link between the two routers will never use more than two valid hosts! This wastes valuable IP address space, and it's the big reason that I'm going to talk to you about VLSM network design.

VLSM Design

Let's take Figure 3.2 and use a classless design . . . which will become the new network shown in Figure 3.3. In the previous example, we wasted address space—one LAN didn't have enough addresses because every router interface and host used the same subnet mask. Not so good. What would be good is to provide only the needed number of hosts on each router interface. To do this, we use what are referred to as Variable Length Subnet Masks (VLSMs).

Now remember that we can use different sized masks on each router interface. And if we use a /30 on our WAN links and a /27, /28, and /29 on our LANs, we'll get 2 hosts per WAN interface, and 30, 14, and 8 hosts per LAN interface—nice! This makes a huge difference—not only can we get just the right number of hosts on each LAN, but we still have room to add more WANs and LANs using this same network!

Remember, in order to implement a VLSM design on your network, you need to have a routing protocol that sends subnet mask information with the route updates. This would be RIPv2, EIGRP, and OSPF. RIPv1 and IGRP will not work in classless networks and are considered classful routing protocols.

FIGURE 3.3   Classless network design

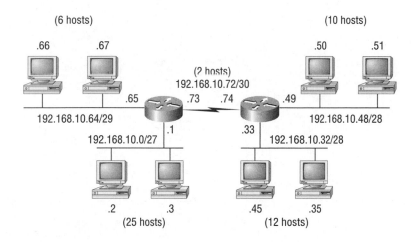

Exam Objectives

Understand the difference between classful and classless networks.   Classful networks are networks that have the same subnet mask on every node. Classless networks are networks that allows different sized masks on each subnets, called variable length subnet masks.

Remember which routing protocols are classful and which routing protocols are classless.   Classful routing protocols are RIP and IGRP, and classless routing protocols are RIPv2, EIGRP, and OSPF.

3.6 Determine the appropriate classless addressing scheme using VLSM and summarization to satisfy addressing requirements in a LAN/WAN environment

To create VLSMs quickly and efficiently, you need to understand how block sizes and charts work together to create the VLSM masks. Table 3.3 shows you the block sizes used when creating VLSMs with Class C networks. For example, if you need 25 hosts, then you'll need a block size of 32. If you need 11 hosts, you'll use a block size of 16. Need 40 hosts? Then you'll need a block of 64. You cannot just make up block sizes—they've got to be the block sizes shown in Table 3.3. So, memorize the block sizes in this table—it's easy. They're the same numbers we used with subnetting!

TABLE 3.3   Block Sizes

Prefix	Mask	Hosts	Block Size
/25	128	126	128
/26	192	62	64
/27	224	30	32
/28	240	14	16
/29	248	6	8
/30	252	2	4

The next step is to create a VLSM table. Figure 3.4 shows you the table used in creating a VLSM network. The reason that we use this table is so that we don't accidentally overlap networks.

You'll find the sheet shown in Figure 3.4 very valuable because it lists every block size you can use for a network address. Notice that the block sizes are listed starting from a block size of 4 all the way to a block size of 128. If you have two networks with block sizes of 128, you'll quickly see that you can have only two networks. With a block size of 64, you can have only four networks, and so on, all the way to having 64 networks if you use only block sizes of 4. Remember that this takes into account that you are using the command ip subnet-zero in your network design.

Now, just fill in the chart in the lower-left corner, and then add the subnets to the worksheet and you're good to go.

So, let's take what we've learned so far about our block sizes and VLSM table and create a VLSM using a Class C network address 192.168.10.0 for the network in Figure 3.5. Then fill out the VLSM table, as shown in Figure 3.6.

In Figure 3.5, we have four WAN links and four LANs connected together. We need to create a VLSM network that will allow us to save address space. Looks like we have two block sizes of 32, a block size of 16, and a block size of 8, and our WANs each have a block size of 4. Take a look and see how I filled out our VLSM chart in Figure 3.6.

We still have plenty of room for growth with this VLSM network design. We never could accomplish that with one subnet mask using classful routing. Let's do another one. Figure 3.7 shows a network with 11 networks, two block sizes of 64, one of 32, five of 16, and three of 4.

FIGURE 3.4   The VLSM table

Variable Length Subnet Masks Worksheet

Subnet	Mask	Subnets	Hosts	Block
/26	192	4	62	64
/27	224	8	30	32
/28	240	16	14	16
/29	248	32	6	8
/30	252	64	2	4

Class C Network   192.168.10.0

Network	Hosts	Block	Subnet	Mask
A				
B				
C				
D				
E				
F				
G				
H				
I				
J				
K				
L				
MNetwork	Hosts	Block	Subnet	Mask

0
4
8
12
16
20
24
28
32
36
40
44
48
52
56
60
64
68
72
76
80
84
88
92
96
100
104
108
112
116
120
124
128
132
136
140
144
148
152
156
160
154
158
172
176
180
184
188
192
196
200
204
208
212
216
220
224
228
232
236
240
244
248
252
256

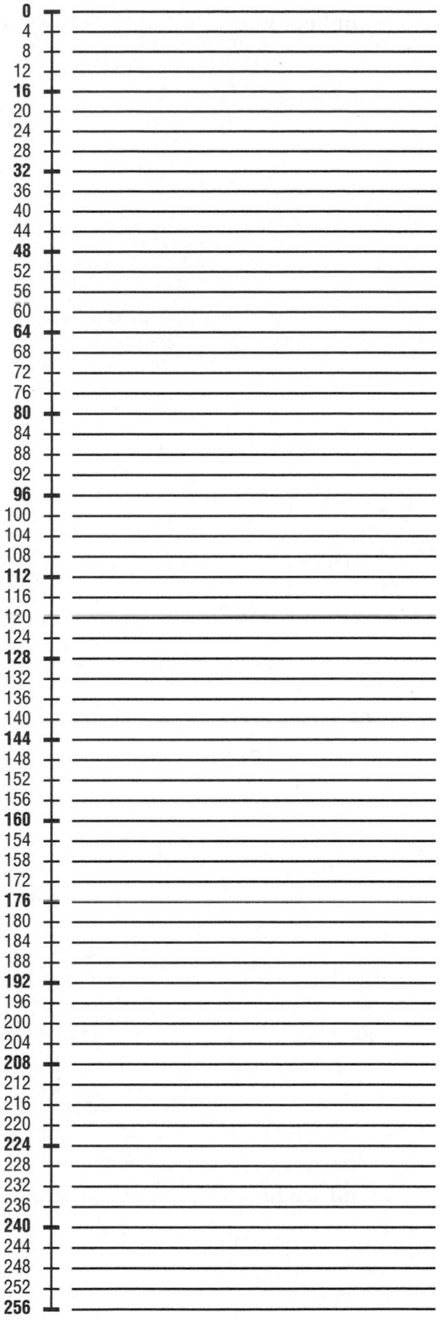

FIGURE 3.5 A VLSM network, example one

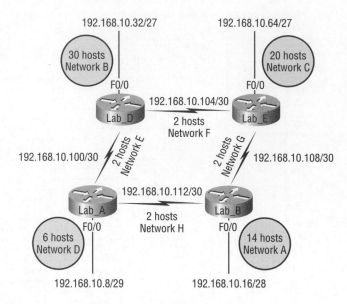

FIGURE 3.6 VLSM network, example two

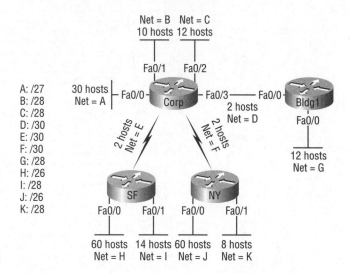

First, create your VLSM table and use your block size chart to fill in the table with the subnets you need. Figure 3.8 shows a possible solution.

Notice that we filled in this entire chart and only have room for one more block size of 4! Only with a VLSM network can you provide this type of address space savings.

FIGURE 3.7   A VLSM table, example one

Variable Length Subnet Masks Worksheet

Subnet	Mask	Subnets	Hosts	Block
/26	192	4	62	64
/27	224	8	30	32
/28	240	16	14	16
/29	248	32	6	8
/30	252	64	2	4

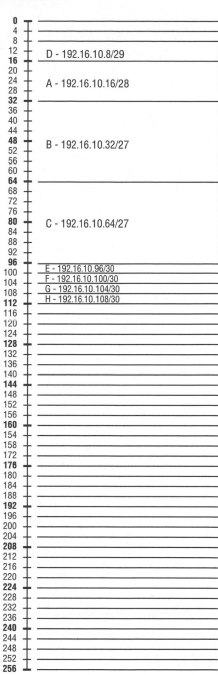

Class C Network   192.16.10.0

Network	Hosts	Block	Subnet	Mask
A	12	16	/28	240
B	20	32	/27	224
C	25	32	/27	224
D	4	8	/29	248
E	2	4	/30	252
F	2	4	/30	252
G	2	4	/30	252
H	2	4	/30	252

FIGURE 3.8   VLSM table, example two

Variable Length Subnet Masks Worksheet

Subnet	Mask	Subnets	Hosts	Block
/26	192	4	62	64
/27	224	8	30	32
/28	240	16	14	16
/29	248	32	6	8
/30	252	64	2	4

Class C Network   192.168.10.0

Network	Hosts	Block	Subnet	Mask
A	30	32	32	224
B	10	16	0	240
C	12	16	16	240
D	2	4	244	252
E	2	4	248	252
F	2	4	252	252
G	12	16	208	240
H	60	64	64	192
I	14	16	192	240
J	60	64	128	192
K	8	16	224	240
L				30
M				10

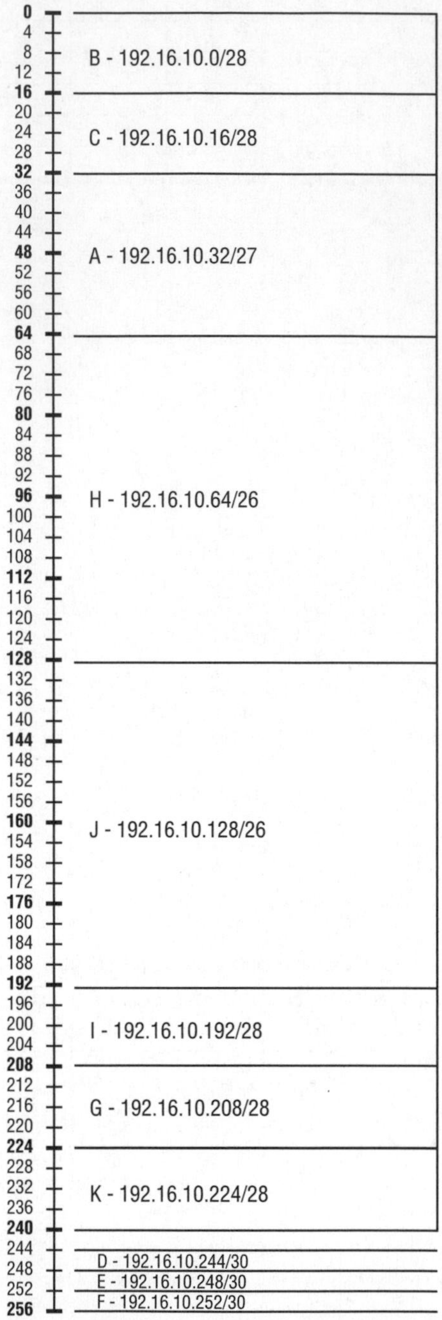

Worksheet block diagram (0–256):

- B - 192.16.10.0/28
- C - 192.16.10.16/28
- A - 192.16.10.32/27
- H - 192.16.10.64/26
- J - 192.16.10.128/26
- I - 192.16.10.192/28
- G - 192.16.10.208/28
- K - 192.16.10.224/28
- D - 192.16.10.244/30
- E - 192.16.10.248/30
- F - 192.16.10.252/30

Keep in mind that it doesn't matter where you start your block sizes as long as you always count from zero. For example, if you had a block size of 16, you must start at 0 and count from there—0, 16, 32, 48, etc. You can't start a block size of 16 from, say, 40 or anything other than increments of 16.

Here's another example. If you have block sizes of 32, you must start at zero like this: 0, 32, 64, 96, and so on. Just remember that you don't get to start wherever you want; you must always start counting from zero. In the example in Figure 3.8, I started at 64 and 128, with my two block sizes of 64. I didn't have much choice, because my options are 0, 64, 128, and 192. However, I was able to add the block sizes of 32, 16, 8, and 4 wherever I wanted just as long as they were in the correct increments of that block size.

Okay—you have three locations you need to address, and the IP network you have received is 192.168.55.0 to use as the addressing for the entire network. You'll use `ip subnet-zero` and RIPv2 as the routing protocol. (RIPv2 supports VLSM networks, RIPv1 does not.) Figure 3.9 shows the network diagram and the IP address of the RouterA S0/0 interface.

FIGURE 3.9   VLSM design example

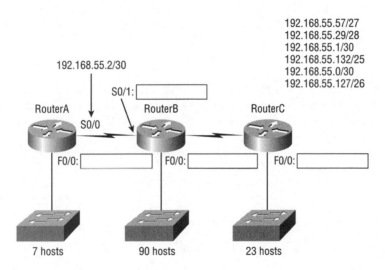

From the list of IP addresses on the right of the figure, which IP address will be placed in each router's FastEthernet 0/0 interface and serial 0/1 of RouterB?

To answer this question, first look for clues in Figure 3.10. The first clue is that interface S0/0 on RouterA has IP address 192.168.55.2/30 assigned, which makes for an easy answer. A /30, as you know, is 255.255.255.252, which gives you a block size of 4. Your subnets are 0, 4, 8, and so on. Since the known host has an IP address of 2, the only other valid host in the zero subnet is 1, so the third answer down is what you want for the s0/1 interface of RouterB.

The next clues are the listed number of hosts for each of the LANs. RouterA needs 7 hosts, a block size of 16 (/28); RouterB needs 90 hosts, a block size of 128 (/25); and RouterC needs 23 hosts, a block size of 32 (/27).

Figure 3.10 shows the answers to this question.

FIGURE 3.10   Solution to VLSM design example

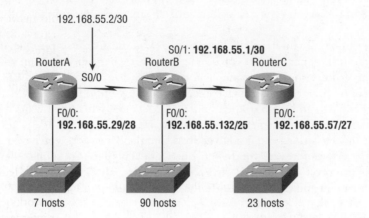

Once you figured out the block size needed for each LAN, this was actually a pretty simple question—all you need to do is look for the right clues and, of course, know your block sizes.

Summarization

Summarization, also called *route aggregation*, allows routing protocols to advertise many networks as one address. The purpose of this is to reduce the size of routing tables on routers to save memory, which also shortens the amount of time it takes for IP to parse the routing table and find the path to a remote network.

Figure 3.11 shows how a summary address would be used in an internetwork.

FIGURE 3.11   Summary address used in an internetwork

Summarization is actually somewhat simple because all you really need to have down are the block sizes that we just used in learning subnetting and VLSM design. For example, if you wanted to summarize the following networks into one network advertisement, you just have to find the block size first; then you can easily find your answer:

192.168.16.0 through network 192.168.31.0

What's the block size? There are exactly 16 Class C networks, so this neatly fits into a block size of 16.

Okay, now that you know the block size, you can find the network address and mask used to summarize these networks into one advertisement. The network address used to advertise the summary address is always the first network address in the block—in this example, 192.168.16.0. To figure out a summary mask, in this same example, what mask is used to get a block size of 16? Yes, 240 is correct. This 240 would be placed in the third octet—the octet where we are summarizing. So, the mask would be 255.255.240.0.

Here's another example:

Networks 172.16.32.0 through 172.16.50.0

This is not as clean as the previous example because there are two possible answers, and here's why: Since you're starting at network 32, your options for block sizes are 4, 8, 16, 32, 64, and so on, and block sizes of 16 and 32 could work as this summary address.

- **Answer #1:** If you used a block size of 16, then the network address is 172.16.32.0 with a mask of 255.255.240.0 (240 provides a block of 16). However, this only summarizes from 32 to 47, which means that networks 48 through 50 would be advertised as single networks. This is probably the best answer, but that depends on your network design. Let's look at the next answer.

- **Answer #2:** If you used a block size of 32, then your summary address would still be 172.16.32.0, but the mask would be 255.255.224.0 (224 provides a block of 32). The possible problem with this answer is that it will summarize networks 32 to 63, and we only have networks 32 to 50. This is no problem if you're planning on adding networks 51 to 63 later into the same network, but you could have serious problems in your internetwork if somehow networks 51 to 63 were to show up and be advertised from somewhere else in your network! This is the reason why answer number one is the safest answer.

Exam Objectives

Remember your block sizes.   Block sizes are used to help you subnet, but they can also be helpful when creating summaries on contiguous boundaries. Block sizes are 1, 2, 4, 8, 16, 32, 64, 128, and so on. However, using a block size larger than 128 is not typical.

Remember how to create classless networks.   Classless networking, also called variable length subnet masking, uses blocks of addresses that can be assigned on each router interface. A different mask can be used on each interface to allow the granular addressing of hosts, which saves address space. In order to use classless networking, you must use a routing protocol like RIPv2, EIGRP or OSPF.

3.7 Describe the technological requirements for running IPv6 in conjunction with IPv4 (including protocols, dual stack, tunneling, etc)

The IPv6 header and address structure has been completely overhauled, and many of the features that were basically just afterthoughts and addendums in IPv4 are now included as full-blown standards in IPv6. It's seriously well equipped, poised, and ready to manage the mind-blowing demands of the Internet to come.

Why Do We Need IPv6?

Well, the short answer is, because we need to communicate, and our current system isn't really cutting it anymore—rather like how the Pony Express can't compete with airmail. Just look at how much time and effort we've invested in coming up with slick new ways to conserve bandwidth and IP addresses. We've even come up with VLSMs in our struggle to overcome the worsening address drought.

It's reality—the number of people and devices that connect to networks increases each and every day. That's not a bad thing at all—we're finding new and exciting ways to communicate with more people all the time, and that's a good thing. In fact, it's a basic human need. But the forecast isn't exactly blue skies and sunshine because, as I alluded to in this chapter's introduction, IPv4, upon which our ability to communicate is presently dependent, is going to run out of addresses for us to use. IPv4 has only about 4.3 billion addresses available—in theory, and we know that we don't even get to use all of those. There really are only about 250 million addresses that can be assigned to devices. Sure, the use of Classless Inter-Domain Routing (CIDR) and NAT has helped to extend the inevitable dearth of addresses, but we will run out of them, and it's going to happen within a few years. China is barely online, and we know there's a huge population of people and corporations there that surely want to be. There are a lot of reports that give us all kinds of numbers, but all you really need to think about to convince yourself that I'm not just being an alarmist is the fact that there are about 6.5 billion people in the world today, and it's estimated that just over 10 percent of that population is connected to the Internet—wow!

That statistic is basically screaming at us the ugly truth that based on IPv4's capacity, every person can't even have a computer—let alone all the other devices we use with them. I have more than one computer, and it's pretty likely you do too. And I'm not even including in the mix phones, laptops, game consoles, fax machines, routers, switches, and a mother lode of other devices we use every day! So, I think I've made it pretty clear that we've got to do something before we run out of addresses and lose the ability to connect with each other as we know it. And that "something" just happens to be implementing IPv6.

The Benefits and Uses for IPv6

So, what's so fabulous about IPv6? Is it really the answer to our coming dilemma? Is it really worth it to upgrade from IPv4? All good questions—you may even think of a few more. Of course, there's going to be that group of people with the time-tested and well-known "resistance to change syndrome," but don't listen to them. If we had done that years ago, we'd still be waiting weeks, even months for our mail to arrive via horseback. Instead, just know that the answer is a resounding YES! Not only does IPv6 give us lots of addresses (3.4×10^{38} = definitely enough), but there are many other features built into this version that make it well worth the cost, time, and effort required to migrate to it.

Today's networks, as well as the Internet, have a ton of unforeseen requirements that simply were not considerations when IPv4 was created. We've tried to compensate with a collection of add-ons that can actually make implementing them more difficult than they would be if they were applied according to a standard. By default, IPv6 has improved upon and included many of those features as standard and mandatory. One of these sweet new standards is *IPSec*. Another little beauty is known as *mobility*, and as its name suggests, it allows a device to roam from one network to another without dropping connections.

But it's the efficiency features that are really going to rock the house! For starters, the header in an IPv6 packet have half the fields, and they are aligned to 64 bits, which gives us some seriously souped-up processing speed—compared to IPv4, lookups happen at light speed! Most of the information that used to be bound into the IPv4 header was taken out, and now you can choose to put it, or parts of it, back into the header in the form of optional extension headers that follow the basic header fields.

And, of course, there's that whole new universe of addresses (3.4×10^{38}) we talked about already. But where did we get them? Did that Criss Angel—Mindfreak dude just show up and, Blammo? I mean, that huge proliferation of address had to come from somewhere! Well it just so happens that IPv6 gives us a substantially larger address space, meaning the address is whole lot bigger—four times bigger as a matter of fact! An IPv6 address is actually 128 bits in length. For now, let me just say that all that additional room permits more levels of hierarchy inside the address space and a more flexible address architecture. It also makes routing much more efficient and scalable because the addresses can be aggregated a lot more effectively. And IPv6 also allows multiple addresses for hosts and networks. This is especially important for enterprises jonesing for availability. Plus, the new version of IP now includes an expanded use of multicast communication (one device sending to many hosts or to a select group), which will also join in to boost efficiency on networks because communications will be more specific.

IPv4 uses broadcasts very prolifically, causing a bunch of problems, the worst of which is of course the dreaded *broadcast storm*—an uncontrolled deluge of forwarded broadcast traffic that can bring an entire network to its knees and devour every last bit of bandwidth. Another nasty thing about broadcast traffic is that it interrupts each and every device on the network. When a broadcast is sent out, every machine has to stop what it's doing and respond to the traffic, whether the broadcast is meant for it or not.

But smile everyone: There is no such thing as a broadcast in IPv6 because it uses multicast traffic instead. And there are two other types of communication as well: unicast, which is the same as it is in IPv4, and a new type called *anycast*. Anycast communication allows the same address to be placed on more than one device so that when traffic is sent to one device addressed in this way, it is routed to the nearest host that shares the same address. This is just the beginning—we'll get more into the various types of communication in the section called "Address Types."

Dual Stacking

This is the most common type of migration strategy because, well, it's the easiest on us—it allows our devices to communicate using either IPv4 or IPv6. *Dual stacking* lets you upgrade your devices and applications on the network one at a time. As more and more hosts and devices on the network are upgraded, more of your communication will happen over IPv6, and after you've arrived—everything's running on IPv6, and you get to remove all the old IPv4 protocol stacks you no longer need.

Plus, configuring dual stacking on a Cisco router is amazingly easy—all you have to do is enable IPv6 forwarding and apply an address to the interfaces already configured with IPv4. It'll look something like this:

```
Corp(config)#ipv6 unicast-routing
Corp(config)#interface fastethernet 0/0
Corp(config-if)#ipv6 address 2001:db8:3c4d:1::/64 eui-64
Corp(config-if)#ip address 192.168.255.1 255.255.255.0
```

But to be honest, it's really a good idea to understand the various tunneling techniques because it'll probably be awhile before we all start running IPv6 as a solo routed protocol.

6to4 Tunneling

6to4 tunneling is really useful for carrying IPv6 data over a network that's still IPv4. It's quite possible that you'll have IPv6 subnets or other portions of your network that are all IPv6, and those networks will have to communicate with each other. Not so complicated, but when you consider that you might find this happening over a WAN or some other network that you don't control, well, that could be a bit ugly. So, what do we do about this if we don't control the whole tamale? Create a tunnel that will carry the IPv6 traffic for us across the IPv4 network, that's what.

The whole idea of tunneling isn't a difficult concept, and creating tunnels really isn't as hard as you might think. All it really comes down to is snatching the IPv6 packet that's happily traveling across the network and sticking an IPv4 header onto the front of it. It's kind of like catch-and-release fishing, except that the fish doesn't get something plastered on its face before being thrown back into the stream.

To get a picture of this, take a look at Figure 3.12.

FIGURE 3.12 Creating a 6to4 tunnel

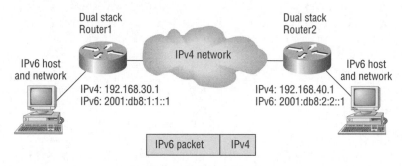

IPv6 packet encapsulated in an IPv4 packet

Nice—but to make this happen we're going to need a couple of dual-stacked routers, which I just demonstrated for you, so you should be good to go. Now we have to add a little configuration to place a tunnel between those routers. Tunnels are pretty simple—we just have to tell each router where the tunnel begins and where we want it to end up. Referring again to Figure 3.12, we'll configure the tunnel on each router:

```
Router1(config)#int tunnel 0
Router1(config-if)#ipv6 address 2001:db8:1:1::1/64
Router1(config-if)#tunnel source 192.168.30.1
Router1(config-if)#tunnel destination 192.168.40.1
Router1(config-if)#tunnel mode ipv6ip

Router2(config)#int tunnel 0
Router2(config-if)#ipv6 address 2001:db8:2:2::1/64
Router2(config-if)#tunnel source 192.168.40.1
Router2(config-if)#tunnel destination 192.168.30.1
Router2(config-if)#tunnel mode ipv6ip
```

With this in place, our IPv6 networks can now communicate over the IPv4 network. Now, I've got to tell you that this is not meant to be a permanent configuration; your end goal should still be to run a total, complete IPv6 network end to end.

One important note here—if the IPv4 network that you're traversing in this situation has a NAT translation point, it would absolutely break the tunnel encapsulation we've just created! Over the years, NAT has been upgraded a lot so that it can handle specific protocols and dynamic connections, and without one of these upgrades, NAT likes to demolish most connections. And since this transition strategy isn't present in most NAT implementations, that means trouble.

But there is a way around this little problem and it's called *Teredo*, which allows all your tunnel traffic to be placed in UDP packets. NAT doesn't blast away at UDP packets, so they won't get broken as other protocols packets do. So, with Teredo in place and your packets disguised under their UDP cloak, the packets will easily slip by NAT alive and well!

Exam Objectives

Understand why we need IPv6.   Without IPv6, the world would be depleted of IP addresses.

Understand link-local.   Link-local is like an IPv4 private IP address, but it can't be routed at all, not even in your organization.

3.8 Describe IPv6 addresses

Just as understanding how IP addresses are structured and used is critical with IPv4 addressing, it's also vital when it comes to IPv6. You've already read about the fact that at 128 bits, an IPv6 address is much larger than an IPv4 address. Because of this, as well as the new ways the addresses can be used, you've probably guessed that IPv6 will be more complicated to manage. But no worries! As I said, I'll break down the basics and show you what the address looks like, how you can write it, and what many of its common uses are. It's going to be a little weird at first, but before you know it, you'll have it nailed!

So, let's take a look at Figure 3.13, which has a sample IPv6 address broken down into sections.

FIGURE 3.13   IPv6 address example

```
2001:0db8:3c4d:0012:0000:0000:1234:56ab
―――――――――|___|―――――――――
Global prefix   Subnet      Interface ID
```

So as you can now see, the address is truly much larger—but what else is different? Well, first, notice that it has eight groups of numbers instead of four and also that those groups are separated by colons instead of periods. And hey wait a second . . . there are letters in that address! Yep, the address is expressed in hexadecimal just like a MAC address is, so you could say this address has eight 16-bit hexadecimal colon-delimited blocks. That's already quite a mouthful, and you probably haven't even tried to say the address out loud yet!

One other thing I want to point out is useful for when you set up your test network to play with IPv6, because I know you're going to want to do that. When you use a web browser to make an HTTP connection to an IPv6 device, you have to type the address into the browser with brackets around the literal address. Why? Well a colon is already being used by the browser for specifying a port number. So, basically, if you don't enclose the address in brackets, the browser will have no way to identify the information.

Here's an example of how this looks:

```
http://[2001:0db8:3c4d:0012:0000:0000:1234:56ab]/default.html
```

Now obviously if you can, you would rather use names to specify a destination (like www.lammle.com), but even though it's definitely going to be a pain in the rear, we just have to accept the fact that sometimes we have to bite the bullet and type in the address number. So, it should be pretty clear that DNS is going to become extremely important when implementing IPv6.

Shortened Expression

The good news is there are a few tricks to help rescue us when writing these monster addresses. For one thing, you can actually leave out parts of the address to abbreviate it, but to get away with doing that you have to follow a couple of rules. First, you can drop any leading zeros in each of the individual blocks. The sample address from earlier would then look like this:

```
2001:db8:3c4d:12:0:0:1234:56ab
```

Okay, that's a definite improvement—at least we don't have to write all of those extra zeros! But what about whole blocks that don't have anything in them except zeros? Well, we can lose those, too—at least some of them. Again referring to our sample address, we can remove the two blocks of zeros by replacing them with double colons, like this:

2001:db8:3c4d:12::1234:56ab

Cool—we replaced the blocks of all zeros with double colons. The rule you have to follow to get away with this is that you can only replace one contiguous block of zeros in an address. So, if my address has four blocks of zeros and each of them were separated, I just don't get to replace them all. Check out this example:

2001:0000:0000:0012:0000:0000:1234:56ab

And just know that you *can't* do this:

2001::12::1234:56ab

Instead, this is the best that you can do:

2001::12:0:0:1234:56ab

The reason why the above example is our best shot is that if we remove two sets of zeros, the device looking at the address will have no way of knowing where the zeros go back in. Basically, the router would look at the incorrect address and say, "Well, do I place two blocks into the first set of double colons and two into the second set, or do I place three blocks into the first set and one block into the second set?" And on and on it would go because the information the router needs just isn't there.

Address Types

We're all familiar with IPv4's unicast, broadcast, and multicast addresses that basically define who or at least how many other devices we're talking to. But as I mentioned, IPv6 adds to that trio and introduces the anycast. Broadcasts, as we know them, have been eliminated in IPv6 because of their cumbersome inefficiency.

So, let's find out what each of these types of IPv6 addressing and communication methods do for us.

Unicast Packets addressed to a unicast address are delivered to a single interface. For load balancing, multiple interfaces can use the same address. There are a few different types of unicast addresses, but we don't need to get into that here.

Global unicast addresses These are your typical publicly routable addresses, and they're the same as they are in IPv4.

Link-local addresses These are like the private addresses in IPv4 in that they're not meant to be routed. Think of them as a handy tool that gives you the ability to throw a temporary LAN together for meetings or for creating a small LAN that's not going to be routed but still needs to share and access files and services locally.

Unique local addresses These addresses are also intended for nonrouting purposes, but they are nearly globally unique, so it's unlikely you'll ever have one of them overlap. Unique local addresses were designed to replace site-local addresses, so they basically do almost exactly what IPv4 private addresses do—allow communication throughout a site while being routable to multiple local networks. Site-local addresses were denounced as of September 2004.

Multicast   Again, same as in IPv4, packets addressed to a multicast address are delivered to all interfaces identified by the multicast address. Sometimes people call them *one-to-many addresses*. It's really easy to spot a multicast address in IPv6 because they always start with *FF*.

Anycast   Like multicast addresses, an anycast address identifies multiple interfaces, but there's a big difference: the anycast packet is only delivered to one address—actually, to the first one it finds defined in terms of routing distance. And again, this address is special because you can apply a single address to more than one interface. You could call them one-to-one-of-many addresses, but just saying "anycast" is a lot easier.

You're probably wondering if there are any special, reserved addresses in IPv6 because you know they're there in IPv4. Well there are—plenty of them! Let's go over them now.

Special Addresses

I'm going to list some of the addresses and address ranges that you should definitely make a point to remember because you'll eventually use them. They're all special or reserved for specific use, but unlike IPv4, IPv6 gives us a galaxy of addresses, so reserving a few here and there doesn't hurt a thing!

0:0:0:0:0:0:0:0   Equals ::. This is the equivalent of IPv4's 0.0.0.0, and is typically the source address of a host when you're using stateful configuration.

0:0:0:0:0:0:0:1   Equals ::1. The equivalent of 127.0.0.1 in IPv4.

0:0:0:0:0:0:192.168.100.1   This is how an IPv4 address would be written in a mixed IPv6/IPv4 network environment.

2000::/3   The global unicast address range.

FC00::/7   The unique local unicast range.

FE80::/10   The link-local unicast range.

FF00::/8   The multicast range.

3FFF:FFFF::/32   Reserved for examples and documentation.

2001:0DB8::/32   Also reserved for examples and documentation.

2002::/16   Used with 6to4, which is the transition system—the structure that allows IPv6 packets to be transmitted over an IPv4 network without the need to configure explicit tunnels.

Exam Objectives

Understand why we need IPv6.   Without IPv6, the world would be depleted of IP addresses.

Understand link-local.   Link-local is like an IPv4 private IP address, but it can't be routed at all, not even in your organization.

Understand unique local.   This, like link-local, is like private IP addresses in IPv4 and cannot be routed to the Internet. However, the difference between link-local and unique local is that unique local can be routed within your organization or company.

Remember IPv6 Addressing.   IPv6 addressing is not like IPv4 addressing. IPv6 addressing has much more address space and is 128 bits long, represented in hexadecimal, unlike IPv4, which is only 32 bits long and represented in decimal.

3.9 Identify and correct common problems associated with IP addressing and host configurations

Troubleshooting IP addressing is obviously an important skill because running into trouble somewhere along the way is pretty much a sure thing, and it's going to happen to you. No— I'm not a pessimist; I'm just keeping it real. Because of this nasty fact, it will be great when you can save the day because you can both figure out (diagnose) the problem and fix it on an IP network whether you're at work or at home!

So, this is where I'm going to show you the "Cisco way" of troubleshooting IP addressing. Let's use Figure 3.14 as an example of your basic IP trouble—poor Sally can't log in to the Windows server. Do you deal with this by calling the Microsoft team to tell them their server is a pile of junk and causing all your problems? Probably not such a great idea—let's first double-check our network instead.

FIGURE 3.14   Basic IP troubleshooting

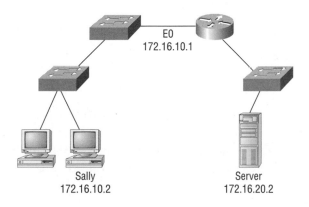

EO
172.16.10.1

Sally
172.16.10.2

Server
172.16.20.2

Okay, let's get started by going over the troubleshooting steps that Cisco follows. They're pretty simple but important nonetheless. Pretend you're at a customer host and they're complaining that they can't communicate to a server that just happens to be on a remote network. Here are the four troubleshooting steps that Cisco recommends:

1. Open a DOS window and ping 127.0.0.1. This is the diagnostic, or loopback, address, and if you get a successful ping, your IP stack is considered to be initialized. If it fails, then you have an IP stack failure and need to reinstall TCP/IP on the host.

    ```
    C:\>ping 127.0.0.1
    Pinging 127.0.0.1 with 32 bytes of data:
    Reply from 127.0.0.1: bytes=32 time<1ms TTL=128
    Reply from 127.0.0.1: bytes=32 time<1ms TTL=128
    Reply from 127.0.0.1: bytes=32 time<1ms TTL=128
    Reply from 127.0.0.1: bytes=32 time<1ms TTL=128
    Ping statistics for 127.0.0.1:
        Packets: Sent = 4, Received = 4, Lost = 0 (0% loss),
    Approximate round trip times in milli-seconds:
        Minimum = 0ms, Maximum = 0ms, Average = 0ms
    ```

2. From the DOS window, ping the IP address of the local host. If that's successful, your network interface card (NIC) is functioning. If it fails, there is a problem with the NIC. Success here doesn't mean that a cable is plugged into the NIC, only that the IP protocol stack on the host can communicate to the NIC (via the LAN driver).

    ```
    C:\>ping 172.16.10.2
    Pinging 172.16.10.2 with 32 bytes of data:
    Reply from 172.16.10.2: bytes=32 time<1ms TTL=128
    Reply from 172.16.10.2: bytes=32 time<1ms TTL=128
    Reply from 172.16.10.2: bytes=32 time<1ms TTL=128
    Reply from 172.16.10.2: bytes=32 time<1ms TTL=128
    Ping statistics for 172.16.10.2:
        Packets: Sent = 4, Received = 4, Lost = 0 (0% loss),
    Approximate round trip times in milli-seconds:
        Minimum = 0ms, Maximum = 0ms, Average = 0ms
    ```

3. From the DOS window, ping the default gateway (router). If the ping works, it means that the NIC is plugged into the network and can communicate on the local network. If it fails, you have a local physical network problem that could be anywhere from the NIC to the router.

    ```
    C:\>ping 172.16.10.1
    Pinging 172.16.10.1 with 32 bytes of data:
    Reply from 172.16.10.1: bytes=32 time<1ms TTL=128
    Reply from 172.16.10.1: bytes=32 time<1ms TTL=128
    Reply from 172.16.10.1: bytes=32 time<1ms TTL=128
    ```

```
Reply from 172.16.10.1: bytes=32 time<1ms TTL=128
Ping statistics for 172.16.10.1:
    Packets: Sent = 4, Received = 4, Lost = 0 (0% loss),
Approximate round trip times in milli-seconds:
    Minimum = 0ms, Maximum = 0ms, Average = 0ms
```

4. If steps 1 through 3 were successful, try to ping the remote server. If that works, then you know that you have IP communication between the local host and the remote server. You also know that the remote physical network is working.

```
C:\>ping 172.16.20.2
Pinging 172.16.20.2 with 32 bytes of data:
Reply from 172.16.20.2: bytes=32 time<1ms TTL=128
Reply from 172.16.20.2: bytes=32 time<1ms TTL=128
Reply from 172.16.20.2: bytes=32 time<1ms TTL=128
Reply from 172.16.20.2: bytes=32 time<1ms TTL=128
Ping statistics for 172.16.20.2:
    Packets: Sent = 4, Received = 4, Lost = 0 (0% loss),
Approximate round trip times in milli-seconds:
    Minimum = 0ms, Maximum = 0ms, Average = 0ms
```

If the user still can't communicate with the server after steps 1 through 4 are successful, you probably have some type of name resolution problem and need to check your Domain Name Service (DNS) settings. But if the ping to the remote server fails, then you know you have some type of remote physical network problem and need to go to the server and work through steps 1 through 3 until you find the snag.

Before we move on to determining IP address problems and how to fix them, I just want to mention some basic DOS commands that you can use to help troubleshoot your network from both a PC and a Cisco router (the commands might do the same thing, but they are implemented differently).

Packet InterNet Groper (ping)   Uses ICMP echo request and replies to test if a node IP stack is initialized and alive on the network.

traceroute   Displays the list of routers on a path to a network destination by using TTL time-outs and ICMP error messages. This command will not work from a DOS prompt.

tracert   Same command as traceroute, but it's a Microsoft Windows command and will not work on a Cisco router.

arp -a   Displays IP-to-MAC-address mappings on a Windows PC.

show ip arp   Same command as arp -a, but displays the ARP table on a Cisco router. Like the commands traceroute and tracert, the two are not interchangeable through DOS and Cisco.

ipconfig /all   Used only from a DOS prompt, shows you the PC network configuration.

Once you've gone through all these steps and used the appropriate DOS commands, if necessary, what do you do if you find a problem? How do you go about fixing an IP address configuration error? Let's move on and discuss how to determine the IP address problems and how to fix them.

Determining IP Address Problems

It's common for a host, router, or other network device to be configured with the wrong IP address, subnet mask, or default gateway. Because this happens way too often, I'm going to teach you how to both determine and fix IP address configuration errors.

Once you've worked through the four basic steps of troubleshooting and determined there's a problem, you obviously need to find and fix it. It really helps to draw out the network and IP addressing scheme. If it's already done, consider yourself lucky and go buy a lottery ticket, because although it should be done, it rarely is. And if it is, it's usually outdated or inaccurate anyway. Typically it is not done, and you'll probably just have to bite the bullet and start from scratch.

Once you have your network accurately drawn out, including the IP addressing scheme, you need to verify each host's IP address, mask, and default gateway address to determine the problem. (I'm assuming that you don't have a physical problem or that if you did, you've already fixed it.)

Let's check out the example illustrated in Figure 3.15. A user in the sales department calls and tells you that she can't get to ServerA in the marketing department. You ask her if she can get to ServerB in the marketing department, but she doesn't know because she doesn't have rights to log on to that server. What do you do?

FIGURE 3.15   IP address problem 1

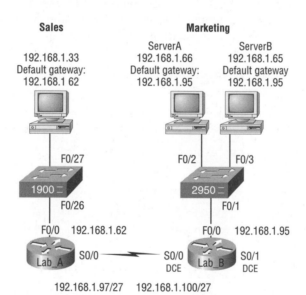

You ask the client to go through the four troubleshooting steps that you learned about in the preceding section. Steps 1 through 3 work, but step 4 fails. By looking at the figure, can you determine the problem? Look for clues in the network drawing. First, the WAN link between the Lab_A router and the Lab_B router shows the mask as a /27. You should already know that this mask is 255.255.255.224 and then determine that all networks are using this mask. The network address is 192.168.1.0. What are our valid subnets and hosts? 256 – 224 = 32, so this makes our subnets 32, 64, 96, 128, and so on. So, by looking at the figure, you can see that subnet 32 is being used by the sales department, the WAN link is using subnet 96, and the marketing department is using subnet 64.

Now you've got to determine what the valid host ranges are for each subnet. From what you learned at the beginning of this chapter, you should now be able to easily determine the subnet address, broadcast addresses, and valid host ranges. The valid hosts for the Sales LAN are 33 through 62—the broadcast address is 63 because the next subnet is 64, right? For the Marketing LAN, the valid hosts are 65 through 94 (broadcast 95), and for the WAN link, 97 through 126 (broadcast 127). By looking at the figure, you can determine that the default gateway on the Lab_B router is incorrect. That address is the broadcast address of the 64 subnet, so there's no way it could be a valid host.

Did you get all that? Maybe we should try another one, just to make sure. Figure 3.16 shows a network problem. A user in the Sales LAN can't get to ServerB. You have the user run through the four basic troubleshooting steps and find that the host can communicate to the local network but not to the remote network. Find and define the IP addressing problem.

FIGURE 3.16   IP address problem 2

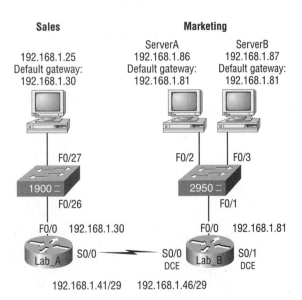

If you use the same steps used to solve the last problem, you can see first that the WAN link again provides the subnet mask to use— /29, or 255.255.255.248. You need to determine what the valid subnets, broadcast addresses, and valid host ranges are to solve this problem.

The 248 mask is a block size of 8 (256 − 248 = 8), so the subnets both start and increment in multiples of 8. By looking at the figure, you see that the Sales LAN is in the 24 subnet, the WAN is in the 40 subnet, and the Marketing LAN is in the 80 subnet. Can you see the problem yet? The valid host range for the Sales LAN is 25–30, and the configuration appears correct. The valid host range for the WAN link is 41–46, and this also appears correct. The valid host range for the 80 subnet is 81–86, with a broadcast address of 87 because the next subnet is 88. ServerB has been configured with the broadcast address of the subnet.

Okay, now that you can figure out misconfigured IP addresses on hosts, what do you do if a host doesn't have an IP address and you need to assign one? What you need to do is look at other hosts on the LAN and figure out the network, mask, and default gateway. Let's take a look at a couple of examples of how to find and apply valid IP addresses to hosts.

You need to assign a server and router IP addresses on a LAN. The subnet assigned on that segment is 192.168.20.24/29, and the router needs to be assigned the first usable address and the server the last valid host ID. What are the IP address, mask, and default gateway assigned to the server?

To answer this, you must know that a /29 is a 255.255.255.248 mask, which provides a block size of 8. The subnet is known as 24, the next subnet in a block of 8 is 32, so the broadcast address of the 24 subnet is 31, which makes the valid host range 25–30.

Server IP address: 192.168.20.30

Server mask: 255.255.255.248

Default gateway: 192.168.20.25 (router's IP address)

Exam Objectives

Remember the four diagnostic steps.   The four simple steps that Cisco recommends for troubleshooting are ping the loopback address, ping the NIC, ping the default gateway, and ping the remote device.

You must be able to find and fix an IP addressing problem.   Once you go through the four troubleshooting steps that Cisco recommends, you must be able to determine the IP addressing problem by drawing out the network and finding the valid and invalid hosts addressed in your network.

Understand the troubleshooting tools that you can use from your host and a Cisco router.   `ping 127.0.0.1` tests your local IP stack. `tracert` is a Windows DOS command to track the path a packet takes through an internetwork to a destination. Cisco routers use the command `traceroute`, or just `trace` for short. Don't confuse the Windows and Cisco commands. Although they produce the same output, they don't work from the same prompts. `ipconfig /all` will display your PC network configuration from a DOS prompt, and `arp -a` (again from a DOS prompt) will display IP to MAC address mapping on a Windows PC.

Review Questions

The following questions are designed to test your understanding of this chapter's material. For more information on how to get additional questions, please see this book's Introduction.

1. On a VLSM network, which mask should you use on point-to-point WAN links in order to reduce the waste of IP addresses?

   A. /27

   B. /28

   C. /29

   D. /30

   E. /31

2. A network administrator is connecting hosts A and B directly through their Ethernet interfaces, as shown in the illustration. Ping attempts between the hosts are unsuccessful. What can be done to provide connectivity between the hosts? (Choose two.)

Straight-through Cable

IP Address: 192.168.1.20   IP Address: 192.168.1.201
Mask 255.255.255.240   Mask 255.255.255.240

   A. A crossover cable should be used in place of the straight-through cable.

   B. A rollover cable should be used in place of the straight-though cable.

   C. The subnet masks should be set to 255.255.255.192.

   D. A default gateway needs to be set on each host.

   E. The subnet masks should be set to 255.255.255.0.

3. Using the following illustration, what would be the IP address of E0 if you were using the eighth subnet? The network ID is 192.168.10.0/28, and you need to use the last available IP address in the range. The zero subnet should not be considered valid for this question.

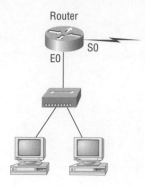

    A. 192.168.10.142

    B. 192.168.10.66

    C. 192.168.100.254

    D. 192.168.10.143

    E. 192.168.10.126

4. Using the illustration from the previous question, what would be the IP address of S0 if you were using the first subnet? The network ID is 192.168.10.0/28, and you need to use the last available IP address in the range. Again, the zero subnet should not be considered valid for this question.

    A. 192.168.10.24

    B. 192.168.10.62

    C. 192.168.10.30

    D. 192.168.10.127

5. To test the IP stack on your local host, which IP address would you ping?

    A. 127.0.0.0

    B. 1.0.0.127

    C. 127.0.0.1

    D. 127.0.0.255

    E. 255.255.255.255

6. Which of the following is true when describing a global unicast address?

    A. Packets addressed to a unicast address are delivered to a single interface.

    B. These are your typical publicly routable addresses, just like a regular publicly routable address in IPv4.

    C. These are like private addresses in IPv4 in they are not meant to be routed.

    D. These addresses are meant for nonrouting purposes, but they are almost globally unique so it is unlikely they will have an address overlap.

7. Which of the following is true when describing a unicast address?

   A. Packets addressed to a unicast address are delivered to a single interface.

   B. These are you typical publicly routable addresses, just like a regular publicly routable address in IPv4.

   C. These are like private addresses in IPv4 in they are not meant to be routed.

   D. These addresses are meant for nonrouting purposes, but they are almost globally unique, so it is unlikely they will have an address overlap.

8. Which of the following is true when describing a link-local address?

   A. Packets addressed to a unicast address are delivered to a single interface.

   B. These are you typical publicly routable addresses, just like a regular publicly routable address in IPv4.

   C. These are like private addresses in IPv4 in they are not meant to be routed.

   D. These addresses are meant for nonrouting purposes, but they are almost globally unique, so it is unlikely they will have an address overlap.

9. Which of the following is true when describing a unique local address?

   A. Packets addressed to a unicast address are delivered to a single interface.

   B. These are you typical publicly routable addresses, just like a regular publicly routable address in IPv4.

   C. These are like private addresses in IPv4 in they are not meant to be routed.

   D. These addresses are meant for nonrouting purposes, but they are almost globally unique, so it is unlikely they will have an address overlap.

10. Which of the following is true when describing a multicast address?

   A. Packets addressed to a unicast address are delivered to a single interface.

   B. Packets are delivered to all interfaces identified by the address. This is also called a one-to-many address.

   C. Identifies multiple interfaces and is only delivered to one address. This address can also be called one-to-one-of-many.

   D. These addresses are meant for nonrouting purposes, but they are almost globally unique, so it is unlikely they will have an address overlap.

Answers to Review Questions

1. D. A point-to-point link uses only two hosts. A /30, or 255.255.255.252, mask provides two hosts per subnet.

2. A, E. First, if you have two hosts directly connected, as shown in the graphic, then you need a crossover cable. A straight-through cable won't work. Second, the hosts have different masks, which puts them in different subnets. The easy solution is just to set both masks to 255.255.255.0 (/24).

3. A. A /28 is a 255.255.255.240 mask. Let's count to the ninth subnet (we need to find the broadcast address of the eighth subnet, so we need to count to the ninth subnet). Starting at 16 (remember, the question stated that we will not use subnet zero so we start at 16, not 0)16, 32, 48, 64, 80, 96, 112, 128, 144. The eighth subnet is 128 and the next subnet is 144, so our broadcast address of the 128 subnet is 143. This makes the host range 129-142.] 142 is the last valid host.

4. C. A /28 is a 255.255.255.240 mask. The first subnet is 16 (remember that the question stated not to use subnet zero), and the next subnet is 32, so our broadcast address is 31. This makes our host range 17–30. 30 is the last valid host.

5. C. To test the local stack on your host, ping the loopback interface of 127.0.0.1.

6. B. Unlike unicast addresses, global unicast addresses are meant to be routed.

7. A. Packets addressed to a unicast address are delivered to a single interface. For load balancing, multiple interfaces can use the same address.

8. C. Link-local addresses are meant for throwing together a temporary LAN for meetings or a small LAN that is not going to be routed but needs to share and access files and services locally.

9. D. These addresses are meant for nonrouting purposes like link-local, but they are almost globally unique, so it is unlikely they will have an address overlap. Unique local addresses where designed as a replacement for site-local addresses

10. B. Packets addressed to a multicast address are delivered to all interfaces identified by the multicast address, the same as in IPv4. It is also called a one-to-many address. You can always tell a multicast address in IPv6 because multicast addresses always start with FF.

Chapter

4

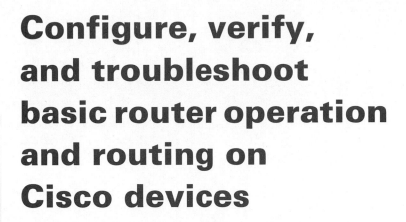

Configure, verify, and troubleshoot basic router operation and routing on Cisco devices

THE CISCO CCNA EXAM OBJECTIVES COVERED IN THIS CHAPTER INCLUDE:

- 4.1 Describe basic routing concepts (including packet forwarding, router lookup process)
- 4.2 Describe the operation of Cisco routers (including router bootup process, POST, router components)
- 4.3 Select the appropriate media, cables, ports, and connectors to connect routers to other network devices and hosts
- 4.4 Configure, verify, and troubleshoot RIPv2
- 4.5 Access and utilize the router to set basic parameters (including CLI/SDM)
- 4.6 Connect, configure, and verify the operational status of a device interface
- 4.7 Verify device configuration and network connectivity using ping, traceroute, Telnet, SSH, or other utilities
- 4.8 Perform and verify routing configuration tasks for a static or default route given specific routing requirements
- 4.9 Manage IOS configuration files. (including save, edit, upgrade, restore)
- 4.10 Manage Cisco IOS
- 4.11 Compare and contrast methods of routing and routing protocols

- 4.12 Configure, verify, and troubleshoot OSPF
- 4.13 Configure, verify, and troubleshoot EIGRP
- 4.14 Verify network connectivity (including: using ping, traceroute, and telnet or SSH)
- 4.15 Troubleshoot routing issues
- 4.16 Verify router hardware and software operation using the SHOW & DEBUG commands
- 4.17 Implement basic router security

In this chapter, I'm going to discuss the IP routing process. This is an important subject to understand, since it pertains to all routers and configurations that use IP. *IP routing* is the process of moving packets from one network to another network using routers. And as before, by routers I mean Cisco routers, of course!

But before you read this chapter, you must understand the difference between a routing protocol and a routed protocol. A *routing protocol* is used by routers to dynamically find all the networks in the internetwork and to ensure that all routers have the same routing table. Basically, a routing protocol determines the path of a packet through an internetwork. Examples of routing protocols are RIP, RIPv2, EIGRP, and OSPF.

Once all routers know about all networks, a *routed protocol* can be used to send user data (packets) through the established enterprise. Routed protocols are assigned to an interface and determine the method of packet delivery. Examples of routed protocols are IP and IPv6.

Enhanced Interior Gateway Routing Protocol (EIGRP) is a proprietary Cisco protocol that runs on Cisco routers. It is important for you to understand EIGRP because it is probably one of the two most popular routing protocols in use today. I'm also going to introduce you to the *Open Shortest Path First* (OSPF) routing protocol, which is the other popular routing protocol in use today. You'll build a solid foundation for understanding OSPF by first becoming familiar with the terminology and internal operation of it and then learning about OSPF's advantages over RIP.

For up-to-the-minute updates on the CCNA objectives covered by this chapter, please see www.lammle.com and/or www.sybex.com.

4.1 Describe basic routing concepts (including packet forwarding, router lookup process)

Once you create an internetwork by connecting your WANs and LANs to a router, you'll need to configure logical network addresses, such as IP addresses, to all hosts on the internetwork so that they can communicate across that internetwork.

The term *routing* is used for taking a packet from one device and sending it through the network to another device on a different network. Routers don't really care about hosts—they only care about networks and the best path to each network. The logical network address of the destination host is used to get packets to a network through a routed network, and then the hardware address of the host is used to deliver the packet from a router to the correct destination host.

If your network has no routers, then it should be apparent that you are not routing. Routers route traffic to all the networks in your internetwork. To be able to route packets, a router must know, at a minimum, the following:

- Destination address

- Neighbor routers from which it can learn about remote networks

- Possible routes to all remote networks

- The best route to each remote network

- How to maintain and verify routing information

The router learns about remote networks from neighbor routers or from an administrator. The router then builds a routing table (a map of the internetwork) that describes how to find the remote networks. If a network is directly connected, then the router already knows how to get to it.

If a network isn't directly connected to the router, the router must use one of two ways to learn how to get to the remote network: *static routing*, meaning that someone must hand-type all network locations into the routing table, or something called dynamic routing. In *dynamic routing*, a protocol on one router communicates with the same protocol running on neighbor routers. The routers then update each other about all the networks they know about and place this information into the routing table. If a change occurs in the network, the dynamic routing protocols automatically inform all routers about the event. If *static routing* is used, the administrator is responsible for updating all changes by hand into all routers. Typically, in a large network, a combination of both dynamic and static routing is used.

Before we jump into the IP routing process, let's take a look at a simple example that demonstrates how a router uses the routing table to route packets out of an interface. We'll be going into a more detailed study of the process in the next section.

Figure 4.1 shows a simple two-router network. Lab_A has one serial interface and three LAN interfaces.

Looking at Figure 4.1, can you see which interface Lab_A will use to forward an IP datagram to a host with an IP address of 10.10.10.10?

By using the command show ip route, we can see the routing table (map of the internetwork) that Lab_A uses to make forwarding decisions:

```
Lab_A#sh ip route
[output cut]
Gateway of last resort is not set
C       10.10.10.0/24 is directly connected, FastEthernet0/0
C       10.10.20.0/24 is directly connected, FastEthernet0/1
C       10.10.30.0/24 is directly connected, FastEthernet0/2
C       10.10.40.0/24 is directly connected, Serial 0/0
```

FIGURE 4.1   A simple routing example

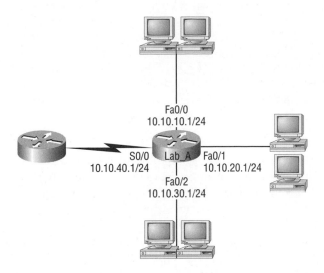

The C in the routing table output means that the networks listed are "directly connected," and until we add a routing protocol—something like RIP, EIGRP, and so on—to the routers in our internetwork (or use static routes), we'll have only directly connected networks in our routing table.

So, let's get back to the original question: By looking at the figure and the output of the routing table, can you tell what IP will do with a received packet that has a destination IP address of 10.10.10.10? The router will packet-switch the packet to interface FastEthernet 0/0, and this interface will frame the packet and then send it out on the network segment.

Because we can, let's do another example: Based on the output of the next routing table, which interface will a packet with a destination address of 10.10.10.14 be forwarded from?

```
Lab_A#sh ip route
[output cut]
Gateway of last resort is not set
C       10.10.10.16/28 is directly connected, FastEthernet0/0
C       10.10.10.8/29 is directly connected, FastEthernet0/1
C       10.10.10.4/30 is directly connected, FastEthernet0/2
C       10.10.10.0/30 is directly connected, Serial 0/0
```

First, you can see that the network is subnetted and each interface has a different mask. And I have to tell you—you just can't answer this question if you can't subnet! 10.10.10.14 would be a host in the 10.10.10.8/29 subnet connected to the FastEthernet0/1 interface.

Using DNS to Resolve Names

If you have a lot of devices and don't want to create a host table in each device, you can use a DNS server to resolve hostnames.

Any time a Cisco device receives a command it doesn't understand, it will try to resolve it through DNS by default. Watch what happens when I type the special command todd at a Cisco router prompt:

```
Corp#todd
Translating "todd"...domain server (255.255.255.255)
Translating "todd"...domain server (255.255.255.255)
Translating "todd"...domain server (255.255.255.255)
% Unknown command or computer name, or unable to find
  computer address
Corp#
```

It doesn't know my name or what command I am trying to type, so it tries to resolve this through DNS. This is really annoying because I need to hang out and wait for the name lookup to time out. You can get around this and prevent a time-consuming DNS lookup by using the no ip domain-lookup command on your router from global configuration mode.

If you have a DNS server on your network, you need to add a few commands to make DNS name resolution work:

- The first command is **ip domain-lookup**, which is turned on by default. It needs to be entered only if you previously turned it off (with the **no ip domain-lookup** command). The command can be used without the hyphen as well (**ip domain lookup**).

- The second command is **ip name-server**. This sets the IP address of the DNS server. You can enter the IP addresses of up to six servers.

- The last command is **ip domain-name**. Although this command is optional, it really should be set. It appends the domain name to the hostname you type in. Since DNS uses a fully qualified domain name (FQDN) system, you must have a full DNS name, in the form **domain.com**.

Here's an example of using these three commands:

```
Corp#config t
Corp(config)#ip domain-lookup
Corp(config)#ip name-server ?
  A.B.C.D  Domain server IP address (maximum of 6)
Corp(config)#ip name-server 192.168.0.70
Corp(config)#ip domain-name lammle.com
Corp(config)#^Z
Corp#
```

After the DNS configurations are set, you can test the DNS server by using a hostname to ping or telnet a device like this:

```
Corp#ping R1
Translating "R1"...domain server (192.168.0.70) [OK]
Type escape sequence to abort.
```

```
Sending 5, 100-byte ICMP Echos to 10.2.2.2, timeout is
  2 seconds:
!!!!!
Success rate is 100 percent (5/5), round-trip min/avg/max
  = 28/31/32 ms
```

Notice that the router uses the DNS server to resolve the name.

Exam Objectives

Understand the basic IP-routing process.   You need to remember that the frame changes at each hop but that the packet is never changed or manipulated in any way until it reaches the destination device.

Understand the term routing.   The term routing is used for taking a packet from one device and sending it through the network to another device on a different network. Routers don't really care about hosts - they only care about networks and the best path to each network.

4.2 Describe the operation of Cisco routers (including router bootup process, POST, router components)

To configure and troubleshoot a Cisco internetwork, you need to know the major components of Cisco routers and understand what each one does. Table 4.1 describes the major Cisco router components.

TABLE 4.1   Cisco Router Components

Component	Description
Bootstrap	Stored in the microcode of the ROM, the bootstrap is used to bring a router up during initialization. It will boot the router and then load the IOS.
POST (power-on self-test)	Stored in the microcode of the ROM, the POST is used to check the basic functionality of the router hardware and determines which interfaces are present.
ROM monitor	Stored in the microcode of the ROM, the ROM monitor is used for manufacturing, testing, and troubleshooting.
Mini-IOS	Called the RXBOOT or bootloader by Cisco, the mini-IOS is a small IOS in ROM that can be used to bring up an interface and load a Cisco IOS into flash memory. The mini-IOS can also perform a few other maintenance operations.

TABLE 4.1   Cisco Router Components *(continued)*

Component	Description
RAM (random access memory)	Used to hold packet buffers, ARP cache, routing tables, and also the software and data structures that allow the router to function. Running-config is stored in RAM, and most routers expand the IOS from flash into RAM upon boot.
ROM (read-only memory)	Used to start and maintain the router. Holds the POST and the Bootstrap program, as well as the mini-IOS.
Flash memory	Stores the Cisco IOS by default. Flash memory is not erased when the router is reloaded. It is EEPROM (electronically erasable programmable read-only memory) created by Intel.
NVRAM (nonvolatile RAM)	Used to hold the router and switch configuration. NVRAM is not erased when the router or switch is reloaded. Does not store an IOS. The configuration register is stored in NVRAM.
Configuration register	Used to control how the router boots up. This value can be found as the last line of the show version command output and by default is set to 0x2102, which tells the router to load the IOS from flash memory as well as to load the configuration from NVRAM.

The Router Boot Sequence

When a router boots up, it performs a series of steps, called the *boot sequence*, to test the hardware and load the necessary software. The boot sequence consists of the following steps:

1. The router performs a POST. The POST tests the hardware to verify that all components of the device are operational and present. For example, the POST checks for the different interfaces on the router. The POST is stored in and run from *ROM (read-only memory)*.

2. The bootstrap then looks for and loads the Cisco IOS software. The *bootstrap* is a program in ROM that is used to execute programs. The bootstrap program is responsible for finding where each IOS program is located and then loading the file. By default, the IOS software is loaded from flash memory in all Cisco routers.

The default order of an IOS loading from a router is Flash, TFTP server, then ROM.

3. The IOS software looks for a valid configuration file stored in NVRAM. This file is called startup-config and is only there if an administrator copies the running-config file into NVRAM. (Cisco's new Integrated Services Router (ISR) have a small startup-config file preloaded.)

4. If a startup-config file is in NVRAM, the router will copy this file and place it in RAM and call the file running-config. The router will use this file to run the router. The router should now be operational. If a startup-config file is not in NVRAM, the router will broadcast out any interface that detects carrier detect (CD) for a TFTP host looking for a configuration, and when that fails (typically it will fail—most people won't even realize the router has attempted this process), it will start the setup mode configuration process.

Managing Configuration Register

All Cisco routers have a 16-bit software register that's written into NVRAM. By default, the *configuration register* is set to load the Cisco IOS from *flash memory* and to look for and load the startup-config file from NVRAM. In the following sections, I am going to discuss the configuration register settings and how to use these settings to provide password recovery on your routers.

Understanding the Configuration Register Bits

The 16 bits (2 bytes) of the configuration register are read from 15 to 0, from left to right. The default configuration setting on Cisco routers is 0x2102. This means that bits 13, 8, and 1 are on, as shown in Table 4.2. Notice that each set of 4 bits (called a *nibble*) is read in binary with a value of 8, 4, 2, 1.

TABLE 4.2 The Configuration Register Bit Numbers

Configuration Register		2					1				0			2	
Bit number	15	14	13	12	11	10	9	8	7	6	5	4	3	2	1	0
Binary	0	0	1	0	0	0	0	1	0	0	0	0	0	0	1	0

Add the prefix *0x* to the configuration register address. The *0x* means that the digits that follow are in hexadecimal.

Table 4.3 lists the software configuration bit meanings. Notice that bit 6 can be used to ignore the NVRAM contents. This bit is used for password recovery.

Remember that in hex, the scheme is 0–9 and A–F (A = 10, B = 11, C = 12, D = 13, E = 14, and F = 15). This means that a 210F setting for the configuration register is actually 210(15), or 1111 in binary.

TABLE 4.3 Software Configuration Meanings

Bit	Hex	Description
0–3	0x0000–0x000F	Boot field (see Table 4.4)
6	0x0040	Ignore NVRAM contents
7	0x0080	OEM bit enabled
8	0x101	Break disabled
10	0x0400	IP broadcast with all zeros
5, 11–12	0x0800–0x1000	Console line speed
13	0x2000	Boot default ROM software if network boot fails
14	0x4000	IP broadcasts do not have net numbers
15	0x8000	Enable diagnostic messages and ignore NVRAM contents

The boot field, which consists of bits 0–3 in the configuration register, controls the router boot sequence. Table 4.4 describes the boot field bits.

TABLE 4.4 The Boot Field (Configuration Register Bits 00–03)

Boot Field	Meaning	Use
00	ROM monitor mode	To boot to ROM monitor mode, set the configuration register to 2100. You must manually boot the router with the b command. The router will show the rommon> prompt.
01	Boot image from ROM	To boot an IOS image stored in ROM, set the configuration register to 2101. The router will show the Router(boot)> prompt.
02–F	Specifies a default boot file name	Any value from 2102 through 210F tells the router to use the boot commands specified in NVRAM.

Exam Objectives

Remember the default configuration register setting. The default configuration register setting is 0x2102, which means "load the IOS from flash and the configuration from NVRAM."

Remember where the IOS is stored by default. The IOS is stored and loaded from flash memory by default on all Cisco routers.

4.3 Select the appropriate media, cables, ports, and connectors to connect routers to other network devices and hosts

Although this will cover the same material as in objective 2.1, I will add one new section on serial (WAN) connection types that a router uses.

Ethernet cabling is an important discussion, especially if you are planning on taking the Cisco exams. Three types of Ethernet cables are available:

- Straight-through cable
- Crossover cable
- Rolled cable

We will look at each in the following sections.

Straight-Through Cable

The *straight-through cable* is used to connect

- Host to switch or hub
- Router to switch or hub

Four wires are used in straight-through cable to connect Ethernet devices. It is relatively simple to create this type; Figure 4.2 shows the four wires used in a straight-through Ethernet cable.

FIGURE 4.2　Straight-through Ethernet cable

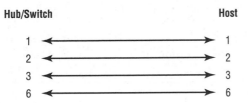

Notice that only pins 1, 2, 3, and 6 are used. Just connect 1 to 1, 2 to 2, 3 to 3, and 6 to 6, and you'll be up and networking in no time. However, remember that this would be an Ethernet-only cable and wouldn't work with voice, Token Ring, ISDN, and so on.

Crossover Cable

The *crossover cable* can be used to connect

- Switch to switch
- Hub to hub
- Host to host
- Hub to switch
- Router direct to host

The same four wires are used in this cable as in the straight-through cable; we just connect different pins together. Figure 4.3 shows how the four wires are used in a crossover Ethernet cable.

Notice that instead of connecting 1 to 1, 2 to 2, and so on, here we connect pins 1 to 3 and 2 to 6 on each side of the cable.

FIGURE 4.3   Crossover Ethernet cable

Rolled Cable

Although *rolled cable* isn't used to connect any Ethernet connections together, you can use a rolled Ethernet cable to connect a host to a router console serial communication (com) port.

If you have a Cisco router or switch, you would use this cable to connect your PC running HyperTerminal to the Cisco hardware. Eight wires are used in this cable to connect serial devices, although not all eight are used to send information, just as in Ethernet networking. Figure 4.4 shows the eight wires used in a rolled cable.

These are probably the easiest cables to make because you just cut the end off on one side of a straight-through cable, turn it over, and put it back on (with a new connector, of course).

FIGURE 4.4   Rolled Ethernet cable

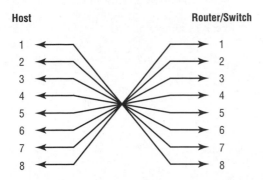

Once you have the correct cable connected from your PC to the Cisco router or switch, you can start HyperTerminal to create a console connection and configure the device. Set the configuration as follows:

1. Open HyperTerminal and enter a name for the connection. It is irrelevant what you name it, but I always just use Cisco. Then click OK.

2. Choose the communications port—either COM1 or COM2, whichever is open on your PC.

3. Now set the port settings. The default values (2400bps and no flow control hardware) will not work; you must set the port settings as shown in Figure 4.5.

FIGURE 4.5   Port settings for a rolled cable connection

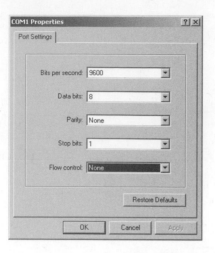

Notice that the bit rate is now set to 9600 and the flow control is set to None. At this point, you can click OK and press the Enter key, and you should be connected to your Cisco device console port.

We've taken a look at the various RJ45 unshielded twisted-pair (UTP) cables. Keeping this in mind, what cable is used between the switches in Figure 4.6?

FIGURE 4.6   RJ45 UTP cable question #1

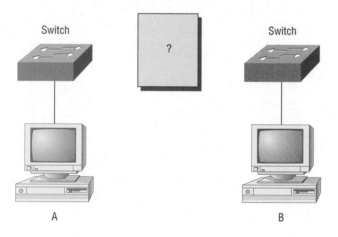

In order for host A to ping host B, you need a crossover cable to connect the two switches. But what types of cables are used in the network shown in Figure 4.7?

FIGURE 4.7   RJ45 UTP cable question #2

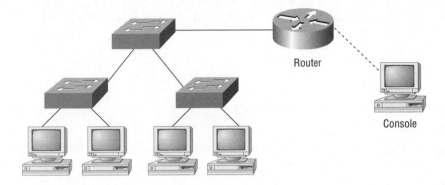

Router

Console

In Figure 4.7, there are a variety of cables in use. For the connection between the switches, we'd obviously use a crossover cable as you saw in Figure 4.3. The trouble is, we have a console connection that uses a rolled cable. Plus, the connection from the router to the switch is a straight-through cable, as is true for the hosts to the switches. Keep in mind that if we had a serial connection (which we don't), it would be a V.35 that we'd use to connect us to a WAN.

Router WAN Connections

As you can imagine, there are a few things that you need to know before connecting your WAN in order to make sure everything goes well. For starters, you have to understand the kind of WAN Physical layer implementation that Cisco provides as well as ensure that you're familiar with the various types of WAN serial connectors involved.

The good news is that Cisco serial connections support almost any type of WAN service. Your typical WAN connection is a dedicated leased line using HDLC, PPP, and Frame Relay with speeds that can kick it up to 45Mbps (T3).

HDLC, PPP, and Frame Relay can use the same Physical layer specifications, and I'll go over the various types of connections and then move on to telling you all about the WAN protocols specified in the CCNA objectives.

Serial Transmission

WAN serial connectors use *serial transmission*, something that takes place 1 bit at a time over a single channel.

Parallel transmission can pass at least 8 bits at a time, but all WANs use serial transmission.

Cisco routers use a proprietary 60-pin serial connector that you have to get from Cisco or a provider of Cisco equipment. Cisco also has a new, smaller proprietary serial connection that's about one-tenth the size of the 60-pin basic serial cable called the "smart-serial"—I'm not sure why. But I do know that you have to make sure that you have the right type of interface in your router before using this cable connector.

The type of connector you have on the other end of the cable depends on your service provider and their particular end-device requirements. There are several different types of ends you'll run into:

- EIA/TIA-232
- EIA/TIA-449
- V.35 (used to connect to a CSU/DSU)
- EIA-530

Make sure that you're clear on these things: Serial links are described in frequency or cycles per second (hertz). The amount of data that can be carried within these frequencies is called *bandwidth*. Bandwidth is the amount of data in bits per second that the serial channel can carry.

Data Terminal Equipment and Data Communication Equipment

By default, router interfaces are *data terminal equipment (DTE)*, and they connect into *data communication equipment (DCE)* like a *channel service unit/data service unit (CSU/DSU)*. The CSU/DSU then plugs into a demarcation location (demarc) and is the service provider's last responsibility. Most of the time, the demarc is a jack that has an RJ-45 (8-pin modular) female connector located in a telecommunications closet.

Actually, you may already have heard of demarcs. If you've ever had the glorious experience of reporting a problem to your service provider, they'll usually tell you everything tests out fine up to the demarc, so the problem must be the CPE, or customer premises equipment. In other words, it's your problem not theirs.

Figure 4.8 shows a typical DTE-DCE-DTE connection and the devices used in the network.

The idea behind a WAN is to be able to connect two DTE networks through a DCE network. The DCE network includes the CSU/DSU, through the provider's wiring and switches, all the way to the CSU/DSU at the other end. The network's DCE device (CSU/DSU) provides clocking to the DTE-connected interface (the router's serial interface).

As mentioned, the DCE network provides clocking to the router; this is the CSU/DSU. If you have a nonproduction network and you're using a WAN crossover type of cable and do not have a CSU/DSU, then you need to provide clocking on the DCE end of the cable by using the `clock rate` command.

Terms such as *EIA/TIA-232*, *V.35*, *X.21*, and *HSSI (High-Speed Serial Interface)* describe the Physical layer between the DTE (router) and DCE device (CSU/DSU).

FIGURE 4.8   DTE-DCE-DTE WAN connection

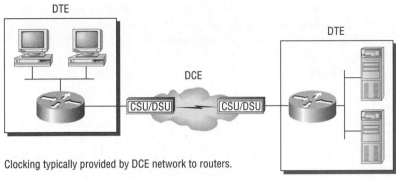

Clocking typically provided by DCE network to routers.

In non-production environments, a DCE network is not always present.

Exam Objectives

Remember the types of Ethernet cabling and when you would use them.   The three types of cables that can be created from an Ethernet cable are straight-through (to connect a PC's or a router's Ethernet interface to a hub or switch), crossover (to connect hub to hub, hub to switch, switch to switch, or PC to PC), and rolled (for a console connection from a PC to a router or switch).

Understand how to connect a console cable from a PC to a router and start HyperTerminal. Take a rolled cable and connect it from the COM port of the host to the console port of a router. Start HyperTerminal and set the BPS to 9600 and flow control to None.

Understand the difference between DTE and DCE connections.   *Data terminal equipment (DTE) is considered your router connected to a WAN and is the customers responsibility. DTE devices connect into data communication equipment (DCE), typically considered the CSU/DSU, which then connects into the providers network.*

4.4 Configure, verify, and troubleshoot RIPv2

RIP version 2 is mostly the same as RIP version 1. Both RIPv1 and RIPv2 are *distance-vector protocols*, which means that each router running RIP sends its complete routing tables out all active interfaces at periodic time intervals. Also, the timers and loop-avoidance schemes are the same in both RIP versions (i.e., holddown timers and split horizon rule). Both RIPv1 and RIPv2 are configured as classful addressing (but RIPv2 is considered classless because subnet information is sent with each route update), and both have the same administrative distance (120).

But there are some important differences that make RIPv2 more scalable than RIPv1. And I've got to add a word of advice here before we move on; I'm definitely not advocating using RIP of either version in your network. But since RIP is an open standard, you can use RIP with any brand of router. You can also use OSPF, since OSPF is an open standard as well. RIP just requires too much bandwidth, making it pretty intensive to use in your network. Why go there when you have other, more elegant options?

Table 4.5 discusses the differences between RIPv1 and RIPv2.

TABLE 4.5   RIPv1 vs. RIPv2

RIPv1	RIPv2
Distance vector	Distance vector
Maximum hop count of 15	Maximum hop count of 15
Classful	Classless
Broadcast based	Uses multicast 224.0.0.9
No support for VLSM	Supports VLSM networks
No authentication	Allows for MD5 authentication
No support for discontiguous networks	Supports discontiguous networks

RIPv2, unlike RIPv1, is a classless routing protocol (even though it is configured as classful, like RIPv1), which means that it sends subnet mask information along with the route updates. By sending the subnet mask information with the updates, RIPv2 can support variable length subnet masks (VLSMs) as well as the summarization of network boundaries. In addition, RIPv2 can support discontiguous networking.

Configuring RIPv2 is pretty straightforward. Here's an example:

```
Lab_C(config)#router rip
Lab_C(config-router)#network 192.168.40.0
Lab_C(config-router)#network 192.168.50.0
Lab_C(config-router)#version 2
```

That's it; just add the command **version 2** under the (config-router)# prompt, and you are now running RIPv2.

RIPv2 is classless and works in VLSM and discontiguous networks.

Let's see if we can find a difference in our routing table after enabling RIPv2.

```
        10.0.0.0/24 is subnetted, 12 subnets
C       10.1.11.0 is directly connected, FastEthernet0/1
C       10.1.10.0 is directly connected, FastEthernet0/0
R       10.1.9.0 [120/2] via 10.1.5.1, 00:00:23, Serial0/0/1
R       10.1.8.0 [120/2] via 10.1.5.1, 00:00:23, Serial0/0/1
R       10.1.12.0 [120/1] via 10.1.11.2, 00:00:18, FastEthernet0/1
R       10.1.3.0 [120/1] via 10.1.5.1, 00:00:23, Serial0/0/1
```

Well, ummm—looks the same to me as the output for RIPv1. I'm going to turn on debugging and see if that shows us anything new:

```
*Mar 17 19:34:00.123: RIP: sending v2 update to 224.0.0.9 via
    Serial0/0/1 (10.1.5.2)
*Mar 17 19:34:00.123: RIP: build update entries
*Mar 17 19:34:00.123:    10.1.10.0/24 via 0.0.0.0, metric 1, tag 0
*Mar 17 19:34:00.123:    10.1.11.0/24 via 0.0.0.0, metric 1, tag 0
*Mar 17 19:34:00.123:    10.1.12.0/24 via 0.0.0.0, metric 2, tag 0col
*Mar 17 19:34:03.795: RIP: received v2 update from 10.1.5.1 on
    Serial0/0/1
[output cut]
```

Bingo! Look at that! The networks are still being advertised every 30 seconds, but they're now sending the advertisements as v2 and as a multicast address of 224.0.0.9. Let's take a look at the show ip protocols output:

```
Router#sh ip protocols
Routing Protocol is "rip"
  Outgoing update filter list for all interfaces is not set
  Incoming update filter list for all interfaces is not set
  Sending updates every 30 seconds, next due in 27 seconds
  Invalid after 180 seconds, hold down 180, flushed after 240
  Redistributing: rip
  Default version control: send version 2, receive version 2
    Interface          Send  Recv  Triggered RIP  Key-chain
    FastEthernet0/1     2     2
    Serial0/0/1         2     2
  Automatic network summarization is not in effect
  Maximum path: 4
  Routing for Networks:
    10.0.0.0
  Passive Interface(s):
```

```
  FastEthernet0/0
  Serial0/0/0
Routing Information Sources:
  Gateway         Distance      Last Update
  10.1.11.2            120      00:00:00
  10.1.5.1             120      00:00:02
Distance: (default is 120)
```

We are now sending and receiving RIPv2.

Exam Objectives

Remember the multicast address of RIPv2.   RIPv2 does not use broadcasts like RIPv1; instead, it uses a multicast address of 224.0.0.9 to communicate with other routers running RIPv2.

Understand how to configure RIPv2.   RIPv2 has a very simple configuration. You just add the command version 2 under the RIP configuration.

4.5 Access and utilize the router to set basic parameters (including CLI/SDM)

If you boot a router, the interface status messages appear, and you press Enter, the Router> prompt will appear. This is called *user exec mode* (user mode), and it's mostly used to view statistics, but it's also a stepping stone to logging in to privileged mode.

You can only view and change the configuration of a Cisco router in *privileged exec mode* (privileged mode), which you can enter with the enable command.

Here's how:

```
Router>enable
Router#
```

You now end up with a Router# prompt, which indicates that you're in *privileged mode*, where you can both view and change the router's configuration. You can go back from privileged mode into user mode by using the disable command, as seen here:

```
Router#disable
Router>
```

At this point, you can type logout from either mode to exit the console:

```
Router>logout

Router con0 is now available
Press RETURN to get started.
```

In the following sections, I am going to show you how to perform some basic administrative configurations.

Overview of Router Modes

To configure from a CLI, you can make global changes to the router by typing **configure terminal** (or **config t** for short), which puts you in global configuration mode and changes what's known as the `running-config`. A global command (a command run from global config) is set only once and affects the entire router.

You can type **config** from the privileged-mode prompt and then just press Enter to take the default of `terminal`, as shown here:

```
yourname#config
Configuring from terminal, memory, or network [terminal]? [press enter]
Enter configuration commands, one per line. End with CNTL/Z.
yourname(config)#
```

At this point, you make changes that affect the router as a whole (globally), hence the term global configuration mode. To change the `running-config`—the current configuration running in dynamic RAM (DRAM)—you use the `configure terminal` command, as I just demonstrated.

To change the `startup-config`—the configuration stored in NVRAM—you use the `configure memory` command (or `config mem` for short), which merges the `startup-config` file into the `running-config` file in RAM. If you want to change a router configuration stored on a TFTP host, you use the `configure network` command (or `config net` for short), which also merges the file with the `running-config` file in RAM.

The `configure terminal`, `configure memory`, and `configure network` are all used to configure information into RAM on a router; however, typically only the `configure terminal` command is used. However, it is possible that the commands `config mem` and `config net` can be useful if you screw up your `running-config` file and don't want to reboot your router.

Some of the other options under the `configure` command are:

```
yourname(config)#exit or press cntl-z
yourname#config ?
  confirm           Confirm replacement of running-config with a new config
file
  memory            Configure from NV memory
  network           Configure from a TFTP network host
  overwrite-network Overwrite NV memory from TFTP network host
  replace           Replace the running-config with a new config file
  terminal          Configure from the terminal
  <cr>
```

As you can see, Cisco has added a few more commands in the 12.4 IOS.

Defining Router Terms

Table 4.6 defines some of the terms we've used so far.

TABLE 4.6   Router Terms

Mode	Definition
User EXEC mode	Limited to basic monitoring commands
Privileged EXEC mode	Provides access to all other router commands
Global configuration mode	Commands that affect the entire system
Specific configuration modes	Commands that affect interfaces/processes only
Setup mode	Interactive configuration dialog

Gathering Basic Routing Information

The show version command will provide basic configuration for the system hardware as well as the software version and the boot images. Here's an example:

```
yourname#show version
Cisco IOS Software, 2800 Software (C2800NM-ADVSECURITYK9-M), Version
    12.4(12), RELEASE SOFTWARE (fc1)
Technical Support: http://www.cisco.com/techsupport
Copyright (c) 1986-2006 by Cisco Systems, Inc.
Compiled Fri 17-Nov-06 12:02 by prod_rel_team
```

The preceding section of output describes the Cisco IOS running on the router. The following section describes the read-only memory (ROM) used, which is used to boot the router and holds the POST:

```
ROM: System Bootstrap, Version 12.4(13r)T, RELEASE SOFTWARE (fc1)
```

The next section shows how long the router has been running, how it was restarted (if you see a system restarted by bus error, that is a very bad thing), where the Cisco IOS was loaded from, and the IOS name. Flash is the default:

```
yourname uptime is 2 hours, 30 minutes
System returned to ROM by power-on
System restarted at 09:04:07 UTC Sat Aug 25 2007
System image file is "flash:c2800nm-advsecurityk9-mz.124-12.bin"
```

This next section displays the processor, the amount of DRAM and flash memory, and the interfaces the POST found on the router:

```
[some output cut]
Cisco 2811 (revision 53.50) with 249856K/12288K bytes of memory.
Processor board ID FTX1049A1AB
2 FastEthernet interfaces
4 Serial(sync/async) interfaces
1 Virtual Private Network (VPN) Module
DRAM configuration is 64 bits wide with parity enabled.
239K bytes of non-volatile configuration memory.
62720K bytes of ATA CompactFlash (Read/Write)
Configuration register is 0x2102
```

The configuration register value is listed last.

In addition, the show interfaces and show ip interface brief commands are very useful in verifying and troubleshooting a router as well as network issues.

Router and Switch Administrative Configurations

Even though this section isn't critical to making a router or switch work on a network, it's still really important; in it, I'm going to lead you through configuring commands that will help you administrate your network.

The administrative functions that you can configure on a router and switch are:

- Hostnames
- Banners
- Passwords
- Interface descriptions

Remember, none of these will make your routers or switches work better or faster, but trust me, your life will be a whole lot better if you just take the time to set these configurations on each of your network devices. That's because doing this makes troubleshooting and maintaining your network sooooo much easier—seriously!

Hostnames

You can set the identity of the router with the hostname command. This is only locally significant, which means that it has no bearing on how the router performs name lookups or how the router works on the internetwork. However, I'll use the hostname in Chapter 8 for authentication purposes when I discuss PPP.

Here's an example:

```
yourname#config t
Enter configuration commands, one per line. End with
   CNTL/Z.
```

```
yourname(config)#hostname Todd
Todd(config)#hostname Atlanta
Atlanta(config)#hostname Todd
Todd(config)#
```

Even though it's pretty tempting to configure the hostname after your own name, it's definitely a better idea to name the router something pertinent to the location. This is because giving it a hostname that's somehow relevant to where the device actually lives will make finding it a whole lot easier. And it also helps you confirm that you are, indeed, configuring the right device.

Banners

A *banner* is more than just a little cool—one very good reason for having a banner is to give any and all who dare attempt to telnet or dial into your internetwork a little security notice. And you can create a banner to give anyone who shows up on the router exactly the information you want them to have.

Make sure that you're familiar with these four available banner types: exec process creation banner, incoming terminal line banner, login banner, and message of the day banner (all illustrated in the following code):

```
Todd(config)#banner ?
  LINE            c banner-text c, where 'c' is a delimiting character
  exec            Set EXEC process creation banner
  incoming        Set incoming terminal line banner
  login           Set login banner
  motd            Set Message of the Day banner
  prompt-timeout  Set Message for login authentication timeout
  slip-ppp        Set Message for SLIP/PPP
```

Message of the day (MOTD) is the most extensively used banner. It provides a message to every person dialing into or connecting to the router via Telnet or auxiliary port, or even through a console port, as shown here:

```
Todd(config)#banner motd ?
LINE c banner-text c, where 'c' is a delimiting character
Todd(config)#banner motd #
Enter TEXT message. End with the character '#'.
$ Acme.com network, then you must disconnect immediately.
#
Todd(config)#^Z
Todd#
00:25:12: %SYS-5-CONFIG_I: Configured from console by
  console
```

```
Todd#exit

Router con0 is now available

Press RETURN to get started.

If you are not authorized to be in Acme.com network, then you must disconnect
immediately.
Todd#
```

The preceding MOTD banner essentially tells anyone connecting to the router that if they're not on the guest list, get lost! The part to understand is the delimiting character—the thing that's used to tell the router when the message is done. You can use any character you want for it, but (I hope this is obvious) you can't use the delimiting character in the message itself. Also, once the message is complete, press Enter, then the delimiting character, and then Enter again. It'll still work if you don't do that, but if you have more than one banner, they'll be combined as one message and put on a single line.

For example, you can set a banner on one line as shown here:

```
Todd(config)#banner motd x Unauthorized access prohibited! x
```

This example will work just fine, but if you add another MOTD banner message, they will end up on a single line.

Setting Passwords

Five passwords are used to secure your Cisco routers: console, auxiliary, Telnet (VTY), enable password, and enable secret. The enable secret and enable password are used to set the password that's used to secure privileged mode. This will prompt a user for a password when the `enable` command is used. The other three are used to configure a password when user mode is accessed through the console port, through the auxiliary port, or via Telnet.

Let's take a look at each of these now.

Enable Passwords

You set the enable passwords from global configuration mode like this:

```
Todd(config)#enable ?
  last-resort Define enable action if no TACACS servers
              respond
  password    Assign the privileged level password
  secret      Assign the privileged level secret
  use-tacacs  Use TACACS to check enable passwords
```

The following points describe the enable password parameters:

last-resort Allows you to still enter the router if you set up authentication through a TACACS server and it's not available. But it isn't used if the TACACS server is working.

password Sets the enable password on older, pre-10.3 systems, and isn't ever used if an enable secret is set.

secret This is the newer, encrypted password that overrides the enable password if it's set.

use-tacacs This tells the router to authenticate through a TACACS server. It's convenient if you have anywhere from a dozen to multitudes of routers because, well, would you like to face the fun task of changing the password on all those routers? If you're sane, no, you wouldn't. So instead, just go through the TACACS server, and you only have to change the password once—yeah!

Here's an example of setting the enable passwords:

```
Todd(config)#enable secret todd
Todd(config)#enable password todd
The enable password you have chosen is the same as your
  enable secret. This is not recommended. Re-enter the
  enable password.
```

If you try to set the enable secret and enable passwords the same, the router will give you a nice, polite warning to change the second password. If you don't have older legacy routers, don't even bother to use the enable password.

User-mode passwords are assigned by using the `line` command:

```
Todd(config)#line ?
  <0-337>  First Line number
  aux      Auxiliary line
  console  Primary terminal line
  tty      Terminal controller
  vty      Virtual terminal
  x/y      Slot/Port for Modems
  x/y/z    Slot/Subslot/Port for Modems
```

Here are the lines to be concerned with:

aux Sets the user-mode password for the auxiliary port. It's usually used for attaching a modem to the router, but it can be used as a console as well.

console Sets a console user-mode password.

vty Sets a Telnet password on the router. If this password isn't set, then Telnet can't be used by default.

To configure the user-mode passwords, you configure the line you want and use either the `login` or `no login` command to tell the router to prompt for authentication. The next section will provide a line-by-line example of each line configuration.

Auxiliary Password

To configure the auxiliary password, go into global configuration mode and type **line aux ?**. You can see here that you only get a choice of 0–0 (that's because there's only one port):

```
Todd#config t
Enter configuration commands, one per line. End with CNTL/Z.
Todd(config)#line aux ?
  <0-0>  First Line number
Todd(config)#line aux 0
Todd(config-line)#login
% Login disabled on line 1, until 'password' is set
Todd(config-line)#password aux
Todd(config-line)#login
```

It's important to remember the login command, or the auxiliary port won't prompt for authentication.

Cisco has begun this process of not letting you set the login command before a password is set on a line because if you set the login command under a line, and then don't set a password, the line won't be usable. And it will prompt for a password that doesn't exist. So, this is a good thing—a feature, not a hassle!

 Definitely remember that although Cisco has this new "password feature" on its routers, starting with its newer IOS (12.2 and above). It's not in all its IOSes.

Console Password

To set the console password, use the line console 0 command. But look at what happened when I tried to type **line console 0 ?** from the (config-line)# prompt—I received an error. You can still type **line console 0** and it will accept it, but the help screens just don't work from that prompt. Type **exit** to get back one level, and you'll find that your help screens now work.

Here's the example:

```
Todd(config-line)#line console ?
% Unrecognized command
Todd(config-line)#exit
Todd(config)#line console ?
  <0-0>  First Line number
Todd(config-line)#password console
Todd(config-line)#login
```

Since there's only one console port, I can only choose line console 0. You can set all your line passwords to the same password, but for security reasons, I'd recommend that you make them different.

Telnet Password

To set the user-mode password for Telnet access into the router, use the `line vty` command. Routers that aren't running the Enterprise edition of the Cisco IOS default to five VTY lines, 0 through 4. But if you have the Enterprise edition, you'll have significantly more. The best way to find out how many lines you have is to use that question mark:

```
Todd(config-line)#line vty 0 ?
% Unrecognized command
Todd(config-line)#exit
Todd(config)#line vty 0 ?
  <1-1180>  Last Line number
  <cr>
Todd(config)#line vty 0 1180
Todd(config-line)#password telnet
Todd(config-line)#login
```

 Please note that Secure Shell (SSH) is the more secure method of connecting to a remote device

Remember: You cannot get help from your (`config-line`)# prompt. You must go back to privilege mode in order to use the question mark (?).

 You may or may not have to set the `login` command before the password on the VTY lines—it depends on the IOS version. The result is the same either way.

So what will happen if you try to telnet into a router that doesn't have a VTY password set? You'll receive an error stating that the connection is refused because, well, the password isn't set. So, if you telnet into a router and receive the message

```
Todd#telnet SFRouter
Trying SFRouter (10.0.0.1)…Open

Password required, but none set
[Connection to SFRouter closed by foreign host]
Todd#
```

then the remote router (SFRouter in this example) does not have the VTY (Telnet) password set. But you can get around this and tell the router to allow Telnet connections without a password by using the `no login` command:

```
SFRouter(config-line)#line vty 0 4
SFRouter(config-line)#no login
```

I do not recommend the above step unless you are in a testing or classroom environment! In a production network, you should always set your VTY password.

After your routers are configured with an IP address, you can use the Telnet program to configure and check your routers instead of having to use a console cable. You can use the Telnet program by typing **telnet** from any command prompt (DOS or Cisco). Anything Telnet is covered more thoroughly in Chapter 5.

Setting Up Secure Shell (SSH)

Instead of telnet, you can use secure shell, which creates a more secure session than the Telnet application that uses an unencrypted data stream. Secure Shell (SSH) uses encrypted keys to send data so that your username and password are not sent in the clear.

Here are the steps to setting up SSH:

1. Set your hostname:

Router(config)#**hostname Todd**

2. Set the domain-name. (Both the hostname and domain-name are required for the encryption keys to be generated.)

Todd(config)#**ip domain-name Lammle.com**

3. Generate the encryption keys for securing the session:

```
Todd(config)#crypto key generate rsa general-keys modulus ?
  <360-2048>  size of the key modulus [360-2048]
Todd(config)#crypto key generate rsa general-keys modulus 1024
The name for the keys will be: Todd.Lammle.com
% The key modulus size is 1024 bits
% Generating 1024 bit RSA keys, keys will be non-exportable...[OK]
*June 24 19:25:30.035: %SSH-5-ENABLED: SSH 1.99 has been enabled
```

4. Set the max idle timer for a SSH session:

```
Todd(config)#ip ssh time-out ?
  <1-120>  SSH time-out interval (secs)
Todd(config)#ip ssh time-out 60
```

5. Set the max failed attempts for a SSH connection:

```
Todd(config)#ip ssh authentication-retries ?
  <0-5>  Number of authentication retries
Todd(config)#ip ssh authentication-retries 2
```

6. Connect to the vty lines of the router:

Todd(config)#**line vty 0 1180**

7. Last, configure SSH and then Telnet as access protocols.

Todd(config-line)#**transport input ssh telnet**

If you do not use the keyword "**telnet**" at the end of the command string, then only SSH will work on the router. It will look like this:

Todd(config-line)#**transport input ssh**

I am not suggesting you use either way, but just understand that SSH is more secure than Telnet.

Descriptions

Setting descriptions on an interface is helpful to the administrator and, like the hostname, only locally significant. The description command is a helpful one because you can, for instance, use it to keep track of circuit numbers.

Here's an example:

Todd#**config t**
Todd(config)#**int s0/0/0**
Todd(config-if)#**description Wan to SF circuit number 6fdda12345678**
Todd(config-if)#**int fa0/0**
Todd(config-if)#**description Sales VLAN**
Todd(config-if)#**^Z**
Todd#

You can view the description of an interface with either the show running-config command or the show interface command:

Todd#**sh run**
[output cut]
!
interface FastEthernet0/0
 description Sales VLAN
 ip address 10.10.10.1 255.255.255.248
 duplex auto
 speed auto
!
interface Serial0/0/0
 description Wan to SF circuit number 6fdda 12345678
 no ip address

```
shutdown
!
```
[output cut]
```
Todd#sh int f0/0
FastEthernet0/0 is up, line protocol is down
  Hardware is MV96340 Ethernet, address is 001a.2f55.c9e8 (bia 001a.2f55.c9e8)
  Description: Sales VLAN
```
[output cut]

```
Todd#sh int s0/0/0
Serial0/0/0 is administratively down, line protocol is down
  Hardware is GT96K Serial
  Description: Wan to SF circuit number 6tdda12345678
```

Exam Objectives

Remember how to configure your administrative functions.   Administrative functions are your hostname, banners, passwords, and interface descriptions.

Remember what is required to configure SSH on your router.   You must configure both your hostname and domain name on the router in order for SSH to be enabled.

4.6 Connect, configure, and verify the operational status of a device interface

Interface configuration is one of the most important router configurations, because without interfaces, a router is pretty much a completely useless object. Plus, interface configurations must be totally precise to enable communication with other devices. Network layer addresses, media type, bandwidth, and other administrator commands are all used to configure an interface.

Different routers use different methods to choose the interfaces used on them. Use the question mark to find your interface numbers:

```
Router(config)#int serial ?
 <0-9> Serial interface number
```

Now it's time to choose the interface you want to configure. Once you do that, you will be in interface configuration for that specific interface. The following command would be used to choose serial port 5, for example:

```
Router(config)#int serial 5
Router(config)-if#
```

The above router has one Ethernet 10BaseT port, and typing **interface ethernet 0** can configure that interface, as shown here:

```
Router(config)#int ethernet ?
 <0-0> Ethernet interface number
Router(config)#int ethernet 0
Router(config-if)#
```

As I showed you above, the 2500 router is a fixed configuration router. This means that when you buy that model, you're stuck with that physical configuration—a huge reason why I don't use them much. I certainly never would use them in a production setting anymore.

To configure an interface, we always used the interface *type number* sequence, but the 2600 and 2800 series routers (actually, any ISR router for that matter), use a physical slot in the router, with a port number on the module plugged into that slot. So on a modular router, the configuration would be interface *type slot/port*, as shown here:

```
Router(config)#int fastethernet ?
 <0-1> FastEthernet interface number
Router(config)#int fastethernet 0
% Incomplete command.
Router(config)#int fastethernet 0?
/
Router(config)#int fastethernet 0/?
 <0-1> FastEthernet interface number
```

Make note of the fact that you can't just type **int fastethernet 0**. You must type the full command: *type slot/port*, or **int fastethernet 0/0** (or **int fa 0/0**).

For the ISR series, it's basically the same, only you get even more options. For example, the built-in Fast Ethernet interfaces work with the same configuration we used with the 2600 series:

```
Todd(config)#int fastEthernet 0/?
 <0-1>  FastEthernet interface number
Todd(config)#int fastEthernet 0/0
Todd(config-if)#
```

But the rest of the modules are different—they use three numbers instead of two. The first 0 is the router itself, and then you choose the slot, and then the port. Here's an example of a serial interface on my 2811:

```
Todd(config)#interface serial ?
 <0-2>  Serial interface number
Todd(config)#interface serial 0/0/?
 <0-1>  Serial interface number
Todd(config)#interface serial 0/0/0
Todd(config-if)#
```

This can look a little dicey, I know, but I promise it's really not that hard! It helps to remember that you should always view a `running-config` output first so that you know what interfaces you have to deal with. Here's my 2801 output:

```
Todd(config-if)#do show run
Building configuration...
[output cut]
!
interface FastEthernet0/0
 no ip address
 shutdown
 duplex auto
 speed auto
!
interface FastEthernet0/1
 no ip address
 shutdown
 duplex auto
 speed auto
!
interface Serial0/0/0
 no ip address
 shutdown
 no fair-queue
!
interface Serial0/0/1
 no ip address
 shutdown
!
interface Serial0/1/0
 no ip address
 shutdown
!
interface Serial0/2/0
 no ip address
 shutdown
 clock rate 2000000
!
 [output cut]
```

For the sake of brevity I didn't include my complete `running-config`, but I've displayed all you need. You can see the two built-in Fast Ethernet interfaces, the two serial interfaces in slot 0 (0/0/0 and 0/0/1), the serial interface in slot 1 (0/1/0), and the serial interface in slot 2 (0/2/0). Once you see the interfaces like this, it makes it a lot easier for you to understand how the modules are inserted into the router.

Just understand that if you type **interface e0** on a 2500, **interface fastethernet 0/0** on a 2600, or **interface serial 0/1/0** on a 2800, all you're doing is choosing an interface to configure, and basically, they're all configured the same way after that.

I'm going to continue with our router interface discussion in the next sections, and I'll include how to bring up the interface and set an IP address on a router interface.

Bringing Up an Interface

You can disable an interface with the interface command shutdown, and enable it with the no shutdown command.

If an interface is shut down, it'll display administratively down when using the show interfaces command (sh int for short):

```
Todd#sh int f0/1
FastEthernet0/1 is administratively down, line protocol is down
[output cut]
```

Another way to check an interface's status is via the show running-config command. All interfaces are shut down by default. You can bring up the interface with the no shutdown command (no shut for short):

```
Todd#config t
Todd(config)#int f0/1
Todd(config-if)#no shutdown
Todd(config-if)#
*Feb 28 22:45:08.455: %LINK-3-UPDOWN: Interface FastEthernet0/1,
    changed state to up
Todd(config-if)#do show int f0/1
FastEthernet0/1 is up, line protocol is up
[output cut]
```

Configuring an IP Address on an Interface

Even though you don't have to use IP on your routers, it's most often what people actually do use. To configure IP addresses on an interface, use the ip address command from interface configuration mode:

```
Todd(config)#int f0/1
Todd(config-if)#ip address 172.16.10.2 255.255.255.0
```

Don't forget to enable the interface with the no shutdown command. Remember to look at the command show interface *int* to see if it's administratively shut down or not. show running-config will also give you this information.

The `ip address` *address mask* command starts the IP processing on the interface.

Serial Interface Commands

Wait! Before you just jump in and configure a serial interface, you need some key information—like knowing that the interface will usually be attached to a CSU/DSU type of device that provides clocking for the line to the router, as I've shown in Figure 4.9.

FIGURE 4.9   A typical WAN connection

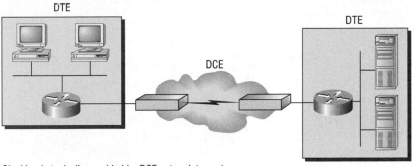

Clocking is typically provided by DCE network to routers.
In nonproduction environments, a DCE network is not always present.

Here you can see that the serial interface is used to connect to a DCE network via a CSU/DSU that provides the clocking to the router interface. But if you have a back-to-back configuration, (for example, one that's used in a lab environment like I've shown you in Figure 4.10), one end—the data communication equipment (DCE) end of the cable—must provide clocking!

FIGURE 4.10   Providing clocking on a nonproduction network

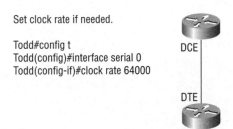

Set clock rate if needed.

Todd#config t
Todd(config)#interface serial 0
Todd(config-if)#clock rate 64000

DCE side determined by cable.
Add clocking to DCE side only.

show controllers will show the cable connection type.

By default, Cisco routers are all data terminal equipment (DTE) devices, which means that you must configure an interface to provide clocking if you need it to act like a DCE device. Again, you would not provide clocking on a production T1 connection, for example, because you would have a CSU/DSU connected to your serial interface, as Figure 4.4 shows.

You configure a DCE serial interface with the clock rate command:

```
Todd#config t
Enter configuration commands, one per line. End with CNTL/Z.
Todd(config)#int s0/0/0
Todd(config-if)#clock rate 1000000
```

The clock rate command is set in bits per second. Besides looking at the cable end to check for a label of DCE or DTE, you can see if a router's serial interface has a DCE cable connected with the show controllers *int* command:

```
Todd#sh controllers s0/0/0
Interface Serial0/0/0
Hardware is GT96K
DTE V.35idb at 0x4342FCB0, driver data structure at 0x434373D4
```

Here is an example of an output that shows a DCE connection:

```
Todd#sh controllers s0/2/0
Interface Serial0/2/0
Hardware is GT96K
DCE V.35, clock rate 1000000
```

The next command you need to get acquainted with is the bandwidth command. Every Cisco router ships with a default serial link bandwidth of T1 (1.544Mbps). But this has nothing to do with how data is transferred over a link. The bandwidth of a serial link is used by routing protocols such as EIGRP and OSPF to calculate the best cost (path) to a remote network. So if you're using RIP routing, then the bandwidth setting of a serial link is irrelevant since RIP uses only hop count to determine that.

Here's an example of using the bandwidth command:

```
Todd#config t
Todd(config)#int s0/0/0
Todd(config-if)#bandwidth ?
  <1-10000000>  Bandwidth in kilobits
  inherit       Specify that bandwidth is inherited
  receive       Specify receive-side bandwidth
Todd(config-if)#bandwidth 1000
```

Did you notice that, unlike the clock rate command, the bandwidth command is configured in kilobits?

OK, after going through all this configuration examples regarding the **clock rate** command, understand that the new ISR router automatically detect DCE connection and set the **clock rate** to 2000000. However, you still need to understand the clock rate command, even though the new routers set it for you automatically!

Viewing, Saving, and Erasing Configurations

You can manually save the file from DRAM to NVRAM by using the copy running-config startup-config command (you can use the shortcut copy run start also):

```
Todd#copy running-config startup-config
Destination filename [startup-config]? [press enter]
Building configuration...
[OK]
Todd#
Building configuration...
```

When you see a question with an answer in [], it means that if you just press Enter, you're choosing the default answer.

Also, when the command asked for the destination filename, the default answer was startup-config. The reason it asks is because you can copy the configuration pretty much anywhere you want. Take a look:

```
Todd#copy running-config ?
  archive:        Copy to archive: file system
  flash:          Copy to flash: file system
  ftp:            Copy to ftp: file system
  http:           Copy to http: file system
  https:          Copy to https: file system
  ips-sdf         Update (merge with) IPS signature configuration
  null:           Copy to null: file system
  nvram:          Copy to nvram: file system
  rcp:            Copy to rcp: file system
  running-config  Update (merge with) current system configuration
  scp:            Copy to scp: file system
  startup-config  Copy to startup configuration
  syslog:         Copy to syslog: file system
  system:         Copy to system: file system
  tftp:           Copy to tftp: file system
```

```
xmodem:          Copy to xmodem: file system
ymodem:          Copy to ymodem: file system
```

We'll take a closer look at how and where to copy files in Chapter 5.

You can view the files by typing **show running-config** or **show startup-config** from privileged mode. The sh run command, which is a shortcut for show running-config, tells us that we are viewing the current configuration:

```
Todd#show running-config
Building configuration...

Current configuration : 3343 bytes
!
version 12.4
[output cut]
```

The sh start command—one of the shortcuts for the show startup-config command— shows us the configuration that will be used the next time the router is reloaded. It also tells us how much NVRAM is being used to store the startup-config file. Here's an example:

```
Todd#show startup-config
Using 1978 out of 245752 bytes
!
version 12.4
[output cut]
```

Verifying Your Configuration

Obviously, **show running-config** would be the best way to verify your configuration and **show startup-config** would be the best way to verify the configuration that'll be used the next time the router is reloaded—right?

Well, once you take a look at the running-config, if all appears well, you can verify your configuration with utilities such as ping and Telnet. Ping is Packet Internet Groper, a program that uses ICMP echo requests and replies. Ping sends a packet to a remote host, and if that host responds, you know that the host is alive. But you don't know if it's alive and also *well*—just because you can ping a Microsoft server does not mean you can log in! Even so, ping is an awesome starting point for troubleshooting an internetwork.

Did you know that you can ping with different protocols? You can, and you can test this by typing **ping ?** at either the router user-mode or privileged-mode prompt:

```
Router#ping ?
  WORD      Ping destination address or hostname
  appletalk Appletalk echo
```

```
clns        CLNS echo
decnet      DECnet echo
ip          IP echo
ipv6        IPv6 echo
ipx         Novell/IPX echo
srb         srb echo
tag         Tag encapsulated IP echo
<cr>
```

If you want to find a neighbor's Network layer address, either you need to go to the router or switch itself or you can type **show cdp entry * protocol** to get the Network layer addresses you need for pinging.

Traceroute uses ICMP with IP time to live (TTL) time-outs to track the path a packet takes through an internetwork, in contrast to ping, which just finds the host and responds. And traceroute can also be used with multiple protocols.

Router#**traceroute ?**
```
WORD        Trace route to destination address or hostname
appletalk   AppleTalk Trace
clns        ISO CLNS Trace
ip          IP Trace
ipv6        IPv6 Trace
ipx         IPX Trace
<cr>
```

Telnet, FTP, or HTTP are really the best tools because they use IP at the Network layer and TCP at the Transport layer to create a session with a remote host. If you can telnet, ftp, or http into a device, your IP connectivity just has to be good.

Router#**telnet ?**
```
WORD IP address or hostname of a remote system
<cr>
```

From the router prompt, you just type a hostname or IP address and it will assume you want to telnet—you don't need to type the actual command, telnet.

In the following sections, I am going to show you how to verify the interface statistics.

Verifying with the show interface Command

Another way to verify your configuration is by typing show interface commands, the first of which is show interface ?. That will reveal all the available interfaces to configure.

The show interfaces command displays the configurable parameters and statistics of all interfaces on a router.

This command is very useful for verifying and troubleshooting router and network issues. The following output is from my freshly erased and rebooted 2811 router:

```
Router#sh int ?
  Async               Async interface
  BVI                 Bridge-Group Virtual Interface
  CDMA-Ix             CDMA Ix interface
  CTunnel             CTunnel interface
  Dialer              Dialer interface
  FastEthernet        FastEthernet IEEE 802.3
  Loopback            Loopback interface
  MFR                 Multilink Frame Relay bundle interface
  Multilink           Multilink-group interface
  Null                Null interface
  Port-channel        Ethernet Channel of interfaces
  Serial              Serial
  Tunnel              Tunnel interface
  Vif                 PGM Multicast Host interface
  Virtual-PPP         Virtual PPP interface
  Virtual-Template    Virtual Template interface
  Virtual-TokenRing   Virtual TokenRing
  accounting          Show interface accounting
  counters            Show interface counters
  crb                 Show interface routing/bridging info
  dampening           Show interface dampening info
  description         Show interface description
  etherchannel        Show interface etherchannel information
  irb                 Show interface routing/bridging info
  mac-accounting      Show interface MAC accounting info
  mpls-exp            Show interface MPLS experimental accounting info
  precedence          Show interface precedence accounting info
  pruning             Show interface trunk VTP pruning information
  rate-limit          Show interface rate-limit info
  stats               Show interface packets & octets, in & out, by switching
                      path
  status              Show interface line status
  summary             Show interface summary
  switching           Show interface switching
  switchport          Show interface switchport information
  trunk               Show interface trunk information
  |                   Output modifiers
  <cr>
```

The only "real" physical interfaces are Fast Ethernet, Serial, and Async; the rest are all logical interfaces or commands to verify with.

The next command is show interface fastethernet 0/0. It reveals to us the hardware address, logical address, and encapsulation method, as well as statistics on collisions, as shown here:

```
Router#sh int f0/0
FastEthernet0/0 is up, line protocol is up
  Hardware is MV96340 Ethernet, address is 001a.2f55.c9e8 (bia 001a.2f55.c9e8)
  Internet address is 192.168.1.33/27
MTU 1500 bytes, BW 100000 Kbit, DLY 100 usec,
    reliability 255/255, txload 1/255, rxload 1/255
  Encapsulation ARPA, loopback not set
  Keepalive set (10 sec)
  Auto-duplex, Auto Speed, 100BaseTX/FX
  ARP type: ARPA, ARP Timeout 04:00:00
  Last input never, output 00:02:07, output hang never
  Last clearing of "show interface" counters never
  Input queue: 0/75/0/0 (size/max/drops/flushes); Total output drops: 0
  Queueing strategy: fifo
  Output queue: 0/40 (size/max)
  5 minute input rate 0 bits/sec, 0 packets/sec
  5 minute output rate 0 bits/sec, 0 packets/sec
     0 packets input, 0 bytes
     Received 0 broadcasts, 0 runts, 0 giants, 0 throttles
     0 input errors, 0 CRC, 0 frame, 0 overrun, 0 ignored
     0 watchdog
     0 input packets with dribble condition detected
     16 packets output, 960 bytes, 0 underruns
     0 output errors, 0 collisions, 0 interface resets
     0 babbles, 0 late collision, 0 deferred
     0 lost carrier, 0 no carrier
     0 output buffer failures, 0 output buffers swapped out
Router#
```

As you probably guessed, we're going to discuss the important statistics from this output, but first, I've got to ask you what subnet is the FastEthernet 0/0 a member of and what's the broadcast address and valid host range?

Just in case you didn't, the address is 192.168.1.33/27. And I've gotta be honest—if you don't know what a /27 is at this point, you'll need a miracle to pass the exam. (A /27 is 255.255.255.224.) The fourth octet is a block size of 32. The subnets are 0, 32, 64, . . .; the Fast Ethernet interface is in the 32 subnet; the broadcast address is 63; and the valid hosts are 33–62.

NOTE If you struggled with any of this, please save yourself from certain doom and get yourself into Chapter 3, "Subnetting, Variable Length Subnet Masks (VLSMs), and Troubleshooting TCP/IP," in the Sybex CCNA Study Guide, 6th Edition. Read and reread it until you've got it dialed in!

The preceding interface is working and looks to be in good shape. The show interfaces command will show you if you are receiving errors on the interface, and it will show you the maximum transmission units (MTUs), bandwidth (BW), reliability (255/255 means perfect!), and load (1/255 means no load).

Continuing to use the output from above, what is the bandwidth of the interface? Well, other than the easy giveaway of the interface being called a "FastEthernet" interface, we can see the bandwidth is 100000Kbit, which is 100,000,000 (Kbit means to add three zeros), which is 100Mbits per second, or FastEthernet. Gigabit would be 1,000,000Kbits per second.

The most important statistic of the show interface command is the output of the line and data-link protocol status. If the output reveals that FastEthernet 0/0 is up and the line protocol is up, then the interface is up and running:

Router#**sh int fa0/0**
FastEthernet0/0 is up, line protocol is up

The first parameter refers to the Physical layer, and it's up when it receives carrier detect. The second parameter refers to the Data Link layer, and it looks for keepalives from the connecting end. (Keepalives are used between devices to make sure that connectivity has not dropped.)

Here's an example of where the problem usually is found—on serial interfaces:

Router#**sh int s0/0/0**
Serial0/0 is up, line protocol is down

If you see that the line is up but the protocol is down, as shown above, you're experiencing a clocking (keepalive) or framing problem—possibly an encapsulation mismatch. Check the keepalives on both ends to make sure that they match, that the clock rate is set, if needed, and that the encapsulation type is the same on both ends. The output above would be considered a Data Link layer problem.

If you discover that both the line interface and the protocol are down, it's a cable or interface problem. The following output would be considered a Physical layer problem:

Router#**sh int s0/0/0**
Serial0/0 is down, line protocol is down

If one end is administratively shut down (as shown next), the remote end would present as down and down:

Router#**sh int s0/0/0**
Serial0/0 is administratively down, line protocol is down

To enable the interface, use the command no shutdown from interface configuration mode.
The next show interface serial 0/0/0 command demonstrates the serial line and the maximum transmission unit (MTU)—1,500 bytes by default. It also shows the default bandwidth (BW) on all Cisco serial links: 1.544Kbps. This is used to determine the bandwidth of the line for routing protocols such as EIGRP and OSPF. Another important configuration to notice is the keepalive, which is 10 seconds by default. Each router sends a keepalive message to its neighbor every 10 seconds, and if both routers aren't configured for the same keepalive time, it won't work.

```
Router#sh int s0/0/0
Serial0/0 is up, line protocol is up
 Hardware is HD64570
 MTU 1500 bytes, BW 1544 Kbit, DLY 20000 usec,
   reliability 255/255, txload 1/255, rxload 1/255
 Encapsulation HDLC, loopback not set, keepalive set
 (10 sec)
 Last input never, output never, output hang never
 Last clearing of "show interface" counters never
 Queueing strategy: fifo
 Output queue 0/40, 0 drops; input queue 0/75, 0 drops
 5 minute input rate 0 bits/sec, 0 packets/sec
 5 minute output rate 0 bits/sec, 0 packets/sec
   0 packets input, 0 bytes, 0 no buffer
   Received 0 broadcasts, 0 runts, 0 giants, 0 throttles
   0 input errors, 0 CRC, 0 frame, 0 overrun, 0 ignored,
   0 abort
   0 packets output, 0 bytes, 0 underruns
   0 output errors, 0 collisions, 16 interface resets
   0 output buffer failures, 0 output buffers swapped out
   0 carrier transitions
   DCD=down DSR=down DTR=down RTS=down CTS=down
```

You can clear the counters on the interface by typing the command **clear counters**:

```
Router#clear counters ?
  Async            Async interface
  BVI              Bridge-Group Virtual Interface
  CTunnel          CTunnel interface
  Dialer           Dialer interface
  FastEthernet     FastEthernet IEEE 802.3
  Group-Async      Async Group interface
  Line             Terminal line
```

```
Loopback          Loopback interface
MFR               Multilink Frame Relay bundle interface
Multilink         Multilink-group interface
Null              Null interface
Serial            Serial
Tunnel            Tunnel interface
Vif               PGM Multicast Host interface
Virtual-Template  Virtual Template interface
Virtual-TokenRing Virtual TokenRing
<cr>
```

Router#**clear counters s0/0/0**
Clear "show interface" counters on this interface
  [confirm]**[Enter]**
Router#
00:17:35: %CLEAR-5-COUNTERS: Clear counter on interface
  Serial0/0/0 by console
Router#

Verifying with the show ip interface Command

The show ip interface command will provide you with information regarding the layer 3 configurations of a router's interfaces:

Router#**sh ip interface**
FastEthernet0/0 is up, line protocol is up
  Internet address is 1.1.1.1/24
  Broadcast address is 255.255.255.255
  Address determined by setup command
  MTU is 1500 bytes
  Helper address is not set
  Directed broadcast forwarding is disabled
  Outgoing access list is not set
  Inbound access list is not set
  Proxy ARP is enabled
  Security level is default
  Split horizon is enabled
[output cut]

The status of the interface, the IP address and mask, information on whether an access list is set on the interface, and basic IP information are included in this output.

Using the show ip interface brief **Command**

The show ip interface brief command is probably one of the most helpful commands that you can ever use on a Cisco router. This command provides a quick overview of the router's interfaces, including the logical address and status:

```
Router#sh ip int brief
Interface IP-Address      OK? Method Status  Protocol
FastEthernet0/0  unassigned      YES unset  up up
FastEthernet0/1  unassigned      YES unset  up up
Serial0/0/0      unassigned      YES unset  up down
Serial0/0/1      unassigned      YES unset  administratively down down
Serial0/1/0      unassigned      YES unset  administratively down down
Serial0/2/0      unassigned      YES unset  administratively down down
```

Remember, the administratively down means that you need to type **no shutdown** under the interface. Notice that Serial0/0/0 is up/down, which means that the physical layer is good and carrier detect is sensed, but no keepalives are being received from the remote end. In a non-production network, like the one I am working with, the clock rate isn't set.

Exam Objectives

Remember how to enable a router interface.   From within the interface configuration, use the no shutdown command to enable a router interface.

Understand the output from the show interface command.   An interface should show Serial0/0 is up, line protocol is up, which means all is operational. If it shows Serial0/0 is up, line protocol is down, then you have a Data Link layer problem. Serial0/0 is down, line protocol is down is a physical layer problem.

4.7 Verify device configuration and network connectivity using ping, traceroute, Telnet, SSH, or other utilities

Before we move on to determining IP address problems and how to fix them, I just want to mention some basic DOS commands that you can use to help troubleshoot your network from both a PC and a Cisco router (the commands might do the same thing, but they are implemented differently).

Packet InterNet Groper (ping)   Uses ICMP echo request and replies to test if a node IP stack is initialized and alive on the network.

traceroute   Displays the list of routers on a path to a network destination by using TTL time-outs and ICMP error messages. This command will not work from a DOS prompt.

tracert   Same command as **traceroute**, but it's a Microsoft Windows command and will not work on a Cisco router.

telnet   Connects a device as a dumb terminal to another device and allows this dumb terminal to run programs on the connected device. All information, including login information, is sent in clear text.

secure shell (SSH)   Same as telnet, however, with one large difference: the connection is a secure connection and certificates are used to authenticate the connection. SSH also secures or encrypts the connection which is what the keys are for.

arp -a   Displays IP-to-MAC-address mappings on a Windows PC.

show ip arp   Same command as **arp -a**, but displays the ARP table on a Cisco router. Like the commands **traceroute** and **tracert**, they are not interchangeable through DOS and Cisco.

ipconfig /all   Used only from a DOS prompt, shows you the PC network configuration.

Once you've gone through all these steps and used the appropriate DOS commands, if necessary, what do you do if you find a problem? How do you go about fixing an IP address configuration error? Let's move on and discuss how to determine the IP address problems and how to fix them.

Checking Network Connectivity

You can use the **ping** and **traceroute** commands to test connectivity to remote devices, and both of them can be used with many protocols, not just IP.

Using the *ping* Command

So far, you've seen many examples of pinging devices to test IP connectivity and name resolution using the DNS server. To see all the different protocols that you can use with **ping**, use the **ping ?** command like this:

```
Todd2509#ping ?
  WORD        Ping destination address or hostname
  apollo      Apollo echo
  appletalk   Appletalk echo
  clns        CLNS echo
  decnet      DECnet echo
  ip          IP echo
  ipx         Novell/IPX echo
  srb         srb echo
  tag         Tag encapsulated IP echo
  vines       Vines echo
  xns         XNS echo
  <cr>
```

The ping output displays the minimum, average, and maximum times it takes for a ping packet to find a specified system and return. Here's another example:

```
Todd2509#ping todd2509
Translating "todd2509"...domain server (192.168.0.70)[OK]
Type escape sequence to abort.
Sending 5, 100-byte ICMP Echos to 192.168.0.121, timeout
  is 2 seconds:
!!!!!
Success rate is 100 percent (5/5), round-trip min/avg/max
  = 32/32/32 ms
Todd2509#
```

You can see that the DNS server was used to resolve the name, and the device was pinged in 32ms (milliseconds).

The ping command can be used in user and privileged mode but not configuration mode.

Using the *traceroute* Command

Traceroute (the traceroute command, or trace for short) shows the path a packet takes to get to a remote device. To see the protocols that you can use with traceroute, use the traceroute ? command, do this:

```
Todd2509#traceroute ?
  WORD       Trace route to destination address or
             hostname
  appletalk  AppleTalk Trace
  clns       ISO CLNS Trace
  ip         IP Trace
  ipx        IPX Trace
  oldvines   Vines Trace (Cisco)
  vines      Vines Trace (Banyan)
  <cr>
```

The trace command shows the hop or hops that a packet traverses on its way to a remote device. Here's an example:

```
Todd2509#trace 2501b
Type escape sequence to abort.
Tracing the route to 2501b.lammle.com (172.16.10.2)

 1 2501b.lammle.com (172.16.10.2) 16 msec *  16 msec
Todd2509#
```

You can see that the packet went through only one hop to find the destination.

> Do not get confused on the exam. You can't use the `tracert` command—it's a Windows command. For a router, use the `traceroute` command!

Using Telnet and SSH

Telnet and SSH are not necessarily used to test network connectivity like ping and traceroute; however, if you can connect to a remote device using Telnet or SSH, this means that you do have good connectivity to the device. This can be considered a better network test than using ping and Telnet because Telnet and SSH are Application layer protocols, whereas ping and traceroute are Network layer protocols.

Telnet, part of the TCP/IP protocol suite, is a virtual terminal protocol that allows you to make connections to remote devices, gather information, and run programs.

After your routers and switches are configured, you can use the Telnet program to reconfigure and/or check up on your routers and switches without using a console cable. You run the Telnet program by typing **telnet** from any command prompt (DOS or Cisco). You need to have VTY passwords set on the routers for this to work.

Remember, you can't use CDP to gather information about routers and switches that aren't directly connected to your device. But you can use the Telnet application to connect to your neighbor devices and then run CDP on those remote devices to get information on them.

You can issue the `telnet` command from any router prompt like this:

```
Corp#telnet 10.2.2.2
Trying 10.2.2.2 ... Open

Password required, but none set

[Connection to 10.2.2.2 closed by foreign host]
Corp#
```

As you can see, I didn't set my passwords—how embarrassing! Remember that the VTY ports on a router are configured as `login`, meaning that we have to either set the VTY passwords or use the `no login` command.

> If you find you can't telnet into a device, it could be that the password on the remote device hasn't been set. It's also possible that an access control list is filtering the Telnet session.

On a Cisco router, you don't need to use the `telnet` command; you can just type in an IP address from a command prompt, and the router will assume that you want to telnet to the device. Here's how that looks by using just the IP address:

```
Corp#10.2.2.2
Trying 10.2.2.2 ... Open
```

```
User Access Verification
```

```
Password:
R1>
```

Remember that the VTY password is the user-mode password, not the enable-mode password. Watch what happens when I try to go into privileged mode after telnetting into router R1:

```
R1>en
% No password set
R1>
```

It is basically saying, "No way!" This is a really good security feature because you don't want anyone telnetting into your device and being able to just type the **enable** command to get into privileged mode. You've got to set your enable-mode password or enable secret password to use Telnet to configure remote devices!

 When you telnet into a remote device, you will not see console messages by default. For example, you will not see debugging output. To allow console messages to be sent to your Telnet session, use the terminal monitor command.

It's different if you want to set the router to use HTTPS and SSH—you need to add a few more commands.

First, enable the HTTP/HTTPS server (your router won't support HTTPS if it doesn't have the advanced services IOS):

```
Router(config)#ip http server
Router(config)#ip http secure-server
% Generating 1024 bit RSA keys, keys will be non-exportable...[OK]
Router(config)#ip http authentication local
```

Second, create a user account using privilege level 15 (the highest level):

```
Router(config)#username cisco privilege ?
  <0-15>  User privilege level

Router(config)#username cisco privilege 15 password ?
  0     Specifies an UNENCRYPTED password will follow
  7     Specifies a HIDDEN password will follow
  LINE  The UNENCRYPTED (cleartext) user password
Router(config)#username cisco privilege 15 password 0 cisco
```

Last, configure console, SSH, and Telnet to provide local login authentication at privilege level access:

```
Router(config)#line console 0
Router(config-line)#login local
Router(config-line)#exit
Router(config)#line vty 0 ?
  <1-1180>  Last Line number
  <cr>
Router(config)#line vty 0 1180
Router(config-line)#privilege level 15
Router(config-line)#login local
Router(config-line)#transport input telnet
Router(config-line)#transport input telnet ssh
Router(config-line)#^Z
```

Exam Objectives

Understand when you would use the *ping* command.   Packet Internet Groper (ping) uses ICMP echo request and ICMP echo replies to verify an active IP address on a network.

Understand what Telnet and SSH provide.   If you can connect to a remote device using Telnet or SSH, this means you do have good connectivity to the device because Telnet and SSH are Application layer protocols, whereas ping and traceroute are Network layer protocols.

4.8 Perform and verify routing configuration tasks for a static or default route given specific routing requirements

You must have a good foundation of routing to pass the CCNA exam. This section will provide a solid foundation on static and default routing.

Static routing occurs when you manually add routes in each router's routing table. There are pros and cons to static routing, but that's true for all routing processes.

Static routing has the following benefits:

- There is no overhead on the router CPU, which means that you could possibly buy a cheaper router than you would use if you were using dynamic routing.

- There is no bandwidth usage between routers, which means that you could possibly save money on WAN links.

- It adds security, because the administrator can choose to allow routing access to certain networks only.

Static routing has the following disadvantages:

- The administrator must really understand the internetwork and how each router is connected in order to configure routes correctly.

- If a network is added to the internetwork, the administrator has to add a route to it on all routers—by hand.

- It's not feasible in large networks because maintaining it would be a full-time job in itself.

Okay—that said, here's the command syntax you use to add a static route to a routing table:

```
ip route [destination_network] [mask] [next-hop_address or
  exitinterface] [administrative_distance] [permanent]
```

This list describes each command in the string:

ip route   The command used to create the static route.

destination_network   The network you're placing in the routing table.

mask   The subnet mask being used on the network.

next-hop_address   The address of the next-hop router that will receive the packet and forward it to the remote network. This is a router interface that's on a directly connected network. You must be able to ping the router interface before you add the route. If you type in the wrong next-hop address or the interface to that router is down, the static route will show up in the router's configuration but not in the routing table.

exitinterface   Used in place of the next-hop address if you want, and shows up as a directly connected route.

administrative_distance   By default, static routes have an administrative distance of 1 (or even 0 if you use an exit interface instead of a next-hop address). You can change the default value by adding an administrative weight at the end of the command. I'll talk a lot more about this subject later in the chapter when we get to the section on dynamic routing.

permanent   If the interface is shut down or the router can't communicate to the next-hop router, the route will automatically be discarded from the routing table. Choosing the **permanent** option keeps the entry in the routing table no matter what happens.

Before we dive into configuring static routes, let's take a look at a sample static route and see what we can find out about it.

```
Router(config)#ip route 172.16.3.0 255.255.255.0 192.168.2.4
```

- The **ip route** command tells us simply that it is a static route.
- 172.16.3.0 is the remote network we want to send packets to.
- 255.255.255.0 is the mask of the remote network.
- 192.168.2.4 is the next hop, or router, we will send packets to.

However, suppose the static route looked like this:

```
Router(config)#ip route 172.16.3.0 255.255.255.0 192.168.2.4 150
```

The 150 at the end changes the default administrative distance (AD) of 1 to 150. No worries—I'll talk much more about AD when we get into dynamic routing. For now, just remember that the AD is the trustworthiness of a route, where 0 is best and 255 is worst.

One more example, then we'll start configuring:

```
Router(config)#ip route 172.16.3.0 255.255.255.0 s0/0/0
```

Instead of using a next-hop address, we can use an exit interface that will make the route show up as a directly connected network. Functionally, the next hop and exit interface work exactly the same.

We use *default routing* to send packets with a remote destination network not in the routing table to the next-hop router. You should only use default routing on stub networks—those with only one exit path out of the network. You can easily create loops with default routing, so be careful!

To configure a default route, you use wildcards in the network address and mask locations of a static route. In fact, you can just think of a default route as a static route that uses wildcards instead of network and mask information.

By using a default route, you can just create one static route entry instead. This sure is easier than typing in all those routes!

```
Router(config)#ip route 0.0.0.0 0.0.0.0 10.1.11.1
Router(config)#ip classless
Router(config)#do show ip route
  Gateway of last resort is 10.1.11.1 to network 0.0.0.0
 10.0.0.0/24 is subnetted, 2 subnets
C      10.1.11.0 is directly connected, Vlan1
C      10.1.12.0 is directly connected, Dot11Radio0
S*   0.0.0.0/0 [1/0] via 10.1.11.1
Router(config)#
```

If you look at the routing table, you'll see only the two directly connected networks plus an S*, which indicates that this entry is a candidate for a default route. I could have completed the default route command another way:

```
Router(config)#ip route 0.0.0.0 0.0.0.0 vlan1
```

What this is telling us is that if you don't have an entry for a network in the routing table, just forward it out Vlan1 (which will send it out FastEthernet0/0). You can choose the IP address of the next-hop router or the exit interface—either way, it will work the same. Remember, I used this exit interface configuration with the R3 static route configs.

Notice also in the routing table that the gateway of last resort is now set. Even so, there's one more command you must be aware of when using default routes: the ip classless command.

All Cisco routers are classful routers, meaning that they expect a default subnet mask on each interface of the router. When a router receives a packet for a destination subnet that's not in the routing table, it will drop the packet by default. If you're using default routing, you must use the `ip classless` command because it is possible that no remote subnets will be in the routing table.

Since I have version 12.4 of the IOS on my routers, the `ip classless` command is on by default. If you're using default routing and this command isn't in your configuration, you will need to add it if you have subnetted networks on your routers. The command is shown here:

Router(config)#**ip classless**

Notice that it's a global configuration mode command. The interesting part of the `ip classless` command is that default routing sometimes works without it but sometimes doesn't. To be on the safe side, you should always turn on the `ip classless` command when you use default routing.

There's another command you can use to configure a gateway of last resort—the `ip default-network` command. Figure 4.11 shows a network that needs to have a gateway of last resort statement configured.

FIGURE 4.11   Configuring a gateway of last resort

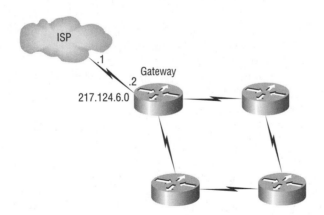

Here are three commands (all providing the same solution) for adding a gateway of last resort on the gateway router to the ISP.

Gateway(config)#**ip route 0.0.0.0 0.0.0.0 217.124.6.1**

Gateway(config)#**ip route 0.0.0.0 0.0.0.0 s0/0**

Gateway(config)#**ip default-network 217.124.6.0**

As I said before, all three of these commands would accomplish the goal of setting the gateway of last resort, but there are some small differences between them. First, the exit interface solution would be used over the other two solutions because it has an AD of 0. Also, the `ip default-network` command would advertise the default network when you configure an IGP (like RIP) on the router. This is so other routers in your internetwork will receive this route as a default route automatically.

Exam Objectives

Understand how to configure a static route.   A static route is configure from global configuration mode. Here is the command structure: `ip route` *remote_network remote_mask next_hop_address/exit_interface.*

Understand how to configure a default route, also called a gateway of last resort.   A default route is configure from global configuration mode. Here is the command structure: `ip route` 0.0.0.0 0.0.0.0 *next_hop_address/exit_interface.*

4.9 Manage IOS configuration files (including save, edit, upgrade, restore)

Any changes that you make to the router configuration are stored in the `running-config` file. And if you don't enter a `copy run start` command after you make a change to `running-config`, that change will go poof if the router reboots or gets powered down. So, you probably want to make another backup of the configuration information just in case the router or switch completely dies on you. Even if your machine is healthy and happy, it's good to have for reference and documentation reasons.

In the following sections, I'll describe how to copy the configuration of a router to a TFTP server and how to restore that configuration.

Backing Up the Cisco Router Configuration

To copy the router's configuration from a router to a TFTP server, you can use either the `copy running-config tftp` or the `copy startup-config tftp` command. Either one will back up the router configuration that's currently running in DRAM or that's stored in NVRAM.

Verifying the Current Configuration

To verify the configuration in DRAM, use the `show running-config` command (`sh run` for short) like this:

```
Router#show running-config
Building configuration...
```

```
Current configuration : 776 bytes
!
version 12.4
```

The current configuration information indicates that the router is running version 12.4 of the IOS.

Verifying the Stored Configuration

Next, you should check the configuration stored in NVRAM. To see this, use the show startup-config command (sh start for short) like this:

```
Router#show startup-config
Using 776 out of 245752 bytes
!
version 12.4
```

The second line shows you how much room your backup configuration is using. Here, you can see that NVRAM is 239KB (again, memory is easier to see with the show version command when using an ISR router) and that only 776 bytes of it are used.

If you're not sure that the files are the same and the running-config file is what you want to use, then use the copy running-config startup-config. This will help you verify that both files are in fact the same. I'll go through this with you in the next section.

Copying the Current Configuration to NVRAM

By copying running-config to NVRAM as a backup, as shown in the following output, you're assured that your running-config will always be reloaded if the router gets rebooted. In the new IOS version 12.0, you're prompted for the filename you want to use.

```
Router#copy running-config startup-config
Destination filename [startup-config]?[enter]
Building configuration...
[OK]
Router#
```

The reason that the filename prompt appears is that there are now so many options you can use when using the copy command:

```
Router#copy running-config ?
  archive:        Copy to archive: file system
  flash:          Copy to flash: file system
  ftp:            Copy to ftp: file system
  http:           Copy to http: file system
  https:          Copy to https: file system
  ips-sdf         Update (merge with) IPS signature configuration
```

```
null:            Copy to null: file system
nvram:           Copy to nvram: file system
rcp:             Copy to rcp: file system
running-config   Update (merge with) current system configuration
scp:             Copy to scp: file system
startup-config   Copy to startup configuration
syslog:          Copy to syslog: file system
system:          Copy to system: file system
tftp:            Copy to tftp: file system
xmodem:          Copy to xmodem: file system
ymodem:          Copy to ymodem: file system
```

We'll go over the copy command again in a minute.

Copying the Configuration to a TFTP Server

Once the file is copied to NVRAM, you can make a second backup to a TFTP server by using the copy running-config tftp command (copy run tftp for short), like this:

```
Router#copy running-config tftp
Address or name of remote host []?1.1.1.2
Destination filename [router-confg]?todd-confg
!!
776 bytes copied in 0.800 secs (970 bytes/sec)
Router#
```

In the preceding example, I named the file todd-confg because I had not set a hostname for the router. If you have a hostname already configured, the command will automatically use the hostname plus the extension -confg as the name of the file.

Restoring the Cisco Router Configuration

If you've changed your router's running-config file and want to restore the configuration to the version in the startup-config file, the easiest way to do this is to use the copy startup-config running-config command (copy start run for short). You can also use the older Cisco command config mem to restore a configuration. Of course, this will work only if you first copied running-config into NVRAM before making any changes!

If you did copy the router's configuration to a TFTP server as a second backup, you can restore the configuration using the copy tftp running-config command (copy tftp run for short) or the copy tftp startup-config command (copy tftp start for short), as shown here (the old command that provides this function is config net):

```
Router#copy tftp running-config
Address or name of remote host []?1.1.1.2
```

```
Source filename []?todd-confg
Destination filename[running-config]?[enter]
Accessing tftp://1.1.1.2/todd-confg...
Loading todd-confg from 1.1.1.2 (via FastEthernet0/0): !
[OK - 776 bytes]
776 bytes copied in 9.212 secs (84 bytes/sec)
Router#
*Mar  7 17:53:34.071: %SYS-5-CONFIG_I: Configured from
    tftp://1.1.1.2/todd-confg by console
Router#
```

The configuration file is an ASCII text file, meaning that before you copy the configuration stored on a TFTP server back to a router, you can make changes to the file with any text editor. Last, notice that the command was changed to a URL of tftp://1.1.1.2/todd-config.

 It is important to remember that when you copy or merge a configuration from a TFTP server to a router's RAM, the interfaces are shut down by default and you must manually enable each interface with the no shutdown command.

Erasing the Configuration

To delete the startup-config file on a Cisco router, use the command erase startup-config, like this:

```
Router#erase startup-config
Erasing the nvram filesystem will remove all configuration files!
    Continue? [confirm][enter]
[OK]
Erase of nvram: complete
*Mar  7 17:56:20.407: %SYS-7-NV_BLOCK_INIT: Initialized the geometry of nvram
Router#reload
System configuration has been modified. Save? [yes/no]:n
Proceed with reload? [confirm][enter]
 *Mar  7 17:56:31.059: %SYS-5-RELOAD: Reload requested by console.
    Reload Reason: Reload Command.
```

This command deletes the contents of NVRAM on the router. Typing **reload** at privileged mode and saying no to saving changes will cause the router to reload and come up into setup mode.

Exam Objectives

Remember how to save the configuration of a router. There are a couple of ways to do this, but the most common, as well as most tested, method is copy running-config startup-config.

Remember how to erase the configuration of a router. Type the privileged-mode command erase startup-config and reload the router.

4.10 Manage Cisco IOS

Before you upgrade or restore a Cisco IOS, you really should copy the existing file to a *TFTP host* as a backup just in case the new image crashes and burns.

And you can use any TFTP host to accomplish this. By default, the flash memory in a router is used to store the Cisco IOS. In the following sections, I'll describe how to check the amount of flash memory, how to copy the Cisco IOS from flash memory to a TFTP host, and how to copy the IOS from a TFTP host to flash memory.

To learn how to use the Cisco IFS, please see Chapter 5 of the Sybex CCNA Study Guide 6th Edition.

But before you back up an IOS image to a network server on your intranet, you've got to do these three things:

- Make sure that you can access the network server.

- Ensure that the network server has adequate space for the code image.

- Verify the file naming and path requirements.

And if you have a laptop or workstation's Ethernet port directly connected to a router's Ethernet interface, as shown in Figure 4.12, you need to verify the following before attempting to copy the image to or from the router:

- TFTP server software must be running on the administrator's workstation.

- The Ethernet connection between the router and the workstation must be made with a crossover cable.

FIGURE 4.12 Copying an IOS from a workstation to a router

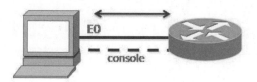

- The workstation must be on the same subnet as the router's Ethernet interface.
- The copy flash tftp command must be supplied the IP address of the workstation if you are copying from the router flash.
- And if you're copying "into" flash, you need to verify that there's enough room in flash memory to accommodate the file to be copied.

Verifying Flash Memory

Before you attempt to upgrade the Cisco IOS on your router with a new IOS file, it's a good idea to verify that your flash memory has enough room to hold the new image. You verify the amount of flash memory and the file or files being stored in flash memory by using the show flash command (sh flash for short):

```
Router#sh flash
-#- --length-- -----date/time------ path
1     21710744 Jan 2 2007 22:41:14 +00:00 c2800nm-advsecurityk9-mz.124-12.bin
[output cut]
32989184 bytes available (31027200 bytes used)
```

The ISR router above has 64MB of RAM, and roughly half of the memory is in use.

 The show flash command will display the amount of memory consumed by the current IOS image, as well as if there's enough room available to hold both current and new images. If there's not enough room for both the old and new image you want to load, understand that the old image will be erased!

The amount of flash is actually easier to tally using the show version command on the ISR routers:

```
Router#show version
[output cut]
Cisco 2811 (revision 49.46) with 249856K/12288K bytes of memory.
Processor board ID FTX1049A1AB
2 FastEthernet interfaces
4 Serial(sync/async) interfaces
1 Virtual Private Network (VPN) Module
DRAM configuration is 64 bits wide with parity enabled.
239K bytes of non-volatile configuration memory.
62720K bytes of ATA CompactFlash (Read/Write)
```

You can see that the amount of flash shows up on the last line. By averaging up, we get the amount of flash to 64MB.

Notice that the filename in this example is c2800nm-advsecurityk9-mz.124-12.bin. The main difference in the output of the show flash and show version commands is that the show flash command displays all files in flash, and the show version command shows the actual name of the file that the router is using to run the router.

Backing Up the Cisco IOS

To back up the Cisco IOS to a TFTP server, you use the copy flash tftp command. It's a straightforward command that requires only the source filename and the IP address of the TFTP server.

The key to success in this backup routine is to make sure that you've got good, solid connectivity to the TFTP server. Check this by pinging the TFTP device from the router console prompt like this:

```
Router#ping 1.1.1.2
Type escape sequence to abort.
Sending 5, 100-byte ICMP Echos to 1.1.1.2, timeout
  is 2 seconds:
!!!!!
Success rate is 100 percent (5/5), round-trip min/avg/max
  = 4/4/8 ms
```

After you ping the TFTP server to make sure that IP is working, you can use the copy flash tftp command to copy the IOS to the TFTP server as shown next:

```
Router#copy flash tftp
Source filename []?c2800nm-advsecurityk9-mz.124-12.bin
Address or name of remote host []?1.1.1.2
Destination filename [c2800nm-advsecurityk9-mz.124-12.bin]?[enter]
!!!!!!!!!!!!!!!!!!!!!!!!!!!!!!!!!!!!!!!!!!!!!!!!!!!!!!!!!!!!!!!!!!!!!!!!!!!!!!!!!!!!!!!
!!!!!!!
21710744 bytes copied in 60.724 secs (357532 bytes/sec)
Router#
```

Just copy the IOS filename from either the show flash or show version command and then paste it when prompted for the source filename.

In the preceding example, the contents of flash memory were copied successfully to the TFTP server. The address of the remote host is the IP address of the TFTP host, and the source filename is the file in flash memory.

WARNING   The copy flash tftp command won't prompt you for the location of any file or ask you where to put the file. TFTP is just a "grab it and place it" program in this situation. This means that the TFTP server must have a default directory specified or it won't work!

Restoring or Upgrading the Cisco Router IOS

What happens if you need to restore the Cisco IOS to flash memory to replace an original file that has been damaged or if you want to upgrade the IOS? You can download the file from a TFTP server to flash memory by using the copy tftp flash command. This command requires the IP address of the TFTP host and the name of the file you want to download.

But before you begin, make sure that the file you want to place in flash memory is in the default TFTP directory on your host. When you issue the command, TFTP won't ask you where the file is, so if the file you want to use isn't in the default directory of the TFTP host, this just won't work.

```
Router#copy tftp flash
Address or name of remote host []?1.1.1.2
Source filename []?c2800nm-advsecurityk9-mz.124-12.bin
Destination filename [c2800nm-advsecurityk9-mz.124-12.bin]?[enter]
%Warning:There is a file already existing with this name
Do you want to over write? [confirm][enter]
Accessing tftp://1.1.1.2/c2800nm-advsecurityk9-mz.124-12.bin...
Loading c2800nm-advsecurityk9-mz.124-12.bin from 1.1.1.2 (via
    FastEthernet0/0):
!!!!!!!!!!!!!!!!!!!!!!!!!!!!!!!!!!!!!!!!!!!!!!!!!!!!!!!!!!!!!!!!!!!!!!!!!!!
!!!!!!
[OK - 21710744 bytes]

21710744 bytes copied in 82.880 secs (261954 bytes/sec)
Router#
```

In the above example, I copied the same file into flash memory, so it asked me if I wanted to overwrite it. Remember that we are "playing" with files in flash memory. If I just corrupted my file by overwriting the file, I won't know this until I reboot the router. Be careful with this command! If the file is corrupted, then you'll need to do an IOS restore from ROMMON.

If you are loading a new file and you don't have enough room in flash memory to store both the new and existing copies, the router will ask to erase the contents of flash memory before writing the new file into flash memory.

Exam Objectives

Remember how to back up an IOS image.   By using the privileged-mode command copy flash tftp, you can back up a file from flash memory to a TFTP (network) server.

Remember how to restore or upgrade an IOS image.   By using the privileged-mode command copy tftp flash, you can restore or upgrade a file from a TFTP (network) server to flash memory.

Remember what you must complete before you back up an IOS image to a network server. Make sure that you can access the network server, ensure that the network server has adequate space for the code image, and verify the file naming and path requirements.

4.11 Compare and contrast methods of routing and routing protocols

A *routing protocol* is used by routers to dynamically find all the networks in the internetwork and to ensure that all routers have the same routing table. Basically, a routing protocol determines the path of a packet through an internetwork. Examples of routing protocols are RIP, RIPv2, EIGRP, and OSPF.

Once all routers know about all networks, a *routed protocol* can be used to send user data (packets) through the established enterprise. Routed protocols are assigned to an interface and determine the method of packet delivery. Examples of routed protocols are IP and IPv6.

The *administrative distance (AD)* is used to rate the trustworthiness of routing information received on a router from a neighbor router. An administrative distance is an integer from 0 to 255, where 0 is the most trusted and 255 means no traffic will be passed via this route.

If a router receives two updates listing the same remote network, the first thing the router checks is the AD. If one of the advertised routes has a lower AD than the other, then the route with the lowest AD will be placed in the routing table.

If both advertised routes to the same network have the same AD, then routing protocol metrics (such as *hop count* or bandwidth of the lines) will be used to find the best path to the remote network. The advertised route with the lowest metric will be placed in the routing table. But if both advertised routes have the same AD as well as the same metrics, then the routing protocol will load-balance to the remote network (which means that it sends packets down each link).

Table 4.7 shows the default administrative distances that a Cisco router uses to decide which route to take to a remote network.

TABLE 4.7   Default Administrative Distances

Route Source	Default AD
Connected interface	0
Static route	1
EIGRP	90
IGRP	100

TABLE 4.7   Default Administrative Distances *(continued)*

Route Source	Default AD
OSPF	110
RIP	120
External EIGRP	170
Unknown	255 (this route will never be used)

If a network is directly connected, the router will always use the interface connected to the network. If you configure a static route, the router will then believe that route over any other learned routes. You can change the administrative distance of static routes, but, by default, they have an AD of 1. In our static route configuration, the AD of each route is set at 150 or 151. This lets us configure routing protocols without having to remove the static routes. They'll be used as backup routes in case the routing protocol experiences a failure of some type.

For example, if you have a static route, a RIP-advertised route, and an IGRP-advertised route listing the same network, then, by default, the router will always use the static route unless you change the AD of the static route—which we did.

Routing Protocols

There are three classes of routing protocols:

Distance vector   The *distance-vector protocols* find the best path to a remote network by judging distance. Each time a packet goes through a router, that's called a *hop*. The route with the least number of hops to the network is determined to be the best route. The vector indicates the direction to the remote network. Both RIP and IGRP are distance-vector routing protocols. They send the entire routing table to directly connected neighbors.

Link state   In *link-state protocols*, also called *shortest-path-first protocols*, the routers each create three separate tables. One of these tables keeps track of directly attached neighbors, one determines the topology of the entire internetwork, and one is used as the routing table. Link-state routers know more about the internetwork than any distance-vector routing protocol. OSPF is an IP routing protocol that is completely link state. Link-state protocols send updates containing the state of their own links to all other routers on the network.

Hybrid   *Hybrid protocols* use aspects of both distance vector and link state—for example, EIGRP.

There's no set way of configuring routing protocols for use with every business. This is something you really have to do on a case-by-case basis. If you understand how the different routing protocols work, you can make good, solid decisions that truly meet the individual needs of any business.

Exam Objectives

Be able to define a routing protocol.   A *routing protocol* is used by routers to dynamically find all the networks in the internetwork and to ensure that all routers have the same routing table. Basically, a routing protocol determines the path of a packet through an internetwork. Examples of routing protocols are RIP, RIPv2, EIGRP, and OSPF.

Be able to define a routed protocol.   Once all routers know about all networks, a *routed protocol* can be used to send user data (packets) through the established enterprise. Routed protocols are assigned to an interface and determine the method of packet delivery. Examples of routed protocols are IP and IPv6.

4.12 Configure, verify, and troubleshoot OSPF

Open Shortest Path First (OSPF) is an open standard routing protocol that's been implemented by a wide variety of network vendors, including Cisco. If you have multiple routers and not all of them are Cisco (what!), then you can't use EIGRP, can you? So, your remaining CCNA objective options are basically RIP, RIPv2, and OSPF.

OSPF works by using the *Dijkstra algorithm*. First, a shortest path tree is constructed, and then the routing table is populated with the resulting best paths. OSPF converges quickly, although perhaps not as quickly as EIGRP, and it supports multiple, equal-cost routes to the same destination. Like EIGRP, it does support both IP and IPv6 routed protocols.

OSPF provides the following features:

- Consists of areas and autonomous systems
- Minimizes routing update traffic
- Allows scalability
- Supports VLSM/CIDR
- Has unlimited hop count
- Allows multi-vendor deployment (open standard)

OSPF is the first link-state routing protocol that most people are introduced to, so it's useful to see how it compares to more traditional distance-vector protocols such as RIPv2 and RIPv1. Table 4.8 gives you a comparison of these three protocols.

TABLE 4.8   OSPF and RIP comparison

Characteristic	OSPF	RIPv2	RIPv1
Type of protocol	Link state	Distance vector	Distance vector
Classless support	Yes	Yes	No

TABLE 4.8   OSPF and RIP comparison *(continued)*

Characteristic	OSPF	RIPv2	RIPv1
VLSM support	Yes	Yes	No
Auto-summarization	No	Yes	Yes
Manual summarization	Yes	No	No
Discontiguous support	Yes	Yes	No
Route propagation	Multicast on change	Periodic multicast	Periodic broadcast
Path metric	Bandwidth	Hops	Hops
Hop count limit	None	15	15
Convergence	Fast	Slow	Slow
Peer authentication	Yes	Yes	No
Hierarchical network	Yes (using areas)	No (flat only)	No (flat only)
Updates	Event triggered	Route table updates	Route table updates
Route computation	Dijkstra	Bellman-Ford	Bellman-Ford

OSPF has many features beyond the few I've listed in Table 4.8, and all of them contribute to a fast, scalable, and robust protocol that can be actively deployed in thousands of production networks.

OSPF is supposed to be designed in a hierarchical fashion, which basically means that you can separate the larger internetwork into smaller internetworks called *areas*. This is the best design for OSPF.

The following are reasons for creating OSPF in a hierarchical design:

- To decrease routing overhead
- To speed up convergence
- To confine network instability to single areas of the network

This does not make configuring OSPF easier, but more elaborate and difficult.

Figure 4.13 shows a typical OSPF simple design. Notice how each router connects to the backbone—called area 0, or the backbone area. OSPF must have an area 0, and all other areas should connect to this area. (Areas that do not connect directly to area 0 by using virtual links are beyond the scope of this book.) Routers that connect other areas to the backbone area within an AS are called *Area Border Routers* (ABRs). Still, at least one interface of the ABR must be in area 0.

FIGURE 4.13   OSPF design example

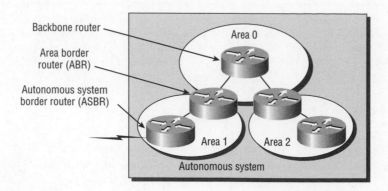

OSPF runs inside an autonomous system, but it can also connect multiple autonomous systems. The router that connects these ASs is called an *Autonomous System Boundary Router* (ASBR).

Ideally, you would create other areas of networks to help keep route updates to a minimum and to keep problems from propagating throughout the network. But that's beyond the scope of this chapter. Just make note of it.

Configuring OSPF Areas

After identifying the OSPF process, you need to identify the interfaces that you want to activate OSPF communications on as well as the area in which each resides. This will also configure the networks you're going to advertise to others. OSPF uses wildcards in the configuration—which are also used in access-list configurations.

Here's an OSPF basic configuration example for you:

```
Lab_A#config t
Lab_A(config)#router ospf 1
Lab_A(config-router)#network 10.0.0.0 0.255.255.255
 area ?
  <0-4294967295>  OSPF area ID as a decimal value
  A.B.C.D         OSPF area ID in IP address format
Lab_A(config-router)#network 10.0.0.0 0.255.255.255
 area 0
```

The areas can be any number from 0 to 4.2 billion. Don't get these numbers confused with the Process ID, which is from 1 to 65,535.

Remember, the OSPF Process ID number is irrelevant. It can be the same on every router on the network, or it can be different—doesn't matter. It's locally significant and just enables the OSPF routing on the router.

There are several ways to verify proper OSPF configuration and operation, and in the following sections I'll show you the OSPF show commands you need to know in order to do this. We're going to start by taking a quick look at the routing table of the Corp router:

So, let's issue a show ip route command on the Corp router:

```
     10.0.0.0/24 is subnetted, 12 subnets
O       10.1.11.0 [110/65] via 10.1.5.2, 00:01:31, Serial0/2/0
O       10.1.10.0 [110/65] via 10.1.5.2, 00:01:31, Serial0/2/0
O       10.1.9.0 [110/74] via 10.1.4.2, 00:01:31, Serial0/1/0
O       10.1.8.0 [110/65] via 10.1.4.2, 00:01:31, Serial0/1/0
O       10.1.12.0 [110/66] via 10.1.5.2, 00:01:31, Serial0/2/0
C       10.1.3.0 is directly connected, Serial0/0/1
C       10.1.2.0 is directly connected, Serial0/0/0
C       10.1.1.0 is directly connected, FastEthernet0/1
O       10.1.7.0 [110/74] via 10.1.3.2, 00:01:32, Serial0/0/1
                 [110/74] via 10.1.2.2, 00:01:32, Serial0/0/0
O       10.1.6.0 [110/74] via 10.1.3.2, 00:01:32, Serial0/0/1
                 [110/74] via 10.1.2.2, 00:01:32, Serial0/0/0
C       10.1.5.0 is directly connected, Serial0/2/0
C       10.1.4.0 is directly connected, Serial0/1/0
```

The Corp router shows the found routes for all 12 of our networks, with the O representing OSPF internal routes (the Cs are obviously our directly connected networks). It also found the dual routes to networks 10.1.6.0 and 10.1.7.0. I removed the bandwidth and delay commands from under the interface, so the defaults are being used to determine the metric. But remember, OSPF only uses bandwidth to determine the best path to a network.

 Important note: OSPF can load-balance only across links of equal costs. It can't load-balance across unequal-cost links as EIGRP can.

It's time to show you all the OSPF verification commands that you need to know.

The *show ip ospf* Command

The show ip ospf command is used to display OSPF information for one or all OSPF processes running on the router. Information contained therein includes the Router ID, area information, SPF statistics, and LSA timer information. Let's check out the output from the Corp router:

```
Corp#sh ip ospf
 Routing Process "ospf 132" with ID 10.1.5.1
 Start time: 04:32:04.116, Time elapsed: 01:27:10.156
 Supports only single TOS(TOS0) routes
```

```
Supports opaque LSA
Supports Link-local Signaling (LLS)
Supports area transit capability
Router is not originating router-LSAs with maximum metric
Initial SPF schedule delay 5000 msecs
Minimum hold time between two consecutive SPFs 10000 msecs
Maximum wait time between two consecutive SPFs 10000 msecs
Incremental-SPF disabled
Minimum LSA interval 5 secs
Minimum LSA arrival 1000 msecs
LSA group pacing timer 240 secs
Interface flood pacing timer 33 msecs
Retransmission pacing timer 66 msecs
Number of external LSA 0. Checksum Sum 0x000000
Number of opaque AS LSA 0. Checksum Sum 0x000000
Number of DCbitless external and opaque AS LSA 0
Number of DoNotAge external and opaque AS LSA 0
Number of areas in this router is 1. 1 normal 0 stub 0 nssa
Number of areas transit capable is 0
External flood list length 0
    Area BACKBONE(0)
        Number of interfaces in this area is 5
        Area has no authentication
        SPF algorithm last executed 00:14:52.220 ago
        SPF algorithm executed 14 times
        Area ranges are
        Number of LSA 6. Checksum Sum 0x03C06F
        Number of opaque link LSA 0. Checksum Sum 0x000000
        Number of DCbitless LSA 0
        Number of indication LSA 0
        Number of DoNotAge LSA 0
        Flood list length 0
```

Notice the Router ID (RID) of 10.1.5.1, which is the highest IP address configured on the router.

The *show ip ospf database* Command

Using the show ip ospf database command will give you information about the number of routers in the internetwork (AS) plus the neighboring router's ID (this is the topology database I mentioned earlier). Unlike the show ip eigrp topology command, this command shows the "OSPF routers," not each and every link in the AS as EIGRP does.

The output is broken down by area. Here's a sample output, again from Corp:

Corp#**sh ip ospf database**

                OSPF Router with ID (10.1.5.1) (Process ID 132)

                    Router Link States (Area 0)

Link ID   ADV Router   Age   Seq#   Checksum Link count
10.1.5.1   10.1.5.1   72   0x80000002 0x00F2CA 9
10.1.7.1   10.1.7.1   83   0x80000004 0x009197 6
10.1.9.1   10.1.9.1   73   0x80000001 0x00DA1C 4
10.1.11.1   10.1.11.1   67   0x80000005 0x00666A 4
10.1.12.1   10.1.12.1   67   0x80000004 0x007631 2

                    Net Link States (Area 0)

Link ID   ADV Router   Age   Seq#   Checksum
10.1.11.2   10.1.12.1   68   0x80000001 0x00A337

You can see all five routers and the RID of each router (the highest IP address on each router). The router output shows the link ID—remember that an interface is also a link—and the RID of the router on that link under the ADV router, or advertising router.

The *show ip ospf interface* Command

The show ip ospf interface command displays all interface-related OSPF information. Data is displayed about OSPF information for all interfaces or for specified interfaces. (I'll bold some of the important things.)

Corp#**sh ip ospf interface f0/1**
FastEthernet0/1 is up, line protocol is up
  Internet Address 10.1.1.1/24, Area 0
  Process ID 132, Router ID 10.1.5.1, Network Type BROADCAST, Cost: 1
  Transmit Delay is 1 sec, State DR, **Priority 1**
  Designated Router (ID) 10.1.5.1, Interface address 10.1.1.1
  No backup designated router on this network
  Timer intervals configured, Hello 10, Dead 40, Wait 40, Retransmit 5
    oob-resync timeout 40
    Hello due in 00:00:01
  Supports Link-local Signaling (LLS)
  Index 1/1, flood queue length 0
  Next 0x0(0)/0x0(0)
  Last flood scan length is 0, maximum is 0

```
Last flood scan time is 0 msec, maximum is 0 msec
Neighbor Count is 0, Adjacent neighbor count is 0
Suppress hello for 0 neighbor(s)
```

The following information is displayed by this command:

- Interface IP address
- Area assignment
- Process ID
- Router ID
- Network type
- Cost
- Priority
- DR/BDR election information (if applicable)
- Hello and Dead timer intervals
- Adjacent neighbor information

The reason I used the `show ip ospf interface f0/1` command is that I knew that there would be a designated router elected on the FastEthernet broadcast multi-access network. We'll get into DR and DBR elections in detail in a minute.

The *show ip ospf neighbor* Command

The `show ip ospf neighbor` command is super-useful because it summarizes the pertinent OSPF information regarding neighbors and the adjacency state. If a DR or BDR exists, that information will also be displayed. Here's a sample:

```
Corp#sh ip ospf neighbor
Neighbor ID  Pri  State     Dead Time   Address    Interface
10.1.11.1     0   FULL/  -  00:00:37    10.1.5.2   Serial0/2/0
10.1.9.1      0   FULL/  -  00:00:34    10.1.4.2   Serial0/1/0
10.1.7.1      0   FULL/  -  00:00:38    10.1.3.2   Serial0/0/1
10.1.7.1      0   FULL/  -  00:00:34    10.1.2.2   Serial0/0/0
```

This is a super-important command to understand because it's extremely useful in production networks. Let's take a look at the R3 and 871W routers outputs:

```
R3#sh ip ospf neighbor
Neighbor ID  Pri  State     Dead Time   Address    Interface
10.1.5.1      0   FULL/  -  00:00:39    10.1.5.1   Serial0/0/1
10.1.11.2     1   FULL/BDR  00:00:31    10.1.11.2  FastEthernet0/1
871W#sh ip ospf nei
Neihbor ID   Pri  State     Dead Time   Address    Interface
10.1.11.1     1   FULL/DR   00:00:30    10.1.11.1  Vlan1
```

Since there's an Ethernet link (broadcast multi-access) on the Corp router, there's going to be an election to determine who will be the designated router and who will be the nondesignated router. You can see that the 871W became the designated router, and it won because it had the highest IP address on the network. You can change this, but that's the default.

The reason that the Corp connections to R1, R2, and R3 don't have a DR or BDR listed in the output is that by default, elections don't happen on point-to-point links. But you can see that the Corp router is fully adjacent to all three routers (and on both connections to R1) from its output.

Debugging OSPF

Debugging is a great tool for any protocol, so let's take a look in Table 4.9 at a few debugging commands for troubleshooting OSPF.

TABLE 4.9   Debugging Commands for Troubleshooting OSPF

Command	Description/Function
debug ip ospf packet	Shows Hello packets being sent and received on your router.
debug ip ospf hello	Shows Hello packets being sent and received on your router. Shows more detail than the debug ip ospf packet output.
debug ip ospf adj	Shows DR and DBR elections on a broadcast and nonbroadcast multi-access network.

I'll start by showing you the output from the Corp router I got using the debug ip ospf packet command:

```
Corp#debug ip ospf packet
OSPF packet debugging is on
*Mar 23 01:20:42.199: OSPF: rcv. v:2 t:1 l:48 rid:172.16.10.3
     aid:0.0.0.0 chk:8075 aut:0 auk: from Serial0/1/0
Corp#
*Mar 23 01:20:45.507: OSPF: rcv. v:2 t:1 l:48 rid:172.16.10.2
     aid:0.0.0.0 chk:8076 aut:0 auk: from Serial0/0/0
*Mar 23 01:20:45.531: OSPF: rcv. v:2 t:1 l:48 rid:172.16.10.2
     aid:0.0.0.0 chk:8076 aut:0 auk: from Serial0/0/1
*Mar 23 01:20:45.531: OSPF: rcv. v:2 t:1 l:48 rid:172.16.10.4
     aid:0.0.0.0 chk:8074 aut:0 auk: from Serial0/2/0
*Mar 23 01:20:52.199: OSPF: rcv. v:2 t:1 l:48 rid:172.16.10.3
     aid:0.0.0.0 chk:8075 aut:0 auk: from Serial0/1/0
*Mar 23 01:20:55.507: OSPF: rcv. v:2 t:1 l:48 rid:172.16.10.2
```

```
        aid:0.0.0.0 chk:8076 aut:0 auk: from Serial0/0/0
*Mar 23 01:20:55.527: OSPF: rcv. v:2 t:1 l:48 rid:172.16.10.2
        aid:0.0.0.0 chk:8076 aut:0 auk: from Serial0/0/1
*Mar 23 01:20:55.531: OSPF: rcv. v:2 t:1 l:48 rid:172.16.10.4
        aid:0.0.0.0 chk:8074 aut:0 auk: from Serial0/2/0
```

In the preceding output, you can see that our router is both sending and receiving Hello packets every 10 seconds from neighbor (adjacent) routers. The next command will provide us with the same information, but with more detail. For example, you can see the multicast address used (224.0.0.5) and the area:

```
Corp#debug ip ospf hello
*Mar 23 01:18:41.103: OSPF: Send hello to 224.0.0.5 area 0 on
    Serial0/1/0 from 10.1.4.1
*Mar 23 01:18:41.607: OSPF: Send hello to 224.0.0.5 area 0 on
    FastEthernet0/1 from 10.1.1.1
*Mar 23 01:18:41.607: OSPF: Send hello to 224.0.0.5 area 0 on
    Serial0/0/0 from 10.1.2.1
*Mar 23 01:18:41.611: OSPF: Send hello to 224.0.0.5 area 0 on
    Serial0/2/0 from 10.1.5.1
*Mar 23 01:18:41.611: OSPF: Send hello to 224.0.0.5 area 0 on
    Serial0/0/1 from 10.1.3.1
*Mar 23 01:18:42.199: OSPF: Rcv hello from 172.16.10.3 area 0 from
    Serial0/1/0 10.1.4.2
*Mar 23 01:18:42.199: OSPF: End of hello processing
*Mar 23 01:18:45.519: OSPF: Rcv hello from 172.16.10.2 area 0 from
    Serial0/0/0 10.1.2.2
*Mar 23 01:18:45.519: OSPF: End of hello processing
*Mar 23 01:18:45.543: OSPF: Rcv hello from 172.16.10.2 area 0 from
    Serial0/0/1 10.1.3.2
*Mar 23 01:18:45.543: OSPF: End of hello processing
*Mar 23 01:18:45.543: OSPF: Rcv hello from 172.16.10.4 area 0 from
    Serial0/2/0 10.1.5.2
*Mar 23 01:18:45.543: OSPF: End of hello processing
```

The last debug command I'm going show you is the debug ip ospf adj command, which will show you elections as they occur on broadcast and nonbroadcast multi-access networks:

```
Corp#debug ip ospf adj
OSPF adjacency events debugging is on
*Mar 23 01:24:34.823: OSPF: Interface FastEthernet0/1 going Down
*Mar 23 01:24:34.823: OSPF: 172.16.10.1 address 10.1.1.1 on
    FastEthernet0/1 is dead, state DOWN
```

```
*Mar 23 01:24:34.823: OSPF: Neighbor change Event on interface
   FastEthernet0/1
*Mar 23 01:24:34.823: OSPF: DR/BDR election on FastEthernet0/1
*Mar 23 01:24:34.823: OSPF: Elect BDR 0.0.0.0
*Mar 23 01:24:34.823: OSPF: Elect DR 0.0.0.0
*Mar 23 01:24:34.823: OSPF: Elect BDR 0.0.0.0
*Mar 23 01:24:34.823: OSPF: Elect DR 0.0.0.0
*Mar 23 01:24:34.823:          DR: none     BDR: none
*Mar 23 01:24:34.823: OSPF: Flush network LSA immediately
*Mar 23 01:24:34.823: OSPF: Remember old DR 172.16.10.1 (id)
*Mar 23 01:24:35.323: OSPF: We are not DR to build Net Lsa for
   interface FastEthernet0/1
*Mar 23 01:24:35.323: OSPF: Build router LSA for area 0, router ID
   172.16.10.1, seq 0x80000006
*Mar 23 01:24:35.347: OSPF: Rcv LS UPD from 172.16.10.2 on Serial0/0/1
   length 148 LSA count 1
*Mar 23 01:24:40.703: OSPF: Interface FastEthernet0/1 going Up
*Mar 23 01:24:41.203: OSPF: Build router LSA for area 0, router ID
   172.16.10.1, seq 0x80000007
*Mar 23 01:24:41.231: OSPF: Rcv LS UPD from 172.16.10.2 on Serial0/0/1
   length 160 LSA count 1
```

Exam Objectives

Be able to configure a single-area OSPF.   A minimal single-area configuration involves only two commands: router ospf *process-id* and network *x.x.x.x y.y.y.y area Z*.

Be able to verify the operation of OSPF.   There are many show commands that provide useful details on OSPF, and it is useful to be completely familiar with the output of each: show ip ospf, show ip ospf database, show ip ospf interface, show ip ospf neighbor, and show ip protocols.

4.13 Configure, verify, and troubleshoot EIGRP

There are two modes from which EIGRP commands are entered: router configuration mode and interface configuration mode. *Router configuration mode* enables the protocol, determines which networks will run EIGRP, and sets global characteristics. *Interface configuration mode* allows customization of summaries, metrics, timers, and bandwidth.

To start an EIGRP session on a router, use the router eigrp command followed by the autonomous system number of your network. You then enter the network numbers connected to the router using the network command followed by the network number.

Let's look at an example of enabling EIGRP for autonomous system 20 on a router connected to two networks, with the network numbers being 10.3.1.0/24 and 172.16.10.0/24:

```
Router#config t
Router(config)#router eigrp 20
Router(config-router)#network 172.16.0.0
Router(config-router)#network 10.0.0.0
```

Remember—as with RIP, you use the classful network address, which is all subnet and host bits turned off.

Understand that the AS number is irrelevant—that is, as long as all routers use the same number! You can use any number from 1 to 65,535.

Verifying EIGRP

There are several commands that can be used on a router to help you troubleshoot and verify the EIGRP configuration. Table 4.10 contains all of the most important commands that are used in conjunction with verifying EIGRP operation and offers a brief description of what each command does.

TABLE 4.10 EIGRP Troubleshooting Commands

Command	Description/Function
show ip route	Shows the entire routing table
show ip route eigrp	Shows only EIGRP entries in the routing table
show ip eigrp neighbors	Shows all EIGRP neighbors
show ip eigrp topology	Shows entries in the EIGRP topology table
debug eigrp packet	Shows Hello packets sent/received between adjacent routers
Debug ip eigrp notification	Shows EIGRP changes and updates as they occur on your network

I'll demonstrate how you would use the commands in Table 4.10 by using them on our internetwork that we just configured—not including the discontiguous network example.

The following router output is from the Corp router in the example:

```
Corp#sh ip route
     10.0.0.0/24 is subnetted, 12 subnets
D       10.1.11.0 [90/2172416] via 10.1.5.2, 00:01:05, Serial0/2/0
D       10.1.10.0 [90/2195456] via 10.1.5.2, 00:01:05, Serial0/2/0
D       10.1.9.0 [90/2195456] via 10.1.4.2, 00:01:05, Serial0/1/0
D       10.1.8.0 [90/2195456] via 10.1.4.2, 00:01:05, Serial0/1/0
D       10.1.12.0 [90/2172416] via 10.1.5.2, 00:01:05, Serial0/2/0
C       10.1.3.0 is directly connected, Serial0/0/1
C       10.1.2.0 is directly connected, Serial0/0/0
C       10.1.1.0 is directly connected, FastEthernet0/1
D       10.1.7.0 [90/2195456] via 10.1.2.2, 00:01:06, Serial0/0/0
D       10.1.6.0 [90/2195456] via 10.1.2.2, 00:01:06, Serial0/0/0
C       10.1.5.0 is directly connected, Serial0/2/0
C       10.1.4.0 is directly connected, Serial0/1/0
```

You can see that all routes are there in the routing table (10.1.3.0 shows that it's directly connected again), and we have only one link to networks 10.1.6.0 and 10.1.7.0! Notice that EIGRP routes are indicated with simply a *D* designation (DUAL) and that the default AD of these routes is 90. This represents internal EIGRP routes. Let's take a look at the R1 router table now that we've changed the metrics:

```
R1#sh ip route
     10.0.0.0/24 is subnetted, 12 subnets
D       10.1.11.0 [90/2684416] via 10.1.2.1, 00:00:09, Serial0/0/0
D       10.1.10.0 [90/2707456] via 10.1.2.1, 00:00:09, Serial0/0/0
D       10.1.9.0 [90/2707456] via 10.1.2.1, 00:00:09, Serial0/0/0
D       10.1.8.0 [90/2707456] via 10.1.2.1, 00:00:09, Serial0/0/0
D       10.1.12.0 [90/2684416] via 10.1.2.1, 00:00:09, Serial0/0/0
C       10.1.3.0 is directly connected, Serial0/0/1
C       10.1.2.0 is directly connected, Serial0/0/0
D       10.1.1.0 [90/2172416] via 10.1.2.1, 00:00:09, Serial0/0/0
C       10.1.7.0 is directly connected, FastEthernet0/1
C       10.1.6.0 is directly connected, FastEthernet0/0
D       10.1.5.0 [90/2681856] via 10.1.2.1, 00:00:09, Serial0/0/0
D       10.1.4.0 [90/2681856] via 10.1.2.1, 00:00:09, Serial0/0/0
```

Now we have only one route to each remote network, and the 10.1.3.0 network is our backup link. Obviously, it would be better if we could use both links at the same time, but in my example, I made the 10.1.3.0 network a backup link.

Let's go back to the Corp router and see what it shows us in the neighbor table:

Corp#**sh ip eigrp neighbors**
IP-EIGRP neighbors for process 10

H	Address	Interface	Hold Uptime (sec)	SRTT (ms)	RTO	Q Cnt	Seq Num
1	10.1.3.2	Se0/0/1	14 00:35:10	1	200	0	81
3	10.1.5.2	Se0/2/0	10 02:51:22	1	200	0	31
2	10.1.4.2	Se0/1/0	13 03:17:20	1	200	0	20
0	10.1.2.2	Se0/0/0	10 03:19:37	1	200	0	80

We read the information in this output like this:

- The H field indicates the order in which the neighbor was discovered.
- The hold time is how long this router will wait for a Hello packet to arrive from a specific neighbor.
- The uptime indicates how long the neighborship has been established.
- The SRTT field is the smooth round-trip timer—an indication of the time it takes for a round-trip from this router to its neighbor and back. This value is used to determine how long to wait after a multicast for a reply from this neighbor. If a reply isn't received in time, the router will switch to using unicasts in an attempt to complete the communication.

Now let's see what's in the Corp topology table by using the show ip eigrp topology command—this should be interesting!

Corp#**sh ip eigrp topology**
IP-EIGRP Topology Table for AS(10)/ID(10.1.5.1)
Codes: P - Passive, A - Active, U - Update, Q - Query, R - Reply,
        r - reply Status, s - sia Status
P 10.1.11.0/24, 1 successors, FD is 2172416
        via 10.1.5.2 (2172416/28160), Serial0/2/0
P 10.1.10.0/24, 1 successors, FD is 2172416
        via 10.1.5.2 (2195456/281600), Serial0/2/0
P 10.1.9.0/24, 1 successors, FD is 2195456
        via 10.1.4.2 (2195456/281600), Serial0/1/0
P 10.1.8.0/24, 1 successors, FD is 2195456
        via 10.1.4.2 (2195456/72960), Serial0/1/0
P 10.1.12.0/24, 1 successors, FD is 2172416
        via 10.1.5.2 (2172416/28160), Serial0/2/0
P 10.1.3.0/24, 1 successors, FD is 76839936
        via Connected, Serial0/0/1
        via 10.1.2.2 (9849856/7719936), Serial0/0/0

```
P 10.1.2.0/24, 1 successors, FD is 2169856
        via Connected, Serial0/0/0
        via 10.1.2.2 (2681856/551936), Serial0/0/0
P 10.1.1.0/24, 1 successors, FD is 28160
        via Connected, FastEthernet0/1
P 10.1.7.0/24, 1 successors, FD is 793600
        via 10.1.2.2 (2195456/281600), Serial0/0/0
        via 10.1.3.2 (77081600/281600), Serial0/0/1
P 10.1.6.0/24, 1 successors, FD is 793600
        via 10.1.2.2 (2195456/281600), Serial0/0/0
        via 10.1.3.2 (77081600/281600), Serial0/0/1
P 10.1.5.0/24, 1 successors, FD is 2169856
        via Connected, Serial0/2/0
P 10.1.4.0/24, 1 successors, FD is 2169856
        via Connected, Serial0/1/0
```

Notice that every route is preceded by a *P*. This means that the route is in the *passive state,* which is a good thing because routes in the *active state (A)* indicate that the router has lost its path to this network and is searching for a replacement. Each entry also indicates the *feasible distance*, or FD, to each remote network plus the next-hop neighbor through which packets will travel to their destination. Plus, each entry also has two numbers in parentheses. The first indicates the feasible distance, and the second the advertised distance to a remote network.

Now here's where things get interesting—notice that under the 10.1.7.0 and 10.1.6.0 outputs there are two links to each network and that the feasible distance and advertised distance are different. What this means is that we have one successor to the networks and one feasible successor—a backup route! So very cool! You need to remember that even though both routes to network 10.1.6.0 and 10.1.7.0 are in the topology table, only the successor route (the one with the lowest metrics) will be copied and placed into the routing table.

 In order for the route to be a feasible successor, its advertised distance must be less than the feasible distance of the successor route.

EIGRP will load-balance across both links automatically when they are of equal variance (equal cost), but EIGRP can also load-balance across unequal-cost links as well if we use the `variance` command. The variance metric is set to 1 by default, meaning that only equal-cost links will load-balance. You can change the metric anywhere up to 128. Changing a variance value enables EIGRP to install multiple, loop-free routes with unequal cost in a local routing table.

So basically, if the variance is set to 1, only routes with the same metric as the successor will be installed in the local routing table. And, for example, if the variance is set to 2, any EIGRP-learned route with a metric less than two times the successor metric will be installed in the local routing table (if it is already a feasible successor).

Now's a great time for us to check out some debugging outputs. First, let's use the debug eigrp packet command that will show our Hello packets being sent between neighbor routers:

```
Corp#debug eigrp packet
EIGRP Packets debugging is on
    (UPDATE, REQUEST, QUERY, REPLY, HELLO, IPXSAP, PROBE, ACK, STUB,
    SIAQUERY, SIAREPLY)
Corp#
*Mar 21 23:17:35.050: EIGRP: Sending HELLO on FastEthernet0/1
*Mar 21 23:17:35.050:    AS 10, Flags 0x0, Seq 0/0 idbQ 0/0 iidbQ un/rely 0/0
*Mar 21 23:17:35.270: EIGRP: Received HELLO on Serial0/1/0 nbr 10.1.4.2
*Mar 21 23:17:35.270:    AS 10, Flags 0x0, Seq 0/0 idbQ 0/0 iidbQ
    un/rely 0/0 peerQ un/rely 0/0
*Mar 21 23:17:35.294: EIGRP: Received HELLO on Serial0/0/0 nbr 10.1.2.2
*Mar 21 23:17:35.294:    AS 10, Flags 0x0, Seq 0/0 idbQ 0/0 iidbQ
    un/rely 0/0 peerQ un/rely 0/0
*Mar 21 23:17:38.014: EIGRP: Received HELLO on Serial0/2/0 nbr 10.1.5.2
*Mar 21 23:17:38.014:    AS 10, Flags 0x0, Seq 0/0 idbQ 0/0 iidbQ
    un/rely 0/0 peerQ un/rely 0/0
```

Exam Objectives

Know EIGRP features.   EIGRP is a classless, advanced distance-vector protocol that supports IP, IPX, AppleTalk, and now IPv6. EIGRP uses a unique algorithm, called DUAL, to maintain route information and uses RTP to communicate with other EIGRP routers reliably.

Know how to configure EIGRP.   Be able to configure basic EIGRP. This is configured the same as IGRP with classful addresses.

Know how to verify EIGRP operation.   Know all of the EIGRP show commands and be familiar with their output and the interpretation of the main components of their output.

4.14 Verify network connectivity (including: using ping, traceroute, and Telnet or SSH)

For information on this objectives, please see objective 4.7 earlier in this chapter.

4.15 Troubleshoot routing issues

The best troubleshooting tools are show and debug commands, specifically show ip protocols and various routing protocol debugging commands. Let's take a look.

First, the show ip protocols command will show you the routing protocols configured on your router. Hopefully you have only one. Here is an example:

```
Router#sh ip protocols
Routing Protocol is "rip"
  Outgoing update filter list for all interfaces is not set
  Incoming update filter list for all interfaces is not set
  Sending updates every 30 seconds, next due in 27 seconds
  Invalid after 180 seconds, hold down 180, flushed after 240
  Redistributing: rip
  Default version control: send version 2, receive version 2
    Interface          Send  Recv  Triggered RIP  Key-chain
    FastEthernet0/1    2     2
    Serial0/0/1        2     2
  Automatic network summarization is not in effect
  Maximum path: 4
  Routing for Networks:
    10.0.0.0
  Passive Interface(s):
    FastEthernet0/0
    Serial0/0/0
  Routing Information Sources:
    Gateway          Distance      Last Update
    10.1.11.2             120       00:00:00
    10.1.5.1              120       00:00:02
  Distance: (default is 120)
```

The above router output shows the router is running RIPv2, the interfaces participating in the routing process, the next hop gateways (neighbors) and the administrative distance. Also, you can see that the maximum path is 4, which means that RIP will load-balance across four equal cost links by default.

There are dozens of debugging commands you can use, and for RIP, the debug ip rip command is the best tool for debugging RIP routing.

```
*Mar 17 19:34:00.123: RIP: sending v2 update to 224.0.0.9 via
    Serial0/0/1 (10.1.5.2)
*Mar 17 19:34:00.123: RIP: build update entries
*Mar 17 19:34:00.123:   10.1.10.0/24 via 0.0.0.0, metric 1, tag 0
```

```
*Mar 17 19:34:00.123:    10.1.11.0/24 via 0.0.0.0, metric 1, tag 0
*Mar 17 19:34:00.123:    10.1.12.0/24 via 0.0.0.0, metric 2, tag 0col
*Mar 17 19:34:03.795: RIP: received v2 update from 10.1.5.1 on
  Serial0/0/1
```

The above debug output shows we are running RIPv2, with multicast address 224.0.0.9.

For EIGRP I am going to show you two commands. The **debug eigrp packet** command and the debug **ip eigrp notification** command:

Router#**debug eigrp packet**
```
EIGRP Packets debugging is on
    (UPDATE, REQUEST, QUERY, REPLY, HELLO, IPXSAP, PROBE, ACK, STUB,
    SIAQUERY, SIAREPLY)
*Mar 21 23:17:35.050: EIGRP: Sending HELLO on FastEthernet0/1
*Mar 21 23:17:35.050:    AS 10, Flags 0x0, Seq 0/0 idbQ 0/0 iidbQ un/rely 0/0
*Mar 21 23:17:35.270: EIGRP: Received HELLO on Serial0/1/0 nbr 10.1.4.2
*Mar 21 23:17:35.270:    AS 10, Flags 0x0, Seq 0/0 idbQ 0/0 iidbQ
  un/rely 0/0 peerQ un/rely 0/0
*Mar 21 23:17:35.294: EIGRP: Received HELLO on Serial0/0/0 nbr 10.1.2.2
*Mar 21 23:17:35.294:    AS 10, Flags 0x0, Seq 0/0 idbQ 0/0 iidbQ
  un/rely 0/0 peerQ un/rely 0/0
*Mar 21 23:17:38.014: EIGRP: Received HELLO on Serial0/2/0 nbr 10.1.5.2
*Mar 21 23:17:38.014:    AS 10, Flags 0x0, Seq 0/0 idbQ 0/0 iidbQ
  un/rely 0/0 peerQ un/rely 0/0
```

The EIGRP 224.0.0.10 multicast is sent out every five seconds, and the Hello packets are sent out of every active interface, as well as all the interfaces that we have neighbors connected to. Did you notice the AS number is provided in the update? This is because if a neighbor doesn't have the same AS number, the Hello update would just be discarded.

The debug **ip eigrp notification** command (called **debug ip eigrp events** on pre 12.4 routers) shouldn't show you anything at all! That's right—the only time you'll see output from this command is if there's a problem on your network, or you've added or deleted a network from a router in your internetwork. Since I have a problem-free network, I'm going to shut down an interface on my router in order to see some output:

Router(config)#**int f0/1**
Router(config-if)#**shut**
```
*Mar 21 23:25:43.506: IP-EIGRP(Default-IP-Routing-Table:10): Callback:
  route_adjust FastEthernet0/1
*Mar 21 23:25:43.506: IP-EIGRP: Callback: ignored connected AS 0 10.1.1.0/24
*Mar 21 23:25:43.506:               into: eigrp AS 10
*Mar 21 23:25:43.506: IP-EIGRP(Default-IP-Routing-Table:10): Callback:
  callbackup_routes 10.1.1.0/24
Corp(config-if)#n
```

```
*Mar 21 23:25:45.506: %LINK-5-CHANGED: Interface FastEthernet0/1,
    changed state to administratively down
*Mar 21 23:25:46.506: %LINEPROTO-5-UPDOWN: Line protocol on Interface
    FastEthernet0/1, changed state to down
Router(config-if)#no shut
Router(config-if)#^Z
*Mar 21 23:25:49.570: %LINK-3-UPDOWN: Interface FastEthernet0/1,
    changed state to up
*Mar 21 23:25:49.570: IP-EIGRP(Default-IP-Routing-Table:10): Callback:
    lostroute 10.1.1.0/24
*Mar 21 23:25:49.570: IP-EIGRP(Default-IP-Routing-Table:0): Callback:
    redist connected (config change) FastEthernet0/1
*Mar 21 23:25:49.570: IP-EIGRP(Default-IP-Routing-Table:0): Callback:
    redist connected (config change) Serial0/0/0
*Mar 21 23:25:49.570: IP-EIGRP(Default-IP-Routing-Table:0): Callback:
    redist connected (config change) Serial0/0/1
*Mar 21 23:25:49.570: IP-EIGRP(Default-IP-Routing-Table:0): Callback:
    redist connected (config change) Serial0/1/0
*Mar 21 23:25:49.570: IP-EIGRP(Default-IP-Routing-Table:0): Callback:
    redist connected (config change) Serial0/2/0
*Mar 21 23:25:49.570: IP-EIGRP(Default-IP-Routing-Table:10): Callback:
    route_adjust FastEthernet0/1
```

Debugging is a great tool for any protocol, so let's take a look in Table 4.11 at a few debugging commands for troubleshooting OSPF.

TABLE 4.11   Table 411: Debugging Commands for Troubleshooting OSPF

Command	Description/Function
debug ip ospf packet	Shows Hello packets being sent and received on your router.
debug ip ospf hello	Shows Hello packets being sent and received on your router. Shows more detail than the debug ip ospf packet output.
debug ip ospf adj	Shows DR and DBR elections on a broadcast and nonbroadcast multi-access network.

I'll start by showing you the output from the router I have, using the debug ip ospf packet command:

```
Router#debug ip ospf packet
OSPF packet debugging is on
```

```
*Mar 23 01:20:42.199: OSPF: rcv. v:2 t:1 l:48 rid:172.16.10.3
    aid:0.0.0.0 chk:8075 aut:0 auk: from Serial0/1/0
*Mar 23 01:20:45.507: OSPF: rcv. v:2 t:1 l:48 rid:172.16.10.2
    aid:0.0.0.0 chk:8076 aut:0 auk: from Serial0/0/0
*Mar 23 01:20:45.531: OSPF: rcv. v:2 t:1 l:48 rid:172.16.10.2
    aid:0.0.0.0 chk:8076 aut:0 auk: from Serial0/0/1
*Mar 23 01:20:45.531: OSPF: rcv. v:2 t:1 l:48 rid:172.16.10.4
    aid:0.0.0.0 chk:8074 aut:0 auk: from Serial0/2/0
*Mar 23 01:20:52.199: OSPF: rcv. v:2 t:1 l:48 rid:172.16.10.3
    aid:0.0.0.0 chk:8075 aut:0 auk: from Serial0/1/0
*Mar 23 01:20:55.507: OSPF: rcv. v:2 t:1 l:48 rid:172.16.10.2
    aid:0.0.0.0 chk:8076 aut:0 auk: from Serial0/0/0
```

In the above output, you can see that the router is both sending and receiving Hello packets every 10 seconds from neighbor (adjacent) routers. The next command will provide the same information, but with more detail. For example, you can see the multicast address used (224.0.0.5) and the area:

```
Router#debug ip ospf hello
*Mar 23 01:18:41.103: OSPF: Send hello to 224.0.0.5 area 0 on
    Serial0/1/0 from 10.1.4.1
*Mar 23 01:18:41.607: OSPF: Send hello to 224.0.0.5 area 0 on
    FastEthernet0/1 from 10.1.1.1
*Mar 23 01:18:41.607: OSPF: Send hello to 224.0.0.5 area 0 on
    Serial0/0/0 from 10.1.2.1
*Mar 23 01:18:41.611: OSPF: Send hello to 224.0.0.5 area 0 on
    Serial0/2/0 from 10.1.5.1
*Mar 23 01:18:41.611: OSPF: Send hello to 224.0.0.5 area 0 on
    Serial0/0/1 from 10.1.3.1
*Mar 23 01:18:42.199: OSPF: Rcv hello from 172.16.10.3 area 0 from
    Serial0/1/0 10.1.4.2
*Mar 23 01:18:42.199: OSPF: End of hello processing
*Mar 23 01:18:45.519: OSPF: Rcv hello from 172.16.10.2 area 0 from
    Serial0/0/0 10.1.2.2
*Mar 23 01:18:45.519: OSPF: End of hello processing
```

The last debug command I'm going show you is the debug ip ospf adj command that will show us elections as they occur on broadcast and nonbroadcast multi-access networks:

```
Router#debug ip ospf adj
OSPF adjacency events debugging is on
*Mar 23 01:24:34.823: OSPF: Interface FastEthernet0/1 going Down
*Mar 23 01:24:34.823: OSPF: 172.16.10.1 address 10.1.1.1 on
   FastEthernet0/1 is dead, state DOWN
```

```
*Mar 23 01:24:34.823: OSPF: Neighbor change Event on interface
    FastEthernet0/1
*Mar 23 01:24:34.823: OSPF: DR/BDR election on FastEthernet0/1
*Mar 23 01:24:34.823: OSPF: Elect BDR 0.0.0.0
*Mar 23 01:24:34.823: OSPF: Elect DR 0.0.0.0
*Mar 23 01:24:34.823: OSPF: Elect BDR 0.0.0.0
*Mar 23 01:24:34.823: OSPF: Elect DR 0.0.0.0
*Mar 23 01:24:34.823:          DR: none    BDR: none
*Mar 23 01:24:34.823: OSPF: Flush network LSA immediately
*Mar 23 01:24:34.823: OSPF: Remember old DR 172.16.10.1 (id)
*Mar 23 01:24:35.323: OSPF: We are not DR to build Net Lsa for
    interface FastEthernet0/1
*Mar 23 01:24:35.323: OSPF: Build router LSA for area 0, router ID
    172.16.10.1, seq 0x80000006
*Mar 23 01:24:35.347: OSPF: Rcv LS UPD from 172.16.10.2 on Serial0/0/1
    length 148 LSA count 1
*Mar 23 01:24:40.703: OSPF: Interface FastEthernet0/1 going Up
*Mar 23 01:24:41.203: OSPF: Build router LSA for area 0, router ID
    172.16.10.1, seq 0x80000007
*Mar 23 01:24:41.231: OSPF: Rcv LS UPD from 172.16.10.2 on Serial0/0/1
    length 160 LSA count 1
```

Exam Objectives

Remember what the command debug ip ospf packet provides to you   Shows Hello packets being sent and received on your router.

Remember what the command debug ip ospf hello provides to you   Shows Hello packets being sent and received on your router. Shows more detail than the `debug ip ospf packet` output.

Remember what the command debug ip ospf adj provides to you   Shows DR and DBR elections on a broadcast and nonbroadcast multi-access network.

4.16 Verify router hardware and software operation using the SHOW and DEBUG commands

You can use the `ping` and `traceroute` commands to test connectivity to remote devices, and both of them can be used with many protocols, not just IP. But don't forget that the `show ip` route command is a good troubleshooting command for verifying your routing table, and the show interfaces command will show you the status of each interface.

I am going to go over both the debug command and the show processes command you need to troubleshoot a router.

Using the ping Command

So far, you've seen many examples of pinging devices to test IP connectivity and name resolution using the DNS server. To see all the different protocols that you can use with the *ping* program, type ping ?:

```
Corp#ping ?
  WORD  Ping destination address or hostname
  clns  CLNS echo
  ip    IP echo
  srb   srb echo
  tag   Tag encapsulated IP echo
  <cr>
```

The ping output displays the minimum, average, and maximum times it takes for a ping packet to find a specified system and return. Here's an example:

```
Corp#ping R1
Translating "R1"...domain server (192.168.0.70)[OK]
Type escape sequence to abort.
Sending 5, 100-byte ICMP Echos to 10.2.2.2, timeout
  is 2 seconds:
!!!!!
Success rate is 100 percent (5/5), round-trip min/avg/max
  = 1/2/4 ms
Corp#
```

You can see that the DNS server was used to resolve the name, and the device was pinged in 1 ms (millisecond), an average of 2 ms, and up to 4 ms.

The ping command can be used in user and privileged mode but not configuration mode.

Pinging with SDM

Unlike the Telnet option in SDM, we at least have a screen we can use to choose an option or two.

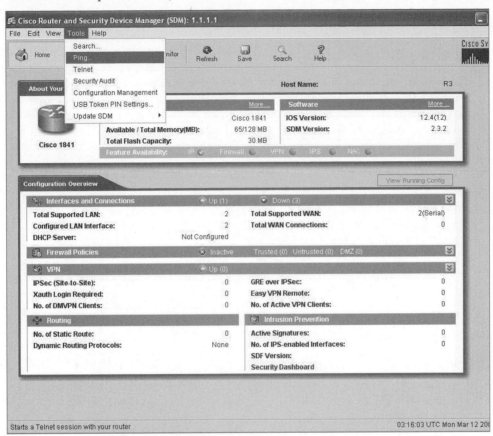

Once you choose Tools➢ Ping, you receive the following screen:

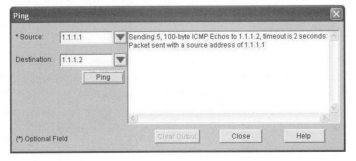

From here you can choose the source interface to ping from, which is a nice option. Enter your destination and then click Ping.

Using the `traceroute` Command

Traceroute (the `traceroute` command, or `trace` for short) shows the path a packet takes to get to a remote device. It uses time to live (TTL) time-outs and ICMP error messages to outline the path a packet takes through an internetwork to arrive at remote host.

Trace (the `trace` command) that can be used from either user mode or privileged mode allows you to figure out which router in the path to an unreachable network host should be examined more closely for the cause of the network's failure.

To see the protocols that you can use with the `traceroute` command, type `traceroute ?`:

```
Corp#traceroute ?
  WORD       Trace route to destination address or hostname
  appletalk  AppleTalk Trace
  clns       ISO CLNS Trace
  ip         IP Trace
  ipv6       IPv6 Trace
  ipx        IPX Trace
  <cr>
```

The `trace` command shows the hop or hops that a packet traverses on its way to a remote device. Here's an example:

```
Corp#traceroute r1

Type escape sequence to abort.
Tracing the route to R1 (10.2.2.2)

  1 R1 (10.2.2.2) 4 msec *  0 msec
Corp#
```

You can see that the packet went through only one hop to find the destination.

 Do not get confused! You can't use the `tracert` command—it's a Windows command. For a router, use the `traceroute` command!

Here's an example of using `tracert` from a Windows DOS prompt (notice the command `tracert`!):

```
C:\>tracert www.whitehouse.gov

Tracing route to a1289.g.akamai.net [69.8.201.107]
```

over a maximum of 30 hops:

```
1      *         *         *         Request timed out.
2     53 ms    61 ms    53 ms    hlrn-dsl-gw15-207.hlrn.qwest.net
         [207.225.112.207]
3     53 ms    55 ms    54 ms    hlrn-agw1.inet.qwest.net [71.217.188.113]
4     54 ms    53 ms    54 ms    hlr-core-01.inet.qwest.net [205.171.253.97]
5     54 ms    53 ms    54 ms    apa-cntr-01.inet.qwest.net [205.171.253.26]
6     54 ms    53 ms    53 ms    63.150.160.34
7     54 ms    54 ms    53 ms    www.whitehouse.gov [69.8.201.107]
```

Trace complete.

Okay, let's move on now and talk about how to troubleshoot your network using the debug command.

Debugging

Debug is a troubleshooting command that's available from the privileged exec mode of Cisco IOS. It's used to display information about various router operations and the related traffic generated or received by the router, plus any error messages.

It's a useful and informative tool, but you really need to understand some important facts about its use. Debug is regarded as a very high-priority task because it can consume a huge amount of resources and the router is forced to process-switch the packets being debugged. So, you don't just use Debug as a monitoring tool—it's meant to be used for a short period of time and only as a troubleshooting tool. By using it, you can really find out some truly significant facts about both working and faulty software and/or hardware components.

Because debugging output takes priority over other network traffic, and because the debug all command generates more output than any other debug command, it can severely diminish the router's performance—even render it unusable. So, in virtually all cases, it's best to use more-specific debug commands.

As you can see from the following output, you can't enable debugging from user mode, only privileged mode:

```
Corp>debug ?
% Unrecognized command
Corp>en
Corp#debug ?
  aaa                  AAA Authentication, Authorization and Accounting
  access-expression    Boolean access expression
  adjacency            adjacency
  all                  Enable all debugging
[output cut]
```

If you've got the freedom to pretty much take out a router and you really want to have some fun with debugging, use the debug all command:

```
Corp#debug all
```

```
This may severely impact network performance. Continue? (yes/[no]):yes
```

```
All possible debugging has been turned on
```

```
2d20h: SNMP: HC Timer 824AE5CC fired
2d20h: SNMP: HC Timer 824AE5CC rearmed, delay = 20000
2d20h: Serial0/0: HDLC myseq 4, mineseen 0, yourseen 0, line down
2d20h:
2d20h: Rudpv1 Sent: Pkts 0,  Data Bytes 0,  Data Pkts 0
2d20h: Rudpv1 Rcvd: Pkts 0,  Data Bytes 0,  Data Pkts 0
2d20h: Rudpv1 Discarded: 0,  Retransmitted 0
2d20h:
2d20h: RIP-TIMER: periodic timer expired
2d20h: Serial0/0: HDLC myseq 5, mineseen 0, yourseen 0, line down
2d20h: Serial0/0: attempting to restart
2d20h: PowerQUICC(0/0): DCD is up.
2d20h: is_up: 0 state: 4 sub state: 1 line: 0
2d20h:
2d20h: Rudpv1 Sent: Pkts 0,  Data Bytes 0,  Data Pkts 0
2d20h: Rudpv1 Rcvd: Pkts 0,  Data Bytes 0,  Data Pkts 0
2d20h: Rudpv1 Discarded: 0,  Retransmitted 0
2d20h: un all
All possible debugging has been turned off
Corp#
```

To disable debugging on a router, just use the command no in front of the debug command:

```
Corp#no debug all
```

But I typically just use the undebug all command, since it is so easy when using the shortcut:

```
Corp#un all
```

Remember that instead of using the debug all command, it's almost always better to use specific commands—and only for short periods of time. Here's an example of deploying debug ip rip that will show you RIP updates being sent and received on a router:

```
Corp#debug ip rip
RIP protocol debugging is on
```

```
Corp#
1w4d: RIP: sending v2 update to 224.0.0.9 via Serial0/0 (192.168.12.1)
1w4d: RIP: build update entries
1w4d:    10.10.10.0/24 via 0.0.0.0, metric 2, tag 0
1w4d:    171.16.125.0/24 via 0.0.0.0, metric 3, tag 0
1w4d:    172.16.12.0/24 via 0.0.0.0, metric 1, tag 0
1w4d:    172.16.125.0/24 via 0.0.0.0, metric 3, tag 0
1w4d: RIP: sending v2 update to 224.0.0.9 via Serial0/2 (172.16.12.1)
1w4d: RIP: build update entries
1w4d:    192.168.12.0/24 via 0.0.0.0, metric 1, tag 0
1w4d:    192.168.22.0/24 via 0.0.0.0, metric 2, tag 0
1w4d: RIP: received v2 update from 192.168.12.2 on Serial0/0
1w4d:    192.168.22.0/24 via 0.0.0.0 in 1 hops
Corp#un all
```

I'm sure you can see that the **debug** command is one powerful command. And because of this, I'm also sure you realize that before you use any of the debugging commands, you should make sure you check the utilization of your router. This is important because in most cases, you don't want to negatively impact the device's ability to process the packets through on your internetwork. You can determine a specific router's utilization information by using the **show processes** command.

Remember, when you telnet into a remote device, you will not see console messages by default! For example, you will not see debugging output. To allow console messages to be sent to your Telnet session, use the **terminal monitor** command.

Using the show processes **Command**

As mentioned in the previous section, you've really got to be careful when using the **debug** command on your devices. If your router's CPU utilization is consistently at 50 percent or more, it's probably not a good idea to type in the **debug all** command unless you want to see what a router looks like when it crashes!

So, what other approaches can you use? Well, the **show processes** (or **show processes cpu**) is a good tool for determining a given router's CPU utilization. Plus, it'll give you a list of active processes along with their corresponding process ID, priority, scheduler test (status), CPU time used, number of times invoked, and so on. Lots of great stuff! Plus, this command is super-handy when you want to evaluate your router's performance and CPU utilization—for instance, when you find yourself otherwise tempted to reach for the **debug** command.

Okay—what do you see in the output below? The first line shows the CPU utilization output for the last 5 seconds, 1 minute, and 5 minutes. The output provides 2%/0% in front of the CPU utilization for the last 5 seconds. The first number equals the total utilization and the second one delimits the utilization due to interrupt routines:

```
Corp#sh processes
CPU utilization for five seconds: 2%/0%; one minute: 0%; five minutes: 0%
 PID QTy         PC Runtime (ms)    Invoked    uSecs    Stacks TTY Process
   1 Cwe 8034470C           0          1        0 5804/6000    0 Chunk Manager
   2 Csp 80369A88           4       1856        2 2616/3000    0 Load Meter
   3 M*         0         112         14 800010656/12000    0 Exec
   5 Lst 8034FD9C      268246      52101     5148 5768/6000    0 Check heaps
   6 Cwe 80355E5C          20          3     6666 5704/6000    0 Pool Manager
   7 Mst 802AC3C4           0          2        0 5580/6000    0 Timers
[output cut]
```

So basically, the output from the show processes command shows that our router is happily able to process debugging commands without being overloaded.

Exam Objectives

Remember the difference between the command traceroute and tracert.   The command trace (or traceroute) is used with Cisco routers, switches, and Unix devices, among others. However, the command tracert is used on Windows devices from the DOS prompt.

Remember the command to use before using debugging on a router.   Before using any debug command on a router, you should verify the CPU utilization, using the show processes command.

4.17 Implement basic router security

An *access list* is essentially a list of conditions that categorize packets. They can be really helpful when you need to exercise control over network traffic. An access list would be your tool of choice for decision making in these situations.

One of the most common and easiest to understand uses of access lists is filtering unwanted packets when implementing security policies. For example, you can set them up to make very specific decisions about regulating traffic patterns so that they'll allow only certain hosts to access web resources on the Internet while restricting others. With the right combination of access lists, network managers arm themselves with the power to enforce nearly any security policy they can invent.

Access lists can even be used in situations that don't necessarily involve blocking packets. For example, you can use them to control which networks will or won't be advertised by dynamic routing protocols. How you configure the access list is the same. The difference here is simply how you apply it—to a routing protocol instead of an interface. When you apply an access list in this way, it's called a distribute list, and it doesn't stop routing advertisements, it just controls their content. You can also use access lists to categorize packets for queuing or QoS-type services and for controlling which types of traffic can activate an ISDN link.

Creating access lists is really a lot like programming a series of `if-then` statements—if a given condition is met, then a given action is taken. If the specific condition isn't met, nothing happens and the next statement is evaluated. Access-list statements are basically packet filters that packets are compared against, categorized by, and acted upon accordingly. Once the lists are built, they can be applied to either inbound or outbound traffic on any interface. Applying an access list causes the router to analyze every packet crossing that interface in the specified direction and take the appropriate action.

There are a few important rules that a packet follows when it's being compared with an access list:

- It's always compared with each line of the access list in sequential order—that is, it'll always start with the first line of the access list, then go to line 2, then line 3, and so on.

- It's compared with lines of the access list only until a match is made. Once the packet matches the condition on a line of the access list, the packet is acted upon and no further comparisons take place.

- There is an implicit "deny" at the end of each access list—this means that if a packet doesn't match the condition on any of the lines in the access list, the packet will be discarded.

Each of these rules has some powerful implications when filtering IP packets with access lists, so keep in mind that creating effective access lists truly takes some practice.

There are two main types of access lists:

Standard access lists   These use only the source IP address in an IP packet as the condition test. All decisions are made based on the source IP address. This means that standard access lists basically permit or deny an entire suite of protocols. They don't distinguish among any of the many types of IP traffic such as web, Telnet, UDP, and so on.

Extended access lists   Extended access lists can evaluate many of the other fields in the layer 3 and layer 4 headers of an IP packet. They can evaluate source and destination IP addresses, the protocol field in the Network layer header, and the port number at the Transport layer header. This gives extended access lists the ability to make much more granular decisions when controlling traffic.

Named access lists   Hey, wait a minute—I said there were two types of access lists but listed three! Well, technically there really are only two since *named access lists* are either standard or extended and not actually a new type. I'm just distinguishing them because they're created and referred to differently than standard and extended access lists, but they're functionally the same.

Once you create an access list, it's not really going to do anything until you apply it. Yes, they're there on the router, but they're inactive until you tell that router what to do with them. To use an access list as a packet filter, you need to apply it to an interface on the router where you want the traffic filtered. And you've got to specify which direction of traffic you want the access list applied to. There's a good reason for this—you may want different controls in place for traffic leaving your enterprise destined for the Internet than you'd want for traffic coming into your enterprise from the Internet. So, by specifying the direction of traffic, you can—and frequently you'll need to—use different access lists for inbound and outbound traffic on a single interface:

Inbound access lists   When an access list is applied to inbound packets on an interface, those packets are processed through the access list before being routed to the outbound interface. Any packets that are denied won't be routed because they're discarded before the routing process is invoked.

Outbound access lists   When an access list is applied to outbound packets on an interface, those packets are routed to the outbound interface and then processed through the access list before being queued.

There are some general access-list guidelines that should be followed when you're creating and implementing access lists on a router:

- You can assign only one access list per interface per protocol per direction. This means that when creating IP access lists, you can have only one inbound access list and one outbound access list per interface.

When you consider the implications of the implicit deny at the end of any access list, it makes sense that you can't have multiple access lists applied on the same interface in the same direction for the same protocol. That's because any packets that don't match some condition in the first access list would be denied, and there wouldn't be any packets left over to compare against a second access list.

- Organize your access lists so that the more specific tests are at the top of the access list.

- Anytime a new entry is added to the access list, it will be placed at the bottom of the list. Using a text editor for access lists is highly suggested.

- You cannot remove one line from an access list. If you try to do this, you will remove the entire list. It is best to copy the access list to a text editor before trying to edit the list. The only exception is when using named access lists.

- Unless your access list ends with a `permit any` command, all packets will be discarded if they do not meet any of the list's tests. Every list should have at least one `permit` statement or it will deny all traffic.

- Create access lists and then apply them to an interface. Any access list applied to an interface without an access list present will not filter traffic.

- Access lists are designed to filter traffic going through the router. They will not filter traffic that has originated from the router.

- Place IP standard access lists as close to the destination as possible. This is the reason we don't really want to use standard access lists in our networks. You cannot put a standard access list close to the source host or network because you can only filter based on source address and nothing would be forwarded.

- Place IP extended access lists as close to the source as possible. Since extended access lists can filter on very specific addresses and protocols, you don't want your traffic to traverse the entire network and then be denied. By placing this list as close to the source address as possible, you can filter traffic before it uses up your precious bandwidth.

Exam Objectives

Remember the standard and extended IP access-list number ranges. The numbered ranges you can use to configure a standard IP access list are 1–99 and 1300–1999. The numbered ranges for an extended IP access list are 100–199 and 2000–2699.

Understand the term "implicit deny." At the end of every access list is an implicit deny. What this means is that if a packet does not match any of the lines in the access list, then it will be discarded. Also, if you have nothing but deny statements in your list, then the list will not permit any packets.

Understand the standard IP access-list configuration command. To configure a standard IP access list, use the access-list numbers 1–99 or 1300–1999 in global configuration mode. Choose permit or deny, then choose the source IP address you want to filter on using one of the three techniques covered earlier.

Understand the extended IP access-list configuration command. To configure an extended IP access list, use the access-list numbers 100–199 or 2000–2699 in global configuration mode. Choose permit or deny, the Network layer protocol field, the source IP address you want to filter on, the destination address you want to filter on, and finally the Transport layer port number (if selected).

Review Questions

1. Network 206.143.5.0 was assigned to the Acme Company to connect to its ISP. The administrator of Acme would like to configure one router with the commands to access the Internet. Which commands could be configured on the Gateway router to allow Internet access to the entire network? (Choose two.)

   A. `Gateway(config)#ip route 0.0.0.0 0.0.0.0 206.143.5.2`

   B. `Gateway(config)#router rip`

   C. `Gateway(config-router)#network 206.143.5.0`

   D. `Gateway(config)#router rip`

   E. `Gateway(config-router)#network 206.143.5.0 default`

   F. `Gateway(config)#ip route 206.143.5.0 255.255.255.0 default`

   G. `Gateway(config)#ip default-network 206.143.5.0`

2. Which statement is true regarding classless routing protocols? (Choose two.)

   A. The use of discontiguous networks is not allowed.

   B. The use of variable length subnet masks is permitted.

   C. RIPv1 is a classless routing protocol.

   D. IGRP supports classless routing within the same autonomous system.

   E. RIPv2 supports classless routing.

3. Which two of the following are true regarding the distance-vector and link-state routing protocols?

   A. Link state sends its complete routing table out all active interfaces on periodic time intervals.

   B. Distance vector sends its complete routing table out all active interfaces on periodic time intervals.

   C. Link state sends updates containing the state of their own links to all routers in the internetwork.

   D. Distance vector sends updates containing the state of their own links to all routers in the internetwork.

4. Which command displays RIP routing updates?

   A. `show ip route`

   B. `debug ip rip`

   C. `show protocols`

   D. `debug ip route`

5. Which of the following is true regarding RIPv2?

   A. It has a lower administrative distance than RIPv1.

   B. It converges faster than RIPv1.

   C. It has the same timers as RIPv1.

   D. It is harder to configure than RIPv1.

6. Which command will copy the IOS to a backup host on your network?

    A. `transfer IOS to 172.16.10.1`

    B. `copy run start`

    C. `copy tftp flash`

    D. `copy start tftp`

    E. `copy flash tftp`

7. You are troubleshooting a connectivity problem in your corporate network and want to isolate the problem. You suspect that a router on the route to an unreachable network is at fault. What IOS user exec command should you issue?

    A. `Router>ping`

    B. `Router>trace`

    C. `Router>show ip route`

    D. `Router>show interface`

    E. `Router>show cdp neighbors`

8. You copy a configuration from a network host to a router's RAM. The configuration looks correct, yet it is not working at all. What could the problem be?

    A. You copied the wrong configuration into RAM.

    B. You copied the configuration into flash memory instead.

    C. The copy did not override the `shutdown` command in `running-config`.

    D. The IOS became corrupted after the `copy` command was initiated.

9. A network administrator wants to upgrade the IOS of a router without removing the image currently installed. What command will display the amount of memory consumed by the current IOS image and indicate whether there is enough room available to hold both the current and new images?

    A. `show version`

    B. `show flash`

    C. `show memory`

    D. `show buffers`

    E. `show running-config`

10. Which command loads a new version of the Cisco IOS into a router?

    A. `copy flash ftp`

    B. `copy ftp flash`

    C. `copy flash tftp`

    D. `copy tftp flash`

Answers to Review Questions

1. A, E. There are actually three different ways to configure the same default route, but only two are shown in the answer. First, you can set a default route with the 0.0.0.0 0.0.0.0 mask and then specify the next hop, as in answer A. Or you can use 0.0.0.0 0.0.0.0 and use the exit interface instead of the next hop. Finally, you can use answer E with the `ip default-network` command.

2. B, E. Classful routing means that all hosts in the internetwork use the same mask. Classless routing means that you can use Variable Length Subnet Masks (VLSMs) and can also support discontiguous networking.

3. B, C. The distance-vector routing protocol sends its complete routing table out all active interfaces on periodic time intervals. Link-state routing protocols send updates containing the state of their own links to all routers in the internetwork.

4. B. `Debug ip rip` is used to show the Internet Protocol (IP) Routing Information Protocol (RIP) updates being sent and received on the router.

5. C. RIPv2 is pretty much just like RIPv1. It has the same administrative distance and timers and is configured just like RIPv1.

6. E. Explanation: To copy the IOS to a backup host, which is stored in flash memory by default, use the `copy flash tftp` command.

7. B. Explanation: The command `traceroute` (`trace` for short), which can be issued from user mode or privileged mode, is used to find the path a packet takes through an internetwork and will also show you where the packet stops because of an error on a router.

8. C. Explanation: Since the configuration looks correct, you probably didn't screw up the copy job. However, when you perform a copy from a network host to a router, the interfaces are automatically shut down and need to be manually enabled with the `no shutdown` command.

9. B. Explanation: The `show flash` command will provide you with the current IOS name and size, and the size of flash memory.

10. D. Explanation: The command `copy tftp flash` will allow you to copy a new IOS into flash memory on your router.

Chapter

5

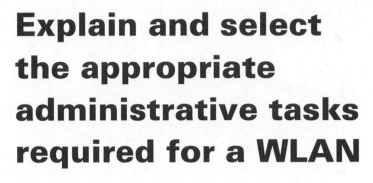

Explain and select the appropriate administrative tasks required for a WLAN

THE CISCO CCNA EXAM OBJECTIVES COVERED IN THIS CHAPTER INCLUDE:

- 5.1 Describe standards associated with wireless media (including: IEEE WI-FI Alliance, ITU/FCC)
- 5. 2 Identify and describe the purpose of the components in a small wireless network (including SSID, BSS, ESS)
- 5.3 Identify the basic parameters to configure on a wireless network to ensure that devices connect to the correct access point
- 5. 4 Compare and contrast wireless security features and capabilities of WPA security (including open, WEP, WPA-1/2)
- 5.5 Identify common issues with implementing wireless networks (including Interface, Miss configuration)

If you want to understand the basic wireless LANs, or WLANs, that are the most commonly used today, just think 10BaseT Ethernet with hubs. What this means is that our WLANs typically run half-duplex communication—everyone is sharing the same bandwidth and only one user is communicating at a time. This isn't necessarily bad—it's just not good enough. Because most people rely upon wireless networks today, it's critical that they evolve faster than greased lightning to keep up with our rapidly escalating needs. The good news is that this is actually happening—Cisco has reacted by coming up with an answer called the *Cisco Unified Wireless Solution* that works with all types of wireless connections. And it works securely too!

My goal in this chapter isn't so much to introduce you to wireless technologies in general; it's to familiarize you with Cisco's wireless technologies because, as you'd probably guess, there are differences—however subtle. Yes, I will cover basic wireless LAN technologies and committees, but the main objective here is to ensure that you understand wireless through Cisco's eyes and solidly grasp the solutions that Cisco provides.

For up-to-the-minute updates on the CCNA objectives covered by Cisco, please see www.lammle.com and/or www.sybex.com.

5.1 Describe standards associated with wireless media (including IEEE WI-FI Alliance, ITU/FCC)

Various agencies have been around for a very long time to help govern the use of wireless devices, frequencies, standards, and how the frequency spectrums are used. Table 5.1 shows the current agencies that help create, maintain, and even enforce wireless standards worldwide.

Because WLANs transmit over radio frequencies, they're regulated by the same types of laws used to govern things like AM/FM radios. It's the Federal Communications Commission (FCC) that regulates the use of wireless LAN devices, and the Institute of Electrical and Electronics Engineers (IEEE) takes it from there and creates standards based on what frequencies the FCC releases for public use.

TABLE 5.1   Wireless Agencies and Standards

Agency	Purpose	Web Site
Institute of Electrical and Electronics Engineers (IEEE)	Creates and maintains operational standards	www.ieee.org
Federal Communications Commission (FCC)	Regulates the use of wireless devices in the U.S.	www.fcc.gov
European Telecommunications Standards Institute (ETSI)	Chartered to produce common standards in Europe	www.etsi.org
Wi-Fi Alliance	Promotes and tests for WLAN interoperability	www.wi-fi.com
WLAN Association (WLANA)	Educates and raises consumer awareness regarding WLANs	www.wlana.org

The FCC has released three unlicensed bands for public use: 900MHz, 2.4GHz, and 5.7GHz. The 900MHz and 2.4GHz bands are referred to as the *Industrial, Scientific, and Medical* (ISM) bands, and the 5GHz band is known as the *Unlicensed National Information Infrastructure* (UNII) band. Figure 5.1 shows where the unlicensed bands sit within the RF spectrum.

FIGURE 5.1   Unlicensed frequencies

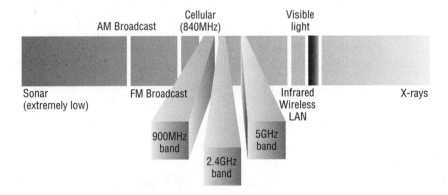

So, it follows that if you opt to deploy wireless in a range outside of the three public bands shown in Figure 5.1, you need to get a specific license from the FCC to do so. Once the FCC opened the three frequency ranges for public use, many manufacturers were able to start offering myriad products that flooded the market, with 802.11b/g being the most widely used wireless network today.

The Wi-Fi Alliance grants certification for interoperability among 802.11 products offered by various vendors. This certification provides a sort of comfort zone for the users purchasing the many types of products, although in my personal experience, it's just a whole lot easier if you buy all your access points from the same manufacturer!

In the current U.S. wireless LAN market, there are several accepted operational standards and drafts created and maintained by the IEEE. Let's take a look at these standards and then talk about how the most commonly used standards work.

The 802.11 Standards

Taking off from what you learned when reading about Ethernet, wireless networking has its own 802 standards group—remember, Ethernet's committee is 802.3. Wireless starts with 802.11, and there are various other up-and-coming standard groups as well, like 802.16 and 802.20. And there's no doubt that cellular networks will become huge players in our wireless future. But for now, we're going to concentrate on the 802.11 standards committee and subcommittees.

IEEE 802.11 was the first, original standardized WLAN at 1 and 2Mbps. It runs in the 2.4GHz radio frequency and was ratified in 1997 even though we didn't see many products pop up until around 1999 when 802.11b was introduced. All the committees listed in Table 5.2 are amendments to the original 802.11 standard except for 802.11F and 802.11T, which are both stand-alone documents.

TABLE 5.2   802.11 Committees and Subcommittees

Committee	Purpose
IEEE 802.11a	54Mbps, 5GHz standard
IEEE 802.11b	Enhancements to 802.11 to support 5.5 and 11Mbps
IEEE 802.11c	Bridge operation procedures; included in the IEEE 802.1D standard
IEEE 802.11d	International roaming extensions
IEEE 802.11e	Quality of service
IEEE 802.11F	Inter-Access Point Protocol
IEEE 802.11g	54Mbps, 2.4GHz standard (backward compatible with 802.11b)
IEEE 802.11h	Dynamic Frequency Selection (DFS) and Transmit Power Control (TPC) at 5Ghz
IEEE 802.11i	Enhanced security

TABLE 5.2   802.11 Committees and Subcommittees *(continued)*

Committee	Purpose
IEEE 802.11j	Extensions for Japan and U.S. public safety
IEEE 802.11k	Radio resource measurement enhancements
IEEE 802.11m	Maintenance of the standard; odds and ends
IEEE 802.11n	Higher throughput improvements using MIMO (multiple input, multiple output antennas)
IEEE 802.11p	Wireless Access for the Vehicular Environment (WAVE)
IEEE 802.11r	Fast roaming
IEEE 802.11s	ESS Extended Service Set Mesh Networking
IEEE 802.11T	Wireless Performance Prediction (WPP)
IEEE 802.11u	Internetworking with non-802 networks (cellular, for example)
IEEE 802.11v	Wireless network management
IEEE 802.11w	Protected management frames
IEEE 802.11y	3650–3700 operation in the U.S.

Exam Objectives

Understand the IEEE 802.11a specification.   802.11a runs in the 5GHz spectrum, and if you use the 802.11h extensions, you have 23 non-overlapping channels. 802.11a can run up to 54Mbps, but only if you are less than 50 feet from an access point.

Understand the IEEE 802.11b specification.   IEEE 802.11b runs in the 2.4GHz range and has three non-overlapping channels. It can handle long distances, but with a maximum data rate of up to 11Mpbs.

Understand the IEEE 802.11g specification.   IEEE 802.11g is 802.11b's big brother and runs in the same 2.4GHz range, but it has a higher data rate of 54Mbps if you are less than 100 feet from an access point.

5.2 Identify and describe the purpose of the components in a small wireless network (including SSID, BSS, ESS)

Transmitting a signal using the typical 802.11 specifications works a lot like it does with a basic Ethernet hub: They're both two-way forms of communication, and they both use the same frequency to both transmit and receive, often referred to as *half-duplex*, as mentioned earlier in the chapter. Wireless LANs (WLANs) use RF's that are radiated into the air from an antenna that creates radio waves. These waves can be absorbed, refracted, or reflected by walls, water, and metal surfaces, resulting in low signal strength. So, because of this innate vulnerability to surrounding environmental factors, it's pretty apparent that wireless will never offer us the same robustness as a wired network can, but that still doesn't mean we're not going to run wireless. Believe me, we definitely will!

We can increase the transmitting power and gain a greater transmitting distance, but doing so can create some nasty distortion, so it has to be done carefully. By using higher frequencies, we can attain higher data rates, but this is, unfortunately, at the cost of decreased transmitting distances. And if we use lower frequencies, we get to transmit greater distances but at lower data rates. This should make it pretty clear to you that understanding all the various types of WLANs you can implement is imperative to creating the LAN solution that best meets the specific requirements of the unique situation you're dealing with.

Also important to note is the fact that the 802.11 specifications were developed so that there would be no licensing required in most countries—to ensure the user the freedom to install and operate without any licensing or operating fees. This means that any manufacturer can create products and sell them at a local computer store or wherever. It also means that all our computers should be able to communicate wirelessly without configuring much, if anything at all.

2.4GHz (802.11b)

First on the menu is the 802.11b standard. It was the most widely deployed wireless standard, and it operates in the 2.4GHz unlicensed radio band that delivers a maximum data rate of 11Mbps. The 802.11b standard has been widely adopted by both vendors and customers who found that its 11Mbps data rate worked pretty well for most applications. But now that 802.11b has a big brother (802.11g), no one goes out and just buys an 802.11b card or access point anymore because why would you buy a 10Mbps Ethernet card when you can score a 10/100 Ethernet card for the same price?

An interesting thing about all Cisco 802.11 WLAN products is that they have the ability to data-rate-shift while moving. This allows the person operating at 11Mbps to shift to 5.5Mbps, 2Mbps, and finally still communicate farthest from the access point at 1Mbps. And furthermore, this rate shifting happens without losing connection and with no interaction from the user. Rate shifting also occurs on a transmission-by-transmission basis. This is important because it means that the access point can support multiple clients at varying speeds depending upon the location of each client.

The problem with 802.11b lies in how the Data Link layer is dealt with. In order to solve problems in the RF spectrum, a type of Ethernet collision detection was created called *CSMA/CA*, or *Carrier Sense Multiple Access with Collision Avoidance*. Check this out in Figure 5.2.

FIGURE 5.2   802.11b CSMA/CA

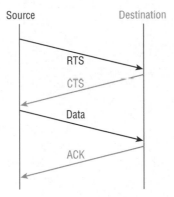

CSMA/CA is also called a *Request to Send, Clear to Send* (RTS/CTS) because of the way that hosts must communicate to the access point (AP). For every packet sent, an RTS/CTS and acknowledgment must be received, and because of this rather cumbersome process, it's kind of hard to believe that it all actually works!

2.4GHz (802.11g)

The 802.11g standard was ratified in June 2003 and is backward compatible to 802.11b. The 802.11g standard delivers the same 54Mbps maximum data rate as 802.11a but runs in the 2.4GHz range—the same as 802.11b.

Because 802.11b/g operates in the same 2.4GHz unlicensed band, migrating to 802.11g is an affordable choice for organizations with existing 802.11b wireless infrastructures. Just keep in mind that 802.11b products can't be "software upgraded" to 802.11g. This limitation is because 802.11g radios use a different chipset in order to deliver the higher data rate.

But still, much like Ethernet and Fast Ethernet, 802.11g products can be co-mingled with 802.11b products in the same network. Yet, for example, completely unlike Ethernet, if you have four users running 802.11g cards and one user starts using an 802.11b card, everyone connected to the same access point is then forced to run the 802.11b CSMA/CA method—an ugly fact that really makes throughput suffer. So to optimize performance, it's recommended that you disable the 802.11b-only modes on all your access points.

To explain this further, 802.11b uses a modulation technique called *Direct Sequence Spread Spectrum* (DSSS) that's just not as robust as the Orthogonal Frequency Division Multiplexing

(OFDM) modulation used by both 802.11g and 802.11a. 802.11g clients using OFDM enjoy much better performance at the same ranges as 802.11b clients do, but—and remember this—when 802.11g clients are operating at the 802.11b rates (11, 5.5, 2, and 1Mbps), they're actually using the same modulation 802.11b does.

Figure 5.3 shows the 14 different channels (each 22Mhz wide) that the FCC released in the 2.4GHz range.

FIGURE 5.3   ISM 2.4GHz channels

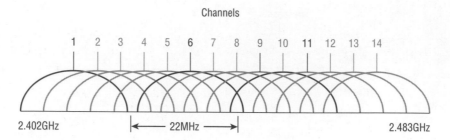

In the U.S., only 11 channels are configurable, with channels 1, 6, and 11 being non-overlapping. This allows you to have three access points in the same area without experiencing interference.

5GHz (802.11a)

The IEEE ratified the 802.11a standard in 1999, but the first 802.11a products didn't begin appearing on the market until late 2001—and boy were they pricey! The 802.11a standard delivers a maximum data rate of 54Mbps with 12 non-overlapping frequency channels. Figure 5.4 shows the UNII bands.

FIGURE 5.4   UNII 5GHz band has 12 non-overlapping channels (U.S.).

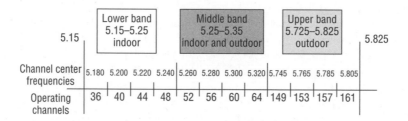

Operating in the 5GHz radio band, 802.11a is also immune to interference from devices that operate in the 2.4GHz band, like microwave ovens, cordless phones, and Bluetooth devices. 802.11a isn't backward compatible with 802.11b because they are different frequencies, so you don't get to just "upgrade" part of your network and expect everything to work together in perfect harmony. But no worries—there are plenty of dual-radio devices that will work in both types of networks. A definite plus for 802.11a is that it can work in the same physical environment without interference from 802.11b users.

Similarly to the 802.11b radios, all 802.11a products also have the ability to data-rate-shift while moving. The 802.11a products allow the person operating at 54Mbps to shift to 48Mbps, 36Mbps, 24Mbps, 18Mbps, 12Mbps, 9Mbps, and finally still communicate farthest from the AP at 6Mbps.

Exam Objectives

Remember the three overlapping channels used with the 2.4Ghz range. In the U.S., only 11 channels are configurable, with channels 1, 6, and 11 being non-overlapping.

Remember how many channels are non-overlapping in the 5Ghz range. The 802.11a standard delivers a maximum data rate of 54Mbps with 12 non-overlapping frequency channels.

5.3 Identify the basic parameters to configure on a wireless network to ensure that devices connect to the correct access point

It's true that a wireless interface can really just be another interface on a router, and it looks just like that in the routing table as well, or a separate device called an access point. In order to bring up the wireless interface, more configurations are needed than for a simple Fast Ethernet interface.

So, check out the following output, and then I'll tell you about the special configuration needs for this wireless interface:

```
R2(config-if)#int dot11radio0/3/0
R2(config-if)#ip address 10.1.8.1 255.255.255.0
R2(config-if)#description Connection to Corp ISR Router
R2(config-if)#no shut
R2(config-if)#ssid ADMIN
R2(config-if-ssid)#guest-mode
R2(config-if-ssid)#authentication open
R2(config-if-ssid)#infrastructure-ssid
R2(config-if-ssid)#no shut
```

So, what we see here is that everything is pretty commonplace until we get to the SSID configuration. This is the Service Set Identifier that creates a wireless network that hosts can connect to.

Unlike access points, the interface on the router is actually a routed interface, which is the reason why the IP address is placed under the physical interface—typically, the IP address would be placed under the management VLAN or Bridge-Group Virtual Interface (BVI).

That guest-mode line means that the interface will broadcast the SSID so that wireless hosts will understand that they can connect to this interface.

Authentication open means just that . . . no authentication. (Even so, you still have to type that command in at minimum to make the wireless interface work.)

Last, the infrastructure-ssid indicates that this interface can be used to communicate to other access points, or other devices on the infrastructure—to the actual wired network itself.

But wait, we're not done yet—we still need to configure the DHCP pool for the wireless clients:

```
R2#config t
R2(config)#ip dhcp pool Admin
R2(dhcp-config)#network 10.1.8.0 255.255.255.0
R2(dhcp-config)#default-router 10.1.8.1
R2(dhcp-config)#exit
R2(config)#ip dhcp excluded-address 10.1.8.1
R2(config)#
```

Creating DHCP pools on a router is actually a pretty simple process. To do so, you just create the pool name, add the network/subnet and the default gateway, and exclude any addresses you don't want handed out (like the default gateway address). And you'd usually add a DNS server as well.

Understand that the pool is basically attached to an interface that has an address from the same subnet created by the DHCP pool. In the above example, this is interface dot11radio 0/3/0. We can easily create another pool and have it connected with a LAN interface as in FastEthernet 0/0 by assigning an address on FastEthernet 0/0 that is from the subnet pool.

Service Sets

There are typically two types of wireless networks that you can create with wired networks:

- Basic Service Set (BSS)
- Extended Service Set (ESS)

Both types of networks define what we call a Service Set ID (SSID) that's used to advertise your wireless network so hosts can connect to the access point (AP). And you can have multiple SSID's configured on an access point for security reasons. For example, you can designate that one SSID is open access for a public hot spot, while another SSID can use WEP or WPA2 for the employees that work at this public hot spot. The SSID name is broadcasted out the AP by default so the clients can find the AP and connect to the wireless network, and of course you can turn this feature off for security reasons.

BSS/IBSS

A BSS only involves a single access point. You create a BSS and by bringing up an AP and creating a name for the service set ID (SSID). Users can then connect to and use this SSID to access the wireless network, which provides connectivity to the wired resources. When the AP connects to a wired network, it then becomes known as an Infrastructure basic service set, or IBSS. Keep in mind that if you have a BSS/IBSS, users won't be able to maintain network connectivity when roaming from AP to AP because each AP is configured with a different SSID name.

BSS wireless networks are also really helpful if you happen to have a couple hosts that need to establish wireless communication directly between just them. You can also make this happen through something we call ad-hoc networking, but if you have an AP between the hosts it's just called a BSS.

Figure 5.5 shows a basic service set using one SSID:

FIGURE 5.5   Basic Service Set (BSS)

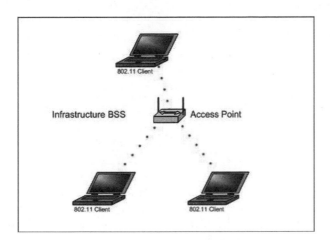

ESS

Mobile wireless clients can roam around within the same network if you set all your access points to the same Service Set ID (SSID). Doing this creates an extended service set (ESS). Figure 5.6 shows four AP's configured with the same SSID in an office thereby creating the ESS network:

For users to be able to roam throughout the wireless network—from AP to AP without losing their connection to the network—all APs must overlap by at least 10% or more, and the channels on each AP shouldn't be set the same either. And remember, in an 802.11b/g network, there are only three non-overlapping channels (1, 6, 11) so design is super important here!

Exam Objectives

Remember how to set a service set identifier (SSID) on a wireless routed interface.   From the interface mode of the wireless routed interface, used the ssid *ssid-name* command. This is the service set identifier that creates a wireless network that hosts can connect to.

FIGURE 5.6 Extended Service Set (ESS)

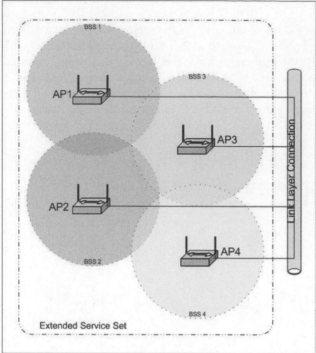

Remember how to configured a wireless interface on a router to allow hosts to communicate to a wired infrastructure. Under the Router(config-if-ssid)# command prompt, use the command infrastructure-ssid to indicate that this interface can be used to communicate to other access points, or to the wired network.

5. 4 Compare and contrast wireless security features and capabilities of WPA security (including open, WEP, WPA-1/2)

By default, wireless security is nonexistent on access points and clients. The original 802.11 committee just didn't imagine that wireless hosts would one day outnumber bounded media hosts, but that's truly where we're headed. Also, and unfortunately, just as with the IPv4 routed protocol, engineers and scientists didn't add security standards that are robust enough to work in a corporate environment. So, we're left with proprietary solution add-ons to aid us in our quest to create a secure wireless network. And no—I'm not just sitting here bashing the standards committees because the security problems we're experiencing were also created by the U.S. government because of export issues with its own security standards. Our world is a complicated place, so it follows that our security solutions are going to be as well.

A good place to start is by discussing the standard basic security that was added into the original 802.11 standards and why those standards are way too flimsy and incomplete to enable us to create a secure wireless network relevant to today's challenges.

Open Access

All Wi-Fi Certified wireless LAN products are shipped in "open-access" mode, with their security features turned off. While open access or no security may be appropriate and acceptable for public hot spots such as coffee shops, college campuses, and maybe airports, it's definitely not an option for an enterprise organization, and likely not even adequate for your private home network.

Security needs to be enabled on wireless devices during their installation in enterprise environments. It may come as quite a shock, but some companies actually don't enable any WLAN security features. Obviously, the companies that don't are exposing their networks to tremendous risk!

The reason that the products are shipped with open access is so that any person who knows absolutely nothing about computers can just buy an access point, plug it into their cable or DSL modem, and voilà—they're up and running. It's marketing, plain and simple, and simplicity sells.

SSIDs, WEP, and MAC Address Authentication

What the original designers of 802.11 did to create basic security was include the use of Service Set Identifiers (SSIDs), open or shared-key authentication, static Wired Equivalency Protocol (WEP), and optional Media Access Control (MAC) authentication. Sounds like a lot, but none of these really offers any type of serious security solution—all they may be close to adequate for is use on a common home network.

SSID is a common network name for the devices in a WLAN system that create the wireless LAN. An SSID prevents access by any client device that doesn't have the SSID. The thing is, by default, an access point broadcasts its SSID in its beacon many times a second. And even if SSID broadcasting is turned off, a bad guy can discover the SSID by monitoring the network and just waiting for a client response to the access point. Why? Because, believe it or not, that information, as regulated in the original 802.11 specifications, must be sent in the clear—how secure!

Two types of authentication were specified by the IEEE 802.11 committee: *open* and *shared-key authentication*. Open authentication involves little more than supplying the correct SSID—but it's the most common method in use today. With shared-key authentication, the access point sends the client device a challenge-text packet that the client must then encrypt with the correct WEP key and return to the access point. Without the correct key, authentication will fail and the client won't be allowed to associate with the access point. But shared-key authentication is still not considered secure because all an intruder has to do to get around this is detect both the clear-text challenge and the same challenge encrypted with a WEP key and then decipher the WEP key. Surprise—shared key isn't used in today's WLANs because of clear-text challenge.

With open authentication, even if a client can complete authentication and associate with an access point, the use of WEP prevents the client from sending and receiving data from the access point unless the client has the correct WEP key. A WEP key is composed of either 40 or 128 bits and, in its basic form, is usually statically defined by the network administrator on the access point and all clients that communicate with that access point. When static WEP keys are used, a network administrator must perform the time-consuming task of entering the same keys on every device in the WLAN. Obviously, we now have fixes for this because this would be administratively impossible in today's huge corporate wireless networks!

Last, client MAC addresses can be statically typed into each access point, and any of them that show up without that MAC addresses in the filter table would be denied access. Sounds good, but of course all MAC layer information must be sent in the clear—anyone equipped with a free wireless sniffer can just read the client packets sent to the access point and spoof their MAC address.

WEP can actually work if administered correctly. But basic static WEP keys are no longer a viable option in today's corporate networks without some of the proprietary fixes that run on top of it. So let's talk about some of these now.

WPA or WPA 2 Pre-Shared Key

Although this is another form of basic security that's really just an add-on to the specifications, *WPA* or *WPA2 Pre-Shared Key* (PSK) is a better form of wireless security than any other basic wireless security method mentioned so far. I did say basic.

The PSK verifies users via a password or identifying code (also called a *passphrase*) on both the client machine and the access point. A client only gains access to the network if its password matches the access point's password. The PSK also provides keying material that TKIP or AES uses to generate an encryption key for each packet of transmitted data. While more secure than static WEP, PSK still has a lot in common with static WEP in that the PSK is stored on the client station and can be compromised if the client station is lost or stolen even though finding this key isn't all that easy to do. It's a definite recommendation to use a strong PSK passphrase that includes a mixture of letters, numbers, and nonalphanumeric characters.

Wi-Fi Protected Access (WPA) is a standard developed in 2003 by the Wi-Fi Alliance, formerly known as WECA. WPA provides a standard for authentication and encryption of WLANs that's intended to solve known security problems existing up to and including the year 2003. This takes into account the well-publicized AirSnort and man-in-the-middle WLAN attacks. Of course, now we'll use WPA2 to help us with today's security issues.

WPA is a step toward the IEEE 802.11i standard and uses many of the same components, with the exception of encryption—802.11i (WPA2) uses AES-CCMP encryption. The IEEE 802.11i standard replaced Wired Equivalent Privacy (WEP) with a specific mode of the Advanced Encryption Standard (AES) known as the Counter Mode Cipher Block Chaining-Message Authentication Code (CBC-MAC) protocol (CCMP). This allows AES-CCMP to provide both data confidentiality (encryption) and data integrity.

WPA's mechanisms are designed to be implementable by current hardware vendors, meaning that users should be able to implement WPA on their systems with only a firmware/software modification.

 The IEEE 802.11i standard has been sanctioned by WPA and is termed WPA version 2.

Exam Objectives

Remember the two types of original 802.11 authentication.   Two types of authentication were specified by the IEEE 802.11 committee: open and shared-key authentication

Remember the standard developed by the Wi-Fi Alliance.   Wi-Fi Protected Access (WPA) is a standard developed by the Wi-Fi Alliance that provides a standard for authentication and encryption of WLANs.

5.5 Identify common issues with implementing wireless networks (including Interface, Miss configuration)

See objective 5.3 for information regarding this objective.

Review Questions

1. What is the frequency range of the IEEE 802.11b standard?
    A. 2.4Gbps
    B. 5Gbps
    C. 2.4GHz
    D. 5GHz

2. What is the frequency range of the IEEE 802.11a standard?
    A. 2.4Gbps
    B. 5Gbps
    C. 2.4GHz
    D. 5GHz

3. What is the frequency range of the IEEE 802.11g standard?
    A. 2.4Gbps
    B. 5Gbps
    C. 2.4GHz
    D. 5GHz

4. What is the encryption used in WPA2?
    A. AES-CCMP
    B. WEP
    C. PSK
    D. TKIP

5. How many non-overlapping channels are available with 802.11g?
    A. 3
    B. 12
    C. 23
    D. 40

6. How many non-overlapping channels are available with 802.11b?
    A. 3
    B. 12
    C. 23
    D. 40

7. How many non-overlapping channels are available with 802.11a?

   A. 3

   B. 12

   C. 23

   D. 40

8. What is the maximum data rate for the 802.11a standard?

   A. 6Mbps

   B. 11Mbps

   C. 22Mbps

   D. 54Mbps

9. What is the maximum data rate for the 802.11g standard?

   A. 6Mbps

   B. 11Mbps

   C. 22Mbps

   D. 54Mbps

10. What is the maximum data rate for the 802.11b standard?

   A. 6Mbps

   B. 11Mbps

   C. 22Mbps

   D. 54Mbps

Answers to Review Questions

1. C. The IEEE 802.11b and IEEE 802.11b both run in the 2.4GHz RF range.

2. D. The IEEE 802.11a standard runs in the 5GHz RF range.

3. C. The IEEE 802.11b and IEEE 802.11b both run in the 2.4GHz RF range.

4. C. WPA2 uses the Advanced Encryption Standard (AES) known as the Counter Mode Cipher Block Chaining-Message Authentication Code (CBC-MAC) protocol (CCMP).

5. A . The IEEE 802.11g standard provides three non-overlapping channels

6. A. The IEEE 802.11b standard provides three non-overlapping channels

7. B. The IEEE 802.11a standard provides up to 12 non-overlapping channels.

8. D. The IEEE 802.11a standard provides a maximum data rate of up to 54Mbps.

9. D. The IEEE 802.11g standard provides a maximum data rate of up to 54Mbps.

10. B. The IEEE 802.11b standard provides a maximum data rate of up to 11Mbps

Chapter

6

Identify security threats to a network and describe general methods to mitigate those threats

THE CISCO CCNA EXAM OBJECTIVES COVERED IN THIS CHAPTER INCLUDE:

- 6. 1 Describe today's increasing network security threats and explain the need to implement a comprehensive security policy to mitigate the threats
- 6. 2 Explain general methods to mitigate common security threats to network devices, hosts, and applications
- 6. 3 Describe the functions of common security appliances and applications
- 6. 4 Describe security recommended practices, including initial steps to secure network devices

If you're a sysadmin, it's my guess that shielding sensitive, critical data, as well as your network's resources, from every possible evil exploit is a top priority. Right? Good to know you're on the right page—Cisco has some really effective security solutions that will arm you with the tools you need to make this happen.

Basically, covering you and your network's posterior is going to be the focus of this chapter. You'll learn a lot about deterring the most common threats to your network's security with Cisco routers and IOS Firewalls that, together, offer quite a powerful, integrated detection package against many types of invasions. I'm going to give you the lowdown on how the Cisco IOS Firewall provides actual security and policy enforcement for both your internal and external networking needs. I'll also show you how to create secure connections to any remote locations you may have living on the fringes.

For up-to-the-minute updates on the CCNA objectives covered by this chapter, please see www.lammle.com and/or www.sybex.com.

6.1 Describe today's increasing network security threats and explain the need to implement a comprehensive security policy to mitigate the threats

You see this a lot—typically, in medium-sized to large enterprise networks, the various strategies for security are based on a some recipe of internal and perimeter routers plus firewall devices. Internal routers provide additional security to the network by screening traffic to various parts of the protected corporate network, and they do this by using access lists. You can see where each of these types of devices is found in Figure 6.1.

I'll use the terms *trusted network* and *untrusted network* throughout this chapter, so it's important that you can see where they are found in a typical secured network. The demilitarized zone (DMZ) can be global (real) Internet addresses or private addresses, depending on how you configure your firewall, but this is typically where you'll find the HTTP, DNS, email, and other Internet-type corporate servers.

FIGURE 6.1   A typical secured network

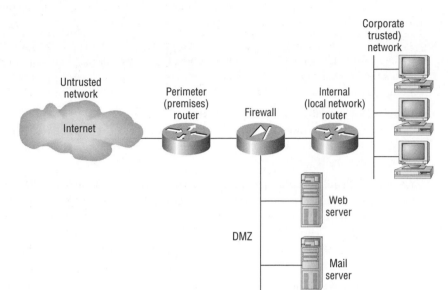

Instead of having routers, we can (as you already know) use virtual local area networks (VLANs) with switches on the inside trusted network. Multilayer switches containing their own security features can sometimes replace internal (LAN) routers to provide higher performance in VLAN architectures.

Let's discuss the security threats a typical secured internetwork faces; then I'll provide some ways of protecting the internetwork using the Cisco IOS Firewall feature set and access lists.

Recognizing Security Threats

Yes, it's true: Security attacks vary considerably in their complexity and threat level, and some even happen because of WUI, or witless user ignorance. (This term isn't an exam objective, but it does occur more than you'd think!)

You see, it all comes down to planning, or rather, lack thereof. Basically, the vital tool that the Internet has become today was absolutely unforeseen by those who brought it into being. This is a big reason why security is now such an issue—most IP implementations are innately insecure. No worries though, because Cisco has a few tricks up its sleeve to help us with this. But first, let's examine some common attack profiles:

Application layer attacks   These attacks commonly zero in on well-known holes in the software that's typically found running on servers. Favorite targets include FTP, sendmail, and HTTP. Because the permissions level granted to these accounts is most often "privileged," bad guys simply access and exploit the machine that's running one of the applications I just mentioned.

Autorooters   You can think of these as a kind of hacker automaton. Bad guys use something called a *rootkit* to probe, scan, and then capture data on a strategically positioned computer that's poised to give them "eyes" into entire systems—automatically!

Backdoors   These are simply paths leading into a computer or network. Through simple invasions, or via more elaborate "Trojan horse" code, bad guys can use their implanted inroads into a specific host or even a network whenever they want to—until you detect and stop them, that is!

Denial of service (DoS) and distributed denial of service (DDoS) attacks   Basically, a service is made unavailable by overwhelming the system that normally provides it. A denial of service attack is characterized by a flood of packets that are requesting a TCP connection to a server and there are several different flavors:

TCP SYN flood   Begins when a client initiates a seemingly run-of-the-mill TCP connection and sends a SYN message to a server. The server predictably responds by sending a SYN-ACK message back to the client machine, which then establishes the connection by returning an ACK message. Sounds fine, but it's actually during this process—when the connection is only halfway open—that the victim machine is literally flooded with a deluge of half-open connections and pretty much becomes paralyzed.

"Ping of death" attacks   You probably know that TCP/IP's maximum packet size is 65,536 octets. It's okay if you didn't know that—just understand that this attack is executed by simply pinging with oversized packets, causing a device to keep rebooting incessantly, freeze up, or just totally crash.

Tribe Flood Network (TFN) and Tribe Flood Network 2000 (TFN2K)   These nasty little numbers are more complex in that they initiate synchronized DoS attacks from multiple sources and can target multiple devices. This is achieved, in part, by something known as "IP spoofing," which I'll be describing soon.

Stacheldraht   This attack is actually a mélange of methods, and it translates from the German term for barbed wire. It basically incorporates TFN and adds a dash of encryption. It all begins with a huge invasion at the root level, followed up with a DoS attack finale.

IP spoofing   This is pretty much what it sounds like it is—a bad guy from within or outside of your network masquerades as a trusted host machine by doing one of two things: presenting with an IP address that's inside your network's scope of trusted addresses or using an approved, trusted external IP address. Because the hacker's true identity is veiled behind the spoofed address, this is often just the beginning of your problems.

Man-in-the-middle attacks   Interception! But it's not a football, it's a bunch of your network's packets—your precious data! A common guilty party could be someone working for your very own ISP using a tool known as a *sniffer* (discussed later) and augmenting it with routing and transport protocols.

Network reconnaissance   Before breaking into a network, hackers often gather all the information they can about it, because the more they know about the network, the better they can compromise it. They accomplish their objectives through methods like port scans, DNS queries, and ping sweeps.

Packet sniffers   This is the tool I mentioned earlier, but I didn't tell you what it is, and it may come as a surprise that it's actually software. Here's how it works—a network adapter card is set to promiscuous mode so that it will send all packets snagged from the network's physical layer through to a special application to be viewed and sorted out. A packet sniffer can nick some highly valuable, sensitive data including, but not limited to, passwords and usernames, making them prized among identity thieves.

Password attacks   These come in many flavors, and even though they can be achieved via more sophisticated types of attacks like IP spoofing, packet sniffing, and Trojan horses, their sole purpose is to—surprise—discover user passwords so that the thief can pretend to be a valid user and then access that user's privileges and resources.

Brute force attack   Another software-oriented attack that employs a program running on a targeted network that tries to log in to some type of shared network resource like a server. For the hacker, it's ideal if the accessed accounts have a lot of privileges because then the bad guys can form backdoors to use to gain access later and bypass the need for passwords entirely.

Port redirection attacks   This approach requires a host machine that the hacker has broken into and uses to get wonky traffic (that normally wouldn't be allowed passage) through a firewall.

Trojan horse attacks and viruses   These two are actually pretty similar—both Trojan horses and viruses infect user machines with malicious code and mess it up with varying degrees of paralysis, destruction, even death! But they do have their differences—viruses are really just nasty programs attached to `command.com`, which just happens to be the main interpreter for all Windows systems. Viruses then run amok, deleting files and infecting any flavor of `command.com` they find on the now-diseased machine. The difference between a virus and a Trojan horse is that Trojans are actually complete applications encased inside code that makes them appear to be completely different entities—say, a simple, innocent game—than the ugly implements of destruction they truly are!

Trust exploitation attacks   These happen when someone exploits a trust relationship inside your network. For example, a company's perimeter network connection usually shelters important things like SMTP, DNS, and HTTP servers, making the servers really vulnerable because they're all on the same segment.

To be honest, I'm not going to go into detail on how to mitigate each and every one of the security threats I just talked about, not only because that would be outside the scope of this book, but also because the methods I am going to teach you will truly protect you from being attacked in general. You will learn enough tricks to make all but the most determined bad guys give up on you and search for easier prey. So basically, think of this as a chapter on how to practice "safe networking."

Exam Objectives

Remember the basic strategy for security.   In medium-sized to large enterprise networks, the various strategies for security are based on some recipe of internal and perimeter routers plus firewall devices.

Remember the four typical denial of service attacks. There are four typical denial of service attacks used on today's networks: TCP SYN flood, ping of death, Tribe Flood Network and Stacheldraht.

6.2 Explain general methods to mitigate common security threats to network devices, hosts, and applications

Cisco has a very cool product called the *Adaptive Security Appliance*, or ASA. But there's a catch or two—it's a pretty pricey little beauty that scales in cost depending on the modules you choose (for example, intrusion prevention). Plus, the ASA is actually above the objectives of this book. I just personally think is the best product on the market.

Cisco IOS software runs on upwards of 80 percent of the Internet backbone routers out there; it's probably the most critical part of network infrastructure. So, let's just keep it real and use the Cisco IOS's software-based security, known as the *Cisco IOS Firewall* feature set, for our end-to-end Internet, intranet, and remote-access network security solutions. Let's take a look.

Cisco's IOS Firewall

Here's where you're going to find out how to mitigate some of the more common security threats on the list I gave you earlier in this chapter by using these Cisco IOS Firewall features:

Stateful IOS Firewall inspection engine This is your perimeter protection feature because it gives your internal users secure access control on a per-application basis. People often call it *Context-based Access Control* (CBAC).

Intrusion detection A deep packet inspection tool that lets you monitor, intercept, and respond to abuse in real time by referencing 102 of the most common attack and intrusion detection signatures.

Firewall voice traversal An application-level feature based on the protocol's understanding of call flow as well as the relevant open channels. It supports both the H.323v2 and Session Initiation Protocol (SIP) voice protocols.

ICMP inspection Basically permits responses to ICMP packets like ping and traceroute that come from inside your firewall while denying other ICMP traffic.

Authentication proxy A feature that makes users authenticate anytime they want to access the network's resources through HTTP, HTTPS, FTP, and Telnet. It keeps personal network access profiles for users and automatically gets them for you from a RADIUS or TACACS+ server and applies them as well.

Destination URL policy management   A buffet of features that's commonly referred to as *URL Filtering*.

Per-user firewalls   Personalized, user-specific, downloadable firewalls obtained through service providers. You can also get personalized ACLs and other settings via AAA server profile storage.

Cisco IOS router and firewall provisioning   Allows for no-touch router provisioning, version updates, and security policies.

Denial of service (DoS) detection and prevention   A feature that checks packet headers and drops any packets it finds suspicious.

Dynamic port mapping   A sort of adapter that permits applications supported by firewalls on nonstandard ports.

Java applet blocking   Protects you from any strange, unrecognized Java applets.

Basic and Advanced Traffic Filtering

You can use standard, extended, even dynamic ACLs like Lock-and-Key traffic filtering with Cisco's IOS Firewall. And you get to apply access controls to any network segment you want. Plus, you can specify the exact kind of traffic you want to allow to pass through any segment.

Policy-based, multi-interface support   Allows you to control user access by IP address and interface depending on your security policy.

Network Address Translation (NAT)   Conceals the internal network from the outside, increasing security.

Time-based access lists   Determine security policies based upon the exact time of day and the particular day of the week.

Peer router authentication   Guarantees that routers are getting dependable routing information from actual, trusted sources. (For this to work, you need a routing protocol that supports authentication, like RIPv2, EIGRP, or OSPF.)

Now that you've been briefed on security threats, relevant features of the Cisco IOS Firewall, and how to use that software to your advantage, let's dive deep into the world of access lists and learn how to use ACLs to mitigate security threats. They really are powerful tools, so pay attention!

Exam Objectives

Remember the basic services that the Cisco IOS Firewall provides.   The Cisco IOS Firewall provides at a minimum stateful IOS firewall inspection engine, intrusion detection, firewall voice traversal, ICMP inspection and authentication proxy, among many other services.

6.3 Describe the functions of common security appliances and applications

In this objective, I'll discuss the most commonly used advanced access control lists and applications used by Cisco routers. But first, I am going to mention two security appliances typically found on network.

Security Appliances

Two technologies that we can use on our networks that provide security are intrusion prevention systems (IPS) and Intrusion detection systems (IDS).

An IPS is an applicance that monitors network and activities for malicious or unwanted behavior and can react, in real-time, to block or prevent those activities. IPS, for example, will operate in-line to monitor all network traffic for malicious code or attacks. When an attack is detected, it can drop the offending packets while still allowing all other traffic to pass.

An IDS generally detects unwanted manipulations to computer systems, mainly through the Internet. The manipulations may take the form of attacks by crackers. An intrusion detection system is used to detect many types of malicious network traffic and computer usage that can't be detected by a conventional firewall. This includes network attacks against vulnerable services, data driven attacks on applications, host based attacks such as privilege escalation, unauthorized logins and access to sensitive files, and malware (viruses, trojan horses, and worms).

Lock and Key (Dynamic ACLs)

This flavor of ACL depends on either remote or local Telnet authentication in combination with extended ACLs.

Before you can configure a dynamic ACL, you need to apply an extended ACL on your router to stop the flow of traffic through it. The only way anyone can get through the blockade is if they telnet the router and gain authentication. It works like this: The Telnet connection the user initiated gets dropped and is replaced with a single-entry dynamic ACL that's appended to the extended ACL already in place. This causes traffic to be allowed through for a specific amount of time, and as you may have guessed, time-outs can and do happen.

Reflexive ACLs

These ACLs filter IP packets depending upon upper-layer session information, and they often permit outbound traffic to pass but place limitations on inbound traffic. You can't define reflexive ACLs with numbered or standard IP ACLs, or any other protocol ACLs for that matter. They can be used along with other standard or static extended ACLs, but they're only defined with extended named IP ACLs—that's it.

Time-Based ACLs

Time-based ACLs work a lot like extended ACLs do, but their type of access control is totally time oriented. Basically, you specify a certain time of day and week and then identify that particular period by giving it a name referenced by a task. So, by necessity, the reference function will fall under whatever time constraints you've dictated. The time period is based upon the router's clock, but I highly recommend using it in conjunction with Network Time Protocol (NTP) synchronization.

Here's an example:

```
Corp#config t
Corp(config)#time-range no-http
Corp(config-time-range)#periodic we?
Wednesday  weekdays  weekend
Corp(config-time-range)#periodic weekend ?
  hh:mm  Starting time
Corp(config-time-range)#periodic weekend 06:00 to 12:00
Corp(config-time-range)#exit
Corp(config)#time-range tcp-yes
Corp(config-time-range)#periodic weekend 06:00 to 12:00
Corp(config-time-range)#exit
Corp(config)#ip access-list extended Time
Corp(config-ext-nacl)#deny tcp any any eq www time-range no-http
Corp(config-ext-nacl)#permit tcp any any time-range tcp-yes
Corp(config-ext-nacl)#interface f0/0
Corp(config-if)#ip access-group Time in
Corp(config-if)#do show time-range
time-range entry: no-http (inactive)
   periodic weekdays 8:00 to 15:00
   used in: IP ACL entry
time-range entry: tcp-yes (inactive)
   periodic weekend 8:00 to 13:00
   used in: IP ACL entry
Corp(config-if)#
```

The `time-range` command is pretty flexible and will drive users crazy if you deny them basic network access or access to the Internet during off-hours. Be careful with the preceding commands—make sure you test your list on a nonproduction network before you implement the lists on your production network.

Remarks

This is the tool you grab to use the `remark` keyword, and it's really important because it arms you with the ability to include comments, or rather *remarks*, regarding the entries you've made in both your IP standard and extended ACLs. Remarks are very cool because they efficiently increase your ability to examine and understand your ACLs to the superhero level. Without them, you'd be caught in a quagmire of meaningless numbers without anything to help you recall what those numbers mean.

Even though you have the option of placing your remarks either before or after a permit or deny statement, I totally recommend that you choose to position them consistently, so you don't get confused about which remark is relevant to which one of your permit or deny statements.

To get this going for both standard and extended ACLs, just use the access-list *access-list number* remark *remark* global configuration command. And if you want to get rid of a remark, just use the command's no form.

Let's take a look at an example of how to use the remark command:

```
R2#config t
R2(config)#access-list 110 remark Permit Bob from Sales Only To Finance
R2(config)#access-list 110 permit ip host 172.16.10.1 172.16.20.0 0.0.0.255
R2(config)#access-list 110 deny ip 172.16.10.0 0.0.0.255
172.16.20.0 0.0.0.255
R2(config)#ip access-list extended No_Telnet
R2(config-ext-nacl)#remark Deny all of Sales from Telnetting
to Marketing
R2(config-ext-nacl)#deny tcp 172.16.30.0 0.0.0.255
172.16.40.0 0.0.0.255 eq 23
R2(config-ext-nacl)#permit ip any any
R2(config-ext-nacl)#do show run
[output cut]
!
ip access-list extended No_Telnet
 remark Stop all of Sales from Telnetting to Marketing
 deny   tcp 172.16.30.0 0.0.0.255 172.16.40.0 0.0.0.255 eq telnet
 permit ip any any
!
access-list 110 remark Permit Bob from Sales Only To Finance
access-list 110 permit ip host 172.16.10.1 172.16.20.0 0.0.0.255
access-list 110 deny    ip 172.16.10.0 0.0.0.255 172.16.20.0 0.0.0.255
!
```

I was able to add a remark to both an extended lists and a named access list. However, you cannot see these remarks in the output of the show access-list command, only in the running-config.

Context-Based Access Control (Cisco IOS Firewall)

You've got to have the Cisco IOS Firewall set in the IOS to make use of CBAC, and the funny thing is, it's rare to hear someone—even Cisco—differentiate between the two. People usually just refer to the Cisco IOS Firewall and leave it at that. But what is it?

Well, the CBAC's job is to scrutinize any and all traffic that's attempting to come through the firewall, so it can find out about and control the state information for TCP and UDP sessions. And it uses that very information it's gathered to determine whether to create a temporary pathway into the firewall's access lists.

To make this happen, just configure `ip inspect` lists in the same direction that the traffic is flowing. If you don't do this, any return traffic won't be able to get back through, which will negatively impact any session connections originating from inside the internal network in a big way.

Take a look at Figure 6.2, which illustrates in a very simple way how the Cisco IOS Firewall (CBAC) works.

FIGURE 6.2   Cisco IOS Firewall (CBAC) example

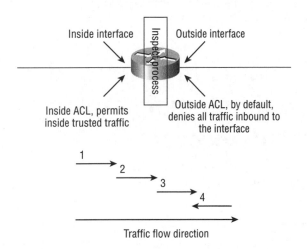

A router that's configured with the Cisco IOS Firewall will process traffic in the following manner:

1. First, if the inside ACL approves, the router will get all inside packets sent to it.

2. Next, the approved traffic is subjected to the firewall's `ip inspect` process, which adds the approved connection's state information into the state table.

3. Finally, the traffic passes through the IP inspect process, which then creates a dynamic ACL entry and puts it into the outside ACL so that the return traffic will be allowed to pass back through the router.

Authentication Proxy

I have this set on all of my routers, but to be able to do that you must also have the Cisco IOS Firewall feature set up. I have the configuration set up this way because the authentication proxy is a good thing to have on your side.

This is true because it authenticates inbound users, outbound users, or both. Those who would normally be blocked by an ACL can just bring up a browser to get through the firewall and then authenticate on a TACACS+ or RADIUS server.

Exam Objectives

Remember the two types of security appliances typically found on a network   The two types of security appliances that you'll typically find on a network that provide security are intrusion prevention systems (IPS) and intrusion detection systems (IDS).

Understand what CBAC's is   Context-Based Access Control scrutinizes any and all traffic that's attempting to come through the firewall, so it can find out about and control the state information for TCP and UDP sessions.

6.4 Describe security recommended practices, including initial steps to secure network devices

Here's a list of the many security threats you can mitigate with ACLs:

- IP address spoofing, inbound
- IP address spoofing, outbound
- Denial of service (DoS) TCP SYN attacks, blocking external attacks
- DoS TCP SYN attacks, using TCP Intercept
- DoS smurf attacks
- Filtering ICMP messages, inbound
- Filtering ICMP messages, outbound
- Filtering traceroute

It's generally wise not to allow into a private network any IP packets that contain the source address of any internal hosts or networks—just don't do it!

Here's a list of rules to live by when configuring ACLs from the Internet to your production network to mitigate security problems:

- Deny any addresses from your internal networks.
- Deny any local host addresses (127.0.0.0/8).

- Deny any reserved private addresses.
- Deny any addresses in the IP multicast address range (224.0.0.0/4).

None of the above addresses should be allowed to enter your internetwork.

Exam Objectives

Remember the list of typical rules when configuring ACLs from the Internet to your production network to mitigate security problems.   Deny any addresses from your internal networks, deny any local host addresses (127.0.0.0/8), deny any reserved private addresses, deny any addresses in the IP multicast address range (224.0.0.0/4).

Review Questions

1. Which Cisco IOS Firewall feature set allows you to use a browser to get through the firewall and then authenticate on a TACACS+ or RADIUS server?

    A. Reflexive ACLs

    B. Authentication proxy

    C. CBAC's

    D. Dynamic ACLs

2. The Cisco IOS uses what to scrutinize any and all traffic that's attempting to come through the firewall so that it can find out about and control the state information for TCP and UDP sessions?

    A. Reflexive ACLs

    B. Authentication proxy

    C. CBAC's

    D. Dynamic ACLs

3. Which type of ACLs filter IP packets depending upon upper-layer session information, and can permit outbound traffic to pass but place limitations on inbound traffic?

    A. Reflexive ACLs

    B. Authentication proxy

    C. CBAC's

    D. Dynamic ACLs

4. Which type of ACL depends on either remote or local Telnet authentication in combination with extended ACLs c?

    A. Reflexive ACLs

    B. Authentication proxy

    C. CBAC's

    D. Dynamic ACLs

5. Which two of the following are considered to be denial of service attacks (DoS)?

    A. TCP SYN Flood

    B. Application Layer attacks

    C. Ping of death attacks

    D. Autorooters

6. Which of the following commonly zero in on well-known holes in the software that's typically found running on servers?

   A. Application layer attacks

   B. Autorooters

   C. Backdoors

   D. Denial of service

7. Which of the following are simply paths leading into a computer or network or can also be a more elaborate Trojan horse code?

   A. Application layer attacks

   B. Autorooters

   C. Backdoors

   D. Denial of service

8. Which of the following probe, scan, and then capture data on a strategically positioned computer?

   A. Application layer attacks

   B. Autorooters

   C. Backdoors

   D. Denial of service

9. Which of the following makes a service unavailable by overwhelming the system that normally provides it?

   A. Application layer attacks

   B. Autorooters

   C. Backdoors

   D. Denial of service

10. Which two of the following are security appliances that can be installed in a network?

    A. IDS

    B. IPS

    C. AAA

    D. SDM

Answers to Review Questions

1. B. Users who would normally be blocked by an ACL can just bring up a browser to get through the firewall and then authenticate on a TACACS+ or RADIUS server.

2. C. Context-based Access Control (CBAC's) job is to scrutinize any and all traffic that's attempting to come through the firewall so it can find out about and control the state information for TCP and UDP sessions. And it uses that very information it's gathered to determine whether to create a temporary pathway into the firewall's access lists.

3. A. Reflexive ACLs filter IP packets depending upon upper-layer session information, and they often permit outbound traffic to pass but place limitations on inbound traffic. You can't define reflexive ACLs with numbered or standard IP ACLs, or any other protocol ACLs for that matter.

4. D. Dynamic ACLs first drop the Telnet connection that the user initiated and replace it with a single-entry dynamic ACL that's appended to the extended ACL already in place. This causes traffic to be allowed through for a specific amount of time.

5. A, C. The four typical types of denial of service attacks are TCP SYN flood, ping of death, Tribe Flood Network and Stacheldraht.

6. A. Application layer attacks commonly zero in on well-known holes in the software that's typically found running on servers. Favorite targets include FTP, sendmail, and HTTP.

7. C. Backdoors are simply paths leading into a computer or network. Through simple invasions, or via more elaborate "Trojan horse" code, bad guys can use them as inroads into a specific host or even a network.

8. B. Bad guys use something called a rootkit to probe, scan, and then capture data on a strategically positioned computer that's poised to give them "eyes" into entire systems.

9. D. Denial of service attacks are attacks that makes a service unavailable by overwhelming the system that normally provides it, and there are several different versions.

10. A, B. The two types of security appliances that you'll typically find on a network that provide security are intrusion prevention systems (IPS), which prevent intrusions, hopefully, and intrusion detection systems (IDS), which only detect them and tells you about it.

Chapter

7

Implement, verify, and troubleshoot NAT and ACLs in a medium-sized Enterprise branch office network.

THE CISCO CCNA EXAM OBJECTIVES COVERED IN THIS CHAPTER INCLUDE:

- 7.1 Describe the purpose and types of ACLs
- 7.2 Configure and apply ACLs based on network filtering requirements (including CLI/SDM)
- 7.3 Configure and apply an ACLs to limit Telnet and SSH access to the router using (including SDM/CLI)
- 7. 4 Verify and monitor ACLs in a network environment
- 7.5 Troubleshoot ACL issues
- 7.6 Explain the basic operation of NAT
- 7.7 Configure NAT for given network requirements using (including CLI/SDM)
- 7.8 Troubleshoot NAT issues

Access control lists (ACLs) are an integral part of Cisco's security solution, and I'll show you the keys of both simple and advanced access lists that will equip you with the ability to ensure internetwork security as well as mitigate most security-oriented network threats.

The proper use and configuration of access lists is a vital part of router configuration because access lists are such versatile networking accessories. Contributing mightily to the efficiency and operation of your network, access lists give network managers a huge amount of control over traffic flow throughout the enterprise. With access lists, managers can gather basic statistics on packet flow and security policies can be implemented. Sensitive devices can also be protected from unauthorized access.

In this chapter, I am also going to give you the skinny on ACLs, Network Address Translation (NAT), Dynamic NAT, and Port Address Translation (PAT), also known as *NAT Overload*. Of course, I'll demonstrate NAT, and then I'm going to finish this chapter by using SDM so that you can see how NAT can be configured the easy way.

For up-to-the-minute updates on the CCNA objectives covered by this chapter, please see www.lammle.com and/or www.sybex.com.

7.1 Describe the purpose and types of ACLs

An *access list* is essentially a list of conditions that categorize packets. They can be really helpful when you need to exercise control over network traffic. An access list would be your tool of choice for decision making in these situations.

One of the most common and easiest to understand uses of access lists is filtering unwanted packets when implementing security policies. For example, you can set them up to make very specific decisions about regulating traffic patterns so that they'll allow only certain hosts to access web resources on the Internet while restricting others. With the right combination of access lists, network managers arm themselves with the power to enforce nearly any security policy they can invent.

Access lists can even be used in situations that don't necessarily involve blocking packets. For example, you can use them to control which networks will or won't be advertised by dynamic routing protocols. How you configure the access list is the same. The difference here is simply how you apply it—to a routing protocol instead of an interface. When you apply an access list in this way, it's called a *distribute list*, and it doesn't stop routing advertisements, it just controls their content. You can also use access lists to categorize packets for queuing or QoS-type services and for controlling which types of traffic can activate a pricey ISDN link.

Creating access lists is really a lot like programming a series of `if-then` statements—if a given condition is met, then a given action is taken. If the specific condition isn't met, nothing happens and the next statement is evaluated. Access-list statements are basically packet filters that packets are compared against, categorized by, and acted upon accordingly. Once the lists are built, they can be applied to either inbound or outbound traffic on any interface. Applying an access list causes the router to analyze every packet crossing that interface in the specified direction and take the appropriate action.

There are a few important rules that a packet follows when it's being compared with an access list:

- It's always compared with each line of the access list in sequential order—that is, it'll always start with the first line of the access list, then go to line 2, then line 3, and so on.

- It's compared with lines of the access list only until a match is made. Once the packet matches the condition on a line of the access list, the packet is acted upon and no further comparisons take place.

- There is an implicit "deny" at the end of each access list—this means that if a packet doesn't match the condition on any of the lines in the access list, the packet will be discarded.

Each of these rules has some powerful implications when filtering IP packets with access lists, so keep in mind that creating effective access lists truly takes some practice.

There are two main types of access lists:

Standard access lists   These use only the source IP address in an IP packet as the condition test. All decisions are made based on the source IP address. This means that standard access lists basically permit or deny an entire suite of protocols. They don't distinguish among any of the many types of IP traffic such as web, Telnet, UDP, and so on.

Extended access lists   Extended access lists can evaluate many of the other fields in the layer 3 and layer 4 headers of an IP packet. They can evaluate source and destination IP addresses, the protocol field in the Network layer header, and the port number at the Transport layer header. This gives extended access lists the ability to make much more granular decisions when controlling traffic.

Named access lists   Hey, wait a minute—I said there were two types of access lists but listed three! Well, technically there really are only two since *named access lists* are either standard or extended and not actually a new type. I'm just distinguishing them because they're created and referred to differently than standard and extended access lists, but they're functionally the same.

Exam Objectives

Understand the differences between standard and extended access lists.   Standard access lists make decisions based on source IP address only. Extended access lists can look at source and destination information at layers 3 and 4, as well as protocol type information.

Know the rules for creating and applying access lists. Access lists are *directional*, meaning that you can only have one access list per direction (inbound or outbound) on an interface. The implicit deny means that any packet not matching any line of an access list will be denied, it is as if every access list ends with a "deny all" function.

7.2 Configure and apply ACLs based on network filtering requirements (including CLI/SDM)

For the CCNA exam prep, we will look at two types of access lists; standard IP access lists, extended IP access lists, and named access lists, which is another way of configuring standard and extended access lists. We will also look at a technique for specifying ranges of addressing called wildcard masking that can be used with all three types of access list. For now, let's get started on standard access lists!

Standard IP Access Lists

Standard IP access lists filter network traffic by examining the source IP address in a packet. You create a *standard IP access list* by using the access-list numbers 1–99 or 1300–1999 (expanded range). Access-list types are generally differentiated using a number. Based on the number used when the access list is created, the router knows which type of syntax to expect as the list is entered. By using numbers 1–99 or 1300–1999, you're telling the router that you want to create a standard IP access list, so the router will expect syntax specifying only the source IP address in the test lines.

The following is an example of the many access-list number ranges that you can use to filter traffic on your network (the protocols for which you can specify access lists depend on your IOS version):

```
Corp(config)#access-list ?
  <1-99>            IP standard access list
  <100-199>         IP extended access list
  <1100-1199>       Extended 48-bit MAC address access list
  <1300-1999>       IP standard access list (expanded range)
  <200-299>         Protocol type-code access list
  <2000-2699>       IP extended access list (expanded range)
  <700-799>         48-bit MAC address access list
  compiled          Enable IP access-list compilation
  dynamic-extended  Extend the dynamic ACL absolute timer
  rate-limit        Simple rate-limit specific access list
```

Let's take a look at the syntax used when creating a standard access list:

```
Corp(config)#access-list 10 ?
  deny    Specify packets to reject
  permit  Specify packets to forward
  remark  Access list entry comment
```

As I said, by using the access-list numbers 1–99 or 1300–1999, you're telling the router that you want to create a standard IP access list.

After you choose the access-list number, you need to decide whether you're creating a permit or deny statement. For this example, you will create a deny statement:

```
Corp(config)#access-list 10 deny ?
  Hostname or A.B.C.D  Address to match
  any                  Any source host
  host                 A single host address
```

The next step requires a more detailed explanation. There are three options available. You can use the any parameter to permit or deny any host or network, you can use an IP address to specify either a single host or a range of them, or you can use the host command to specify a specific host only. The any command is pretty obvious—any source address matches the statement, so every packet compared against this line will match. The host command is relatively simple. Here's an example using it:

```
Corp(config)#access-list 10 deny host ?
  Hostname or A.B.C.D  Host address
Corp(config)#access-list 10 deny host 172.16.30.2
```

This tells the list to deny any packets from host 172.16.30.2. The default parameter is host. In other words, if you type **access-list 10 deny 172.16.30.2**, the router assumes you that mean host 172.16.30.2.

But there's another way to specify either a particular host or a range of hosts—you can use wildcard masking. In fact, to specify any range of hosts, you have to use wildcard masking in the access list.

Wildcard Masking

Wildcards are used with access lists to specify an individual host, a network, or a certain range of a network or networks. To understand a *wildcard*, you need to understand what a *block size* is; it's used to specify a range of addresses. Some of the different block sizes available are 64, 32, 16, 8, and 4.

When you need to specify a range of addresses, you choose the next-largest block size for your needs. For example, if you need to specify 34 networks, you need a block size of 64. If you want to specify 18 hosts, you need a block size of 32. If you only specify 2 networks, then a block size of 4 would work.

Wildcards are used with the host or network address to tell the router a range of available addresses to filter. To specify a host, the address would look like this:

172.16.30.5 0.0.0.0

The four zeros represent each octet of the address. Whenever a zero is present, it means that octet in the address must match exactly. To specify that an octet can be any value, the value of 255 is used. As an example, here's how a /24 subnet is specified with a wildcard:

172.16.30.0 0.0.0.255

This tells the router to match up the first three octets exactly, but the fourth octet can be any value.

Now, that was the easy part. What if you want to specify only a small range of subnets? This is where the block sizes come in. You have to specify the range of values in a block size. In other words, you can't choose to specify 20 networks. You can only specify the exact amount as the block size value. For example, the range would have to be either 16 or 32, but not 20.

Let's say that you want to block access to part of the network that is in the range from 172.16.8.0 through 172.16.15.0. That is a block size of 8. Your network number would be 172.16.8.0, and the wildcard would be 0.0.7.255. Whoa! What is that? The 7.255 is what the router uses to determine the block size. The network and wildcard tell the router to start at 172.16.8.0 and go up a block size of eight addresses to network 172.16.15.0.

Seriously—it really is easier than it looks—really! I could certainly go through the binary math for you, but no one needs that. Actually, all you have to do is remember that the wildcard is always one number less than the block size. So, in our example, the wildcard would be 7 since our block size is 8. If you used a block size of 16, the wildcard would be 15. Easy, huh?

But just in case, we'll go through some examples to help you nail it. The following example tells the router to match the first three octets exactly but that the fourth octet can be anything:

Corp(config)#**access-list 10 deny 172.16.10.0 0.0.0.255**

The next example tells the router to match the first two octets and that the last two octets can be any value:

Corp(config)#**access-list 10 deny 172.16.0.0**
  0.0.255.255

Try to figure out this next line:

Corp(config)#**access-list 10 deny 172.16.16.0 0.0.3.255**

This configuration tells the router to start at network 172.16.16.0 and use a block size of 4. The range would then be 172.16.16.0 through 172.16.19.0.

The following example shows an access list starting at 172.16.16.0 and going up a block size of 8 to 172.16.23.0:

Corp(config)#**access-list 10 deny 172.16.16.0 0.0.7.255**

The next example starts at network 172.16.32.0 and goes up a block size of 16 to 172.16.47.0:

```
Corp(config)#access-list 10 deny 172.16.32.0 0.0.15.255
```

The next example starts at network 172.16.64.0 and goes up a block size of 64 to 172.16.127.0:

```
Corp(config)#access-list 10 deny 172.16.64.0 0.0.63.255
```

The last example starts at network 192.168.160.0 and goes up a block size of 32 to 192.168.191.255:

```
Corp(config)#access-list 10 deny 192.168.160.0 0.0.31.255
```

Here are two more things to keep in mind when working with block sizes and wildcards:

- Each block size must start at 0 or a multiple of the block size. For example, you can't say that you want a block size of 8 and then start at 12. You must use 0–7, 8–15, 16–23, and so on. For a block size of 32, the ranges are 0–31, 32–63, 64–95, and so on.
- The command any is the same thing as writing out the wildcard 0.0.0.0255.255.255.255.

 Wildcard masking is a crucial skill to master when creating IP access lists. It's used identically when creating standard and extended IP access lists.

Standard Access List Example

In this section, you'll learn how to use a standard access list to stop specific users from gaining access to the Finance department LAN.

In Figure 7.1, a router has three LAN connections and one WAN connection to the Internet. Users on the Sales LAN should not have access to the Finance LAN, but they should be able to access the Internet and the marketing department. The Marketing LAN needs to access the Finance LAN for application services.

On the router in the figure, the following standard IP access list is configured:

```
Lab_A#config t
Lab_A(config)#access-list 10 deny 172.16.40.0 0.0.0.255
Lab_A(config)#access-list 10 permit any
```

It's very important to know that the any command is the same thing as saying the following using wildcard masking:

```
Lab_A(config)#access-list 10 permit 0.0.0.0 255.255.255.255
```

Since the wildcard mask says that none of the octets is to be evaluated, every address matches the test condition. So, this is functionally the same as using the any keyword.

FIGURE 7.1 IP access list example with three LANs and a WAN connection

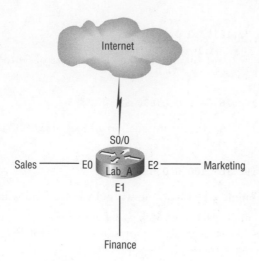

At this point, the access list is configured to deny source addresses from the Sales LAN access to the Finance LAN and allow everyone else. But remember, no action will be taken until the access list is applied on an interface in a specific direction. But where should this access list be placed? If you place it as an incoming access list on E0, you might as well shut down the Ethernet interface because all of the Sales LAN devices will be denied access to all networks attached to the router. The best place to apply this access list is on the E1 interface as an outbound list:

```
Lab_A(config)#int e1
Lab_A(config-if)#ip access-group 10 out
```

This completely stops traffic from 172.16.40.0 from getting out Ethernet 1. It has no effect on the hosts from the Sales LAN accessing the Marketing LAN and the Internet since traffic to those destinations doesn't go through interface E1. Any packet trying to exit out E1 will have to go through the access list first. If there were an inbound list placed on E0, then any packet trying to enter interface E0 would have to go through the access list before being routed to an exit interface.

Let's take a look at another example of a standard access list. Figure 7.2 shows an inter-network of two routers with three LANs and one serial WAN connection.

You want to stop the Accounting users from accessing the Human Resources server attached to the Lab_B router but allow all other users access to that LAN. What standard access list would you create and where would you place it?

The real answer is that you should use an extended access list and place it closest to the source, but the question specifies that you should use a standard access list. Standard access lists, by rule of thumb, are placed closest to the destination—in this example,

Ethernet 0 outbound on the Lab_B router. Here is the access list that should be placed on the Lab_B router:

```
Lab_B#config t
Lab_B(config)#access-list 10 deny 192.168.10.128 0.0.0.31
Lab_B(config)#access-list 10 permit any
Lab_B(config)#interface Ethernet 0
Lab_B(config-if)#ip access-group 10 out
```

FIGURE 7.2   IP standard access list example 2

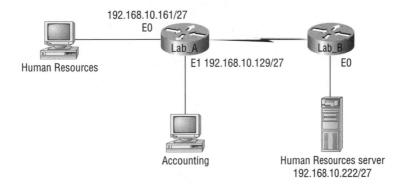

Before we move on to restricting Telnet access on a router, let's take a look at one more standard access list example, but it will require some thought. In Figure 7.3 you have a router with four LAN connections and one WAN connection to the Internet.

You need to write an access list that will stop access from each of the four LANs shown in the diagram to the Internet. Each of the LANs shows a single host's IP address, and from that you need to determine the subnet and use wildcards to configure the access list.

Here is an example of what your answer should look like (starting with the network on E0 and working through to E3):

```
Router(config)#access-list 1 deny 172.16.128.0 0.0.31.255
Router(config)#access-list 1 deny 172.16.48.0 0.0.15.255
Router(config)#access-list 1 deny 172.16.192.0 0.0.63.255
Router(config)#access-list 1 deny 172.16.88.0 0.0.7.255
Router(config)#access-list 1 permit any
Router(config)#interface serial 0
Router(config-if)#ip access-group 1 out
```

Okay, what would be the purpose of creating this list? If you actually applied this access list on the router, you'd effectively shut down access to the Internet, so what's the purpose of even having an Internet connection? I wrote this exercise so you can practice how to use block sizes with access lists—which is critical for your success when studying the CCNA objectives.

FIGURE 7.3 IP standard access list example 3

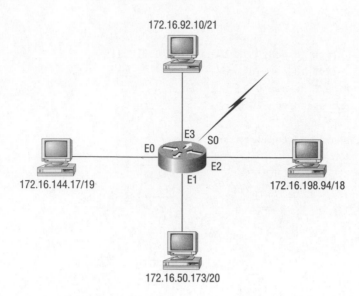

172.16.92.10/21

E3 / S0
EO
E2
172.16.144.17/19   E1   172.16.198.94/18

172.16.50.173/20

Controlling VTY (Telnet) Access

You'll probably have a difficult time trying to stop users from telnetting to a large router because any active interface on a router is fair game for VTY access. You could try to create an extended IP access list that limits Telnet access to every IP address on the router. But if you did that, you'd have to apply it inbound on every interface, and that really wouldn't scale well to a large router with dozens, even hundreds, of interfaces, would it? Here's a much better solution: Use a standard IP access list to control access to the VTY lines themselves.

Why does this work? Because when you apply an access list to the VTY lines, you don't need to specify the Telnet protocol since access to the VTY implies terminal access. You also don't need to specify a destination address, since it really doesn't matter which interface address the user used as a target for the Telnet session. You really only need to control where the user is coming from—their source IP address.

To perform this function, follow these steps:

1. Create a standard IP access list that permits only the host or hosts you want to be able to telnet into the routers.

2. Apply the access list to the VTY line with the access-class command.

Here is an example of allowing only host 172.16.10.3 to telnet into a router:

```
Lab_A(config)#access-list 50 permit 172.16.10.3
Lab_A(config)#line vty 0 4
Lab_A(config-line)#access-class 50 in
```

Because of the implied deny any at the end of the list, the access list stops any host from telnetting into the router except the host 172.16.10.3, regardless of which individual IP address on the router is used as a target.

 Cisco recommends that you use Secure Shell (SSH) instead of Telnet on the VTY lines of a router.

Extended Access Lists

In the standard IP access list example earlier, notice how you had to block all access from the Sales LAN to the finance department. What if you needed Sales to gain access to a certain server on the Finance LAN but not to other network services, for security reasons? With a standard IP access list, you can't allow users to get to one network service and not another. Said another way, when you need to make decisions based on both source and destination addresses, a standard access list won't allow you to do that since it only makes decisions based on source address.

But an *extended access list* will hook you up. That's because extended access lists allow you to specify source and destination address as well as the protocol and port number that identify the upper-layer protocol or application. By using extended access lists, you can effectively allow users access to a physical LAN and stop them from accessing specific hosts—or even specific services on those hosts.

Here's an example of an extended IP access list:

```
Corp(config)#access-list ?
  <1-99>            IP standard access list
  <100-199>         IP extended access list
  <1100-1199>       Extended 48-bit MAC address access list
  <1300-1999>       IP standard access list (expanded range)
  <200-299>         Protocol type-code access list
  <2000-2699>       IP extended access list (expanded range)
  <700-799>         48-bit MAC address access list
  compiled          Enable IP access-list compilation
  dynamic-extended  Extend the dynamic ACL absolute timer
  rate-limit        Simple rate-limit specific access list
```

The first command shows the access-list numbers available. You'll use the extended access-list range from 100 to 199. Be sure to notice that the range 2000–2699 is also available for extended IP access lists.

At this point, you need to decide what type of list entry you are making. For this example, you'll choose a deny list entry.

```
Corp(config)#access-list 110 ?
  deny    Specify packets to reject
```

```
dynamic  Specify a DYNAMIC list of PERMITs or DENYs
permit   Specify packets to forward
remark   Access list entry comment
```

Once you choose the access-list type, you then need to select a protocol field entry.

```
Corp(config)#access-list 110 deny ?
<0-255>  An IP protocol number
ahp      Authentication Header Protocol
eigrp    Cisco's EIGRP routing protocol
esp      Encapsulation Security Payload
gre      Cisco's GRE tunneling
icmp     Internet Control Message Protocol
igmp     Internet Gateway Message Protocol
ip       Any Internet Protocol
ipinip   IP in IP tunneling
nos      KA9Q NOS compatible IP over IP tunneling
ospf     OSPF routing protocol
pcp      Payload Compression Protocol
pim      Protocol Independent Multicast
tcp      Transmission Control Protocol
udp      User Datagram Protocol
```

> If you want to filter by Application layer protocol, you have to choose the appropriate layer 4 transport protocol after the permit or deny statement. For example, to filter Telnet or FTP, you choose TCP since both Telnet and FTP use TCP at the Transport layer. If you were to choose IP, you wouldn't be allowed to specify a specific application protocol later.

Here, you'll choose to filter an Application layer protocol that uses TCP by selecting TCP as the protocol. You'll specify the specific TCP port later. Next, you will be prompted for the source IP address of the host or network (you can choose the any command to allow any source address):

```
Corp(config)#access-list 110 deny tcp ?
A.B.C.D  Source address
any      Any source host
host     A single source host
```

After the source address is selected, the destination address is chosen:

```
Corp(config)#access-list 110 deny tcp any ?
A.B.C.D  Destination address
```

```
any        Any destination host
eq         Match only packets on a given port number
gt         Match only packets with a greater port number
host       A single destination host
lt         Match only packets with a lower port number
neq        Match only packets not on a given port number
range      Match only packets in the range of port numbers
```

In the following example, any source IP address that has a destination IP address of 172.16.30.2 has been denied.

Corp(config)#**access-list 110 deny tcp any host 172.16.30.2 ?**

```
ack          Match on the ACK bit
dscp         Match packets with given dscp value
eq           Match only packets on a given port number
established  Match established connections
fin          Match on the FIN bit
fragments    Check non-initial fragments
gt           Match only packets with a greater port number
log          Log matches against this entry
log-input    Log matches against this entry, including input interface
lt           Match only packets with a lower port number
neq          Match only packets not on a given port number
precedence   Match packets with given precedence value
psh          Match on the PSH bit
range        Match only packets in the range of port numbers
rst          Match on the RST bit
syn          Match on the SYN bit
time-range   Specify a time-range
tos          Match packets with given TOS value
urg          Match on the URG bit
<cr>
```

You can press Enter here and leave the access list as is. But if you do that, all TCP traffic to host 172.16.30.2 will be denied, regardless of destination port. You can be even more specific: Once you have the host addresses in place, just specify the type of service you are denying. The following help screen shows you the available options. You can choose a port number or use the application or protocol name:

Corp(config)#**access-list 110 deny tcp any host 172.16.30.2 eq ?**

```
<0-65535>    Port number
bgp          Border Gateway Protocol (179)
chargen      Character generator (19)
```

cmd	Remote commands (rcmd, 514)
daytime	Daytime (13)
discard	Discard (9)
domain	Domain Name Service (53)
drip	Dynamic Routing Information Protocol (3949)
echo	Echo (7)
exec	Exec (rsh, 512)
finger	Finger (79)
ftp	File Transfer Protocol (21)
ftp-data	FTP data connections (20)
gopher	Gopher (70)
hostname	NIC hostname server (101)
ident	Ident Protocol (113)
irc	Internet Relay Chat (194)
klogin	Kerberos login (543)
kshell	Kerberos shell (544)
login	Login (rlogin, 513)
lpd	Printer service (515)
nntp	Network News Transport Protocol (119)
pim-auto-rp	PIM Auto-RP (496)
pop2	Post Office Protocol v2 (109)
pop3	Post Office Protocol v3 (110)
smtp	Simple Mail Transport Protocol (25)
sunrpc	Sun Remote Procedure Call (111)
syslog	Syslog (514)
tacacs	TAC Access Control System (49)
talk	Talk (517)
telnet	Telnet (23)
time	Time (37)
uucp	Unix-to-Unix Copy Program (540)
whois	Nicname (43)
www	World Wide Web (HTTP, 80)

At this point, let's block Telnet (port 23) to host 172.16.30.2 only. If the users want to FTP, fine—that's allowed. The log command is used to log messages every time the access list is hit. This can be an extremely cool way to monitor inappropriate access attempts. Here is how to do this:

```
Corp(config)#access-list 110 deny tcp any host 172.16.30.2 eq 23 log
```

You need to keep in mind that the next line is an implicit deny any by default. If you apply this access list to an interface, you might as well just shut the interface down, since by default there is an implicit deny all at the end of every access list. You've got to follow up the access list with the following command:

Corp(config)#**access-list 110 permit ip any any**

Remember, the 0.0.0.0 255.255.255.255 is the same command as any, so the command could look like this:

Corp(config)#**access-list 110 permit ip 0.0.0.0 255.255.255.255 0.0.0.0 255.255.255.255**

Once the access list is created, you need to apply it to an interface (it's the same command as the IP standard list):

Corp(config-if)#**ip access-group 110 in**

Or this:

Corp(config-if)#**ip access-group 110 out**

In the following section, we'll look at an example of how to use an extended access list.

Extended Access List Example 1

Using Figure 7.1 from the IP standard access list example earlier, let's use the same network and deny access to a host at 172.16.30.5 on the Finance department LAN for both Telnet and FTP services. All other services on this and all other hosts are acceptable for the sales and marketing departments to access.

The following access list should be created:

Lab_A#**config t**
Lab_A(config)#**access-list 110 deny tcp any host**
  172.16.30.5 eq 21
Lab_A(config)#**access-list 110 deny tcp any host**
  172.16.30.5 eq 23
Lab_A(config)#**access-list 110 permit ip any any**

The access-list 110 tells the router you are creating an extended IP access list. The tcp is the protocol field in the Network layer header. If the list doesn't say tcp here, you cannot filter by port numbers 21 and 23 as shown in the example. (These are FTP and Telnet, and they both use TCP for connection-oriented services.) The any command is the source, which means any IP address, and the host is the destination IP address.

Remember that instead of using the **host 172.16.30.5** command when we created the extended access list, we could have entered **172.16.30.5 0.0.0.0** and there would be no difference in the result—other than the router would change the command to **host 172.16.30.5** in the running-config.

After the list is created, it needs to be applied to the Ethernet 1 interface outbound. This applies the policy we created to all hosts and effectively blocks all FTP and Telnet access to 172.16.30.5 from outside the local LAN. If this list were created to only block access from the Sales LAN, then we'd have put this list closer to the source, or on Ethernet interface 0. So, in this situation, we'd apply the list to inbound traffic.

Let's go ahead and apply the list to interface E1 and block all outside FTP and Telnet access to the host:

```
Lab_A(config-if)#ip access-group 110 out
```

Extended Access List Example 2

In this example, we'll again use Figure 7.3, which has four LANs and a serial connection. What we need to do is stop Telnet access to the networks attached to the Ethernet 1 and Ethernet 2 interfaces. If we only used one access list, it would not be a very effective one because of the latency that will be caused on the Ethernet 1 and 2 interfaces (since every packet going out these interfaces must be looked at), but if we used two lists, the latency could be less on each interface if configured correctly. However, since we're studying the CCNA objectives, we're going to look at this with only one access list.

The configuration on the router would look something like this, although the answer can vary:

```
Router(config)#access-list 110 deny tcp any 172.16.48.0 0.0.15.255
eq 23
Router(config)#access-list 110 deny tcp any 172.16.192.0 0.0.63.255
eq 23
Router(config)#access-list 110 permit ip any any
Router(config)#interface Ethernet 1
Router(config-if)#ip access-group 110 out
Router(config-if)#interface Ethernet 2
Router(config-if)#ip access-group 110 out
```

The important information that you need to understand from this list is as follows: First, you need to verify that the number range is correct for the type of access list you are creating—in this example it's extended, so the range must be 100–199. Second, you need to verify that the protocol field matches the upper-layer process or application—in this example, port 23 (Telnet).

The protocol parameter must be TCP since Telnet uses TCP. If the question stated to use TFTP, for example, then the protocol parameter would have to be UDP since TFTP uses UDP. Third, verify that the destination port number matches the application you are filtering for—in this case, port 23 matches Telnet, which is correct. Finally, the test statement permit ip any any is important to have at the end of the list to enable all packets other than Telnet packets destined for the LANs connected to Ethernet 1 and Ethernet 2.

Exam Objectives

Understand the standard IP access list configuration command.   To configure a standard IP access list, use the access-list numbers 1–99 or 1300-1999 in global configuration mode. Choose permit or deny, then choose the source IP address you want to filter on using one of the three techniques covered earlier.

Understand the extended IP access list configuration command.   To configure an extended IP access list, use the access-list numbers 100–199 or 2000-2699 in global configuration mode. Choose permit or deny, the Network layer protocol, the source IP address you want to filter on, the destination address you want to filer on, and finally the Transport layer protocol (if selected).

7.3 Configure and apply ACLs to limit telnet and SSH access to the router using (including: SDM/CLI)

You'll probably have a difficult time trying to stop users from telnetting to a large router because any active interface on a router is fair game for VTY access. You could try to create an extended IP access list that limits Telnet access to every IP address on the router. But if you did that, you'd have to apply it inbound on every interface, and that really wouldn't scale well to a large router with dozens, even hundreds, of interfaces, would it? Here's a much better solution: Use a standard IP access list to control access to the VTY lines themselves.

Why does this work? Because when you apply an access list to the VTY lines, you don't need to specify the Telnet protocol since access to the VTY implies terminal access. You also don't need to specify a destination address, since it really doesn't matter which interface address the user used as a target for the Telnet session. You really only need to control where the user is coming from—their source IP address.

To perform this function, follow these steps:

1. Create a standard IP access list that permits only the host or hosts you want to be able to telnet into the routers.

2. Apply the access list to the VTY line with the access-class command.

Here is an example of allowing only host 172.16.10.3 to telnet into a router:

```
Lab_A(config)#access-list 50 permit 172.16.10.3
Lab_A(config)#line vty 0 4
Lab_A(config-line)#access-class 50 in
```

Because of the implied deny any at the end of the list, the access list stops any host from telnetting into the router except the host 172.16.10.3, regardless of which individual IP address on the router is used as a target.

> Cisco recommends that you use Secure Shell (SSH) instead of Telnet on the VTY lines of a router.

Secure Shell (SSH)

Instead of Telnet, you can use *Secure Shell* (SSH), which creates a more secure session than the Telnet application that uses an unencrypted data stream. SSH uses encrypted keys to send data so that your username and password are not sent in the clear.

Here are the steps to setting up SSH:

1. Set your hostname:

   `Router(config)#hostname Todd`

2. Set the domain name (both the hostname and domain name are required for the encryption keys to be generated):

   `Todd(config)#ip domain-name Lammle.com`

3. Generate the encryption keys for securing the session:

   ```
   Todd(config)#crypto key generate rsa general-keys modulus ?
     <360-2048>  size of the key modulus [360-2048]
   Todd(config)#crypto key generate rsa general-keys modulus 1024
   The name for the keys will be: Todd.Lammle.com
   % The key modulus size is 1024 bits
   % Generating 1024 bit RSA keys, keys will be non-exportable...[OK]
   *June 24 19:25:30.035: %SSH-5-ENABLED: SSH 1.99 has been enabled
   ```

4. Set the max idle timer for a SSH session:

   ```
   Todd(config)#ip ssh time-out ?
     <1-120>  SSH time-out interval (secs)
   Todd(config)#ip ssh time-out 60
   ```

5. Set the max failed attempts for an SSH connection:

   ```
   Todd(config)#ip ssh authentication-retries ?
     <0-5>  Number of authentication retries
   Todd(config)#ip ssh authentication-retries 2
   ```

6. Connect to the VTY lines of the router:

   `Todd(config)#line vty 0 1180`

7. Last, configure SSH and then Telnet as access protocols:

   `Todd(config-line)#transport input ssh telnet`

If you do not use the keyword `telnet` at the end of the command string, then only SSH will work on the router. I am not suggesting you use either way, but just understand that SSH is more secure than Telnet.

Exam Objectives

Remember the command on a VTY line that enables you to use SSH on a Cisco router. The command to set SSH on a VTY line is `transport input ssh telnet`, although, the command `telnet` at the end of the line is optional.

7. 4 Verify and monitor ACLs in a network environment

Again, it's always good to be able to verify a router's configuration. Table 7.1 lists the commands that can be used to verify the configuration.

TABLE 7.1   Commands Used to Verify Access List Configuration

Command	Effect
show access-list	Displays all access lists and their parameters configured on the router. This command does not show you which interface the list is set on.
show access-list 110	Shows only the parameters for the access list 110. This command does not show you the interface the list is set on.
show ip access-list	Shows only the IP access lists configured on the router.
show ip interface	Shows which interfaces have access lists set.
show running-config	Shows the access lists and which interfaces have access lists set.
Show mac access-group	Displays MAC access lists applied to all layer 2 interfaces or the specified layer 2 interface (used on layer 2 switches only).

We've already used the `show running-config` command to verify that a named access list was in the router as well as a MAC access list on a layer 2 switch. So, now let's take a look at the output from some of the other commands.

The show access-list command will list all access lists on the router, whether they're applied to an interface or not:

```
Lab_A#show access-list
Standard IP access list 10
    deny    172.16.40.0, wildcard bits 0.0.0.255
    permit any
Standard IP access list BlockSales
    deny    172.16.40.0, wildcard bits 0.0.0.255
    permit any
Extended IP access list 110
    deny tcp any host 172.16.30.5 eq ftp
    deny tcp any host 172.16.30.5 eq telnet
    permit ip any any
Lab_A#
```

First, notice that both access list 10 and our named access list appear on this list. Second, notice that even though I entered actual numbers for TCP ports in access list 110, the show command gives us the protocol names rather than TCP ports for readability. (Hey, not everyone has them all memorized!)

Here's the output of the show ip interface command:

```
Lab_A#show ip interface e1
Ethernet1 is up, line protocol is up
  Internet address is 172.16.30.1/24
  Broadcast address is 255.255.255.255
  Address determined by non-volatile memory
  MTU is 1500 bytes
  Helper address is not set
  Directed broadcast forwarding is disabled
  Outgoing access list is BlockSales
  Inbound  access list is not set
  Proxy ARP is enabled
  Security level is default
  Split horizon is enabled
  ICMP redirects are always sent
  ICMP unreachables are always sent
  ICMP mask replies are never sent
  IP fast switching is disabled
  IP fast switching on the same interface is disabled
  IP Null turbo vector
  IP multicast fast switching is disabled
```

```
    IP multicast distributed fast switching is disabled
    Router Discovery is disabled
    IP output packet accounting is disabled
    IP access violation accounting is disabled
    TCP/IP header compression is disabled
    RTP/IP header compression is disabled
    Probe proxy name replies are disabled
    Policy routing is disabled
    Network address translation is disabled
    Web Cache Redirect is disabled
    BGP Policy Mapping is disabled
Lab_A#
```

Be sure to notice the bold line indicating that the outgoing list on this interface is BlockSales but the inbound access list isn't set. One more verification command and then we'll move on to using the SDM to configure firewall security.

As I've already mentioned, you can use the show running-config command to see any and all access lists. However, on a layer 2 switch, you can verify your interface configurations with the show mac access-group command:

```
S1#sh mac access-group
Interface FastEthernet0/1:
    Inbound access-list is not set
    Outbound access-list is not set
Interface FastEthernet0/2:
    Inbound access-list is not set
    Outbound access-list is not set
S1#
```

Depending on how many interfaces you set your MAC access lists on, you can use the interface command to view individual interfaces:

```
S1#sh mac access-group interface f0/6
Interface FastEthernet0/6:
    Inbound access-list is Todd_MAC_List
    Outbound access-list is not set
```

Exam Objectives

Remember the command to verify an access list on an interface.   To see whether an access list is set on an interface and in which direction it is filtering, use the show ip interface command. This command will not show you the contents of the access list, merely which access lists are applied on the interface.

Remember the command to verify the access lists configuration. To see the configured access lists on your router, use the show access-list command. This command will not show you which interfaces have an access list set.

7.5 Troubleshoot ACL issues

When working on a problem, one item to eliminate is the possibility of an access list blocking traffic. It is a crucial troubleshooting skill to be able to quickly view both the contents of access lists, and where they are applied.

 For information concerning this objective, please see the objective 7.4.

7.6 Explain the basic operation of NAT

Similar to Classless Inter-Domain Routing (CIDR), the original intention for NAT was to slow the depletion of available IP address space by allowing many private IP addresses to be represented by some smaller number of public IP addresses.

Since then, it's been discovered that NAT is also a useful tool for network migrations and mergers, server load sharing, and creating "virtual servers." So, in this section, I'm going to describe the basics of NAT functionality and the terminology common to NAT.

At times, NAT really decreases the overwhelming amount of public IP addresses required in your networking environment. And NAT comes in really handy when two companies that have duplicate internal addressing schemes merge. NAT is also great to have around when an organization changes its Internet service provider (ISP) and the networking manager doesn't want the hassle of changing the internal address scheme.

Here's a list of situations when it's best to have NAT on your side:

- You need to connect to the Internet and your hosts don't have globally unique IP addresses.

- You change to a new ISP that requires you to renumber your network.

- You need to merge two intranets with duplicate addresses.

You typically use NAT on a border router. For an illustration of this, see Figure 7.4.

Now you may be thinking, "NAT's totally cool. It's the grooviest greatest network gadget, and I just gotta have it." Well, hang on a minute. There are truly some serious snags related to NAT use. Oh—don't get me wrong: It really can save you sometimes, but there's a dark side you need to know about, too. For a visual of the pros and cons linked to using NAT, check out Table 7.2.

FIGURE 7.4 Where to configure NAT

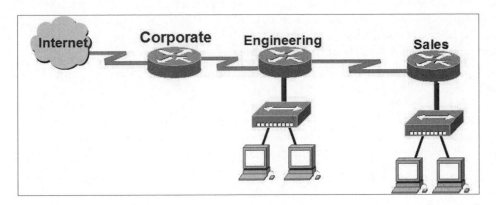

TABLE 7.2 Advantages and Disadvantages of Implementing NAT

Advantages	Disadvantages
Conserves legally registered addresses.	Translation introduces switching path delays.
Reduces address overlap occurrence.	Loss of end-to-end IP traceability.
Increases flexibility when connecting to Internet.	Certain applications will not function with NAT enabled.
Eliminates address renumbering as network changes.	

 The most obvious advantage associated with NAT is that it allows you to conserve your legally registered address scheme. This is why we haven't run out of IPv4 addresses—think about it.

Types of Network Address Translation

In this section, I'm going to go over the three types of NAT:

Static NAT   This type of NAT is designed to allow one-to-one mapping between local and global addresses. Keep in mind that the static version requires you to have one real Internet IP address for every host on your network.

Dynamic NAT This version gives you the ability to map an unregistered IP address to a registered IP address from out of a pool of registered IP addresses. You don't have to statically configure your router to map an inside to an outside address as you would using static NAT, but you do have to have enough real, bona fide IP addresses for everyone who's going to be sending packets to and receiving them from the Internet.

Overloading This is the most popular type of NAT configuration. Understand that overloading really is a form of dynamic NAT that maps multiple unregistered IP addresses to a single registered IP address—many-to-one—by using different ports. Now, why is this so special? Well, because it's also known as *Port Address Translation (PAT)*. And by using PAT (NAT Overload), you get to have thousands of users connect to the Internet using only one real global IP address—pretty slick, yeah? Seriously, NAT Overload is the real reason we haven't run out of valid IP address on the Internet. Really—I'm not joking.

Exam Objectives

Remember the best advantage to using Network Address Translation The largest advantage to using NAT on your network is that it conserves legally registered addresses.

Remember the three types of NAT. The three types of NAT are static, dynamic, and NAT overload.

7.7 Configure NAT for given network requirements using (including CLI/SDM)

This first section will show you how to configure static, dynamic and NAT overload on a Cisco router using the command line interface (CLI). Then I'll show you how to configure NAT on a Cisco router using the Secure Device Manager (SDM).

Static NAT Configuration

Let's take a look at a simple basic static NAT configuration:

```
ip nat inside source static 10.1.1.1 170.46.2.2
!
interface Ethernet0
 ip address 10.1.1.10 255.255.255.0
 ip nat inside
!
interface Serial0
 ip address 170.46.2.1 255.255.255.0
 ip nat outside
!
```

Dynamic NAT Configuration

Dynamic NAT means that we have a pool of addresses that we will use to provide real IP addresses to a group of users on the inside. We do not use port numbers, so we have to have real IP addresses for every user trying to get outside the local network.

Here is a sample output of a dynamic NAT configuration:

```
ip nat pool todd 170.168.2.2 170.168.2.254
    netmask 255.255.255.0
ip nat inside source list 1 pool todd
!
interface Ethernet0
 ip address 10.1.1.10 255.255.255.0
 ip nat inside
!
interface Serial0
 ip address 170.168.2.1 255.255.255.0
 ip nat outside
!
access-list 1 permit 10.1.1.0 0.0.0.255
!
```

PAT (Overloading) Configuration

This last example shows how to configure inside global address overloading. This is the typical NAT that we would use today. It is rare that we would use static or dynamic NAT unless we were statically mapping a server, for example.

Here is a sample output of a PAT configuration:

```
ip nat pool globalnet 170.168.2.1 170.168.2.1
    netmask 255.255.255.0
ip nat inside source list 1 pool globalnet overload
!
interface Ethernet0/0
 ip address 10.1.1.10 255.255.255.0
 ip nat inside
!
interface Serial0/0
 ip address 170.168.2.1 255.255.255.0
 ip nat outside
!
access-list 1 permit 10.1.1.0 0.0.0.255
```

Configuring NAT using the SDM

Configuring NAT using the SDM is really much easier that anyone would think—except for you of course, because you've already seen it in earlier chapters. Anyway, all you have to do is click Configure ➢ NAT and you get a handy wizard that does a lot more that just hold your hand to create a NAT rule. You get to pick between a basic and advanced wizard:

Basic NAT   Use this wizard if you have some basic PCs/hosts on your trusted network that need access to the Internet. This wizard will guide you through the process of creating a basic NAT configuration.

Advanced NAT   If you have a DMZ, or servers on your inside network that users from the outside need to access, you definitely want to opt for the Advanced NAT configuration.

The first screen is the Create NAT Configuration screen (see Figure 7.5).

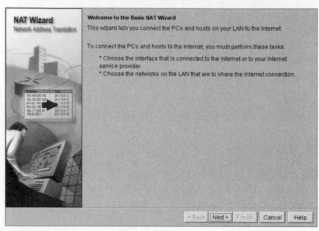

From here, I'm just going to simply connect up and create a basic NAT. After that, I click Launch the Selected Task, and get the next screen, which tells me what the Basic NAT Wizard is going to do (see Figure 7.6).

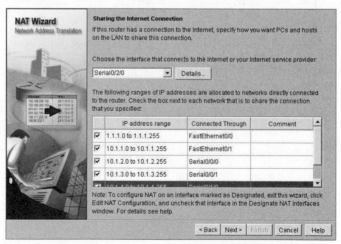

As you might guess, it rocks—all I have to do is to click Next to get to a screen from which I'm able to select all my inside and outside addresses.

Exam Objectives

Remember the command to enable NAT on your inside network.   On your inside interface(s) use the command `ip nat inside`.

Remember the command to enable NAT on your outside network.   On your outside interface(s) use the command `ip nat outside`.

Understand the two types of NAT wizards in SDM.   The two wizards are Basic NAT and Advanced NAT. Basic NAT is used if you have some basic PCs/hosts on your trusted network that need access to the Internet. Advanced NAT is used if you have a DMZ, or servers on your inside network that users from the outside need to access.

7.8 Troubleshoot NAT issues

Before we move on to the configuration section and actually use the commands I just talked about, let's go through a couple of NAT examples and see if you can figure out the configuration that needs to be used. To start, look at Figure 7.7 and ask yourself two things: Where would you implement NAT in this design, and what type of NAT would you configure?

FIGURE 7.5   NAT example

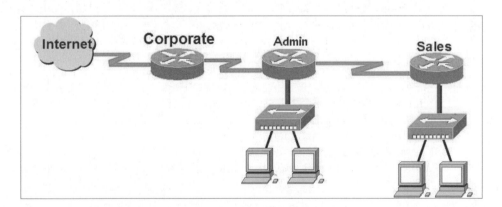

In Figure 7.4, the NAT configuration would be placed on the corporate router and the configuration would be dynamic NAT with overload (PAT). In this NAT example, what type of NAT is being used?

```
ip nat pool todd-nat 170.168.10.10 170.168.10.20 netmask 255.255.255.0
```

The above command uses dynamic NAT. The `pool` in the command gives the answer away, plus there is more then one address in the pool, which means we probably are not using PAT. In the next NAT example, we'll use Figure 7.8 to see if we can figure out the configuration needed.

FIGURE 7.6   Another NAT example

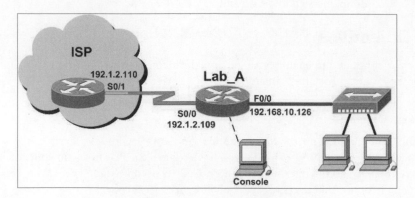

The example in Figure 7.6 shows a border router that needs to be configured with NAT and will allow the use of six public IP addresses, 192.1.2.109 through 114. However, on the inside network, you have 63 hosts that use the private addresses of 192.168.10.65 through 126. What would your NAT configuration be on the border router?

Two different answers would work here, but the following would be my first choice:

```
ip nat pool Todd 192.1.2.109 192.1.2.109 netmask 255.255.255.248
access-list 1 permit 192.168.10.64 0.0.0.63
ip nat inside source list 1 pool Todd overload
```

The command `ip nat pool Todd 192.1.2.109 192.1.2.109 netmask 255.255.255.248` sets the pool name as Todd and creates a dynamic pool of addresses for the NAT to use address 192.1.2.109. Instead of the `netmask` command, you can use the `prefix-length` 29 statement. (And I know what you're thinking, but no, you cannot do this on router interfaces as well.) The second answer would end up with the exact same result of having only 192.1.2.109 as your inside global, but you can type this in and have it work too: `ip nat pool Todd 102.1.2.109 192.1.2.114 netmask 255.255.255.248`. This is a waste because the second through sixth addresses would only be used if there was a conflict with a TCP port number.

The command `ip nat inside source list 1 pool Todd overload` command sets the dynamic pool to use PAT by using the `overload` command.

Be sure to add the `ip nat inside` and `ip nat outside` statements on the appropriate interfaces.

Exam Objectives

Remember to always check your interface configurations when troubleshooting NAT.   Be sure to add the `ip nat inside` and `ip nat outside` statements on the appropriate interfaces.

Remember to check for the overload command if using Port Address Translation (PAT). The command `ip nat inside source list` *list-number* `pool` *pool-name* `overload` command sets the dynamic pool to use PAT by using the `overload` command.

Review Questions

1. Which of the following commands connect access list 110 inbound to interface ethernet0?

    A. Router(config)#`ip access-group 110 in`

    B. Router(config)#`ip access-list 110 in`

    C. Router(config-if)#`ip access-group 110 in`

    D. Router(config-if)#`ip access-list 110 in`

2. What command will permit SMTP mail to only host 1.1.1.1?

    A. `access-list 10 permit smtp host 1.1.1.1`

    B. `access-list 110 permit ip smtp host 1.1.1.1`

    C. `access-list 10 permit tcp any host 1.1.1.1 eq smtp`

    D. `access-list 110 permit tcp any host 1.1.1.1 eq smtp`

3. You configure the following access list:

```
access-list 110 deny tcp 10.1.1.128 0.0.0.63 any eq smtp
access-list 110 deny tcp any eq 23
int ethernet 0
ip access-group 110 out
```

What will the result of this access list be?

    A. Email and Telnet will be allowed out E0.

    B. Email and Telnet will be allowed in E0.

    C. Everything but email and Telnet will be allowed out E0.

    D. No IP traffic will be allowed out E0.

4. Which of the following series of commands will restrict Telnet access to the router?

    A. Lab_A(config)#`access-list 10 permit 172.16.1.1`
        Lab_A(config)#`line con 0`
        Lab_A(config-line)#`ip access-group 10 in`

    B. Lab_A(config)#`access-list 10 permit 172.16.1.1`
        Lab_A(config)#`line vty 0 4`
        Lab_A(config-line)#`access-class 10 out`

    C. Lab_A(config)#`access-list 10 permit 172.16.1.1`
        Lab_A(config)#`line vty 0 4`
        Lab_A(config-line)#`access-class 10 in`

    D. Lab_A(config)#`access-list 10 permit 172.16.1.1`
        Lab_A(config)#`line vty 0 4`
        Lab_A(config-line)#`ip access-group 10 in`

5. Which of the following is true regarding access lists applied to an interface?

    A. You can place as many access lists as you want on any interface until you run out of memory.

    B. You can apply only one access list on any interface.

    C. One access list may be configured, per direction, for each layer 3 protocol configured on an interface.

    D. You can apply two access lists to any interface.

6. You are working on a router that has established privilege levels that restrict access to certain functions. You discover that you are not able to execute the command `show running-configuration`. How can you view and confirm the access lists that have been applied to the Ethernet 0 interface on your router?

    A. `show access-lists`

    B. `show interface Ethernet 0`

    C. `show ip access-lists`

    D. `show ip interface Ethernet 0`

7. Which command would you place on interface on a private network?

    A. `ip nat inside`

    B. `ip nat outside`

    C. `ip outside global`

    D. `ip inside local`

8. Which command would you place on interface connected to the Internet?

    A. `ip nat inside`

    B. `ip nat outside`

    C. `ip outside global`

    D. `ip inside local`

9. Pat Address Translation is also termed what?

    A. NAT Fast

    B. NAT Static

    C. NAT Overload

    D. Overloading Static

10. Which of the following are disadvantages of using NAT? (Choose three.)

    A. Translation introduces switching path delays.

    B. Conserves legally registered addresses.

    C. Causes loss of end-to-end IP traceability.

    D. Increases flexibility when connecting to the Internet.

    E. Certain applications will not function with NAT enabled.

    F. Reduces address overlap occurrence.

Answers to Review Questions

1. C. To place an access list on an interface, use the `ip access-group` command in interface configuration mode.

2. D. When trying to find the best answer to an access-list question, always check the access-list number and then the protocol. When filtering to an upper-layer protocol, you must use an extended list, numbers 100–199 and 2000–2699. Also, when you filter to an upper-layer protocol, you must use either `tcp` or `udp` in the protocol field. If it says `ip` in the protocol field, you cannot filter to an upper-layer protocol. SMTP uses TCP.

3. D. If you add an access list to an interface and you do not have at least one `permit` statement, then you will effectively shut down the interface because of the implicit `deny any` at the end of every list.

4. C. Telnet access to the router is restricted by using either a standard or extended IP access list inbound on the VTY lines of the router. The command `access-class` is used to apply the access list to the VTY lines.

5. C. A Cisco router has rules regarding the placement of access lists on a router interface. You can place one access list per direction for each layer 3 protocol configured on an interface.

6. D. The only command that shows which access lists have been applied to an interface is `show ip interface Ethernet 0`. The command `show access-lists` displays all configured access lists, and `show ip access-lists` displays all configured IP access lists, but neither command indicates whether the displayed access lists have been applied to an interface.

7. A. As with access lists, you must configure your interfaces before NAT will provide any translations. On the inside networks, you would use the command `ip nat inside`. On the outside interface, you will use the command `ip nat outside`.

8. B. As with access lists, you must configure your interfaces before NAT will provide any translations. On the inside networks, you would use the command `ip nat inside`. On the outside interface, you will use the command `ip nat outside`.

9. C. Another term for port address translation is NAT Overload because that is the command used to enable port address translation.

10. A, C, E. NAT is not perfect and can cause some issues in some networks, but most networks work just fine. NAT can cause delays and troubleshooting problems, and some applications just won't work.

Chapter

8

Implement and verify WAN links

THE CISCO CCNA EXAM OBJECTIVES COVERED IN THIS CHAPTER INCLUDE:

- 8.1 Describe different methods for connecting to a WAN
- 8.2 Configure and verify a basic WAN serial connection
- 8.3 Configure and verify Frame Relay on Cisco routers
- 8.3 Troubleshoot WAN implementation issues
- 8.4 Describe VPN technology (including importance, benefits, role, impact, components)
- 8.5 Configure and verify a PPP connection between Cisco routers

The Cisco IOS supports a ton of different wide area network (WAN) protocols that help you extend your local LANs to other LANs at remote sites. And I don't think I have to tell you how positively essential information exchange between disparate sites is these days—it's vital! But even so, it wouldn't exactly be cost-effective or efficient to install your own cable and connect all of your company's remote locations yourself, now would it? A much better way to go about doing this is to simply lease the existing installations that service providers already have in place, and save big time.

So, it follows that I'm going to discuss the various types of connections, technologies, and devices used in accordance with WANs in this chapter. We'll also get into how to implement and configure High-Level Data-Link Control (HDLC), Point-to-Point Protocol (PPP), and Frame Relay. I'll also introduce you to WAN security concepts, tunneling, and virtual private network basics.

For up-to-the-minute updates on the CCNA objectives covered by this chapter, please see www.lammle.com and/or www.sybex.com.

8.1 Describe different methods for connecting to a WAN

Basically, Cisco just supports HDLC, PPP, and Frame Relay on its serial interfaces, and you can see this with the encapsulation ? command from any serial interface (your output may vary depending on the IOS version you are running):

```
Corp#config t
Corp(config)#int s0/0/0
Corp(config-if)#encapsulation ?
  atm-dxi      ATM-DXI encapsulation
  frame-relay  Frame Relay networks
  hdlc         Serial HDLC synchronous
  lapb         LAPB (X.25 Level 2)
  ppp          Point-to-Point protocol
  smds         Switched Megabit Data Service (SMDS)
  x25          X.25
```

Understand that if I had other types of interfaces on my router, I would have other encapsulation options, like ISDN or ADSL. And remember, you can't configure Ethernet or Token Ring encapsulation on a serial interface.

Next, I'm going to define the most prominently known WAN protocols used today: Frame Relay, ISDN, LAPB, LAPD, HDLC, PPP, PPPoE, Cable, DSL, MPLS, and ATM. Just so you know, the only WAN protocols you'll usually find configured on a serial interface are HDLC, PPP, and Frame Relay, but who said we're stuck with using only serial interfaces for wide area connections?

Frame Relay   A packet-switched technology that made its debut in the early 1990s, *Frame Relay* is a high-performance Data Link and Physical layer specification. It's pretty much a successor to X.25, except that much of the technology in X.25 used to compensate for physical errors (noisy lines) has been eliminated. An upside to Frame Relay is that it can be more cost-effective than point-to-point links, plus it typically runs at speeds of 64Kbps up to 45Mbps (T3). Another Frame Relay benefit is that it provides features for dynamic bandwidth allocation and congestion control.

ISDN   *Integrated Services Digital Network (ISDN)* is a set of digital services that transmits voice and data over existing phone lines. ISDN offers a cost-effective solution for remote users who need a higher-speed connection than analog dial-up links can give them, and it's also a good choice to use as a backup link for other types of links like Frame Relay or T1 connections.

LAPB   *Link Access Procedure, Balanced (LAPB)* was created to be a connection-oriented protocol at the Data Link layer for use with X.25, but it can also be used as a simple data link transport. A not-so-good characteristic of LAPB is that it tends to create a tremendous amount of overhead due to its strict time-out and windowing techniques.

LAPD   *Link Access Procedure, D-Channel (LAPD)* is used with ISDN at the Data Link layer (layer 2) as a protocol for the D (signaling) channel. LAPD was derived from the Link Access Procedure, Balanced (LAPB) protocol and is designed primarily to satisfy the signaling requirements of ISDN basic access.

HDLC   *High-Level Data-Link Control (HDLC)* was derived from Synchronous Data Link Control (SDLC), which was created by IBM as a Data Link connection protocol. HDLC works at the Data Link layer and creates very little overhead compared to LAPB.

It wasn't intended to encapsulate multiple Network layer protocols across the same link—the HDLC header doesn't contain any identification about the type of protocol being carried inside the HDLC encapsulation. Because of this, each vendor that uses HDLC has its own way of identifying the Network layer protocol, meaning that each vendor's HDLC is proprietary with regard to its specific equipment.

PPP   *Point-to-Point Protocol (PPP)* is a pretty famous, industry-standard protocol. Because all multiprotocol versions of HDLC are proprietary, PPP can be used to create point-to-point links between different vendors' equipment. It uses a Network Control Protocol field in the Data Link header to identify the Network layer protocol and allows authentication and multilink connections to be run over asynchronous and synchronous links.

PPPoE   *Point-to-Point Protocol over Ethernet* (PPoE) encapsulates PPP frames in Ethernet frames and is usually used in conjunction with ADSL services. It gives you a lot of the familiar PPP features like authentication, encryption, and compression, but there's a downside—it has a lower maximum transmission unit (MTU) than standard Ethernet does, and if your firewall isn't solidly configured, this little attribute can really give you some grief!

Still somewhat popular in the United States, PPPoE on Ethernet's main feature is that it adds a direct connection to Ethernet interfaces, while providing DSL support. It's often used by many hosts on a shared Ethernet interface for opening PPP sessions to various destinations via at least one bridging modem.

In a modern HFC network, typically 500 to 2,000 active data subscribers are connected to a certain cable network segment, all sharing the upstream and downstream bandwidth. (*Hybrid fibre-coaxial*, or HFC, is a telecommunications industry term for a network that incorporates both optical fiber and coaxial cable to create a broadband network.) The actual bandwidth for Internet service over a cable TV (CATV) line can be up to about 27Mbps on the download path to the subscriber, with about 2.5Mbps of bandwidth on the upload path. Typically, users get an access speed from 256Kbps to 6Mbps. This data rate varies greatly throughout the U.S.

DSL   *Digital subscriber line* (DSL) is a technology used by traditional telephone companies to deliver advanced services (high-speed data and sometimes video) over twisted-pair copper telephone wires. It typically has a lower data-carrying capacity than HFC networks, and data speeds can be range limited by line lengths and quality. DSL is not a complete end-to-end solution but rather a Physical layer transmission technology like dial-up, cable, or wireless. DSL connections are deployed in the last mile of a local telephone network—the local loop. The connection is set up between a pair of modems on either end of a copper wire that is run between the customer premises equipment (CPE) and the *Digital Subscriber Line Access Multiplexer* (DSLAM). A DSLAM is the device located at the provider's central office (CO) and concentrates connections from multiple DSL subscribers.

MPLS   *MultiProtocol Label Switching (MPLS)* is a data-carrying mechanism that emulates some properties of a circuit-switched network over a packet-switched network. MPLS is a switching mechanism that imposes labels (numbers) to packets and then uses those labels to forward packets. The labels are assigned on the edge MPLS of the network, and forwarding inside the MPLS network is done solely based on labels. Labels usually correspond to a path to layer 3 destination addresses (equal to IP destination-based routing). MPLS was designed to support forwarding of protocols other than TCP/IP. Because of this, label switching within the network is performed the same regardless of the layer 3 protocol. In larger networks, the result of MPLS labeling is that only the edge routers perform a routing lookup. All the core routers forward packets based on the labels, which makes forwarding the packets through the service provider's network faster. (Most companies are replacing their Frame Relay networks with MPLS today).

ATM   *Asynchronous Transfer Mode* (ATM) was created for time-sensitive traffic, providing simultaneous transmission of voice, video, and data. ATM uses cells that are a fixed 53 bytes long instead of packets. It also can use isochronous clocking (external clocking) to help the data move faster. Typically, if you are running Frame Relay today, you will be running Frame Relay over ATM.

Exam Objectives

Remember the default serial encapsulation on Cisco routers.   Cisco routers use a proprietary High-Level Data Link Control (HDLC) encapsulation on all their serial links by default.

Remember what encapsulation you can use if you need basic dial-up, authentication and multiple Network layer protocols.   PPP is a non-vendor-specific circuit-switching protocol, and PPP can be used to create point-to-point links. It uses a Network Control Protocol field in the Data Link header to identify the Network layer protocol and allows authentication and multilink connections to be run over asynchronous and synchronous links.

8.2 Configure and verify a basic WAN serial connection

As you can imagine, there are a few things that you need to know before connecting your WAN in order to make sure that everything goes well. For starters, you have to understand the kind of WAN Physical layer implementation that Cisco provides as well as ensure that you're familiar with the various types of WAN serial connectors involved.

   The good news is that Cisco serial connections support almost any type of WAN service. Your typical WAN connection is a dedicated leased line using HDLC, PPP, and Frame Relay with speeds that can kick it up to 45Mbps (T3).

   HDLC, PPP, and Frame Relay can use the same Physical layer specifications, and I'll go over the various types of connections and then move on to telling you all about the WAN protocols specified in the CCNA objectives.

Serial Transmission

WAN serial connectors use *serial transmission*, something that takes place 1 bit at a time over a single channel.

 Parallel transmission can pass at least 8 bits at a time, but all WANs use serial transmission.

   Cisco routers use a proprietary 60-pin serial connector that you have to get from Cisco or a provider of Cisco equipment. Cisco also has a new, smaller proprietary serial connection that's about one-tenth the size of the 60-pin basic serial cable, called the "*smart-serial*"—I'm not sure why. But I do know that you have to make sure that you have the right type of interface in your router before using this cable connector.

The type of connector you have on the other end of the cable depends on your service provider and its particular end-device requirements. There are several different types of ends you'll run into:

- EIA/TIA-232

- EIA/TIA-449

- V.35 (used to connect to a CSU/DSU)

- EIA-530

Make sure that you're clear on these things: Serial links are described in frequency or cycles per second (hertz). The amount of data that can be carried within these frequencies is called *bandwidth*. Bandwidth is the amount of data in bits per second that the serial channel can carry.

Data Terminal Equipment and Data Communication Equipment

By default, router interfaces are *data terminal equipment (DTE)*, and they connect into *data communication equipment (DCE)* like a *channel service unit/data service unit (CSU/DSU)*. The CSU/DSU then plugs into a demarcation location (demarc) and is the service provider's last responsibility. Most of the time, the demarc is a jack that has an RJ-45 (8-pin modular) female connector, located in a telecommunications closet.

Actually, you may already have heard of demarcs. If you've ever had the glorious experience of reporting a problem to your service provider, they'll usually tell you everything tests out fine up to the demarc, so the problem must be the CPE, or customer premises equipment. In other words, it's your problem not theirs.

Figure 8.1 shows a typical DTE-DCE-DTE connection and the devices used in the network.

FIGURE 8.1 DTE-DCE-DTE WAN connection

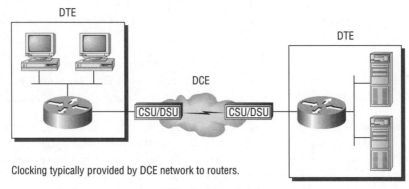

Clocking typically provided by DCE network to routers.

In non-production environments, a DCE network is not always present.

The idea behind a WAN is to be able to connect two DTE networks through a DCE network. The DCE network includes the CSU/DSU, through the provider's wiring and switches, all the way to the CSU/DSU at the other end. The network's DCE device (CSU/DSU) provides clocking to the DTE-connected interface (the router's serial interface).

As mentioned, the DCE network provides clocking to the router; this is the CSU/DSU. If you have a nonproduction network and you're using a WAN crossover type of cable and do not have a CSU/DSU, then you need to provide clocking on the DCE end of the cable by using the clock rate command.

Terms such as *EIA/TIA-232, V.35, X.21*, and *HSSI (High-Speed Serial Interface)* describe the Physical layer between the DTE (router) and DCE device (CSU/DSU).

High-Level Data-Link Control (HDLC) Protocol

The High-Level Data-Link Control (HDLC) protocol is a popular ISO-standard, bit-oriented, Data Link layer protocol. It specifies an encapsulation method for data on synchronous serial data links using frame characters and checksums. HDLC is a point-to-point protocol used on leased lines. No authentication can be used with HDLC.

In byte-oriented protocols, control information is encoded using entire bytes. On the other hand, bit-oriented protocols use single bits to represent the control information. Some common bit-oriented protocols include SDLC, LLC, HDLC, TCP, and IP.

HDLC is the default encapsulation used by Cisco routers over synchronous serial links. And Cisco's HDLC is proprietary—it won't communicate with any other vendor's HDLC implementation. But don't give Cisco grief for it—*everyone's* HDLC implementation is proprietary. Figure 8.2 shows the Cisco HDLC format.

FIGURE 8.2   Cisco HDLC frame format

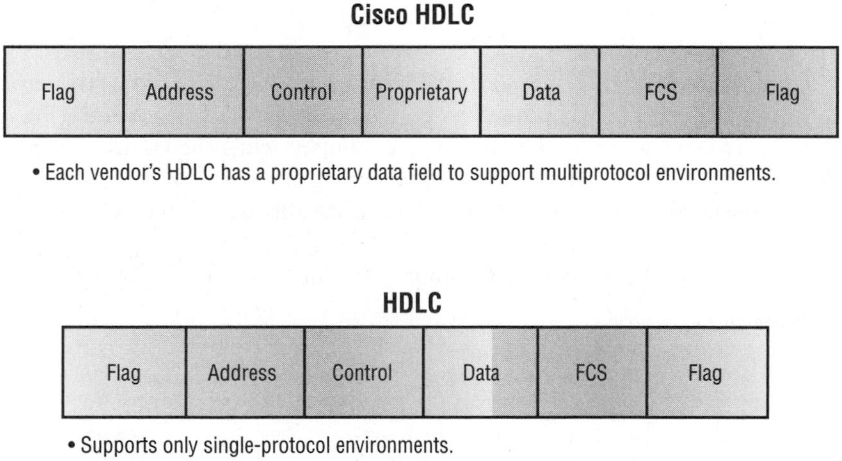

Cisco HDLC

Flag	Address	Control	Proprietary	Data	FCS	Flag

• Each vendor's HDLC has a proprietary data field to support multiprotocol environments.

HDLC

Flag	Address	Control	Data	FCS	Flag

• Supports only single-protocol environments.

As shown in the figure, the reason that every vendor has a proprietary HDLC encapsulation method is that each vendor has a different way for the HDLC protocol to encapsulate multiple Network layer protocols. If the vendors didn't have a way for HDLC to communicate the different layer 3 protocols, then HDLC would only be able to carry one protocol. This proprietary header is placed in the data field of the HDLC encapsulation.

Configuring HDLC on Cisco Routers

Configuring HDLC encapsulation on an interface is really pretty straightforward. To configure it from the CLI, follow these simple router commands:

```
Router#config t
Enter configuration commands, one per line. End with CNTL/Z.
Router(config)#int s0
Router(config-if)#encapsulation hdlc
Router(config-if)#^Z
Router#
```

So, let's say you only have one Cisco router, and you need to connect to a non-Cisco router because your other Cisco router is on order. What would you do? You couldn't use the default HDLC serial encapsulation because it wouldn't work. Instead, you would use something like PPP, an ISO-standard way of identifying the upper-layer protocols. You can check out RFC 1661 for more information on the origins and standards of PPP. Let's discuss PPP in more detail and how to connect to routers using the PPP encapsulation.

Point-to-Point Protocol (PPP)

Let's spend a little time on Point-to-Point Protocol (PPP). Remember that it's a Data Link layer protocol that can be used over either asynchronous serial (dial-up) or synchronous serial (ISDN) media. It uses Link Control Protocol (LCP) to build and maintain data-link connections. Network Control Protocol (NCP) is used to allow multiple Network layer protocols (routed protocols) to be used on a point-to-point connection.

Since HDLC is the default serial encapsulation on Cisco serial links and it works great, why and when would you choose to use PPP? Well, the basic purpose of PPP is to transport layer 3 packets across a Data Link layer point-to-point link, and it's nonproprietary. So, unless you have all Cisco routers, you need PPP on your serial interfaces—the HDLC encapsulation is Cisco proprietary, remember? Plus, since PPP can encapsulate several layer 3 routed protocols and provide authentication, dynamic addressing, and callback, PPP could be the best encapsulation solution for you instead of HDLC.

Figure 8.3 shows the protocol stack compared to the OSI reference model.

FIGURE 8.3   Point-to-Point Protocol stack

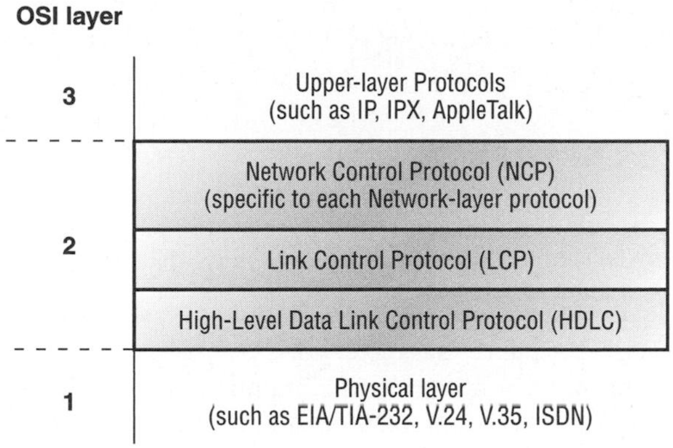

OSI layer

3	Upper-layer Protocols (such as IP, IPX, AppleTalk)
2	Network Control Protocol (NCP) (specific to each Network-layer protocol)
	Link Control Protocol (LCP)
	High-Level Data Link Control Protocol (HDLC)
1	Physical layer (such as EIA/TIA-232, V.24, V.35, ISDN)

PPP contains four main components:

EIA/TIA-232-C, V.24, V.35, and ISDN   A Physical layer international standard for serial communication.

HDLC   A method for encapsulating datagrams over serial links.

LCP   A method of establishing, configuring, maintaining, and terminating the point-to-point connection.

NCP   A method of establishing and configuring different Network layer protocols. NCP is designed to allow the simultaneous use of multiple Network layer protocols. Some examples of protocols here are IPCP (Internet Protocol Control Protocol) and IPXCP (Internetwork Packet Exchange Control Protocol).

Burn it into your mind that the PPP protocol stack is specified at the Physical and Data Link layers only. NCP is used to allow communication of multiple Network layer protocols by encapsulating the protocols across a PPP data link.

Remember that if you have a Cisco router and a non-Cisco router connected with a serial connection, you must configure PPP or another encapsulation method, such as Frame Relay, because the HDLC default just won't work!

Configuring PPP on Cisco Routers

Configuring PPP encapsulation on an interface is the same as HDLC. To configure it from the CLI, follow these simple router commands:

```
Router#config t
Enter configuration commands, one per line. End with CNTL/Z.
```

```
Router(config)#int s0
Router(config-if)#encapsulation ppp
Router(config-if)#^Z
Router#
```

Exam Objectives

Remember the default serial encapsulation on Cisco routers.   Cisco routers use a proprietary High-Level Data Link Control (HDLC) encapsulation on all their serial links by default.

Remember the PPP Data Link layer protocols.   The three Data Link layer protocols are: Network Control Protocol (NCP), which defines the Network layer protocols; Link Control Protocol (LCP), a method of establishing, configuring, maintaining, and terminating the point-to-point connection; and High-Level Data Link Control (HDLC), the MAC layer protocol that encapsulates the packets.

8.3 Configure and verify Frame Relay on Cisco routers

Frame Relay is still one of the most popular WAN services deployed over the past decade, and there's a good reason for this—cost. And it's a rare network design or designer that has the privilege to ignore that all-important cost factor!

By default, Frame Relay is classified as a non-broadcast multi-access (NBMA) network, meaning it doesn't send any broadcasts like RIP updates across the network.

Frame Relay has at its roots a technology called X.25, and it essentially incorporates the components of X.25 that are still relevant to today's reliable and relatively "clean" telecommunications networks, while leaving out the no-longer-needed error-correction components. It's substantially more complex than the simple leased-line networks you learned about when I discussed the HDLC and PPP protocols. The leased-line networks are easy to conceptualize— but not as much when it comes to Frame Relay. It can be significantly more complex and versatile, which is why it's often represented as a "cloud" in networking graphics. I'll get to that in a minute—for right now, I'm going to introduce Frame Relay in concept and show you how it differs from simpler leased-line technologies.

Frame Relay Implementation and Monitoring

As I've said, there are a ton of Frame Relay commands and configuration options, but I'm going to zero in on the ones you really need to know when studying for the CCNA exam objectives. I'm going to start with one of the simplest configuration options—two routers with a single PVC between them. Next, I'll show you a more complex configuration using subinterfaces, and demonstrate some of the monitoring commands available to verify the configuration.

Single Interface

Let's get started by looking at a simple example. Say that we just want to connect two routers with a single PVC. Here's how that configuration would look:

```
RouterA#config t
Enter configuration commands, one per line.  End with CNTL/Z.
RouterA(config)#int s0/0
RouterA(config-if)#encapsulation frame-relay
RouterA(config-if)#ip address 172.16.20.1 255.255.255.0
RouterA(config-if)#frame-relay lmi-type ansi
RouterA(config-if)#frame-relay interface-dlci 101
RouterA(config-if)#^Z
RouterA#
```

The first step is to specify the encapsulation as Frame Relay. Notice that since I didn't specify a particular encapsulation type—either Cisco or IETF—the Cisco default type was used. If the other router were non-Cisco, I would've specified IETF. Next, I assigned an IP address to the interface, then I specified the LMI type of ANSI (the default being Cisco) based on information provided by the telecommunications provider. Finally, I added the Data Link Connection Identifier (DLCI) of 101, which indicates the PVC we want to use (again, given to me by my ISP) and assumes that there's only one PVC on this physical interface.

That's all there is to it—if both sides are configured correctly, the circuit will come up.

Subinterfaces

You probably know by now that we can have multiple virtual circuits on a single serial interface and yet treat each as a separate interface—I did mention this earlier. We can make this happen by creating *subinterfaces*. Think of a subinterface as a logical interface defined by the IOS software. Several subinterfaces will share a single hardware interface, yet for configuration purposes they operate as if they were separate physical interfaces, something known as multiplexing.

To configure a router in a Frame Relay network so that it will avoid split horizon issues by not permitting routing updates, just configure a separate subinterface for each PVC, with a unique DLCI and subnet assigned to the subinterface.

You define subinterfaces using a command like int s0.*subinterface number*. First, you have to set the encapsulation on the physical serial interface, and then you can define the subinterfaces—generally one subinterface per PVC. Here's an example:

```
RouterA(config)#int s0
RouterA(config-if)#encapsulation frame-relay
RouterA(config-if)#int s0.?
  <0-4294967295>  Serial interface number
RouterA(config-if)#int s0.16 ?
  multipoint      Treat as a multipoint link
  point-to-point  Treat as a point-to-point link
RouterA(config-if)#int s0.16 point-to-point
```

Make sure that you don't have an IP address under the physical interface if you have configured subinterfaces!

You can define a serious amount of subinterfaces on any given physical interface, but keep in mind that there are only about a thousand available DLCIs. In the preceding example, I chose to use subinterface 16 because that represents the DLCI number assigned to that PVC by the carrier. There are two types of subinterfaces:

Point-to-point   Used when a single virtual circuit connects one router to another. Each point-to-point subinterface requires its own subnet.

A point-to-point subinterface maps a single IP subnet per DLCI and addresses and resolves NBMA split horizon issues.

Multipoint   This is when the router is the center of a star of virtual circuits that are using a single subnet for all routers' serial interfaces connected to the frame switch. You'll usually find this implemented with the hub router in this mode and the spoke routers in physical interface (always point-to-point) or point-to-point subinterface mode.

Monitoring Frame Relay

Several commands are used frequently to check the status of your interfaces and PVCs once you have Frame Relay encapsulation set up and running. To list them, use the show frame ? command, as shown here:

```
RouterA>sho frame ?
end-to-end      Frame-relay end-to-end VC information
fragment        show frame relay fragmentation information
ip              show frame relay IP statistics
lapf            show frame relay lapf status/statistics
lmi             show frame relay lmi statistics
map             Frame-Relay map table
pvc             show frame relay pvc statistics
qos-autosense   show frame relay qos-autosense information
route           show frame relay route
svc             show frame relay SVC stuff
traffic         Frame-Relay protocol statistics
vofr            Show frame-relay VoFR statistics
```

The most common parameters that you view with the show frame-relay command are lmi, pvc, and map.

Now, let's take a look at the most frequently used commands and the information they provide.

The *show frame-relay lmi* Command

The show frame-relay lmi command will give you the LMI traffic statistics exchanged between the local router and the Frame Relay switch. Here's an example:

```
Router#sh frame lmi

LMI Statistics for interface Serial0 (Frame Relay DTE)
LMI TYPE = CISCO
  Invalid Unnumbered info 0      Invalid Prot Disc 0
  Invalid dummy Call Ref 0       Invalid Msg Type 0
  Invalid Status Message 0       Invalid Lock Shift 0
  Invalid Information ID 0        Invalid Report IE Len 0
  Invalid Report Request 0       Invalid Keep IC Len 0
  Num Status Enq. Sent 0         Num Status msgs Rcvd 0
  Num Update Status Rcvd 0       Num Status Timeouts 0
Router#
```

The router output from the show frame-relay lmi command shows you any LMI errors, plus the LMI type.

The *show frame pvc* Command

The show frame pvc command will present you with a list of all configured PVCs and DLCI numbers. It provides the status of each PVC connection and traffic statistics too. It will also give you the number of BECN and FECN (BECN and FECN and discussed in detail in the CCNA Study Guide) packets received on the router per PVC.

Here is an example:

```
RouterA#sho frame pvc

PVC Statistics for interface Serial0 (Frame Relay DTE)

DLCI = 16,DLCI USAGE = LOCAL,PVC STATUS =ACTIVE,
INTERFACE = Serial0.1
 input pkts 50977876     output pkts 41822892
  in bytes 3137403144
 out bytes 3408047602    dropped pkts 5
  in FECN pkts 0
 in BECN pkts 0        out FECN pkts 0       out BECN pkts 0
 in DE pkts 9393       out DE pkts 0
 pvc create time 7w3d, last time pvc status changed 7w3d

DLCI = 18,DLCI USAGE =LOCAL,PVC STATUS =ACTIVE,
```

```
INTERFACE = Serial0.3
 input pkts 30572401    output pkts 31139837
  in bytes 1797291100
 out bytes 3227181474    dropped pkts 5
  in FECN pkts 0
 in BECN pkts 0        out FECN pkts 0        out BECN pkts 0
 in DE pkts 28        out DE pkts 0
 pvc create time 7w3d, last time pvc status changed 7w3d
```

If you only want to see information about PVC 16, you can type the command **show frame-relay pvc 16**.

The *show interface* Command

You can use the show interface command to check for LMI traffic. The show interface command displays information about the encapsulation, as well as layer 2 and layer 3 information. It also displays line, protocol, DLCI, and LMI information. Check it out:

```
RouterA#sho int s0
Serial0 is up, line protocol is up
 Hardware is HD64570
 MTU 1500 bytes, BW 1544 Kbit, DLY 20000 usec, rely
  255/255, load 2/255
 Encapsulation FRAME-RELAY, loopback not set, keepalive
  set (10 sec)
 LMI enq sent 451751,LMI stat recvd 451750,LMI upd recvd
  164,DTE LMI up
 LMI enq recvd 0, LMI stat sent 0, LMI upd sent 0
 LMI DLCI 1023 LMI type is CISCO frame relay DTE
 Broadcast queue 0/64, broadcasts sent/dropped 0/0,
  interface broadcasts 839294
```

The LMI DLCI above is used to define the type of LMI being used. If it happens to be 1023, it's the default LMI type of Cisco. If LMI DLCI is zero, then it's the ANSI LMI type (Q.933A uses 0 as well). If LMI DLCI is anything other than 0 or 1023, it's a 911—call your provider; they've got major issues!

The *show frame map* Command

The show frame map command displays the Network layer–to–DLCI mappings. Here's how that looks:

```
RouterB#show frame map
Serial0 (up): ipx 20.0007.7842.3575 dlci 16(0x10,0x400),
              dynamic, broadcast,, status defined, active
```

```
Serial0 (up): ip 172.16.20.1 dlci 16(0x10,0x400),
              dynamic, broadcast,, status defined, active
Serial1 (up): ipx 40.0007.7842.153a dlci 17(0x11,0x410),
              dynamic, broadcast,, status defined, active
Serial1 (up): ip 172.16.40.2 dlci 17(0x11,0x410),
              dynamic, broadcast,, status defined, active
```

Notice that the serial interfaces have two mappings—one for IP and one for IPX. Also important is that the Network layer addresses were resolved with the dynamic protocol Inverse ARP (IARP). After the DLCI number is listed, you can see some numbers in parentheses. The first one is 0x10, which is the hex equivalent for the DLCI number 16, used on serial 0. And the 0x11 is the hex for DLCI 17 used on serial 1. The second numbers, 0x400 and 0x410, are the DLCI numbers configured in the Frame Relay frame. They're different because of the way the bits are spread out in the frame.

The *debug frame lmi* Command

The debug frame lmi command will show output on the router consoles by default (as with any debug command). The information this command gives you will enable you to verify and trouble-shoot the Frame Relay connection by helping you determine whether the router and switch are exchanging the correct LMI information. Here's an example:

```
Router#debug frame-relay lmi
Serial3/1(in): Status, myseq 214
RT IE 1, length 1, type 0
KA IE 3, length 2, yourseq 214, myseq 214
PVC IE 0x7 , length 0x6 , dlci 130, status 0x2 , bw 0
Serial3/1(out): StEnq, myseq 215, yourseen 214, DTE up
datagramstart = 0x1959DF4, datagramsize = 13
FR encap = 0xFCF10309
00 75 01 01 01 03 02 D7 D6

Serial3/1(in): Status, myseq 215
RT IE 1, length 1, type 1
KA IE 3, length 2, yourseq 215, myseq 215
Serial3/1(out): StEnq, myseq 216, yourseen 215, DTE up
datagramstart = 0x1959DF4, datagramsize = 13
FR encap = 0xFCF10309
00 75 01 01 01 03 02 D8 D7
```

Exam Objectives

Understand what the LMI is in Frame Relay.   The LMI is a signaling standard between a CPE device (router) and a frame switch. The LMI is responsible for managing and maintaining the status between these devices. This also provides transmission keepalives to ensure that the PVC does not shut down because of inactivity.

Understand the different Frame Relay encapsulations.   Cisco uses two different Frame Relay encapsulation methods on their routers. Cisco is the default, and means that the router is connected to a Cisco Frame Relay switch; Internet Engineering Task Force (IETF) means that your router is connecting to anything except a Cisco Frame Relay switch.

Remember what the CIR is in Frame Relay.   The CIR is the rate, in bits per second, at which the Frame Relay switch agrees to transfer data.

8.3 Troubleshoot WAN implementation issues

If you have a point-to-point link, but the encapsulations aren't the same, the link will never come up. Figure 8.4 shows one link with PPP and one with HDLC.

FIGURE 8.4   Mismatched WAN encapsulations

hostname Pod1R1	hostname Pod1R2
username Pod1R2 password Cisco	username Pod1R1 password cisco
interface serial 0	interface serial 0
ip address 10.0.1.1 255.255.255.0	ip address 10.0.1.2 255.255.255.0
encapsulation ppp	encapsulation HDLC

Look at router Pod1R1 in this output:

```
Pod1R1#sh int s0/0
Serial0/0 is up, line protocol is down
  Hardware is PowerQUICC Serial
  Internet address is 10.0.1.1/24
  MTU 1500 bytes, BW 1544 Kbit, DLY 20000 usec,
     reliability 254/255, txload 1/255, rxload 1/255
  Encapsulation PPP, loopback not set
  Keepalive set (10 sec)
  LCP REQsent
Closed: IPCP, CDPCP
```

The serial interface is down, and LCP is sending requests but will never receive any responses because router Pod1R2 is using the HDLC encapsulation. To fix this problem, you would have to go to router Pod1R2 and configure the PPP encapsulation on the serial interface. One more thing—even though the usernames are configured and they're wrong, it doesn't matter because the command `ppp authentication chap` isn't used under the serial interface configuration and the username command isn't relevant in this example.

NOTE   Always remember that you just can't have PPP on one side and HDLC on the other—they don't get along!

Mismatched IP Addresses

A tricky problem to spot is if you have HDLC or PPP configured on your serial interface, but your IP addresses are wrong. Things seem to be just fine because the interfaces will show that they are up. Take a look at Figure 8.5, and see if you can see what I mean—the two routers are connected with different subnets—router Pod1R1 with 10.0.1.1/24 and router Pod1R2 with 10.2.1.2/24.

FIGURE 8.5   Mismatched IP addresses

```
hostname Pod1R1                         hostname Pod1R2
username Pod1R2 password cisco          username Pod1R1 password cisco
  interface serial 0                      interface serial 0
  ip address 10.0.1.1 255.255.255.0       ip address 10.2.1.2 255.255.255.0
  encapsulation ppp                       encapsulation ppp
  ppp authentication chap                 ppp authentication chap
```

This will never work. But as I said, take a look at the output:

```
Pod1R1#sh int s0/0
Serial0/0 is up, line protocol is up
  Hardware is PowerQUICC Serial
  Internet address is 10.0.1.1/24
  MTU 1500 bytes, BW 1544 Kbit, DLY 20000 usec,
     reliability 255/255, txload 1/255, rxload 1/255
  Encapsulation PPP, loopback not set
  Keepalive set (10 sec)
  LCP Open
  Open: IPCP, CDPCP
```

See that? The IP addresses between the routers are wrong, but the link looks like it's working fine. This is because PPP, like HDLC and Frame Relay, is a layer 2 WAN encapsulation and doesn't care about IP addresses at all. So, yes, the link is up, but you can't use IP across this link since it's misconfigured.

To find and fix this problem, you can use the show running-config or the show interfaces command on each router, or you can use the show cdp neighbors detail command:

```
Pod1R1#sh cdp neighbors detail
-------------------------
Device ID: Pod1R2
Entry address(es):
  IP address: 10.2.1.2
```

You can view and verify the directly connected neighbor's IP address and then solve your problem.

Troubleshooting Frame Relay Networks

Troubleshooting Frame Relay networks isn't any harder than troubleshooting any other type of network as long as you know what to look for, which is what I'm going to cover now. We'll go over some basic problems that commonly occur in Frame Relay configuration and how to solve them.

First on the list are serial encapsulation problems. As you learned recently, there are two Frame Relay encapsulations: Cisco and IETF. Cisco is the default, and it means that you have a Cisco router on each end of the Frame Relay network. If you don't have a Cisco router on the remote end of your Frame Relay network, then you need to run the IETF encapsulation as shown here:

```
RouterA(config)#int s0
RouterA(config-if)#encapsulation frame-relay ?
  ietf  Use RFC1490 encapsulation
  <cr>
RouterA(config-if)#encapsulation frame-relay ietf
```

Once you verify that you're using the correct encapsulation, you then need to check out your Frame Relay mappings. For example, take a look at Figure 8.6.

So, why can't RouterA talk to RouterB across the Frame Relay network? To find that out, take a close look at the frame-relay map statement. See the problem now? You cannot use a remote DLCI to communicate to the Frame Relay switch; you must use *your* DLCI number! The mapping should have included DLCI 100 instead of DLCI 200.

Now that you know how to ensure that you have the correct Frame Relay encapsulation, and that DLCIs are only locally significant, let's look into some routing protocol problems typically associated with Frame Relay. See if you can find a problem with the two configurations in Figure 8.7.

FIGURE 8.6   Frame Relay mappings

```
RouterA#show running-config
interface s0/0
ip address 172.16.100.2 255.255.0.0
encapsulation frame-relay
frame-relay map ip 172.16.100.1 200 broadcast
```

FIGURE 8.7   Frame Relay routing problems

```
RouterA#show running-config          RouterB#show running-config
interface s0/0                       interface s0/0
ip address 172.16.100.2 255.255.0.0  ip address 172.16.100.1 255.255.0.0
encapsulation frame-relay            encapsulation frame-relay
frame-relay map ip 172.16.100.1 100  frame-relay map ip 172.16.100.2 200
router rip                           router rip
     network 172.16.0.0                   network 172.16.0.0
```

Hmmmm, well, the configs look pretty good. Actually, they look great, so what's the problem? Well, remember that Frame Relay is a NBMA network by default, meaning that it doesn't send any broadcasts across the PVC. So, because the mapping statements do not have the broadcast argument at the end of the line, broadcasts, like RIP updates, won't be sent across the PVC.

Exam Objectives

Remember the two Frame Relay encapsulation methods.   There are two Frame Relay encapsulations: Cisco and IETF. Cisco is the default, and it means that you have a Cisco router on each end of the Frame Relay network. If you don't have a Cisco router on the remote end of your Frame Relay network, then you need to run the IETF encapsulation.

Remember that DLCI numbers are considered locally significant.   You cannot use a remote DLCI to communicate to the Frame Relay switch; you must use *your* DLCI number.

8.4 Describe VPN technology (including importance, benefits, role, impact, components)

I'd be pretty willing to bet you've heard the term *VPN* more than once before. Maybe you even know what one is, but just in case, a *virtual private network (VPN)* allows the creation of private networks across the Internet, enabling privacy and tunneling of non-TCP/IP protocols. VPNs are used daily to give remote users and disjointed networks connectivity over a public medium like the Internet instead of using more expensive permanent means.

Types of VPNs are named based upon the role they play in a business. There are three different categories of VPNs:

Remote access VPNs   *Remote access VPNs* allow remote users like telecommuters to securely access the corporate network wherever and whenever they need to.

Site-to-site VPNs   *Site-to-site VPNs*, or, intranet VPNs, allow a company to connect its remote sites to the corporate backbone securely over a public medium like the Internet instead of requiring more expensive WAN connections like Frame Relay.

Extranet VPNs   *Extranet VPNs* allow an organization's suppliers, partners, and customers to be connected to the corporate network in a limited way for business-to-business (B2B) communications.

Now you're interested, huh! And since VPNs are inexpensive and secure, I'm guessing you're really jonesing to find out how VPNs are created, right? Well, there's more than one way to bring a VPN into being. The first approach uses IPSec to create authentication and encryption services between endpoints on an IP network. The second way is via tunneling protocols, allowing you to establish a tunnel between endpoints on a network. And understand that the tunnel itself is a means for data or protocols to be encapsulated inside another protocol—pretty clean!

I'm going to go over the first, IPSec way in a minute, but first, I really want to describe four of the most common tunneling protocols in use:

Layer 2 Forwarding (L2F)   *Layer 2 Forwarding (L2F)* is a Cisco-proprietary tunneling protocol, and it was their first tunneling protocol created for virtual private dial-up networks (VPDNs). VPDN allows a device to use a dial-up connection to create a secure connection to a corporate network. L2F was later replaced by L2TP, which is backward compatible with L2F.

Point-to-Point Tunneling Protocol (PPTP)   *Point-to-Point Tunneling Protocol (PPTP)* was created by Microsoft to allow the secure transfer of data from remote networks to the corporate network.

Layer 2 Tunneling Protocol (L2TP)   *Layer 2 Tunneling Protocol (L2TP)* was created by Cisco and Microsoft to replace L2F and PPTP. L2TP merged the capabilities of both L2F and PPTP into one tunneling protocol.

Generic Routing Encapsulation (GRE)   *Generic Routing Encapsulation (GRE)* is another Cisco-proprietary tunneling protocol. It forms virtual point-to-point links, allowing for a variety of protocols to be encapsulated in IP tunnels.

Exam Objectives

Understand the term virtual private network (VPN).   A *virtual private network (VPN)* allows the creation of private networks across the Internet, enabling privacy and tunneling of non-TCP/IP protocols. VPNs are used daily to give remote users and disjointed networks connectivity over a public medium like the Internet instead of using more expensive permanent means.

Remember the three categories of VPN's.   Types of VPNs are named based upon the role they play in a business. There are three different categories of VPNs: remote access VPNs, site-to-site VPNs and extranet VPNs

8.5 Configure and verify a PPP connection between Cisco routers

After you configure your serial interface to support PPP encapsulation, you can configure authentication using PPP between routers. First, you need to set the hostname of the router, if it's not already set. Then you set the username and password for the remote router that will be connecting to your router:

Here's an example:

```
Router#config t
Enter configuration commands, one per line. End with CNTL/Z.
Router(config)#hostname RouterA
RouterA(config)#username RouterB password cisco
```

When using the hostname command, remember that the username is the hostname of the remote router that's connecting to your router. And it's case sensitive, too. Also, the password on both routers must be the same. It's a plain-text password that you can see with a show run command; you can encrypt the password by using the command service password-encryption. You must have a username and password configured for each remote system you plan to connect to. The remote routers must also be configured with usernames and passwords.

Now, after you've set the hostname, usernames, and passwords, choose the authentication type, either CHAP or PAP (discussed in detail in the CCNA Study Guide):

```
RouterA#config t
Enter configuration commands, one per line. End with CNTL/Z.
RouterA(config)#int s0
RouterA(config-if)#ppp authentication chap pap
RouterA(config-if)#^Z
RouterA#
```

If both methods are configured on the same line, as shown here, then only the first method will be used during link negotiation—the second acts as a backup just in case the first method fails.

Verifying PPP Encapsulation

Okay—now that PPP encapsulation is enabled, let me show you how to verify that it's up and running. First, let's take a look at a figure of a sample network. Figure 8.8 shows two routers connected with either a point-to-point serial or ISDN connection.

FIGURE 8.8   PPP authentication example

Pod1R1   Pod1R2

hostname Pod1R1   hostname Pod1R2
username Pod1R2 password cisco username Pod1R1 password cisco
  interface serial 0   interface serial 0
  ip address 10.0.1.1 255.255.255.0   ip address 10.0.1.2 255.255.255.0
  encapsulation ppp   encapsulation ppp
  ppp authentication chap   ppp authentication chap

You can start verifying the configuration with the show interface command:

```
Pod1R1#sh int s0/0
Serial0/0 is up, line protocol is up
  Hardware is PowerQUICC Serial
  Internet address is 10.0.1.1/24
  MTU 1500 bytes, BW 1544 Kbit, DLY 20000 usec,
     reliability 239/255, txload 1/255, rxload 1/255
  Encapsulation PPP
  loopback not set
  Keepalive set (10 sec)
  LCP Open
  Open: IPCP, CDPCP
[output cut]
```

Notice that the sixth line lists encapsulation as PPP and the eighth line shows that the LCP is open. This means that it has negotiated the session establishment and all is good! The ninth line tells us that NCP is listening for the protocols IP and CDP.

But what will you see if everything isn't perfect? I'm going to type in the configuration shown in Figure 8.9 and find out.

FIGURE 8.9   Failed PPP authentication

hostname Pod1R1
username Pod1R2 password Cisco
  interface serial 0
    ip address 10.0.1.1 255.255.255.0
    encapsulation ppp
    ppp authentication chap

hostname Pod1R2
username Pod1R1 password cisco
  interface serial 0
    ip address 10.0.1.2 255.255.255.0
    encapsulation ppp
    ppp authentication chap

Okay—what's wrong here? Take a look at the usernames and passwords. Do you see the problem now? That's right, the C is capitalized on the Pod1R2 username command found in the configuration of router Pod1R1. This is wrong because the usernames and passwords are case sensitive, remember? Let's take a look at the show interface command and see what happens:

```
Pod1R1#sh int s0/0
Serial0/0 is up, line protocol is down
  Hardware is PowerQUICC Serial
  Internet address is 10.0.1.1/24
  MTU 1500 bytes, BW 1544 Kbit, DLY 20000 usec,
     reliability 243/255, txload 1/255, rxload 1/255
  Encapsulation PPP, loopback not set
  Keepalive set (10 sec)
  LCP Closed
  Closed: IPCP, CDPCP
```

First, notice in the first line of output that Serial0/0 is up, line protocol is down. This is because there are no keepalives coming from the remote router. Next, notice that the LCP is closed because the authentication failed.

Debugging PPP Authentication

To display the CHAP authentication process as it occurs between two routers in the network, just use the command debug ppp authentication.

If your PPP encapsulation and authentication are set up correctly on both routers, and your usernames and passwords are all good, then the debug ppp authentication command will display output that looks like this:

```
d16h: Se0/0 PPP: Using default call direction
1d16h: Se0/0 PPP: Treating connection as a dedicated line
1d16h: Se0/0 CHAP: O CHALLENGE id 219 len 27 from "Pod1R1"
1d16h: Se0/0 CHAP: I CHALLENGE id 208 len 27 from "Pod1R2"
```

```
1d16h: Se0/0 CHAP: O RESPONSE id 208 len 27 from "Pod1R1"
1d16h: Se0/0 CHAP: I RESPONSE id 219 len 27 from "Pod1R2"
1d16h: Se0/0 CHAP: O SUCCESS id 219 len 4
1d16h: Se0/0 CHAP: I SUCCESS id 208 len 4
```

But if you have the username wrong, as we did previously in the PPP authentication failure example back in Figure 14.11, the output would look something like this:

```
1d16h: Se0/0 PPP: Using default call direction
1d16h: Se0/0 PPP: Treating connection as a dedicated line
1d16h: %SYS-5-CONFIG_I: Configured from console by console
1d16h: Se0/0 CHAP: O CHALLENGE id 220 len 27 from "Pod1R1"
1d16h: Se0/0 CHAP: I CHALLENGE id 209 len 27 from "Pod1R2"
1d16h: Se0/0 CHAP: O RESPONSE id 209 len 27 from "Pod1R1"
1d16h: Se0/0 CHAP: I RESPONSE id 220 len 27 from "Pod1R2"
1d16h: Se0/0 CHAP: O FAILURE id 220 len 25 msg is "MD/DES compare failed"
```

PPP with CHAP authentication is a three-way authentication, and if the username and passwords are not configured exactly the way they should be, then the authentication will fail and the link will be down.

Exam Objectives

Remember the PPP Data Link layer protocols.   The three Data Link layer protocols are: Network Control Protocol (NCP), which defines the Network layer protocols; Link Control Protocol (LCP), a method of establishing, configuring, maintaining, and terminating the point-to-point connection; and High-Level Data Link Control (HDLC), the MAC layer protocol that encapsulates the packets.

Review Questions

1. Which command will display the CHAP authentication process as it occurs between two routers in the network?

    A. `show chap authentication`

    B. `show interface serial 0`

    C. `debug ppp authentication`

    D. `debug chap authentication`

2. Suppose that you have a customer who has a central HQ and six branch offices. They anticipate adding six more branches in the near future. They wish to implement a WAN technology that will allow the branches to economically connect to HQ and you have no free ports on the HQ router. Which of the following would you recommend?

    A. PPP

    B. HDLC

    C. Frame Relay

    D. ISDN

3. How should a router that is being used in a Frame Relay network be configured to keep split horizon issues from preventing routing updates?

    A. Configure a separate subinterface for each PVC with a unique DLCI and subnet assigned to the subinterface.

    B. Configure each Frame Relay circuit as a point-to-point line to support multicast and broadcast traffic.

    C. Configure many subinterfaces in the same subnet.

    D. Configure a single subinterface to establish multiple PVC connections to multiple remote router interfaces.

4. Which encapsulations can be configured on a serial interface? (Choose three.)

    A. Ethernet

    B. Token Ring

    C. HDLC

    D. Frame Relay

    E. PPP

5. The Acme Corporation is implementing dial-up services to enable remote-office employees to connect to the local network. The company uses multiple routed protocols, needs authentication of users connecting to the network, and since some calls will be long distance, needs callback support. Which of the following protocols is the best choice for these remote services?

    A. 802.1

    B. Frame Relay

    C. HDLC

    D. PPP

    E. PAP

6. Which WAN encapsulations can be configured on an asynchronous serial connection? (Choose two.)

   A. PPP

   B. ATM

   C. HDLC

   D. SDLC

   E. Frame Relay

7. Why won't the serial link between the Corp router and the Remote router come up?

   ```
   Corp#sh int s0/0
   Serial0/0 is up, line protocol is down
     Hardware is PowerQUICC Serial
     Internet address is 10.0.1.1/24
     MTU 1500 bytes, BW 1544 Kbit, DLY 20000 usec,
         reliability 254/255, txload 1/255, rxload 1/255
     Encapsulation PPP, loopback not set


   Remote#sh int s0/0
   Serial0/0 is up, line protocol is down
     Hardware is PowerQUICC Serial
     Internet address is 10.0.1.2/24
     MTU 1500 bytes, BW 1544 Kbit, DLY 20000 usec,
         reliability 254/255, txload 1/255, rxload 1/255
     Encapsulation HDLC, loopback not set
   ```

   A. The serial cable is faulty.

   B. The IP addresses are not in the same subnet.

   C. The subnet masks are not correct.

   D. The keepalive settings are not correct.

   E. The layer 2 frame types are not compatible.

8. A remote site has just been connected to the central office. However, remote users cannot access applications at the central office. The remote router can be pinged from the central office router. After reviewing the command output shown below, which do you think is the most likely reason for the problem?

   ```
   Central#show running-config
   !
   interface Serial0
    ip address 10.0.8.1 255.255.248.0
    encapsulation frame-relay
    frame-relay map ip 10.0.15.2 200
   !
   Router rip
   Network 10.0.0.0
   ```

```
Remote#show running-config
!
interface Serial0
 ip address 10.0.15.2 255.255.248.0
 encapsulation frame-relay
 frame-relay map ip 10.0.8.1 100
!
Router rip
Network 10.0.0.0
```

A. The Frame Relay PVC is down.

B. The IP addressing on the Central/Remote router link is incorrect.

C. RIP routing information is not being forwarded.

D. Frame Relay Inverse ARP is not properly configured.

9. Which of the following describes an industry-wide standard suite of protocols and algorithms that allows for secure data transmission over an IP-based network that functions at the layer 3 Network layer of the OSI model?

A. HDLC

B. Cable

C. VPN

D. IPSec

E. xDSL

10. Which of the following describes the creation of private networks across the Internet, enabling privacy and tunneling of non-TCP/IP protocols?

A. HDLC

B. Cable

C. VPN

D. IPSec

E. xDSL

Answers to Review Questions

1. C. The command `debug ppp authentication` will show you the authentication process that PPP uses between point-to-point connections.

2. C. The key is "there are no free ports" on your router. Only Frame Relay can provide a connection to multiple locations with one interface, and in an economical manner no less.

3. A. If you have a serial port configured with multiple DLCIs connected to multiple remote sites, split horizon rules stop route updates received on an interface from being sent out the same interface. By creating subinterfaces for each PVC, you can avoid the split horizon issues when using Frame Relay.

4. C, D, E. Ethernet and Token Ring are LAN technologies and cannot be configured on a serial interface. PPP, HDLC, and Frame Relay are layer 2 WAN technologies that are typically configured on a serial interface.

5. D. PPP is your only option, as HDLC and Frame Relay do not support these types of business requirements. PPP provides dynamic addressing, authentication using PAP or CHAP, and callback services.

6. A, B. Please do not freak out because ATM is an answer to this question. ATM is not covered in depth on the CCNA exam. PPP is mostly used for dial-up (async) services, but ATM could be used as well, although it typically is not used anymore, since PPP is so efficient.

7. E. This is an easy question because the Remote router is using the default HDLC serial encapsulation and the Corp router is using the PPP serial encapsulation. You should go to the Remote router and set that encapsulation to PPP or change the Corp router back to the default of HDLC.

8. C. Even though the IP addresses don't look correct, they are in the same subnet, so answer B is not correct. The question states that you can ping the other side, so the PVC must be up—answer A can't be correct. You cannot configure IARP, so only answer C can be correct. Since a Frame Relay network is a non-broadcast multi-access network by default, broadcasts such as RIP updates cannot be sent across the PVC unless you use the broadcast statement at the end of the `frame-relay map` command.

9. D. IPSec is an industry-wide standard suite of protocols and algorithms that allows for secure data transmission over an IP-based network that functions at the layer 3 Network layer of the OSI model.

10. C. A *virtual private network (VPN)* allows the creation of private networks across the Internet, enabling privacy and tunneling of non-TCP/IP protocols. A VPN can be set up across any type of link.

Appendix A

About the Companion CD

IN THIS APPENDIX:

✓ What you'll find on the CD

✓ System requirements

✓ Using the CD

✓ Troubleshooting

What You'll Find on the CD

The following sections are arranged by category and provide a summary of the software and other goodies you'll find on the CD. If you need help with installing the items provided on the CD, refer to the installation instructions in the "Using the CD" section of this appendix.

Some programs on the CD might fall into one of these categories:

Shareware programs are fully functional, free, trial versions of copyrighted programs. If you like particular programs, register with their authors for a nominal fee and receive licenses, enhanced versions, and technical support.

Freeware programs are free, copyrighted games, applications, and utilities. You can copy them to as many computers as you like—for free—but they offer no technical support.

GNU software is governed by its own license, which is included inside the folder of the GNU software. There are no restrictions on distribution of GNU software. See the GNU license at the root of the CD for more details.

Trial, demo, or *evaluation* versions of software are usually limited either by time or functionality (such as not letting you save a project after you create it).

Sybex Test Engine

For Windows and Mac

The CD contains the Sybex Test Engine, which includes all of the Assessment Test and Chapter Review questions in electronic format, as well as two bonus exams located only on the CD.

PDF of Glossary of Terms

For Windows and Mac

We have included an electronic version of the a Glossary of Terms in .pdf format. You can view the electronic version of the Glossary with Adobe Reader.

Adobe Reader

For Windows and Mac

We've also included a copy of Adobe Reader, so you can view PDF files that accompany the book's content. For more information on Adobe Reader or to check for a newer version, visit Adobe's website at `http://www.adobe.com/products/reader/`.

Electronic Flashcards

For PC, Pocket PC and Palm

These handy electronic flashcards are just what they sound like. One side contains a question or fill in the blank, and the other side shows the answer.

System Requirements

Make sure that your computer meets the minimum system requirements shown in the following list. If your computer doesn't match up to most of these requirements, you may have problems using the software and files on the companion CD. For the latest and greatest information, please refer to the ReadMe file located at the root of the CD-ROM.

- A PC running Microsoft Windows 98, Windows 2000, Windows NT4 (with SP4 or later), Windows Me, Windows XP, or Windows Vista.

- An Internet connection

- A CD-ROM drive

Using the CD

To install the items from the CD to your hard drive, follow these steps.

1. Insert the CD into your computer's CD-ROM drive. The license agreement appears.

Windows users: The interface won't launch if you have autorun disabled. In that case, click Start ➤ Run (for Windows Vista, Start ➤ All Programs ➤ Accessories ➤ Run). In the dialog box that appears, type **D:\Start.exe**. (Replace *D* with the proper letter if your CD drive uses a different letter. If you don't know the letter, see how your CD drive is listed under My Computer.) Click OK.

2. Read through the license agreement, and then click the Accept button if you want to use the CD.

The CD interface appears. The interface allows you to access the content with just one or two clicks.

Troubleshooting

Wiley has attempted to provide programs that work on most computers with the minimum system requirements. Alas, your computer may differ, and some programs may not work properly for some reason.

The two likeliest problems are that you don't have enough memory (RAM) for the programs you want to use, or you have other programs running that are affecting installation or running of a program. If you get an error message such as "Not enough memory" or "Setup cannot continue," try one or more of the following suggestions and then try using the software again:

Turn off any antivirus software running on your computer. Installation programs sometimes mimic virus activity and may make your computer incorrectly believe that it's being infected by a virus.

Close all running programs. The more programs you have running, the less memory is available to other programs. Installation programs typically update files and programs; so if you keep other programs running, installation may not work properly.

Have your local computer store add more RAM to your computer. This is, admittedly, a drastic and somewhat expensive step. However, adding more memory can really help the speed of your computer and allow more programs to run at the same time.

Customer Care

If you have trouble with the book's companion CD-ROM, please call the Wiley Product Technical Support phone number at (800) 762-2974. Outside the United States, call +1(317) 572-3994. You can also contact Wiley Product Technical Support at http://sybex.custhelp.com. John Wiley & Sons will provide technical support only for installation and other general quality control items. For technical support on the applications themselves, consult the program's vendor or author.

To place additional orders or to request information about other Wiley products, please call (877) 762-2974.

Glossary

10BaseT   Part of the original IEEE 802.3 standard, 10BaseT is the Ethernet specification of 10Mbps baseband that uses two pairs of twisted-pair, Category 3, 4, or 5 cabling—using one pair to send data and the other to receive. 10BaseT has a distance limit of about 100 meters per segment. *See also: Ethernet* and *IEEE 802.3.*

100BaseT   Based on the IEEE 802.3u standard, 100BaseT is the Fast Ethernet specification of 100Mbps baseband that uses UTP wiring. 100BaseT sends link pulses (containing more information than those used in 10BaseT) over the network when no traffic is present. *See also: 10BaseT, Fast Ethernet,* and *IEEE 802.3.*

100BaseTX   Based on the IEEE 802.3u standard, 100BaseTX is the 100Mbps baseband Fast Ethernet specification that uses two pairs of UTP or STP wiring. The first pair of wires receives data; the second pair sends data. To ensure correct signal timing, a 100BaseTX segment cannot be longer than 100 meters.

A&B bit signaling   Used in T1 transmission facilities and sometimes called "24th channel signaling." Each of the 24 T1 subchannels in this procedure uses one bit of every sixth frame to send supervisory signaling information.

AAA   Authentication, Authorization, and Accounting: A system developed by Cisco to provide network security. *See also: authentication, authorization,* and *accounting.*

AAL   ATM Adaptation Layer: A service-dependent sublayer of the Data Link layer, which accepts data from other applications and brings it to the ATM layer in 48-byte ATM payload segments. CS and SAR are the two sublayers that form AALs. Currently, the four types of AAL recommended by the ITU-T are AAL1, AAL2, AAL3/4, and AAL5. AALs are differentiated by the source-destination timing they use, whether they are CBR or VBR, and whether they are used for connection-oriented or connectionless mode data transmission. *See also: AAL1, AAL2, AAL3/4, AAL5, ATM,* and *ATM layer.*

AAL1   ATM Adaptation Layer 1: One of four AALs recommended by the ITU-T, it is used for connection-oriented, time-sensitive services that need constant bit rates, such as isochronous traffic and uncompressed video. *See also: AAL.*

AAL2   ATM Adaptation Layer 2: One of four AALs recommended by the ITU-T, it is used for connection-oriented services that support a variable bit rate, such as compressed voice traffic. *See also: AAL.*

AAL3/4   ATM Adaptation Layer 3/4: One of four AALs (a product of two initially distinct layers) recommended by the ITU-T, supporting both connectionless and connection-oriented links. Its primary use is in sending SMDS packets over ATM networks. *See also: AAL.*

AAL5   ATM Adaptation Layer 5: One of four AALs recommended by the ITU-T, it is used to support connection-oriented VBR services primarily to transfer classical IP over ATM and LANE traffic. This least complex of the AAL recommendations uses SEAL, offering lower bandwidth costs and simpler processing requirements but also providing reduced bandwidth and error-recovery capacities. *See also: AAL.*

AARP   AppleTalk Address Resolution Protocol: The protocol in an AppleTalk stack that maps data-link addresses to network addresses.

AARP probe packets   Packets sent by the AARP to determine whether a given node ID is being used by another node in a nonextended AppleTalk network. If the node ID is not in use, the sending node appropriates that node's ID. If the node ID is in use, the sending node will select a different ID and then send out more AARP probe packets. *See also: AARP.*

ABM   Asynchronous Balanced Mode: When two stations can initiate a transmission, ABM is an HDLC (or one of its derived protocols) communication technology that supports peer-oriented, point-to-point communications between both stations.

ABR   Area Border Router: An OSPF router that is located on the border of one or more OSPF areas. ABRs are used to connect OSPF areas to the OSPF backbone area.

access layer   One of the layers in Cisco's three-layer hierarchical model. The access layer provides users with access to the internetwork.

access link   A link used with switches that is part of only one virtual LAN (VLAN). Trunk links carry information from multiple VLANs.

access list   A set of test conditions kept by routers that determines "interesting traffic" to and from the router for various services on the network.

access method   The manner in which network devices approach gaining access to the network itself.

access rate   Defines the bandwidth rate of the circuit. For example, the access rate of a T1 circuit is 1.544Mbps. In Frame Relay and other technologies, there may be a fractional T1 connection—256Kbps, for example—however, the access rate and clock rate are still 1.544Mbps.

access server   Also known as a "network access server," it is a communications process connecting asynchronous devices to a LAN or WAN through network and terminal emulation software, providing synchronous or asynchronous routing of supported protocols.

accounting   One of the three components in AAA. Accounting provides auditing and logging functionalities to the security model.

acknowledgment   Verification sent from one network device to another signifying that an event has occurred. May be abbreviated as ACK. *Contrast with: NAK.*

ACR   Allowed cell rate: A designation defined by the ATM Forum for managing ATM traffic. Dynamically controlled using congestion control measures, the ACR varies between the minimum cell rate (MCR) and the peak cell rate (PCR). *See also: MCR and PCR.*

active monitor   The mechanism used to manage a token ring. The network node with the highest MAC address on the ring becomes the active monitor and is responsible for management tasks such as preventing loops and ensuring that tokens are not lost.

active state   In regard to an EIGRP routing table, a route will be in active state when a router is undergoing a route convergence.

address learning   Used with transparent bridges to learn the hardware addresses of all devices on a network. The switch then filters the network with the known hardware (MAC) addresses.

address mapping   By translating network addresses from one format to another, this methodology permits different protocols to operate interchangeably.

address mask   A bit combination descriptor identifying which portion of an address refers to the network or subnet and which part refers to the host. Sometimes simply called the mask. *See also: subnet mask.*

address resolution   The process used for resolving differences between computer addressing schemes. Address resolution typically defines a method for tracing Network layer (layer 3) addresses to Data Link layer (layer 2) addresses. *See also: address mapping.*

adjacency   The relationship made to exchange routing information between defined neighboring routers and end nodes using a common media segment.

administrative distance (AD)   A number between 0 and 255 that expresses the level of trustworthiness of a routing information source. The lower the number, the higher the integrity rating.

administrative weight   A value designated by a network administrator to rate the preference given to a network link. It is one of four link metrics exchanged by PTSPs to test ATM network resource availability.

ADSU   ATM Data Service Unit: The terminal adapter used to connect to an ATM network through an HSSI-compatible mechanism. *See also: DSU.*

advertising   The process whereby routing or service updates are transmitted at given intervals, allowing other routers on the network to maintain a record of viable routes.

AEP   AppleTalk Echo Protocol: A test for connectivity between two AppleTalk nodes where one node sends a packet to another and receives an echo, or copy, in response.

AFI   Authority and Format Identifier: The part of an NSAP ATM address that delineates the type and format of the IDI section of an ATM address.

AFP   AppleTalk Filing Protocol: A Presentation layer protocol, supporting AppleShare and Mac OS File Sharing, that permits users to share files and applications on a server.

AIP   ATM Interface Processor: Supporting AAL3/4 and AAL5, this interface for Cisco 7000 series routers minimizes performance bottlenecks at the UNI. *See also: AAL3/4 and AAL5.*

algorithm   A set of rules or processes used to solve a problem. In networking, algorithms are typically used for finding the best route for traffic from a source to its destination.

alignment error   An error occurring in Ethernet networks, in which a received frame has extra bits—that is, a number not divisible by eight. Alignment errors are generally the result of frame damage caused by collisions.

all-routes explorer packet   An explorer packet that can move across an entire SRB network, tracing all possible paths to a given destination. Also known as an all-rings explorer packet. *See also: explorer packet, local explorer packet,* and *spanning explorer packet.*

AM   Amplitude modulation: A modulation method that represents information by varying the amplitude of the carrier signal. *See also: modulation.*

AMI   Alternate Mark Inversion: A line-code type on T1 and E1 circuits that shows zeros as 01 during each bit cell and ones as 11 or 00, alternately, during each bit cell. The sending device must maintain ones density in AMI but not independently of the data stream. Also known as binary-coded, alternate mark inversion. *Contrast with: B8ZS. See also: ones density.*

amplitude   An analog or digital waveform's highest value.

analog transmission   Signal messaging whereby information is represented by various combinations of signal amplitude, frequency, and phase.

ANSI   American National Standards Institute: The organization of corporate, government, and volunteer members that coordinates standards-related activities, approves U.S. national standards, and develops U.S. positions in international standards organizations. ANSI assists in the creation of international and U.S. standards in disciplines such as communications, networking, and a variety of technical fields. It publishes over 13,000 standards for engineered products and technologies ranging from screw threads to networking protocols. ANSI is a member of the International Electrotechnical Commission (IEC) and International Organization for Standardization (ISO).

anycast   An ATM address that can be shared by more than one end system, allowing requests to be routed to a node that provides a particular service.

AppleTalk   Currently in two versions, the group of communication protocols designed by Apple Computer for use in Macintosh environments. The earlier Phase 1 protocols support one physical network with only one network number that resides in one zone. The later Phase 2 protocols support more than one logical network on a single physical network, allowing networks to exist in more than one zone. *See also: zone.*

Application layer   Layer 7 of the OSI reference network model, supplying services to application procedures (such as electronic mail and file transfer) that are outside the OSI model. This layer chooses and determines the availability of communicating partners along with the resources necessary to make the connection, coordinates partnering applications, and forms a consensus on procedures for controlling data integrity and error recovery. *See also: Data Link layer, Network layer, Physical layer, Presentation layer, Session layer,* and *Transport layer.*

ARA   AppleTalk Remote Access: A protocol for Macintosh users establishing their access to resources and data from a remote AppleTalk location.

area   A logical, rather than physical, set of segments (based on CLNS, DECnet, or OSPF) along with their attached devices. Areas are commonly connected to others using routers to create a single autonomous system. *See also: autonomous system.*

ARM   Asynchronous Response Mode: An HDLC communication mode using one primary station and at least one additional station, in which transmission can be initiated from either the primary or one of the secondary units.

ARP   Address Resolution Protocol: Defined in RFC 826, the protocol that traces IP addresses to MAC addresses. *See also: RARP.*

AS   autonomous system: A group of networks under mutual administration that share the same routing methodology. Autonomous systems are subdivided by areas and must be assigned an individual 16-bit number by the IANA. *See also: area.*

AS path prepending   The use of route maps in BGP to lengthen the autonomous system path by adding false ASNs.

ASBR   Autonomous System Boundary Router: An Area Border Router placed between an OSPF autonomous system and a non-OSPF network that operates both OSPF and an additional routing protocol, such as RIP. ASBRs must be located in a non-stub OSPF area. *See also: ABR, non-stub area,* and *OSPF.*

ASCII   American Standard Code for Information Interchange: An 8-bit code for representing characters, consisting of 7 data bits plus 1 parity bit.

ASICs   Application-specific integrated circuits: Used in layer 2 switches to make filtering decisions. The ASIC looks in the filter table of MAC addresses and determines which port the destination hardware address of a received hardware address is destined for. The frame will be allowed to traverse only that one segment. If the hardware address is unknown, the frame is forwarded out all ports.

ASN.1   Abstract Syntax Notation One: An OSI language used to describe types of data that are independent of computer structures and depicting methods. Described by ISO International Standard 8824.

ASP   AppleTalk Session Protocol: A protocol employing ATP to establish, maintain, and tear down sessions as well as sequence requests. *See also: ATP.*

AST   Automatic Spanning Tree: A function that supplies one path for spanning explorer frames traveling from one node in the network to another, supporting the automatic resolution of spanning trees in SRB networks. AST is based on the IEEE 802.1d standard. *See also: IEEE 802.1* and *SRB.*

asynchronous transmission   Digital signals sent without precise timing, usually with different frequencies and phase relationships. Asynchronous transmissions generally enclose individual characters in control bits (called start and stop bits) that show the beginning and end of each character. *Contrast with: isochronous transmission* and *synchronous transmission.*

ATCP   AppleTalk Control Program: The protocol for establishing and configuring AppleTalk over PPP, defined in RFC 1378. *See also: PPP.*

ATDM   Asynchronous Time-Division Multiplexing: A technique for sending information, it differs from normal TDM in that the time slots are assigned when necessary rather than preassigned to certain transmitters. *Contrast with: FDM, statistical multiplexing,* and *TDM.*

ATG Address Translation Gateway: The mechanism within Cisco DECnet routing software that enables routers to route multiple, independent DECnet networks and to establish a user-designated address translation for chosen nodes between networks.

ATM Asynchronous Transfer Mode: The international standard, identified by fixed-length 53-byte cells, for transmitting cells in multiple service systems, such as voice, video, or data. Transit delays are reduced because the fixed-length cells permit processing to occur in the hardware. ATM is designed to maximize the benefits of high-speed transmission media, such as SONET, E3, and T3.

ATM ARP server A device that supplies logical subnets running classical IP over ATM with address-resolution services.

ATM endpoint The initiating or terminating connection in an ATM network. ATM endpoints include servers, workstations, ATM to LAN switches, and ATM routers.

ATM Forum The international organization founded jointly by Northern Telecom, Sprint, Cisco Systems, and NET/ADAPTIVE in 1991 to develop and promote standards-based implementation agreements for ATM technology. The ATM Forum broadens official standards developed by ANSI and ITU-T and creates implementation agreements before official standards are published.

ATM layer A sublayer of the Data Link layer in an ATM network that is service independent. To create standard 53-byte ATM cells, the ATM layer receives 48-byte segments from the AAL and attaches a 5-byte header to each. These cells are then sent to the physical layer for transmission across the physical medium. *See also: AAL.*

ATMM ATM Management: A procedure that runs on ATM switches, managing rate enforcement and VCI translation. *See also: ATM.*

ATM user-user connection A connection made by the ATM layer to supply communication between at least two ATM service users, such as ATMM processes. These communications can be uni- or bidirectional, using one or two VCs, respectively. *See also: ATM layer and ATMM.*

ATP AppleTalk Transaction Protocol: A transport-level protocol that enables reliable transactions between two sockets; one requests the other to perform a given task and to report the results. ATP fastens the request and response together, assuring a loss-free exchange of request-response pairs.

attenuation In communication, weakening or loss of signal energy, typically caused by distance.

AURP AppleTalk Update-based Routing Protocol: A technique for encapsulating AppleTalk traffic in the header of a foreign protocol that allows the connection of at least two noncontiguous AppleTalk internetworks through a foreign network (such as TCP/IP) to create an AppleTalk WAN. The connection made is called an AURP tunnel. By exchanging routing information between exterior routers, the AURP maintains routing tables for the complete AppleTalk WAN. *See also: AURP tunnel.*

AURP tunnel   A connection made in an AURP WAN that acts as a single, virtual link between AppleTalk internetworks separated physically by a foreign network such as a TCP/IP network. *See also: AURP.*

authentication   The first component in the AAA model. Users are typically authenticated via a username and password, which are used to uniquely identify them.

authority zone   A portion of the domain-name tree associated with DNS for which one name server is the authority. *See also: DNS.*

authorization   The act of permitting access to a resource based on authentication information in the AAA model.

auto-detect mechanism   Used in Ethernet switch, hub, and interface cards to determine the duplex and speed that can be used.

auto duplex   A setting on layer 1 and layer 2 devices that sets the duplex of a switch or hub port automatically.

automatic call reconnect   A function that enables automatic call rerouting away from a failed trunk line.

autonomous confederation   A collection of self-governed systems that depend more on their own network accessibility and routing information than on information received from other systems or groups.

autonomous switching   The ability of Cisco routers to process packets more quickly by using the ciscoBus to switch packets independently of the system processor.

autonomous system   *See: AS.*

autoreconfiguration   A procedure executed by nodes within the failure domain of a token ring wherein nodes automatically perform diagnostics, trying to reconfigure the network around failed areas.

auxiliary port   The console port on the back of Cisco routers that allows you to connect a modem and dial the router and make console configuration settings.

B8ZS   Binary 8-Zero Substitution: A line-code type, interpreted at the remote end of the connection, that uses a special code substitution whenever eight consecutive zeros are transmitted over the link on T1 and E1 circuits. This technique assures ones density independent of the data stream. Also known as bipolar 8-zero substitution. *Contrast with: AMI. See also: ones density.*

backbone   The basic portion of the network that provides the primary path for traffic sent to and initiated from other networks.

back end   A node or software program supplying services to a front end. *See also: server.*

bandwidth   The gap between the highest and lowest frequencies employed by network signals. More commonly, it refers to the rated throughput capacity of a network protocol or medium.

bandwidth on demand (BoD)   This function allows an additional B channel to be used to increase the amount of bandwidth available for a particular connection.

baseband   A feature of a network technology that uses only one carrier frequency. Ethernet is an example. Also named "narrowband." *Compare with: broadband.*

baseline   Baseline information includes historical data about the network and routine utilization information. This information can be used to determine whether there were recent changes made to the network that may contribute to the problem at hand.

Basic Management Setup   Used with Cisco routers when in setup mode. Only provides enough management and configuration to get the router working so someone can telnet into the router and configure it.

baud   Synonymous with bits per second (bps), if each signal element represents 1 bit. It is a unit of signaling speed equivalent to the number of separate signal elements transmitted per second.

B channel   Bearer channel: A full-duplex, 64Kbps channel in ISDN that transmits user data. *Compare with: D channel, E channel,* and *H channel.*

BDR   Backup designated router: This is used in an OSPF network to back up the designated router in case of failure.

beacon   An FDDI frame or Token Ring frame that points to a serious problem with the ring, such as a broken cable. The beacon frame carries the address of the station thought to be down. *See also: failure domain.*

BECN   Backward Explicit Congestion Notification: BECN is the bit set by a Frame Relay network in frames moving away from frames headed into a congested path. A DTE that receives frames with the BECN may ask higher-level protocols to take necessary flow control measures. *Compare with: FECN.*

BGP4   BGP version 4: Version 4 of the interdomain routing protocol most commonly used on the Internet. BGP4 supports CIDR and uses route-counting mechanisms to decrease the size of routing tables. *See also: CIDR.*

BGP Identifier   This field contains a value that identifies the BGP speaker. This is a random value chosen by the BGP router when sending an OPEN message.

BGP neighbors   Two routers running BGP that begin a communication process to exchange dynamic routing information; they use a TCP port at layer 4 of the OSI reference model. Specifically, TCP port 179 is used. Also known as "BGP peers."

BGP peers   *See: BGP neighbors.*

BGP speaker   A router that advertises its prefixes or routes.

bidirectional shared tree   A method of shared tree multicast forwarding. This method allows group members to receive data from the source or the RP, whichever is closer. *See also: RP (rendezvous point).*

binary   A two-character numbering method that uses ones and zeros. The binary numbering system underlies all digital representation of information.

binding   Configuring a Network layer protocol to use a certain frame type on a LAN.

BIP   Bit Interleaved Parity: A method used in ATM to monitor errors on a link, sending a check bit or word in the link overhead for the previous block or frame. This allows bit errors in transmissions to be found and delivered as maintenance information.

BISDN   Broadband ISDN: ITU-T standards created to manage high-bandwidth technologies such as video. BISDN presently employs ATM technology along SONET-based transmission circuits, supplying data rates typically between 155Mbps and 622Mbps and now even into the gigabyte range (if you have the big bucks). *See also: BRI, ISDN,* and *PRI.*

bit   One binary digit; either a 1 or a 0. Eight bits make a byte.

bit-oriented protocol   Regardless of frame content, the class of Data Link layer communication protocols that transmits frames. Bit-oriented protocols, as compared with byte-oriented, supply more efficient and trustworthy full-duplex operation. *Compare with: byte-oriented protocol.*

block size   Number of hosts that can be used in a subnet. Block sizes typically can be used in increments of 4, 8, 16, 32, 64, and 128.

Boot ROM   Used in routers to put the router into bootstrap mode. Bootstrap mode then boots the device with an operating system. The ROM can also hold a small Cisco IOS.

boot sequence   Defines how a router boots. The configuration register tells the router where to boot the IOS from as well as how to load the configuration.

bootstrap protocol   A protocol used to dynamically assign IP addresses and gateways to requesting clients.

border gateway   A router that facilitates communication with routers in different autonomous systems.

border peer   The device in charge of a peer group; it exists at the edge of a hierarchical design. When any member of the peer group wants to locate a resource, it sends a single explorer to the border peer. The border peer then forwards this request on behalf of the requesting router, thus eliminating duplicate traffic.

border router   Typically defined within Open Shortest Path First (OSPF) as a router that connected an area to the backbone area. However, a border router can be a router that connects a company to the Internet as well. *See also: OSPF.*

BPDU   Bridge Protocol Data Unit: A Spanning Tree Protocol initializing packet that is sent at definable intervals for the purpose of exchanging information among bridges in networks.

BRI   Basic Rate Interface: The ISDN interface that facilitates circuit-switched communication between video, data, and voice; it is made up of two B channels (64Kbps each) and one D channel (16Kbps). *Compare with: PRI. See also: BISDN.*

bridge   A device for connecting two segments of a network and transmitting packets between them. Both segments must use identical protocols to communicate. Bridges function at the Data Link layer, layer 2 of the OSI reference model. The purpose of a bridge is to filter, send, or flood any incoming frame, based on the MAC address of that particular frame.

bridge group   Used in the router configuration of bridging, bridge groups are defined by a unique number. Network traffic is bridged between all interfaces that are members of the same bridge group.

bridge identifier   Used to elect the root bridge in a layer 2 switched internetwork. The bridge ID is a combination of the bridge priority and base MAC address.

bridge priority   Sets the STP priority of the bridge. All bridge priorities are set to 32768 by default.

bridging loop   Loops occur in a bridged network if more than one link to a network exists and the STP protocol is not turned on.

broadband   A transmission methodology for multiplexing several independent signals onto one cable. In telecommunications, broadband is classified as any channel with bandwidth greater than 4kHz (typical voice grade). In LAN terminology, it is classified as a coaxial cable on which analog signaling is employed. Also known as "wideband."

broadcast   A data frame or packet that is transmitted to every node on the local network segment (as defined by the broadcast domain). Broadcasts are known by their broadcast address, which is a destination network and host address with all the bits turned on. Also called "local broadcast." *Compare with: directed broadcast.*

broadcast address   Used in both logical addressing and hardware addressing. In logical addressing, the host addresses will be all ones. With hardware addressing, the hardware address will be all ones in binary (all Fs in hex).

broadcast domain   A group of devices receiving broadcast frames initiating from any device within the group. Because routers do not forward broadcast frames, broadcast domains are not forwarded from one broadcast to another.

broadcast (multi-access) networks   Broadcast (multi-access) networks such as Ethernet allow multiple devices to connect to (or access) the same network, as well as provide a broadcast ability in which a single packet is delivered to all nodes on the network

broadcast storm   An undesired event on the network caused by the simultaneous transmission of any number of broadcasts across the network segment. Such an occurrence can overwhelm network bandwidth, resulting in time-outs.

buffer   A storage area dedicated to handling data while in transit. Buffers are used to receive/store sporadic deliveries of data bursts, usually received from faster devices, compensating for the variations in processing speed. Incoming information is stored until everything is received prior to sending data on. Also known as an "information buffer."

bursting Some technologies, including ATM and Frame Relay, are considered burstable. This means that user data can exceed the bandwidth normally reserved for the connection; however, it cannot exceed the port speed. An example of this would be a 128Kbps Frame Relay CIR on a T1—depending on the vendor, it may be possible to send more than 128Kbps for a short time.

bus Any common physical path, typically wires or copper, through which a digital signal can be used to send data from one part of a computer to another.

BUS Broadcast and unknown servers: In LAN emulation, the hardware or software responsible for resolving all broadcasts and packets with unknown (unregistered) addresses into the point-to-point virtual circuits required by ATM. *See also: LANE, LEC, LECS,* and *LES.*

bus topology A linear LAN architecture in which transmissions from various stations on the network are reproduced over the length of the medium and are accepted by all other stations. *Compare with: ring topology* and *star topology.*

BX.25 AT&T's use of X.25. *See also: X.25.*

bypass mode An FDDI and Token Ring network operation that deletes an interface.

bypass relay A device that enables a particular interface in the token ring to be closed down and effectively taken off the ring.

byte Eight bits. *See also: octet.*

byte-oriented protocol Any type of data-link communication protocol that, in order to mark the boundaries of frames, uses a specific character from the user character set. These protocols have generally been superseded by bit-oriented protocols. *Compare with: bit-oriented protocol.*

cable range In an extended AppleTalk network, the range of numbers allotted for use by existing nodes on the network. The value of the cable range can be anywhere from a single network number to a sequence of several touching network numbers. Node addresses are determined by their cable range value.

CAC Connection Admission Control: The sequence of actions executed by every ATM switch while connection setup is performed in order to determine if a request for connection is violating the guarantees of QoS for established connections. Also, CAC is used to route a connection request through an ATM network.

call admission control A device for managing traffic in ATM networks, determining the possibility of a path containing adequate bandwidth for a requested VCC.

call establishment Used to reference an ISDN call setup scheme when the call is working.

call priority In circuit-switched systems, the defining priority given to each originating port; it specifies in which order calls will be reconnected. Additionally, call priority identifies which calls are allowed during a bandwidth reservation.

call setup   Handshaking scheme that defines how a source and destination device will establish a call to each other.

call setup time   The length of time necessary to effect a switched call between DTE devices.

CBR   Constant bit rate: An ATM Forum QoS class created for use in ATM networks. CBR is used for connections that rely on precision clocking to guarantee trustworthy delivery. *Compare with: ABR* and *VBR.*

CD   Carrier detect: A signal indicating that an interface is active or that a connection generated by a modem has been established.

CDP   Cisco Discovery Protocol: Cisco's proprietary protocol that is used to tell a neighbor Cisco device about the type of hardware, software version, and active interfaces the Cisco device is using. It uses a SNAP frame between devices and is not routable.

CDP holdtime   The amount of time a router will hold Cisco Discovery Protocol information received from a neighbor router before discarding it if the information is not updated by the neighbor. This timer is set to 180 seconds by default.

CDP timer   The amount of time between Cisco Discovery Protocol advertisements transmitted out of all router interfaces, by default. The CDP timer is 90 seconds by default.

CDVT   Cell Delay Variation Tolerance: A QoS parameter for traffic management in ATM networks specified when a connection is established. The allowable fluctuation levels for data samples taken by the PCR in CBR transmissions are determined by the CDVT. *See also: CBR* and *PCR.*

cell   In ATM networking, the basic unit of data for switching and multiplexing. Cells have a defined length of 53 bytes, including a 5-byte header that identifies the cell's data stream and 48 bytes of payload. *See also: cell relay.*

cell payload scrambling   The method by which an ATM switch maintains framing on some medium-speed edge and trunk interfaces (T3 or E3 circuits). Cell payload scrambling rearranges the data portion of a cell to maintain the line synchronization with certain common bit patterns.

cell relay   A technology that uses small packets of fixed size, known as cells. Their fixed length enables cells to be processed and switched in hardware at high speeds, making this technology the foundation for ATM and other high-speed network protocols. *See also: cell.*

Centrex   A local exchange carrier service providing local switching that resembles that of an on-site PBX. Centrex has no on-site switching capability. Therefore, all customer connections return to the central office (CO). *See also: CO.*

CER   Cell error ratio: In ATM, the ratio of transmitted cells having errors to the total number of cells transmitted within a certain span of time.

CGMP   Cisco Group Management Protocol: A proprietary protocol developed by Cisco. The router uses CGMP to send multicast membership commands to Catalyst switches.

channelized E1 Operating at 2.048Mpbs, an access link that is sectioned into 29 B channels and one D channel, supporting DDR, Frame Relay, and X.25. *Compare with: channelized T1.*

channelized T1 Operating at 1.544Mbps, an access link that is sectioned into 23 B channels and one D channel of 64Kbps each, where individual channels or groups of channels connect to various destinations, supporting DDR, Frame Relay, and X.25. *Compare with: channelized E1.*

CHAP Challenge Handshake Authentication Protocol: Supported on lines using PPP encapsulation, it is a security feature that identifies the remote end, helping keep out unauthorized users. After CHAP is performed, the router or access server determines whether a given user is permitted access. It is a newer, more secure protocol than PAP. *Compare with: PAP.*

checksum A test for ensuring the integrity of sent data. It is a number calculated from a series of values taken through a sequence of mathematical functions, typically placed at the end of the data from which it is calculated, and then recalculated at the receiving end for verification. *Compare with: CRC.*

choke packet When congestion exists, it is a packet sent to inform a transmitter that it should decrease its sending rate.

CIDR Classless Inter-Domain Routing It allows a group of IP networks to appear to other networks as a unified, larger entity. In CIDR, IP addresses and their subnet masks are written as four dotted octets, followed by a forward slash and the number of masking bits (a form of subnet notation shorthand). *See also: BGP4.*

CIP Channel Interface Processor: A channel attachment interface for use in Cisco 7000 series routers that connects a host mainframe to a control unit. This device eliminates the need for an FBP to attach channels.

CIR Committed information rate: Averaged over a minimum span of time and measured in bps, a Frame Relay network's agreed-upon minimum rate of transferring information.

circuit switching Used with dial-up networks such as PPP and ISDN. Passes data, but needs to set up the connection first—just like making a phone call.

Cisco FRAD Cisco Frame Relay Access Device: A Cisco product that supports Cisco IPS Frame Relay SNA services, connecting SDLC devices to Frame Relay without requiring an existing LAN. May be upgraded to a fully functioning multiprotocol router. Can activate conversion from SDLC to Ethernet and Token Ring, but does not support attached LANs. *See also: FRAD.*

CiscoFusion Cisco's name for the internetworking architecture under which its Cisco IOS operates. It is designed to "fuse" together the capabilities of its disparate collection of acquired routers and switches.

Cisco IOS Cisco Internet Operating System software. The kernel of the Cisco line of routers and switches that supplies shared functionality, scalability, and security for all products under its CiscoFusion architecture. *See also: CiscoFusion.*

CiscoView   GUI-based management software for Cisco networking devices, enabling dynamic status, statistics, and comprehensive configuration information. Displays a physical view of the Cisco device chassis and provides device-monitoring functions and fundamental troubleshooting capabilities. May be integrated with a number of SNMP-based network management platforms.

Class A network   Part of the Internet Protocol hierarchical addressing scheme. Class A networks have only 8 bits for defining networks and 24 bits for defining hosts and subnets on each network.

Class B network   Part of the Internet Protocol hierarchical addressing scheme. Class B networks have 16 bits for defining networks and 16 bits for defining hosts and subnets on each network.

Class C network   Part of the Internet Protocol hierarchical addressing scheme. Class C networks have 24 bits for defining networks and only 8 bits for defining hosts and subnets on each network.

classful routing   Routing protocols that do not send subnet mask information when a route update is sent out.

classical IP over ATM   Defined in RFC 1577, the specification for running IP over ATM that maximizes ATM features. Also known as "CIA."

classless routing   Routing that sends subnet mask information in the routing updates. Classless routing allows Variable-Length Subnet Masking (VLSM) and supernetting. Routing protocols that support classless routing are RIP version 2, EIGRP, and OSPF.

CLI   Command-line interface: Allows you to configure Cisco routers and switches with maximum flexibility.

CLP   Cell Loss Priority: The area in the ATM cell header that determines the likelihood of a cell being dropped during network congestion. Cells with CLP = 0 are considered insured traffic and are not apt to be dropped. Cells with CLP = 1 are considered best-effort traffic that may be dropped during congested episodes, delivering more resources to handle insured traffic.

CLR   Cell Loss Ratio: The ratio of discarded cells to successfully delivered cells in ATM. CLR can be designated a QoS parameter when establishing a connection.

CO   Central office: The local telephone company office where all loops in a certain area connect and where circuit switching of subscriber lines occurs.

collapsed backbone   A nondistributed backbone where all network segments are connected to each other through an internetworking device. A collapsed backbone can be a virtual network segment at work in a device such as a router, hub, or switch.

collision   The effect of two nodes sending transmissions simultaneously in Ethernet. When they meet on the physical media, the frames from each node collide and are damaged. *See also: collision domain.*

collision domain   The network area in Ethernet over which frames that have collided will be detected. Collisions are propagated by hubs and repeaters, but not by LAN switches, routers, or bridges. *See also: collision.*

composite metric   Used with routing protocols, such as IGRP and EIGRP, that use more than one metric to find the best path to a remote network. IGRP and EIGRP both use bandwidth and delay of the line by default. However, maximum transmission unit (MTU), load, and reliability of a link can be used as well.

compression   A technique to send more data across a link than would be normally permitted by representing repetitious strings of data with a single marker.

configuration register   A 16-bit configurable value stored in hardware or software that determines how Cisco routers function during initialization. In hardware, the bit position is set using a jumper. In software, it is set by specifying specific bit patterns used to set startup options, configured using a hexadecimal value with configuration commands.

congestion   Traffic that exceeds the network's ability to handle it.

congestion avoidance   To minimize delays, the method a network uses to control traffic entering the system. Lower-priority traffic is discarded at the edge of the network when indicators signal it cannot be delivered, thus using resources efficiently.

congestion collapse   The situation that results from the retransmission of packets in ATM networks where little or no traffic successfully arrives at destination points. It usually happens in networks made of switches with ineffective or inadequate buffering capabilities combined with poor packet discard or ABR congestion feedback mechanisms.

connection ID   Identifications given to each Telnet session into a router. The show sessions command will give you the connections a local router will have to a remote router. The show users command will show the connection IDs of users telnetted into your local router.

connectionless   Data transfer that occurs without the creation of a virtual circuit. It has low overhead, uses best-effort delivery, and is not reliable. *Contrast with: connection-oriented. See also: virtual circuit.*

Connectionless Network Service (CLNS)   See *connectionless.*

connection-oriented   Data transfer method that sets up a virtual circuit before any data is transferred. Uses acknowledgments and flow control for reliable data transfer. *Contrast with: connectionless. See also: virtual circuit.*

console port   Typically an RJ-45 (8-pin modular) port on a Cisco router and switch that allows command-line interface capability.

control direct VCC   One of two control connections defined by Phase I LAN emulation; a bidirectional virtual control connection (VCC) established in ATM by an LEC to an LES. *See also: control distribute VCC.*

control distribute VCC   One of two control connections defined by Phase 1 LAN emulation; a unidirectional virtual control connection (VCC) set up in ATM from an LES to an LEC. Usually, the VCC is a point-to-multipoint connection. *See also: control direct VCC.*

convergence   The process required for all routers in an internetwork to update their routing tables and create a consistent view of the network using the best possible paths. No user data is passed during an STP convergence time.

core layer   Top layer in the Cisco three-layer hierarchical model, which helps you design, build, and maintain Cisco hierarchical networks. The core layer passes packets quickly to distribution layer devices only. No packet filtering should take place at this layer.

cost   Also known as path cost, an arbitrary value, based on hop count, bandwidth, or another calculation, that is typically assigned by a network administrator and used by the routing protocol to compare different routes through an internetwork. Routing protocols use cost values to select the best path to a certain destination: the lowest cost identifies the best path. Also known as "path cost." *See also: routing metric.*

count to infinity   A problem occurring in routing algorithms that are slow to converge where routers keep increasing the hop count to particular networks. To avoid this problem, various solutions have been implemented into each of the different routing protocols. Some of those solutions include defining a maximum hop count (defining infinity), route poising, poison reverse, and split horizon.

CPCS   Common Part Convergence Sublayer: One of two AAL sublayers that is service dependent, it is further segmented into the CS and SAR sublayers. The CPCS prepares data for transmission across the ATM network; it creates the 48-byte payload cells that are sent to the ATM layer. *See also: AAL and ATM layer.*

CPE   Customer premises equipment: Items such as telephones, modems, and terminals installed at customer locations and connected to the service provider network.

crankback   In ATM, a correction technique used when a node somewhere on a chosen path cannot accept a connection setup request, blocking the request. The path is rolled back to an intermediate node, which then uses GCAC to attempt to find an alternate path to the final destination.

CRC   Cyclic redundancy check: A methodology that detects errors, whereby the frame recipient makes a calculation by dividing frame contents with a prime binary divisor and compares the remainder to a value stored in the frame by the sending node. *Contrast with: checksum.*

crossover cable   Type of Ethernet cable that connects a switch to switch, host to host, hub to hub, or switch to hub.

CSMA/CD   Carrier Sense Multiple Access with Collision Detection: A technology defined by the Ethernet IEEE 802.3 committee. Each device senses the cable for a digital signal before transmitting. Also, CSMA/CD allows all devices on the network to share the same cable, but one at a time. If two devices transmit at the same time, a frame collision will occur and a jamming pattern will be sent; the devices will stop transmitting, wait a predetermined as well as a self-imposed random amount of time, and then try to transmit again.

CSU Channel service unit: A digital mechanism that connects end-user equipment to the local digital telephone loop. Frequently referred to along with the data service unit as CSU/DSU. *See also: DSU.*

CSU/DSU Channel service unit/data service unit: Physical layer device used in wide area networks to convert the CPE digital signals to what is understood by the provider's switch. A CSU/DSU is typically one device that plugs into a RJ-45 (8-pin modular) jack, known as the demarcation point.

CTD Cell Transfer Delay: For a given connection in ATM, the time period between a cell exit event at the source user-network interface (UNI) and the corresponding cell entry event at the destination. The CTD between these points is the sum of the total inter-ATM transmission delay and the total ATM processing delay.

cumulative interface delay This is a Cisco term for delay of the line. The composite metric in IGRP and EIGRP is calculated by using the bandwidth and delay of the line by default.

cut-through frame switching A frame-switching technique that flows data through a switch so that the leading edge exits the switch at the output port before the packet finishes entering the input port. Frames will be read, processed, and forwarded by devices that use cut-through switching as soon as the destination address of the frame is confirmed and the outgoing port is identified.

data circuit-terminating equipment DCE is used to provide clocking to DTE equipment.

data compression *See: compression.*

data direct VCC A bidirectional point-to-point virtual control connection (VCC) set up between two LECs in ATM and one of three data connections defined by Phase 1 LAN emulation. Because data direct VCCs do not guarantee QoS, they are generally reserved for UBR and ABR connections. *Compare with: control distribute VCC and control direct VCC.*

data encapsulation The process in which the information in a protocol is wrapped, or contained, in the data section of another protocol. In the OSI reference model, each layer encapsulates the layer immediately above it as the data flows down the protocol stack.

data frame Protocol Data Unit encapsulation at the Data Link layer of the OSI reference model. Encapsulates packets from the Network layer and prepares the data for transmission on a network medium.

datagram A logical collection of information transmitted as a Network layer unit over a medium without a previously established virtual circuit. IP datagrams have become the primary information unit of the Internet. At various layers of the OSI reference model, the terms *cell, frame, message, packet,* and *segment* also define these logical information groupings.

Data Link Control layer Layer 2 of the SNA architectural model, it is responsible for the transmission of data over a given physical link and compares somewhat to the Data Link layer of the OSI model.

Data Link layer   Layer 2 of the OSI reference model, it ensures the trustworthy transmission of data across a physical link and is primarily concerned with physical addressing, line discipline, network topology, error notification, ordered delivery of frames, and flow control. The IEEE has further segmented this layer into the MAC sublayer and the LLC sublayer. Also known as the link layer. Can be compared somewhat to the data link control layer of the SNA model. *See also: Application layer, LLC, MAC, Network layer, Physical layer, Presentation layer, Session layer,* and *Transport layer.*

data terminal equipment   *See: DTE.*

DCC   Data Country Code: Developed by the ATM Forum, one of two ATM address formats designed for use by private networks. *Compare with: ICD.*

DCE   Data communications equipment (as defined by the EIA) or data circuit-terminating equipment (as defined by the ITU T): The mechanisms and links of a communications network that make up the network portion of the user-to-network interface, such as modems. The DCE supplies the physical connection to the network, forwards traffic, and provides a clocking signal to synchronize data transmission between DTE and DCE devices. *Compare with: DTE.*

D channel   (1) Data channel: A full-duplex, 16Kbps (BRI) or 64Kbps (PRI) ISDN channel. *Compare with: B channel, E channel,* and *H channel.* (2) In SNA, anything that provides a connection between the processor and main storage with any peripherals.

DDP   Datagram Delivery Protocol: Used in the AppleTalk suite of protocols as a connectionless protocol that is responsible for sending datagrams through an internetwork.

DDR   Dial-on-demand routing: A technique that allows a router to automatically initiate and end a circuit-switched session per the requirements of the sending station. By mimicking keepalives, the router fools the end station into treating the session as active. DDR permits routing over ISDN or telephone lines via a modem or external ISDN terminal adapter.

DE   Discard Eligibility: Used in Frame Relay networks to tell a switch that a frame can be preferentially discarded if the switch is too busy. The DE is a field in the frame that is turned on by transmitting routers if the committed information rate (CIR) is oversubscribed or set to 0.

dedicated line   Point-to-point connection that does not share any bandwidth.

de-encapsulation   The technique used by layered protocols in which a layer removes header information from the Protocol Data Unit (PDU) from the layer below. *See: encapsulation.*

default route   The static routing table entry used to direct frames whose next hop is not otherwise spelled out in the routing table.

delay   The time elapsed between a sender's initiation of a transaction and the first response they receive. Also, the time needed to move a packet from its source to its destination over a path. *See also: latency.*

demarc The demarcation point between the customer premises equipment (CPE) and the telco's carrier equipment.

demodulation A series of steps that return a modulated signal to its original form. When receiving, a modem demodulates an analog signal to its original digital form (and, conversely, modulates the digital data it sends into an analog signal). *See also: modulation.*

demultiplexing The process of converting a multiplexed signal comprising more than one input stream back into separate output streams. *See also: multiplexing.*

designated bridge In the process of forwarding a frame from a segment to the root bridge, the bridge with the lowest root path cost.

designated port Used with the Spanning Tree Protocol (STP) to designate forwarding ports. If there are multiple links to the same network, STP will shut a port down to stop network loops.

designated router (DR) An OSPF router that creates LSAs for a multi-access network and is required to perform other special tasks in OSPF operations. Multi-access OSPF networks that maintain a minimum of two attached routers identify one router that is chosen by the OSPF Hello protocol, which makes possible a decrease in the number of adjacencies necessary on a multi-access network. This in turn reduces the quantity of routing protocol traffic and the physical size of the database.

desktop layer The access layer is sometimes referred to as the desktop layer. The access layer controls user and workgroup access to internetwork resources.

destination address The address for the network device(s) that will receive a packet.

DHCP Dynamic Host Configuration Protocol: DHCP is a superset of the BootP protocol. This means that it uses the same protocol structure as BootP, but it has enhancements added. Both of these protocols use servers that dynamically configure clients when requested. The two major enhancements are address pools and lease times.

dial backup Dial backup connections are typically used to provide redundancy to Frame Relay connections. The backup link is activated over an analog modem or ISDN.

directed broadcast A data frame or packet that is transmitted to a specific group of nodes on a remote network segment. Directed broadcasts are known by their broadcast address, which is a destination subnet address with all the host bits turned on.

discovery mode Also known as dynamic configuration, this technique is used by an AppleTalk interface to gain information from a working node about an attached network. The information is subsequently used by the interface for self-configuration.

distance-vector protocols The distance-vector protocols find the best path to a remote network by judging distance. Each time a packet goes through a router, that's called a hop. The route with the least number of hops to the network is determined to be the best route. However, Cisco's IGRP is considered distance vector and uses a composite metric of bandwidth and delay of the line to determine the best path to a remote network.

distance-vector routing algorithm   In order to find the shortest path, this group of routing algorithms reports on the number of hops in a given route, requiring each router to send its complete routing table with each update, but only to its neighbors. Routing algorithms of this type tend to generate loops, but they are fundamentally simpler than their link-state counterparts. *See also: link-state routing algorithm and SPF.*

distribution layer   Middle layer of the Cisco three-layer hierarchical model, which helps you design, install, and maintain Cisco hierarchical networks. The distribution layer is the point where access layer devices connect. Routing is performed at this layer.

DLCI   Data Link Connection Identifier: Used to identify virtual circuits in a Frame Relay network.

DLSw   Data Link Switching: IBM developed Data Link Switching (DLSw) in 1992 to provide support for SNA (Systems Network Architecture) and NetBIOS protocols in router-based networks. SNA and NetBIOS are nonroutable protocols that do not contain any logical layer 3 network information. DLSw encapsulates these protocols into TCP/IP messages that can be routed and is an alternative to Remote Source-Route Bridging (RSRB).

DLSw+   Cisco's implementation of DLSw. In addition to support for the RFC standards, Cisco added enhancements intended to increase scalability and to improve performance and availability.

DNS   Domain Name System: Used to resolve hostnames to IP addresses.

DSAP   Destination Service Access Point: The service access point of a network node, specified in the destination field of a packet. *See also: SSAP and SAP.*

DSR   Data Set Ready: When a DCE is powered up and ready to run, this EIA/TIA-232 interface circuit is also engaged.

DSU   Data service unit: This device is used to adapt the physical interface on a data terminal equipment (DTE) mechanism to a transmission facility such as T1 or E1 and is also responsible for signal timing. It is commonly grouped with the channel service unit and referred to as the CSU/DSU. *See also: CSU.*

DTE   Data terminal equipment: Any device located at the user end of a user-network interface serving as a destination, a source, or both. DTE includes devices such as multiplexers, routers, protocol translators, and computers. The connection to a data network is made through data communication equipment (DCE) such as a modem, using the clocking signals generated by that device. *See also: DCE.*

DTR   Data Terminal Ready: An activated EIA/TIA-232 circuit communicating to the DCE the state of preparedness of the DTE to transmit or receive data.

DUAL   Diffusing Update Algorithm: Used in Enhanced IGRP, this convergence algorithm provides loop-free operation throughout an entire route's computation. DUAL grants routers involved in a topology revision the ability to synchronize simultaneously, while routers unaffected by this change are not involved. *See also: Enhanced IGRP.*

DVMRP Distance Vector Multicast Routing Protocol: Based primarily on the Routing Information Protocol (RIP), this Internet gateway protocol implements a common, condensed-mode IP multicast scheme, using IGMP to transfer routing datagrams between its neighbors. *See also: IGMP.*

DXI Data Exchange Interface: DXI defines the effectiveness of a network device such as a router, bridge, or hub to act as an FEP to an ATM network by using a special DSU that accomplishes packet encapsulation.

dynamic entries Used in layer 2 and layer 3 devices to dynamically create a table of either hardware addresses or logical addresses dynamically.

dynamic routing Also known as "adaptive routing," this technique automatically adapts to traffic or physical network revisions.

dynamic VLAN An administrator will create an entry in a special server with the hardware addresses of all devices on the internetwork. The server will then report the associated VLAN to a switch that requests it based on the new device's hardware address.

E1 Generally used in Europe, a wide-area digital transmission scheme carrying data at 2.048Mbps. E1 transmission lines are available for lease from common carriers for private use.

E.164 (1) Evolved from standard telephone numbering system, the standard recommended by ITU-T for international telecommunication numbering, particularly in ISDN, SMDS, and BISDN. (2) Label of field in an ATM address containing numbers in E.164 format.

eBGP External Border Gateway Protocol: Used to exchange route information between different autonomous systems.

E channel Echo channel: A 64Kbps ISDN control channel used for circuit switching. Specific description of this channel can be found in the 1984 ITU-T ISDN specification, but it was dropped from the 1988 version. *See also: B channel, D channel,* and *H channel.*

edge device A device that enables packets to be forwarded between legacy interfaces (such as Ethernet and Token Ring) and ATM interfaces based on information in the Data Link and Network layers. An edge device does not take part in the running of any Network layer routing protocol; it merely uses the route description protocol in order to get the forwarding information required.

EEPROM Electronically erasable programmable read-only memory: Programmed after their manufacture, these nonvolatile memory chips can be erased if necessary using electric power and reprogrammed. *See also: EPROM* and *PROM.*

EFCI Explicit Forward Congestion Indication: A congestion feedback mode permitted by ABR service in an ATM network. The EFCI may be set by any network element that is in a state of immediate or certain congestion. The destination end system is able to carry out a protocol that adjusts and lowers the cell rate of the connection based on value of the EFCI. *See also: ABR.*

EIGRP   *See: Enhanced IGRP.*

EIP   Ethernet Interface Processor: A Cisco 7000 series router interface processor card, supplying 10Mbps AUI ports to support Ethernet Version 1 and Ethernet Version 2 or IEEE 802.3 interfaces with a high-speed data path to other interface processors.

ELAN   Emulated LAN: An ATM network configured using a client/server model in order to emulate either an Ethernet or Token Ring LAN. Multiple ELANs can exist at the same time on a single ATM network and are made up of a LAN emulation client (LEC), a LAN emulation server (LES), a broadcast and unknown server (BUS), and a LAN emulation configuration server (LECS). ELANs are defined by the LANE specification. *See also: LANE, LEC, LECS,* and *LES.*

ELAP   EtherTalk Link Access Protocol: In an EtherTalk network, the link-access protocol constructed above the standard Ethernet Data Link layer.

encapsulation   The technique used by layered protocols in which a layer adds header information to the Protocol Data Unit (PDU) from the layer above. As an example, in Internet terminology, a packet would contain a header from the Data Link layer, followed by a header from the Network layer (IP), followed by a header from the Transport layer (TCP), followed by the application protocol data.

encryption   The conversion of information into a scrambled form that effectively disguises it to prevent unauthorized access. Every encryption scheme uses some well-defined algorithm, which is reversed at the receiving end by an opposite algorithm in a process known as decryption.

Endpoints   *See: BGP neighbors.*

end-to-end VLANs   VLANs that span the switch fabric from end to end; all switches in end-to-end VLANs understand about all configured VLANs. End-to-end VLANs are configured to allow membership based on function, project, department, and so on.

Enhanced IGRP (EIGRP)   Enhanced Interior Gateway Routing Protocol: An advanced routing protocol created by Cisco combining the advantages of link-state and distance-vector protocols. Enhanced IGRP has superior convergence attributes, including high operating efficiency. *See also: IGP, OSPF,* and *RIP.*

enterprise network   A privately owned and operated network that joins most major locations in a large company or organization.

EPROM   Erasable programmable read-only memory: Programmed after their manufacture, these nonvolatile memory chips can be erased if necessary using high-power light and reprogrammed. *See also: EEPROM* and *PROM.*

ESF   Extended Superframe: Made up of 24 frames with 192 bits each, with the 193rd bit providing other functions including timing. This is an enhanced version of SF. *See also: SF.*

Ethernet   A baseband LAN specification created by the Xerox Corporation and then improved through joint efforts of Xerox, Digital Equipment Corporation, and Intel. Ethernet is similar to the IEEE 802.3 series standard and, using CSMA/CD, operates over various types of cables at 10Mbps. Also called DIX (Digital/Intel/Xerox) Ethernet. *See also: 10BaseT, Fast Ethernet,* and *IEEE.*

EtherTalk   A data-link product from Apple Computer that permits AppleTalk networks to be connected by Ethernet.

excess burst size   The amount of traffic by which the user may exceed the committed burst size.

excess rate   In ATM networking, traffic exceeding a connection's insured rate. The excess rate is the maximum rate less the insured rate. Depending on the availability of network resources, excess traffic can be discarded during congestion episodes. *Compare with: maximum rate.*

EXEC session   Cisco term used to describe the command-line interface. The EXEC session exists in user mode and privileged mode.

expansion   The procedure of directing compressed data through an algorithm, restoring information to its original size.

expedited delivery   Specified by one protocol layer communicating either with other layers or with the identical protocol layer in a different network device, an option that requires that identified data be processed faster.

explorer frame   Used with source route bridging to find the route to the remote bridged network before a frame is transmitted.

explorer packet   An SNA packet transmitted by a source Token Ring device to find the path through a source-route-bridged network.

extended IP access list   IP access list that filters the network by logical address, protocol field in the Network layer header, and even the port field in the Transport layer header.

extended IPX access list   IPX access list that filters the network by logical IPX address, protocol field in the Network layer header, or even socket number in the Transport layer header.

Extended Setup   Used in setup mode to configure the router with more detail than Basic Setup mode. Allows multiple-protocol support and interface configuration.

external EIGRP route   Normally, the administrative distance of an EIGRP route is 90, but this is true only for what is known as an internal EIGRP route. These are routes originated within a specific autonomous system by EIGRP routers that are members of the same autonomous system. The other type of route is called an external EIGRP route and has an administrative distance of 170, which is not so good. These routes appear within EIGRP route tables courtesy of either manual or automatic redistribution, and they represent networks that originated outside of the EIGRP autonomous system.

failure domain   The region in which a failure has occurred in a token ring. When a station gains information that a serious problem, such as a cable break, has occurred with the network, it sends a beacon frame that includes the station reporting the failure, its NAUN and everything between. This defines the failure domain. Beaconing then initiates the procedure known as autoreconfiguration. *See also: autoreconfiguration* and *beacon.*

fallback   In ATM networks, this mechanism is used for scouting a path if it isn't possible to locate one using customary methods. The device relaxes requirements for certain characteristics, such as delay, in an attempt to find a path that meets a certain set of the most important requirements.

Fast Ethernet   Any Ethernet specification with a speed of 100Mbps. Fast Ethernet is 10 times faster than 10BaseT while retaining qualities such as MAC mechanisms, MTU, and frame format. These similarities make it possible for existing 10BaseT applications and management tools to be used on Fast Ethernet networks. Fast Ethernet is based on an extension of IEEE 802.3 specification (IEEE 802.3u). *Compare with: Ethernet. See also: 100BaseT, 100BaseTX,* and *IEEE.*

fast switching   A Cisco feature that uses a route cache to speed packet switching through a router. *Contrast with: process switching.*

fault tolerance   The extent to which a network device or a communication link can fail without communication being interrupted. Fault tolerance can be provided by added secondary routes to a remote network.

FDDI   Fiber Distributed Data Interface: A LAN standard, defined by ANSI X3T9.5, that can run at speeds up to 200Mbps and uses token-passing media access on fiber-optic cable. For redundancy, FDDI can use a dual-ring architecture.

FDM   Frequency-Division Multiplexing: A technique that permits information from several channels to be assigned bandwidth on one wire based on frequency. *See also: TDM, ATDM,* and *statistical multiplexing.*

FECN   Forward Explicit Congestion Notification: A bit set by a Frame Relay network that informs the DTE receptor that congestion was encountered along the path from source to destination. A device receiving frames with the FECN bit set can ask higher-priority protocols to take flow-control action as needed. *See also: BECN.*

FEIP   Fast Ethernet Interface Processor: An interface processor employed on Cisco 7000 series routers, supporting up to two 100Mbps 100BaseT ports.

filtering   Used to provide security on the network with access lists. LAN switches filter the network by MAC (hardware) address.

firewall   A barrier purposefully erected between any connected public networks and a private network—made up of a router or access server or several routers or access servers—that uses access lists and other methods to ensure the security of the private network.

fixed configuration router   A router that cannot be upgraded with any new interfaces.

flapping   Term used to describe a serial interface that is going up and down.

Flash   Electronically erasable programmable read-only memory (EEPROM). Used to hold the Cisco IOS in a router by default.

flash memory   Developed by Intel and licensed to other semiconductor manufacturers, it is nonvolatile storage that can be erased electronically and reprogrammed, physically located on an EEPROM chip. Flash memory permits software images to be stored, booted, and rewritten as needed. Cisco routers and switches use flash memory to hold the IOS by default. *See also: EPROM and EEPROM.*

flat network   Network that is one large collision domain and one large broadcast domain.

floating routes   Used with dynamic routing to provide backup routes (static routes) in case of failure.

flooding   When traffic is received on an interface, it is then transmitted to every interface connected to that device except the interface from which the traffic originated. This technique can be used for traffic transfer by bridges and switches throughout the network.

flow control   A methodology used to ensure that receiving units are not overwhelmed with data from sending devices. Pacing, as it is called in IBM networks, means that when buffers at a receiving unit are full, a message is transmitted to the sending unit to temporarily halt transmissions until all the data in the receiving buffer has been processed and the buffer is again ready for action.

forward/filter decisions   When a frame is received on an interface, the switch looks at the destination hardware address and finds the exit interface in the MAC database. The frame is only forwarded out the specified destination port.

FQDN   Fully qualified domain name: Used within the DNS domain structure to provide name-to-IP-address resolution on the Internet. An example of an FQDN is `bob.acme.com`.

FRAD   Frame Relay access device: Any device affording a connection between a LAN and a Frame Relay WAN. *See also: Cisco FRAD and FRAS.*

fragment   Any portion of a larger packet that has been intentionally segmented into smaller pieces. A packet fragment does not necessarily indicate an error and can be intentional. *See also: fragmentation.*

fragmentation   The process of intentionally segmenting a packet into smaller pieces when sending data over an intermediate network medium that cannot support the larger packet size.

FragmentFree   LAN switch type that reads into the data section of a frame to make sure fragmentation did not occur. Sometimes called modified cut-through.

frame   A logical unit of information sent by the Data Link layer over a transmission medium. The term often refers to the header and trailer, employed for synchronization and error control, that surround the data contained in the unit.

frame filtering   Frame filtering is used on a layer 2 switch to provide more bandwidth. A switch reads the destination hardware address of a frame and then looks for this address in the filter table, built by the switch. It then sends the frame out only the port where the hardware address is located, and the other ports do not see the frame.

frame identification (frame tagging)   VLANs can span multiple connected switches, which Cisco calls a switch fabric. Switches within this switch fabric must keep track of frames as they are received on the switch ports, and they must keep track of the VLAN they belong to as the frames traverse this switch fabric. Frame tagging performs this function. Switches can then direct frames to the appropriate port.

Frame Relay   A more efficient replacement of the X.25 protocol (an unrelated packet relay technology that guarantees data delivery). Frame Relay is an industry-standard, shared-access, best-effort, switched Data Link layer encapsulation that services multiple virtual circuits and protocols between connected mechanisms.

Frame Relay bridging   Defined in RFC 1490, this bridging method uses the identical spanning-tree algorithm as other bridging operations but permits packets to be encapsulated for transmission across a Frame Relay network.

Frame Relay switching   Packet switching for Frame Relay packets that is provided by a service provider.

frame tagging   *See: frame identification.*

frame types   Used in LANs to determine how a packet is put on the local network. Ethernet provides four different frame types. These are not compatible with each other, so for two hosts to communicate, they must use the same frame type.

framing   Encapsulation at the Data Link layer of the OSI model. It is called framing because the packet is encapsulated with both a header and a trailer.

FRAS   Frame Relay Access Support: A feature of Cisco IOS software that enables SDLC, Ethernet, Token Ring, and Frame Relay-attached IBM devices to be linked with other IBM mechanisms on a Frame Relay network. *See also: FRAD.*

frequency   The number of cycles of an alternating current signal per time unit, measured in hertz (cycles per second).

FSIP   Fast Serial Interface Processor: The Cisco 7000 routers' default serial interface processor, it provides four or eight high-speed serial ports.

FTP   File Transfer Protocol: The TCP/IP protocol used for transmitting files between network nodes, it supports a broad range of file types and is defined in RFC 959. *See also: TFTP.*

full-duplex   The capacity to transmit information between a sending station and a receiving unit at the same time. *See also: half-duplex.*

full mesh   A type of network topology where every node has either a physical or a virtual circuit linking it to every other network node. A full mesh supplies a great deal of redundancy but is typically reserved for network backbones because of its expense. *See also: partial mesh.*

global command   Cisco term used to define commands that are used to change the router configuration and that affect the whole router. In contrast, an interface command only affects the interface on which it's configured.

GMII   Gigabit MII: Media Independent Interface that provides 8 bits at a time of data transfer.

GNS   Get Nearest Server: On an IPX network, a request packet sent by a customer for determining the location of the nearest active server of a given type. An IPX network client launches a GNS request to get either a direct answer from a connected server or a response from a router disclosing the location of the service on the internetwork to the GNS. GNS is part of IPX and SAP. *See also: IPX* and *SAP.*

grafting   A process that activates an interface that has been deactivated by the pruning process. It is initiated by an IGMP membership report sent to the router.

GRE   Generic Routing Encapsulation: A tunneling protocol created by Cisco with the capacity for encapsulating a wide variety of protocol packet types inside IP tunnels, thereby generating a virtual point-to-point connection to Cisco routers across an IP network at remote points. IP tunneling using GRE permits network expansion across a single-protocol backbone environment by linking multiprotocol subnetworks in a single-protocol backbone environment.

guardband   The unused frequency area found between two communications channels, furnishing the space necessary to avoid interference between the two.

half-duplex   The capacity to transfer data in only one direction at a time between a sending unit and receiving unit. *See also: full-duplex.*

handshake   Any series of transmissions exchanged between two or more devices on a network to ensure synchronized operations.

H channel   High-speed channel: A full-duplex, ISDN primary rate channel operating at a speed of 384Kbps. *See also: B channel, D channel,* and *Echannel.*

HDLC   High-Level Data-Link Control: Using frame characters, including checksums, HDLC designates a method for data encapsulation on synchronous serial links and is the default encapsulation for Cisco routers. HDLC is a bit-oriented synchronous Data Link layer protocol created by ISO and derived from SDLC. However, most HDLC vendor implementations (including Cisco's) are proprietary. *See also: SDLC.*

helper address   The unicast address specified, which configures the Cisco router to change the client's local broadcast request for a service into a directed unicast to the server.

hierarchical addressing   Any addressing plan employing a logical chain of commands to determine location. IP addresses are made up of a hierarchy of network numbers, subnet numbers, and host numbers to direct packets to the appropriate destination.

hierarchy   Term used in defining IP addressing; in hierarchical addressing, some bits are used for networking and some bits for host addressing. Also used in the DNS structure and the Cisco design model.

HIP HSSI Interface Processor: An interface processor used on Cisco 7000 series routers, providing one HSSI port that supports connections to ATM, SMDS, Frame Relay, or private lines at speeds up to T3 or E3.

holddown The state a route is placed in so that routers can neither advertise the route nor accept advertisements about it for a defined time period. Holddowns are used to avoid accepting bad information. The actual information might be good, but it is not trusted. A route is generally placed in holddown when one of its links fails.

hop The movement of a packet between any two network nodes. *See also: hop count.*

hop count A routing metric that calculates the distance between a source and a destination based on the number of routers in the path. RIP employs hop count as its sole metric. *See also: hop and RIP.*

host address Logical address configured by an administrator or server on a device. Logically identifies this device on an internetwork.

Host-to-Host layer Layer in the Internet Protocol suite that is equal to the Transport layer of the OSI model.

HSCI High-Speed Communication Interface: Developed by Cisco, a single-port interface that provides full-duplex synchronous serial communications capability at speeds up to 52Mbps.

HSRP Hot Standby Router Protocol: A protocol that provides high network availability and nearly instantaneous hardware fail-over without administrator intervention. It generates a Hot Standby router group, including a lead router that lends its services to any packet being transferred to the Hot Standby address. If the lead router fails, it will be replaced by any of the other routers—the standby routers—that monitor it.

HSSI High-Speed Serial Interface: A network standard physical connector for high-speed serial linking over a WAN at speeds of up to 52Mbps.

hubs Physical layer devices that are really just multiple port repeaters. When an electronic digital signal is received on a port, the signal is reamplified or regenerated and forwarded out all segments except the segment from which the signal was received.

hybrid routing protocol Routing protocol that uses the attributes of both distance-vector and link-state. Enhanced Interior Gateway Routing Protocol (Enhanced IGRP).

ICD International Code Designator: Adapted from the subnetwork model of addressing, this assigns the mapping of Network layer addresses to ATM addresses. ICD is one of two ATM formats for addressing created by the ATM Forum to be utilized with private networks. *See also: DCC.*

ICMP Internet Control Message Protocol: Documented in RFC 792, it is a Network layer Internet protocol for the purpose of reporting errors and providing information pertinent to IP packet procedures.

IEEE   Institute of Electrical and Electronics Engineers: A professional organization that, among other activities, defines standards in a number of fields within computing and electronics, including networking and communications. IEEE standards are the predominant LAN standards used today throughout the industry. Many protocols are commonly known by the reference number of the corresponding IEEE standard.

IEEE 802.1   The IEEE committee specification that defines the bridging group. The specification for STP (Spanning Tree Protocol) is IEEE 802.1D. The STP uses STA (spanning-tree algorithm) to find and prevent network loops in bridged networks. The specification for VLAN trunking is IEEE 802.1Q.

IEEE 802.3   The IEEE committee specification that defines the Ethernet group, specifically the original 10Mbps standard. Ethernet is a LAN protocol that specifies physical layer and MAC sublayer media access. IEEE 802.3 uses CSMA/CD to provide access for many devices on the same network. Fast Ethernet is defined as 802.3U, and Gigabit Ethernet is defined as 802.3Q. *See also: CSMA/CD.*

IEEE 802.5   IEEE committee that defines Token Ring media access.

IGMP   Internet Group Management Protocol: Employed by IP hosts, the protocol that reports their multicast group memberships to an adjacent multicast router.

IGP   Interior gateway protocol: Any protocol used by an internetwork to exchange routing data within an independent system. Examples include RIP, IGRP, and OSPF.

IGRP   Interior Gateway Routing Protocol: Cisco proprietary distance-vector routing algorithm. Upgrade from the RIP protocol.

ILMI   Integrated (or Interim) Local Management Interface. A specification created by the ATM Forum, designated for the incorporation of network-management capability into the ATM UNI. Integrated Local Management Interface cells provide for automatic configuration between ATM systems. In LAN emulation, ILMI can provide sufficient information for the ATM end station to find an LECS. In addition, ILMI provides the ATM NSAP (Network Service Access Point) prefix information to the end station.

in-band management   In-band management is the management of a network device "through" the network. Examples include using Simple Network Management Protocol (SNMP) and Telnet directly via the local LAN. *Compare with: out-of-band management.*

in-band signaling   In-band signaling is the use of the bearer channel to deliver signaling, as call waiting in analog POTS lines. This is as opposed to out-of-band signaling, as in the case of the D channel being used to present a second active call in an ISDN circuit.

inside network   In NAT terminology, the inside network is the set of networks that are subject to translation. The outside network refers to all other addresses—usually those located on the Internet.

insured burst   In an ATM network, it is the largest, temporarily permitted data burst exceeding the insured rate on a PVC and not tagged by the traffic policing function for being dropped if network congestion occurs. This insured burst is designated in bytes or cells.

interarea routing   Routing between two or more logical areas. *Contrast with: intra-area routing. See also: area.*

interface configuration mode   Mode that allows you to configure a Cisco router or switch port with specific information, such as an IP address and mask.

interface processor   Any of several processor modules used with Cisco 7000 series routers. *See also: AIP, CIP, EIP, FEIP, HIP, MIP, and TRIP.*

Intermediate System to Intermediate System (IS-IS)   Intermediate System-to-Intermediate System: An OSI link-state hierarchical routing protocol.

internal EIGRP route   These are routes originated within a specific autonomous system by EIGRP routers that are members of the same autonomous system.

Internet   The global "network of networks," whose popularity has exploded starting in the mid 1990's. Originally a tool for collaborative academic research, it has become a medium for exchanging and distributing information of all kinds. The Internet's need to link disparate computer platforms and technologies has led to the development of uniform protocols and standards that have also found widespread use within corporate LANs. *See also: TCP/IP and MBONE.*

Internet   Before the rise of the Internet, this lowercase form was shorthand for "internetwork" in the generic sense. Now rarely used. *See also: internetwork.*

Internet layer   Layer in the Internet Protocol suite of protocols that provides network addressing and routing through an internetwork.

Internet protocol (IP)   Any protocol belonging to the TCP/IP protocol stack. *See also: TCP/IP.*

internetwork   Any group of networks interconnected by routers and other mechanisms, typically operating as a single entity.

internetworking   Broadly, anything associated with the general task of linking networks to each other. The term encompasses technologies, procedures, and products. When you connect networks to a router, you are creating an internetwork.

intra-area routing   Routing that occurs within a logical area. *Contrast with: interarea routing.*

Inverse ARP   Inverse Address Resolution Protocol: A technique by which dynamic mappings are constructed in a network, allowing a device such as a router to locate the logical network address and associate it with a permanent virtual circuit (PVC). Commonly used in Frame Relay to determine the far-end node's TCP/IP address by sending the Inverse ARP request across the local DLCI.

IP   Internet Protocol: Defined in RFC 791, it is a Network layer protocol that is part of the TCP/IP stack and offers connectionless service. IP furnishes an array of features for addressing, type-of-service specification, fragmentation and reassembly, and security.

IP address   Often called an Internet address, this is an address uniquely identifying any device (host) on the Internet (or any TCP/IP network). Each address consists of four octets

(32 bits), represented as decimal numbers separated by periods (a format known as "dotted-decimal"). Every address is made up of a network number, an optional subnetwork number, and a host number. The network and subnetwork numbers together are used for routing, while the host number addresses an individual host within the network or subnetwork. The network and subnetwork information is extracted from the IP address using the subnet mask. There are five classes of IP addresses (A–E), in which classes A through C allocate different numbers of bits to the network, subnetwork, and host portions of the address. *See also: CIDR, IP,* and *subnet mask.*

IPCP   IP Control Program: The protocol used to establish and configure IP over PPP. *See also: IP* and *PPP.*

IP multicast   A technique for routing that enables IP traffic to be reproduced from one source to several endpoints or from multiple sources to many destinations. Instead of transmitting one packet to each individual point of destination, one packet is sent to a multicast group specified by only one IP endpoint address for the group.

IPX   Internetwork Packet eXchange: Network layer protocol (layer 3) used in Novell NetWare networks for transferring information from servers to workstations. Similar to IP and XNS.

IPXCP   IPX Control Protocol: The protocol used to establish and configure IPX over PPP. *See also: IPX* and *PPP.*

IPXWAN   Protocol used for new WAN links to provide and negotiate line options on the link using IPX. After the link is up and the options have been agreed upon by the two end-to-end links, normal IPX transmission begins.

ISDN   Integrated Services Digital Network: Offered as a service by telephone companies, a communication protocol that allows telephone networks to carry data, voice, and other digital traffic. *See also: BISDN, BRI,* and *PRI.*

IS-IS   *See: Intermediate System-to-Intermediate System (IS-IS).*

ISL routing   Inter-Switch Link routing: A Cisco proprietary method of frame tagging in a switched internetwork. Frame tagging is a way to identify the VLAN membership of a frame as it traverses a switched internetwork.

isochronous transmission   Asynchronous data transfer over a synchronous data link, requiring a constant bit rate for reliable transport. *Compare with: asynchronous transmission* and *synchronous transmission.*

ITU-T   International Telecommunication Union-Telecommunication Standardization Sector: This is a group of engineers that develops worldwide standards for telecommunications technologies.

Kerberos   An authentication and encryption method that can be used by Cisco routers to ensure that data cannot be "sniffed" off of the network. Kerberos was developed at MIT and was designed to provide strong security using the Data Encryption Standard (DES) cryptographic algorithm.

LAN   Local area network: Broadly, any network linking two or more computers and related devices within a limited geographical area (up to a few kilometers). LANs are typically high-speed, low-error networks within a company. Cabling and signaling at the Physical and Data Link layers of the OSI are dictated by LAN standards. Ethernet, FDDI, and Token Ring are among the most popular LAN technologies. *Compare with: MAN.*

LANE   LAN emulation: The technology that allows an ATM network to operate as a LAN backbone. To do so, the ATM network is required to provide multicast and broadcast support, address mapping (MAC-to-ATM), and SVC management, in addition to an operable packet format. Additionally, LANE defines Ethernet and Token Ring ELANs. *See also: ELAN.*

LAN switch   A high-speed, multiple-interface transparent bridging mechanism, transmitting packets between segments of data links, usually referred to specifically as an Ethernet switch. LAN switches transfer traffic based on MAC addresses. *See also: multilayer switch* and *store-and-forward packet switching.*

LAPB   Link Accessed Procedure, Balanced: A bit-oriented Data Link layer protocol that is part of the X.25 stack and has its origin in SDLC. *See also: SDLC* and *X.25.*

LAPD   Link Access Procedure on the D channel: The ISDN Data Link layer protocol used specifically for the D channel and defined by ITU-T Recommendations Q.920 and Q.921. LAPD evolved from LAPB and is created to comply with the signaling requirements of ISDN basic access.

latency   Broadly, the time it takes a data packet to get from one location to another. In specific networking contexts, it can mean either (1) the time elapsed (delay) between the execution of a request for access to a network by a device and the time the mechanism actually is permitted transmission, or (2) the time elapsed between when a mechanism receives a frame and the time that frame is forwarded out of the destination port.

layer   Term used in networking to define how the OSI model works to encapsulate data for transmission on the network.

layer 3 switch   *See: multilayer switch.*

layered architecture   Industry standard way of creating applications to work on a network. Layered architecture allows the application developer to make changes in only one layer instead of the whole program.

LCP   Link Control Protocol: The protocol designed to establish, configure, and test data-link connections for use by PPP. *See also: PPP.*

leaky bucket   An analogy for the generic cell rate algorithm (GCRA) used in ATM networks for checking the conformance of cell flows from a user or network. The bucket's "hole" is understood to be the prolonged rate at which cells can be accommodated, and the "depth" is the tolerance for cell bursts over a certain time period.

learning bridge   A bridge that transparently builds a dynamic database of MAC addresses and the interfaces associated with each address. Transparent bridges help to reduce traffic congestion on the network.

LE ARP   LAN Emulation Address Resolution Protocol: The protocol providing the ATM address that corresponds to a MAC address.

leased line   Permanent connection between two points leased from the telephone companies.

LEC   LAN emulation client: Software providing the emulation of the link layer interface that allows the operation and communication of all higher-level protocols and applications to continue. The LEC runs in all ATM devices, which include hosts, servers, bridges, and routers. *See also: ELAN and LES.*

LECS   LAN emulation configuration server: An important part of emulated LAN services, providing the configuration data that is furnished upon request from the LES. These services include address registration for Integrated Local Management Interface (ILMI) support, configuration support for the LES addresses and their corresponding emulated LAN identifiers, and an interface to the emulated LAN. *See also: LES and ELAN.*

LES   LAN emulation server: The central LANE component that provides the initial configuration data for each connecting LEC. The LES typically is located on either an ATM-integrated router or a switch. Responsibilities of the LES include configuration and support for the LEC, address registration for the LEC, database storage and response concerning ATM addresses, and interfacing to the emulated LAN. *See also: ELAN, LEC, and LECS.*

link   A link is a network or router interface assigned to any given network. When an interface is added to the OSPF process, it's considered by OSPF to be a link. This link, or interface, will have state information associated with it (up or down) as well as one or more IP addresses.

link-state protocols   In link-state protocols, also called shortest-path-first protocols, the routers each create three separate tables. One of these tables keeps track of directly attached neighbors, one determines the topology of the entire internetwork, and one is used as the routing table. Link-state routers know more about the internetwork than any distance-vector routing protocol

link-state routing algorithm   A routing algorithm that allows each router to broadcast or multicast information regarding the cost of reaching all its neighbors to every node in the internetwork. Link-state algorithms provide a consistent view of the network and are therefore not vulnerable to routing loops. However, this loop-free network is achieved at the cost of somewhat greater difficulty in computation and more widespread traffic (compared with distance-vector routing algorithms). *See also: distance-vector routing algorithm.*

LLAP   LocalTalk Link Access Protocol: In a LocalTalk environment, the data link–level protocol that manages node-to-node delivery of data. This protocol provides node addressing and management of bus access, and it also controls data sending and receiving to ensure packet length and integrity.

LLC Logical Link Control: Defined by the IEEE, the higher of two Data Link layer sub-layers. LLC is responsible for error detection (but not correction), flow control, framing, and software-sublayer addressing. The predominant LLC protocol, IEEE 802.2, defines both connectionless and connection-oriented operations. *See also: Data Link layer* and *MAC.*

LMI Local Management Interface: An enhancement to the original Frame Relay specification. Among the features it provides are a keepalive mechanism, a multicast mechanism, global addressing, and a status mechanism.

LNNI LAN Emulation Network-to-Network Interface: In the Phase 2 LANE specification, an interface that supports communication between the server components within one ELAN.

load Like IGRP, EIGRP uses only bandwidth and delay of the line to determine the best path to a remote network by default. However, EIGRP can use a combination of bandwidth, delay, load, and reliability in its quest to find the best path to a remote network. Load refers to the amount of data on the link.

load balancing The act of balancing packet load over multiple links to the same remote network.

local explorer packet In a Token Ring SRB network, a packet generated by an end system to find a host linked to the local ring. If no local host can be found, the end system will produce one of two solutions: a spanning explorer packet or an all-routes explorer packet.

local loop Connection from a demarcation point to the closest switching office.

LocalTalk Utilizing CSMA/CD, in addition to supporting data transmission at speeds of 230.4Kbps, LocalTalk is Apple Computer's proprietary baseband protocol, operating at the Data Link and Physical layers of the OSI reference model.

logical address Network layer address that defines how data is sent from one network to another. Examples of logical addresses are IP and IPX.

loop avoidance If multiple connections between switches are created for redundancy purposes, network loops can occur. Spanning Tree Protocol (STP) is used to stop network loops while still permitting redundancy.

loopback address The IP address 127.0.0.1 is called the diagnostic or loopback address, and if you get a successful ping to this address, your IP stack is then considered to be initialized. If it fails, then you have an IP stack failure and need to reinstall TCP/IP on the host.

loopback interface Loopback interfaces are logical interfaces, which means they are not real router interfaces. They can be used for diagnostic purposes as well as OSPF configuration.

LPD Line Printer Daemon: Used in the Unix world to allow printing to an IP address.

LSA Link-State Advertisement: Contained inside of link-state packets (LSPs), these advertisements are usually multicast packets, containing information about neighbors and path costs, that are employed by link-state protocols. Receiving routers use LSAs to maintain their link-state databases and, ultimately, routing tables.

LUNI   LAN Emulation User-to-Network Interface: Defining the interface between the LAN emulation client (LEC) and the LAN emulation server (LES), LUNI is the ATM Forum's standard for LAN emulation on ATM networks. *See also: LES* and *LECS.*

MAC   Media Access Control: The lower sublayer in the Data Link layer, it is responsible for hardware addressing, media access, and error detection of frames. *See also: Data Link layer* and *LLC.*

MAC address   A Data Link layer hardware address that every port or device needs in order to connect to a LAN segment. These addresses are used by various devices in the network for accurate location of logical addresses. MAC addresses are defined by the IEEE standard and their length is six characters, typically using the burned-in address (BIA) of the local LAN interface. Variously called hardware address, physical address, burned-in address, or MAC layer address.

MacIP   In AppleTalk, the Network layer protocol encapsulating IP packets in Datagram Delivery Protocol (DDP) packets. MacIP also supplies substitute ARP services.

MAN   Metropolitan area network: Any network that encompasses a metropolitan area; that is, an area typically larger than a LAN but smaller than a WAN. *See also: LAN.*

Manchester encoding   A method for digital coding in which a mid-bit-time transition is employed for clocking, and a 1 (one) is denoted by a high voltage level during the first half of the bit time. This scheme is used by Ethernet and IEEE 802.3.

maximum burst   Specified in bytes or cells, the largest burst of information exceeding the insured rate that will be permitted on an ATM permanent virtual connection for a short time and will not be dropped even if it goes over the specified maximum rate. *Compare with: insured burst. See also: maximum rate.*

maximum hop count   Number of routers a packet is allowed to pass before it is terminated. This is created to prevent a packet from circling a network forever.

maximum rate   The maximum permitted data throughput on a particular virtual circuit, equal to the total of insured and uninsured traffic from the traffic source. Should traffic congestion occur, uninsured information may be deleted from the path. Measured in bits or cells per second, the maximum rate represents the highest throughput of data the virtual circuit is ever able to deliver and cannot exceed the media rate. *Compare with: excess rate. See also: maximum burst.*

MBONE   The multicast backbone of the Internet, it is a virtual multicast network made up of multicast LANs, including point-to-point tunnels interconnecting them.

MBS   Maximum Burst Size: In an ATM signaling message, this metric, coded as a number of cells, is used to convey the burst tolerance.

MCDV   Maximum Cell Delay Variation: The maximum two-point CDV objective across a link or node for the identified service category in an ATM network.

MCLR   Maximum Cell Loss Ratio: The maximum ratio of cells in an ATM network that fail to transit a link or node compared with the total number of cells that arrive at the link or node. MCLR is one of four link metrics that are exchanged using PTSPs to verify the available resources of an ATM network. The MCLR applies to cells in VBR and CBR traffic classes whose CLP bit is set to zero. *See also: CBR, CLP,* and *VBR.*

MCR   Minimum cell rate: A parameter determined by the ATM Forum for traffic management of the ATM networks. MCR is specifically defined for ABR transmissions and specifies the minimum value for the allowed cell rate (ACR). *See also: ACR* and *PCR.*

MCTD   Maximum Cell Transfer Delay: In an ATM network, the total of the maximum cell delay variation and the fixed delay across the link or node. MCTD is one of four link metrics that are exchanged using PNNI topology state packets to verify the available resources of an ATM network. There is one MCTD value assigned to each traffic class. *See also: MCDV.*

media translation   A router property that allows two different types of LAN to communicate— for example, Ethernet to Token Ring.

MIB   Management Information Base: Used with SNMP management software to gather information from remote devices. The management station can poll the remote device for information, or the MIB running on the remote station can be programmed to send information on a regular basis.

MII   Media Independent Interface: Used in Fast Ethernet and Gigabit Ethernet to provide faster bit transfer rates of 4 and 8 bits at a time. Contrast to AUI interface, which is 1 bit at a time.

MIP   Multichannel Interface Processor: The resident interface processor on Cisco 7000 series routers, providing up to two channelized T1 or E1 connections by serial cables connected to a CSU. The two controllers are capable of providing 24 T1 or 30 E1 channel groups, with each group being introduced to the system as a serial interface that can be configured individually.

mips   Millions of instructions per second: A measure of processor speed.

MLP   Multilink PPP: A technique used to split, recombine, and sequence datagrams across numerous logical data links.

MMP   Multichassis Multilink PPP: A protocol that supplies MLP support across multiple routers and access servers. MMP enables several routers and access servers to work as a single, large dial-up pool with one network address and ISDN access number. MMP successfully supports packet fragmenting and reassembly when the user connection is split between two physical access devices.

modem   Modulator-demodulator: A device that converts digital signals to analog and vice versa so that digital information can be transmitted over analog communication facilities such as voice-grade telephone lines. This is achieved by converting digital signals at the source to analog for transmission and reconverting the analog signals back into digital form at the destination. *See also: modulation* and *demodulation.*

modem eliminator   A mechanism that makes possible a connection between two DTE devices without modems by simulating the commands and physical signaling required.

modulation   The process of modifying some characteristic of an electrical signal, such as amplitude (AM) or frequency (FM), in order to represent digital or analog information. *See also: AM.*

MOSPF   Multicast OSPF: An extension of the OSPF unicast protocol that enables IP multicast routing within the domain. *See also: OSPF.*

MPOA   Multiprotocol over ATM: An effort by the ATM Forum to standardize how existing and future Network layer protocols such as IP, IPv6, AppleTalk, and IPX run over an ATM network with directly attached hosts, routers, and multilayer LAN switches.

MTU   Maximum transmission unit: The largest packet size, measured in bytes, that an interface can handle.

multicast   Broadly, any communication between a single sender and multiple receivers. Unlike broadcast messages, which are sent to all addresses on a network, multicast messages are sent to a defined subset of the network addresses; this subset has a group multicast address, which is specified in the packet's destination address field. *See also: broadcast* and *directed broadcast.*

multicast address   A single address that points to more than one device on the network by specifying a special nonexistent MAC address transmitted in that particular multicast protocol. Identical to group address. *See also: multicast.*

multicast group   Multicast works by sending messages or data to IP multicast group addresses. The group is a defined set of users or hosts that are allowed to read or view the data sent via multicast.

multicast send VCC   A two-directional point-to-point virtual control connection (VCC) arranged by an LEC to a BUS, it is one of the three types of informational links specified by phase 1 LANE. *See also: control distribute VCC* and *control direct VCC.*

multilayer switch   A highly specialized, high-speed, hardware-based type of LAN router, the device filters and forwards packets based on their layer 2 MAC addresses and layer 3 network addresses. It's possible that even layer 4 can be read. Sometimes called a layer 3 switch. *See also: LAN switch.*

multilink   Used to combine multiple async or ISDN links to provide combined bandwidth.

multiplexing   The process of converting several logical signals into a single physical signal for transmission across one physical channel. *Contrast with: demultiplexing.*

NAK   Negative acknowledgment: A response sent from a receiver, telling the sender that the information was not received or contained errors. *Compare with: acknowledgment.*

named access list   Used in both standard and extended lists to help with administration of access lists by allowing you to name the lists instead of using numbers. This also allows you to change a single line of an access list, which isn't possible in regular, numbered access lists.

NAT   Network Address Translation: An algorithm instrumental in minimizing the requirement for globally unique IP addresses, permitting an organization whose addresses are not all globally unique to connect to the Internet nevertheless by translating those addresses into globally routable address space.

native VLAN   Cisco switches all have a native VLAN called VLAN 1. This cannot be deleted or changed in any way. All switch ports are in VLAN 1 by default.

NBP   Name Binding Protocol: In AppleTalk, the transport-level protocol that interprets a socket client's name, entered as a character string, into the corresponding DDP address. NBP gives AppleTalk protocols the capacity to discern user-defined zones and names of mechanisms by showing and keeping translation tables that map names to their corresponding socket addresses.

neighboring routers   Two routers in OSPF that have interfaces to a common network. On networks with multi-access, these neighboring routers are dynamically discovered using the Hello protocol of OSPF.

neighbors   EIGRP and OSPF routers become neighbors when each router sees the other's Hello packets.

neighborship table   In OSPF and EIGRP routing protocols, each router keeps state information about adjacent neighbors. When newly discovered neighbors are learned, the address and interface of the neighbor is recorded. This information is stored in the neighbor data structure and the neighbor table holds these entries. Neighborship table can also be referred to as neighbor table or neighborship database.

NetBEUI   NetBIOS Extended User Interface: An improved version of the NetBIOS protocol used in a number of network operating systems including LAN Manager, Windows NT, LAN Server, and Windows for Workgroups, implementing the OSI LLC2 protocol. NetBEUI formalizes the transport frame not standardized in NetBIOS and adds more functions. *See also: OSI.*

NetBIOS   Network Basic Input/Output System: The API employed by applications residing on an IBM LAN to ask for services, such as session termination or information transfer, from lower-level network processes.

NetView   A mainframe network product from IBM used for monitoring SNA (Systems Network Architecture) networks. It runs as a VTAM (Virtual Telecommunications Access Method) application.

NetWare   A widely used NOS created by Novell, providing a number of distributed network services and remote file access.

Network Access layer   Bottom layer in the Internet Protocol suite that provides media access to packets.

network address   Used with the logical network addresses to identify the network segment in an internetwork. Logical addresses are hierarchical in nature and have at least two parts: network and host. An example of a hierarchical address is 172.16.10.5, where 172.16 is the network and 10.5 is the host address.

network control protocol A method of establishing and configuring different Network layer protocols. NCP is designed to allow the simultaneous use of multiple Network layer protocols. Some examples of protocols here are IPCP (Internet Protocol Control Protocol) and IPXCP (Internetwork Packet Exchange Control Protocol).

Network layer In the OSI reference model, it is layer 3—the layer in which routing is implemented, enabling connections and path selection between two end systems. *See also: Application layer, Data Link layer, Physical layer, Presentation layer, Session layer,* and *Transport layer.*

network segmentation Breaking up a large network into smaller networks. Routers, switches, and bridges are used to create network segmentation.

NFS Network File System: One of the protocols in Sun Microsystems's widely used file system protocol suite, allowing remote file access across a network. The name is loosely used to refer to the entire Sun protocol suite, which also includes RPC, XDR (External Data Representation), and other protocols.

NHRP Next Hop Resolution Protocol: In a nonbroadcast multi-access (NBMA) network, the protocol employed by routers in order to dynamically locate MAC addresses of various hosts and routers. It enables systems to communicate directly without requiring an intermediate hop, thus facilitating increased performance in ATM, Frame Relay, X.25, and SMDS systems.

NHS Next Hop Server: Defined by the NHRP protocol, this server maintains the next-hop resolution cache tables, listing IP-to-ATM address maps of related nodes and nodes that can be reached through routers served by the NHS.

nibble Four bits.

NIC Network interface card: An electronic circuit board placed in a computer. The NIC provides network communication to a LAN.

NLSP NetWare Link Services Protocol: Novell's link-state routing protocol, based on the IS-IS model.

NMP Network Management Processor: A Catalyst 5000 switch processor module used to control and monitor the switch.

node address Used to identify a specific device in an internetwork. Can be a hardware address, which is burned into the network interface card, or a logical network address, which an administrator or server assigns to the node.

non-broadcast multi-access (NBMA) networks Non-broadcast multi-access (NBMA) networks are types such as Frame Relay, X.25, and Asynchronous Transfer Mode (ATM). These networks allow for multi-access, but have no broadcast ability like Ethernet. So, NBMA networks require special OSPF configuration to function properly and neighbor relationships must be defined.

non-designated port A switch port that will not forward frames in order to prevent a switching loop. Spanning Tree Protocol (STP) is responsible for deciding whether a port is designated (forwarding) or non-designated (blocking).

non-stub area   In OSPF, a resource-consuming area carrying a default route, intra-area routes, interarea routes, static routes, and external routes. Non-stub areas are the only areas that can have virtual links configured across them and exclusively contain an autonomous system border router (ASBR). *Compare with: stub area. See also: ASBR and OSPF.*

NRZ   Nonreturn to zero: One of several encoding schemes for transmitting digital data. NRZ signals sustain constant levels of voltage with no signal shifting (no return to zero-voltage level) during a bit interval. If there is a series of bits with the same value (1 or 0), there will be no state change. The signal is not self-clocking. *See also: NRZI.*

NRZI   Nonreturn to zero inverted: One of several encoding schemes for transmitting digital data. A transition in voltage level (either from high to low or vice versa) at the beginning of a bit interval is interpreted as a value of 1; the absence of a transition is interpreted as a 0. Thus, the voltage assigned to each value is continually inverted. NRZI signals are not self-clocking. *See also: NRZ.*

NT   Network termination: A point in an ISDN network. *See: NT1 and NT2.*

NT1   NT1 is the device that converts the two-wire "U" interface to the four-wire "S/T."

NT2   NT2 is an ISDN-compliant switching device, like a PBX, that splits the "S/T" bus into two separate, but electrically equivalent, interfaces. The "T" interface connects to the NT1, while the "S" interface connects to TE1 devices.

NVRAM   Nonvolatile RAM: Random-access memory that keeps its contents intact while power is turned off.

OC   Optical Carrier: A series of physical protocols, designated as OC-1, OC-2, OC-3, and so on, for SONET optical signal transmissions. OC signal levels place STS frames on a multi-mode fiber-optic line at various speeds, of which 51.84Mbps is the lowest (OC-1). Each subsequent protocol runs at a speed divisible by 51.84. *See also: SONET.*

octet   Base-8 numbering system used to identify a section of a dotted decimal IP address. Also referred to as a byte.

ones density   Also known as pulse density, this is a method of signal clocking. The CSU/DSU retrieves the clocking information from data that passes through it. For this scheme to work, the data needs to be encoded to contain at least one binary 1 for each 8 bits transmitted. *See also: CSU and DSU.*

OSI   Open Systems Interconnection: International standardization program designed by ISO and ITU-T for the development of data networking standards that make multivendor equipment interoperability a reality.

OSI reference model   Open Systems Interconnection reference model: A conceptual model defined by the International Organization for Standardization (ISO), describing how any combination of devices can be connected for the purpose of communication. The OSI model divides the task into seven functional layers, forming a hierarchy with the applications at the top and the physical medium at the bottom, and it defines the functions each layer must provide. *See also: Application layer, Data Link layer, Network layer, Physical layer, Presentation layer, Session layer,* and *Transport layer.*

OSPF   Open Shortest Path First: A link-state, hierarchical routing algorithm derived from an earlier version of the IS-IS protocol, whose features include multipath routing, load balancing, and least-cost routing. OSPF is the suggested successor to RIP in the Internet environment. *See also: Enhanced IGRP, IGP,* and *IP.*

OSPF area   An OSPF area is a grouping of contiguous networks and routers. All routers in the same area share a common Area ID. Because a router can be a member of more than one area at a time, the Area ID is associated with specific interfaces on the router. This would allow some interfaces to belong to area 1, while the remaining interfaces can belong to area 0. All of the routers within the same area have the same topology table.

OUI   Organizationally unique identifier: Code assigned by the IEEE to an organization that makes network interface cards. The organization then puts this OUI on each and every card it manufactures. The OUI is 3 bytes (24 bits) long. The manufacturer then adds a 3-byte identifier to uniquely identify the host. The total length of the address is 48 bits (6 bytes) and is called a hardware address or MAC address.

out-of-band management   Management "outside" of the network's physical channels—for example, using a console connection not directly interfaced through the local LAN or WAN or a dial-in modem. *Compare to: in-band management.*

out-of-band signaling   Within a network, any transmission that uses physical channels or frequencies separate from those ordinarily used for data transfer.

outside network   In NAT terminology, the inside network is the set of networks that are subject to translation. The outside network refers to all other addresses—usually those located on the Internet

packet   In data communications, the basic logical unit of information transferred. A packet consists of a certain number of data bytes, wrapped or encapsulated in headers and/or trailers that contain information about where the packet came from, where it's going, and so on. The various protocols involved in sending a transmission add their own layers of header information, which the corresponding protocols in receiving devices then interpret.

packet switch   A physical device that makes it possible for a communication channel to share several connections; its functions include finding the most efficient transmission path for packets.

packet switching   A networking technology based on the transmission of data in packets. Dividing a continuous stream of data into small units—packets—enables data from multiple devices on a network to share the same communication channel simultaneously but also requires the use of precise routing information.

PAP   Password Authentication Protocol: In Point-to-Point Protocol (PPP) networks, a method of validating connection requests. The requesting (remote) device must send an authentication request, containing a password and ID, to the local router when attempting to connect. Unlike the more secure CHAP (Challenge Handshake Authentication Protocol), PAP sends the password unencrypted and does not attempt to verify whether the user is authorized to access the requested resource; it merely identifies the remote end. *See also: CHAP.*

parity checking   A method of error checking in data transmissions. An extra bit (the parity bit) is added to each character or data word so that the sum of the bits will be either an odd number (in odd parity) or an even number (even parity).

partial mesh   A type of network topology in which some network nodes form a full mesh (where every node has either a physical or a virtual circuit linking it to every other network node), but others are attached to only one or two nodes in the network. A typical use of partial-mesh topology is in peripheral networks linked to a fully meshed backbone. *See also: full mesh.*

passive state   Regarding an EIGRP routing table, a route is considered to be in the passive state when a router is not performing a route convergence.

PAT   Port Address Translation: This process allows a single IP address to represent multiple resources by altering the source TCP or UDP port number.

PCM   Pulse code modulation: Process by which an analog signal is converted into digital information.

PCR   Peak cell rate: As defined by the ATM Forum, the parameter specifying, in cells per second, the maximum rate at which a source may transmit.

PDN   Public data network: Generally for a fee, a PDN offers the public access to a computer communication network operated by private concerns or government agencies. Small organizations can take advantage of PDNs, aiding them to create WANs without investing in long-distance equipment and circuitry.

PDU   Protocol Data Unit: The processes at each layer of the OSI model. PDUs at the Transport layer are called segments; PDUs at the Network layer are called packets or datagrams; and PDUs at the Data Link layer are called frames. The Physical layer uses bits.

PGP   Pretty Good Privacy: A popular public-key/private-key encryption application offering protected transfer of files and messages.

phantom router   Used in a Hot Standby Routing Protocol (HSRP) network to provide an IP default gateway address to hosts.

Physical layer   The lowest layer—layer 1—in the OSI reference model, it is responsible for converting data frames from the Data Link layer (layer 2) into electrical signals. Physical layer protocols and standards define, for example, the type of cable and connectors to be used, including their pin assignments and the encoding scheme for signaling 0 and 1 values. *See also: Application layer, Data Link layer, Network layer, Presentation layer, Session layer,* and *Transport layer.*

PIM   Protocol Independent Multicast: A multicast protocol that handles the IGMP requests as well as requests for multicast data forwarding.

PIM-DM   Protocol Independent Multicast Dense Mode: PIM-DM utilizes the unicast route table and relies on the source root distribution architecture for multicast data forwarding.

PIM-SM   Protocol Independent Multicast Sparse Mode: PIM-SM utilizes the unicast route table and relies on the shared root distribution architecture for multicast data forwarding.

ping   Packet Internet Groper: A Unix-based Internet diagnostic tool consisting of a message sent to test the accessibility of a particular device on the IP network. The term's acronym reflects the underlying metaphor of submarine sonar. Just as the sonar operator sends out a signal and waits to hear it echo ("ping") back from a submerged object, the network user can ping another node on the network and wait to see if it responds.

pinhole congestion   A problem associated with distance-vector routing protocols if more than one connection to a remote network is known, but they are different bandwidths.

plesiochronous   Nearly synchronous, except that clocking comes from an outside source instead of being embedded within the signal as in synchronous transmissions.

PLP   Packet Level Protocol: Occasionally called X.25 level 3 or X.25 Protocol, a Network layer protocol that is part of the X.25 stack.

PNNI   Private Network-Network Interface: An ATM Forum specification for offering topology data used for the calculation of paths through the network, among switches and groups of switches. It is based on well-known link-state routing procedures and allows for automatic configuration in networks whose addressing scheme is determined by the topology.

point-to-multipoint connection   In ATM, a communication path going only one way, connecting a single system at the starting point, called the "root node," to systems at multiple points of destination, called "leaves." *See also: point-to-point connection.*

point-to-point connection   In ATM, a channel of communication that can be directed either one way or two ways between two ATM end systems. Also refers to a point-to-point WAN serial connection. *See also: point-to-multipoint connection.*

poison reverse updates   These update messages are transmitted by a router back to the originator (thus ignoring the split-horizon rule) after route poisoning has occurred. Typically used with DV routing protocols in order to overcome large routing loops and offer explicit information when a subnet or network is not accessible (instead of merely suggesting that the network is unreachable by not including it in updates). *See also: route poisoning.*

polling   The procedure of orderly inquiry used by a primary network mechanism to determine if secondary devices have data to transmit. A message is sent to each secondary, granting the secondary the right to transmit.

POP   (1) Point of presence: The physical location where an interexchange carrier has placed equipment to interconnect with a local exchange carrier. (2) Post Office Protocol: A protocol used by client email applications for recovery of mail from a mail server.

port security   Used with layer 2 switches to provide some security. Not typically used in production because it is difficult to manage. Allows only certain frames to traverse administrator-assigned segments.

port numbers   Used at the transport layer with TCP and UDP to keep track of host-to-host virtual circuits.

positive acknowledgment with retransmission   A connection-oriented session that provides acknowledgment and retransmission of the data if it is not acknowledged by the receiving host within a certain time frame.

POTS   Plain old telephone service: This refers to the traditional analog phone service that is found in most installations.

PPP   Point-to-Point Protocol: The protocol most commonly used for dial-up Internet access, superseding the earlier SLIP. Its features include address notification, authentication via CHAP or PAP, support for multiple protocols, and link monitoring. PPP has two layers: the Link Control Protocol (LCP) establishes, configures, and tests a link; and then any of various Network Control Protocols (NCPs) transport traffic for a specific protocol suite, such as IPX. *See also: CHAP, PAP,* and *SLIP.*

prefix routing   Method of defining how many bits are used in a subnet and how this information is sent in a routing update. For example, RIP version 1 does not send subnet mask information in the route updates. However, RIP version 2 does. This means that RIP v2 updates will send /24, /25, /26, etc., with a route update, which RIP v1 will not.

Presentation layer   Layer 6 of the OSI reference model, it defines how data is formatted, presented, encoded, and converted for use by software at the Application layer. *See also: Application layer, Data Link layer, Network layer, Physical layer, Session layer,* and *Transport layer.*

PRI   Primary Rate Interface: A type of ISDN connection between a PBX and a long-distance carrier, which is made up of a single 64Kbps D channel in addition to 23 (T1) or 30 (E1) B channels. *See also: ISDN.*

priority queuing   A routing function in which frames temporarily placed in an interface output queue are assigned priorities based on traits such as packet size or type of interface.

privileged mode   Command-line EXEC mode used in Cisco routers and switches that provides both viewing and changing of configurations.

Process/Application layer   Upper layer in the Internet Protocol stack. Responsible for network services.

process switching   As a packet arrives on a router to be forwarded, it's copied to the router's process buffer, and the router performs a lookup on the layer 3 address. Using the route table, an exit interface is associated with the destination address. The processor forwards the packet with the added new information to the exit interface, while the router initializes the fast-switching cache. Subsequent packets bound for the same destination address follow the same path as the first packet.

PROM Programmable read-only memory: ROM that is programmable only once, using special equipment. *Compare with: EPROM.*

propagation delay The time it takes data to traverse a network from its source to its destination.

protocol In networking, the specification of a set of rules for a particular type of communication. The term is also used to refer to the software that implements a protocol.

protocol-dependent modules The protocol-dependent modules, used in the EIGRP routing protocol, are responsible for network layer, protocol-specific requirements that allow multiple protocol support for IP, IPX and AppleTalk.

protocol stack A collection of related protocols.

Proxy Address Resolution Protocol Proxy ARP: Used to allow redundancy in case of a failure with the configured default gateway on a host. Proxy ARP is a variation of the ARP protocol in which an intermediate device, such as a router, sends an ARP response on behalf of an end node to the requesting host.

pruning The act of trimming down the shortest-path tree. This deactivates interfaces that do not have group participants.

PSE Packet switching exchange: The X.25 term for a switch.

PSN Packet-switched network: Any network that uses packet-switching technology. Also known as packet-switched data network (PSDN). *See also: packet switching.*

PSTN Public switched telephone network: Colloquially referred to as "plain old telephone service" (POTS). A term that describes the assortment of telephone networks and services available globally.

PVC Permanent virtual circuit: In a Frame Relay or ATM network, a logical connection, defined in software, that is maintained permanently. *Compare with: SVC. See also: virtual circuit.*

PVP Permanent virtual path: A virtual path made up of PVCs. *See also: PVC.*

PVP tunneling Permanent virtual path tunneling: A technique that links two private ATM networks across a public network using a virtual path, wherein the public network transparently trunks the complete collection of virtual channels in the virtual path between the two private networks.

QoS Quality of service: A set of metrics used to measure the quality of transmission and service availability of any given transmission system.

queue Broadly, any list of elements arranged in an orderly fashion and ready for processing, such as a line of people waiting to enter a movie theater. In routing, it refers to a backlog of information packets waiting in line to be transmitted over a router interface.

R reference point Used with ISDN networks to identify the connection between an NT1 and an S/T device. The S/T device converts the four-wire network to the two-wire ISDN standard network.

RADIUS   Remote Authentication Dial-In User Service: A protocol that is used to communicate between the remote access device and an authentication server. Sometimes an authentication server running RADIUS will be called a RADIUS server.

RAM   Random-access memory: Used by all computers to store information. Cisco routers use RAM to store packet buffers and routing tables, along with the hardware addresses cache.

RARP   Reverse Address Resolution Protocol: The protocol within the TCP/IP stack that maps MAC addresses to IP addresses. *See also: ARP.*

RARP server   A Reverse Address Resolution Protocol server is used to provide an IP address from a known MAC address.

rate queue   A value, assigned to one or more virtual circuits, that specifies the speed at which an individual virtual circuit will transmit data to the remote end. Every rate queue identifies a segment of the total bandwidth available on an ATM link. The sum of all rate queues should not exceed the total available bandwidth.

RCP   Remote Copy Protocol: A protocol for copying files to or from a file system that resides on a remote server on a network, using TCP to guarantee reliable data delivery.

redundancy   In internetworking, the duplication of connections, devices, or services that can be used as a backup in the event that the primary connections, devices, or services fail.

reference model   Used by application developers to create applications that work on any type of network. The most popular reference model is the Open Systems Interconnection (OSI) model.

reliability   Like IGRP, EIGRP uses only bandwidth and delay of the line to determine the best path to a remote network by default. However, EIGRP can use a combination of bandwidth, delay, load and reliability in its quest to find the best path to a remote network. Reliability refers to the reliability of the link to each remote network.

reliable multicast   When EIGRP sends multicast traffic it uses the Class D address 224.0.0.10. As I said, each EIGRP router is aware of who its neighbors are, and for each multicast it sends out, it maintains a list of the neighbors who have replied. If EIGRP doesn't get a reply from a neighbor, it will switch to using unicasts to resend the same data. If it still doesn't get a reply after 16 unicast attempts, the neighbor is declared dead. People often refer to this process as reliable multicast.

Reliable Transport Protocol (RTP)   The reliable transport protocol, used in the EIGRP routing protocol, is responsible for guaranteed, ordered delivery of EIGRP packets to all neighbors

reload   An event or command that causes Cisco routers to reboot.

RIF   Routing Information Field: In source-route bridging, a header field that defines the path direction of the frame or token. If the Route Information Indicator (RII) bit is not set, the RIF is read from source to destination (left to right). If the RII bit is set, the RIF is read from the destination back to the source, so the RIF is read right to left. It is defined as part of the token ring frame header for source-routed frames, which contains path information.

ring   Two or more stations connected in a logical circular topology. In this topology, which is the basis for Token Ring, FDDI, and CDDI, information is transferred from station to station in sequence.

ring topology   A network logical topology comprising a series of repeaters that form one closed loop by connecting unidirectional transmission links. Individual stations on the network are connected to the network at a repeater. Physically, ring topologies are generally organized in a closed-loop star. *Compare with: bus topology* and *star topology.*

RIP   Routing Information Protocol: The most commonly used interior gateway protocol in the Internet. RIP employs hop count as a routing metric. *See also: Enhanced IGRP, IGP, OSPF,* and *hop count.*

RJ connector   Registered jack connector: Used with twisted-pair wiring to connect the copper wire to network interface cards, switches, and hubs.

rolled cable   Type of wiring cable that is used to connect a PC's COM port to a router or switch console port.

ROM   Read-only memory: Chip used in computers to help boot the device. Cisco routers use a ROM chip to load the bootstrap, which runs a power-on self-test, and then find and load the IOS in flash memory by default.

root bridge   Used with Spanning Tree Protocol to stop network loops from occurring. The root bridge is elected by having the lowest bridge ID. The bridge ID is determined by the priority (32,768 by default on all bridges and switches) and the main hardware address of the device.

route flap   A route that is being announced in an up/down fashion.

route poisoning   Used by various DV routing protocols in order to overcome large routing loops and offer explicit information about when a subnet or network is not accessible (instead of merely suggesting that the network is unreachable by not including it in updates). Typically, this is accomplished by setting the hop count to one more than maximum. *See also: poison reverse updates.*

route summarization   In various routing protocols, such as OSPF, EIGRP, and IS-IS, the consolidation of publicized subnetwork addresses so that a single summary route is advertised to other areas by an area border router.

routed protocol   Routed protocols (such as IP and IPX) are used to transmit user data through an internetwork. By contrast, routing protocols (such as RIP, IGRP, and OSPF) are used to update routing tables between routers.

router   A Network layer mechanism, either software or hardware, using one or more metrics to decide on the best path to use for transmission of network traffic. Sending packets between networks by routers is based on the information provided on Network layers. Historically, this device has sometimes been called a gateway.

Router ID (RID)   The Router ID (RID) is an IP address used to identify the router. Cisco chooses the Router ID by using the highest IP address of all configured loopback interfaces.

If no loopback interfaces are configured with addresses, OSPF will choose the highest IP address of all active physical interfaces.

routing   The process of forwarding logically addressed packets from their local subnetwork toward their ultimate destination. In large networks, the numerous intermediary destinations a packet might travel before reaching its destination can make routing very complex.

routing domain   Any collection of end systems and intermediate systems that operate under an identical set of administrative rules. Every routing domain contains one or several areas, all individually given a certain area address.

routing metric   Any value that is used by routing algorithms to determine whether one route is superior to another. Metrics include such information as bandwidth, delay, hop count, path cost, load, MTU, reliability, and communication cost. Only the best possible routes are stored in the routing table, while all other information may be stored in link-state or topological databases. *See also: cost.*

routing protocol   Any protocol that defines algorithms to be used for updating routing tables between routers. Examples include IGRP, RIP, and OSPF.

routing table   A table kept in a router or other internetworking mechanism that maintains a record of only the best possible routes to certain network destinations and the metrics associated with those routes.

RP   Route processor: Also known as a supervisory processor; a module on Cisco 7000 series routers that holds the CPU, system software, and most of the memory components used in the router.

RSP   Route/Switch Processor: A processor module combining the functions of RP and SP used in Cisco 7500 series routers. *See also: RP and SP.*

RTS   Request To Send: An EIA/TIA-232 control signal requesting permission to transmit data on a communication line.

S reference point   ISDN reference point that works with a T reference point to convert a four-wire ISDN network to the two-wire ISDN network needed to communicate with the ISDN switches at the network provider.

sampling rate   The rate at which samples of a specific waveform amplitude are collected within a specified period of time.

SAP   (1) Service Access Point: A field specified by IEEE 802.2 that is part of an address specification. (2) Service Advertising Protocol: The Novell NetWare protocol that supplies a way to inform network clients of resources and services availability on network, using routers and servers. *See also: IPX.*

SCR   Sustainable cell rate: An ATM Forum parameter used for traffic management, it is the long-term average cell rate for VBR connections that can be transmitted.

SDH   Synchronous Digital Hierarchy: One of the standards developed for Fiber Optics Transmission Systems (FOTS).

SDLC   Synchronous Data Link Control: A protocol used in SNA Data Link layer communications. SDLC is a bit-oriented, full-duplex serial protocol that is the basis for several similar protocols, including HDLC and LAPB. *See also: HDLC* and *LAPB.*

seed router   In an AppleTalk network, the router that is equipped with the network number or cable range in its port descriptor. The seed router specifies the network number or cable range for other routers in that network section and answers to configuration requests from nonseed routers on its connected AppleTalk network, permitting those routers to affirm or modify their configurations accordingly. Every AppleTalk network needs at least one seed router physically connected to each network segment.

sequencing   Used in virtual circuits and segmentation to number segments so they can be put back together again in the correct order.

serial transmission   WAN serial connectors use serial transmission, which takes place one bit at a time, over a single channel.

server   Hardware and software that provide network services to clients.

Session layer   Layer 5 of the OSI reference model, responsible for creating, managing, and terminating sessions between applications and overseeing dataexchange between presentation layer entities. *See also: Application layer, Data Link layer, Network layer, Physical layer, Presentation layer,* and *Transport layer.*

set-based   Set-based routers and switches use the `set` command to configure devices. Cisco is moving away from set-based commands and is using the command-line interface (CLI) on all new devices.

setup mode   Mode that a router will enter if no configuration is found in nonvolatile RAM when the router boots. Allows the administrator to configure a router step-by-step. Not as robust or flexible as the command-line interface.

SF   A super frame (also called a D4 frame) consists of 12 frames with 192 bits each, and the 193rd bit providing other functions including error checking. SF is frequently used on T1 circuits. A newer version of the technology is Extended Super Frame (ESF), which uses 24 frames. *See also: ESF.*

shared tree   A method of multicast data forwarding. Shared trees use an architecture in which multiple sources share a common rendezvous point.

Shortest Path First (SPF)   A type of routing algorithm. The only true SPF protocol is Open Shortest Path First (OSPF).

signaling packet   An informational packet created by an ATM-connected mechanism that wants to establish connection with another such mechanism. The packet contains the QoS parameters needed for connection and the ATM NSAP address of the endpoint. The endpoint responds with a message of acceptance if it is able to support the desired QoS, and the connection is established. *See also: QoS.*

silicon switching   A type of high-speed switching used in Cisco 7000 series routers, based on the use of a separate processor (the Silicon Switch Processor, or SSP). *See also: SSE.*

simplex   A mode at which data or a digital signal is transmitted. Simplex is a way of transmitting in only one direction. Half-duplex transmits in two directions but only one direction at a time. Full-duplex transmits both directions simultaneously.

sliding window   The method of flow control used by TCP, as well as several Data Link layer protocols. This method places a buffer between the receiving application and the network data flow. The "window" available for accepting data is the size of the buffer minus the amount of data already there. This window increases in size as the application reads data from it and decreases as new data is sent. The receiver sends the transmitter announcements of the current window size, and it may stop accepting data until the window increases above a certain threshold.

SLIP   Serial Line Internet Protocol: An industry standard serial encapsulation for point-to-point connections that supports only a single routed protocol, TCP/IP. SLIP is the predecessor to PPP. *See also: PPP.*

SMDS   Switched Multimegabit Data Service: A packet-switched, datagram-based WAN networking technology offered by telephone companies that provides high speed.

SMTP   Simple Mail Transfer Protocol: A protocol used on the Internet to provide electronic mail services.

SNA   System Network Architecture: A complex, feature-rich, network architecture similar to the OSI reference model but with several variations; created by IBM in the 1970s and essentially composed of seven layers.

SNAP   Subnetwork Access Protocol: SNAP is a frame used in Ethernet, Token Ring, and FDDI LANs. Data transfer, connection management, and QoS selection are three primary functions executed by the SNAP frame.

snapshot routing   Snapshot routing takes a point-in-time capture of a dynamic routing table and maintains it even when the remote connection goes down. This allows the use of a dynamic routing protocol without requiring the link to remain active, which might incur per-minute usage charges.

SNMP   Simple Network Management Protocol: This protocol polls SNMP agents or devices for statistical and environmental data. This data can include device temperature, name, performance statistics, and much more. SNMP works with MIB objects that are present on the SNMP agent. This information is queried, then sent to the SNMP server.

socket   (1) A software structure that operates within a network device as a destination point for communications. (2) In AppleTalk networks, an entity at a specific location within a node; AppleTalk sockets are conceptually similar to TCP/IP ports.

software address   Also called a logical address. This is typically an IP address, but can also be an IPX address.

SOHO   Small office/home office: A contemporary term for remote users.

SONET   Synchronous Optical Network: The ANSI standard for synchronous transmission on fiber-optic media, developed at Bell Labs. It specifies a base signal rate of 51.84Mbps and a set of multiples of that rate, known as Optical Carrier levels, up to 2.5Gbps.

source tree   A method of multicast data forwarding. Source trees use the architecture of the source of the multicast traffic as the root of the tree.

SP   Switch processor: Also known as a ciscoBus controller, it is a Cisco 7000 series processor module acting as governing agent for all CxBus activities.

span   A full-duplex digital transmission line connecting two facilities.

SPAN   Switched Port Analyzer: A feature of the Catalyst 5000 switch, offering freedom to manipulate within a switched Ethernet environment by extending the monitoring ability of the existing network analyzers into the environment. At one switched segment, the SPAN mirrors traffic onto a predetermined SPAN port, while a network analyzer connected to the SPAN port is able to monitor traffic from any other Catalyst switched port.

spanning explorer packet   Sometimes called limited-route or single-route explorer packet, it pursues a statically configured spanning tree when searching for paths in a source-route bridging network. *See also: all-routes explorer packet, explorer packet,* and *local explorer packet.*

spanning tree   A subset of a network topology, within which no loops exist. When bridges are interconnected into a loop, the bridge, or switch, cannot identify a frame that has been forwarded previously, so there is no mechanism for removing a frame as it passes the interface numerous times. Without a method of removing these frames, the bridges continuously forward them—consuming bandwidth and adding overhead to the network. Spanning trees prune the network to provide only one path for any packet. *See also: Spanning Tree Protocol* and *spanning-tree algorithm.*

spanning-tree algorithm (STA)   An algorithm that creates a spanning tree using the Spanning Tree Protocol (STP). *See also: spanning tree* and *Spanning Tree Protocol.*

Spanning Tree Protocol (STP)   The bridge protocol (IEEE 802.1D) that enables a learning bridge to dynamically avoid loops in the network topology by creating a spanning tree using the spanning-tree algorithm. Spanning-tree frames called Bridge Protocol Data Units (BPDUs) are sent and received by all switches in the network at regular intervals. The switches participating in the spanning tree don't forward the frames; instead, they're processed to determine the spanning-tree topology itself. Cisco Catalyst series switches use STP 802.1D to perform this function. *See also: BPDU, learning bridge, MAC address, spanning tree,* and *spanning-tree algorithm.*

SPF   Shortest Path First algorithm: A routing algorithm used to decide on the shortest-path. Sometimes called Dijkstra's algorithm and frequently used in link-state routing algorithms. *See also: link-state routing algorithm.*

SPID   Service Profile Identifier: A number assigned by service providers or local telephone companies and configured by administrators to a BRI port. SPIDs are used to determine subscription services of a device connected via ISDN. ISDN devices use SPID when accessing the telephone company switch that initializes the link to a service provider.

split horizon   Useful for preventing routing loops, a type of distance-vector routing rule where information about routes is prevented from leaving the router interface through which that information was received.

spoofing   (1) In dial-on-demand routing (DDR), where a circuit-switched link is taken down to save toll charges when there is no traffic to be sent, spoofing is a scheme used by routers that causes a host to treat an interface as if it were functioning and supporting a session. The router pretends to send "spoof" replies to keepalive messages from the host in an effort to convince the host that the session is up and running. *See also: DDR.* (2) The illegal act of sending a packet labeled with a false address, in order to deceive network security mechanisms such as filters and access lists.

spooler   A management application that processes requests submitted to it for execution in a sequential fashion from a queue. A good example is a print spooler.

SPX   Sequenced Packet Exchange: A Novell NetWare transport protocol that augments the datagram service provided by Network layer (layer 3) protocols, it was derived from the Switch-to-Switch Protocol of the XNS protocol suite.

SQE   Signal Quality Error: In an Ethernet network, a message sent from a transceiver to an attached machine that the collision-detection circuitry is working.

SRB   Source-Route Bridging: Created by IBM, the bridging method used in Token Ring networks. The source determines the entire route to a destination before sending the data and includes that information in routing information fields (RIF) within each packet. *Contrast with: transparent bridging.*

SRT   Source-Route Transparent bridging: A bridging scheme developed by IBM, merging source-route and transparent bridging. SRT takes advantage of both technologies in one device, fulfilling the needs of all end nodes. Translation between bridging protocols is not necessary. *Compare with: SR/TLB.*

SR/TLB   Source-Route Translational Bridging: A bridging method that allows source-route stations to communicate with transparent bridge stations aided by an intermediate bridge that translates between the two bridge protocols. Used for bridging between Token Ring and Ethernet. *Compare with: SRT.*

SSAP   Source Service Access Point: The SAP of the network node identified in the Source field of the packet identifying the Network layer protocol. *See also: DSAP and SAP.*

SSE   Silicon Switching Engine: The software component of Cisco's silicon switching technology, hard-coded into the Silicon Switch Processor (SSP). Silicon switching is available only on the Cisco 7000 with an SSP. Silicon-switched packets are compared to the silicon-switching cache on the SSE. The SSP is a dedicated switch processor that offloads the switching process from the route processor, providing a fast-switching solution, but packets must still traverse the backplane of the router to get to the SSP and then back to the exit interface.

standard IP access list IP access list that uses only the source IP addresses to filter a network.

standard IPX access list IPX access list that uses only the source and destination IPX address to filter a network.

star topology A LAN physical topology with endpoints on the network converging at a common central device (known as a hub) using point-to-point links. A logical ring topology can be configured as a physical star topology using a unidirectional closed-loop star rather than point-to-point links. That is, connections within the hub are arranged in an internal ring. *See also: bus topology* and *ring topology*.

startup range If an AppleTalk node does not have a number saved from the last time it was booted, then the node selects from the range of values from 65,280 to 65,534.

state transitions Digital signaling scheme that reads the "state" of the digital signal in the middle of the bit cell. If it is five volts, the cell is read as a one. If the state of the digital signal is zero volts, the bit cell is read as a zero.

static route A route whose information is purposefully entered into the routing table by an administrator and takes priority over those chosen by dynamic routing protocols.

static VLAN A VLAN that is manually configured port-by-port. This is the method typically used in production networks.

statistical multiplexing Multiplexing in general is a technique that allows data from multiple logical channels to be sent across a single physical channel. Statistical multiplexing dynamically assigns bandwidth only to input channels that are active, optimizing available bandwidth so that more devices can be connected than with other multiplexing techniques. Also known as statistical time-division multiplexing or stat mux.

STM-1 Synchronous Transport Module Level 1. In the European SDH standard, one of many formats identifying the frame structure for the 155.52Mbps lines that are used to carry ATM cells.

store-and-forward packet switching A technique in which the switch first copies each packet into its buffer and performs a cyclic redundancy check (CRC). If the packet is error-free, the switch then looks up the destination address in its filter table, determines the appropriate exit port, and sends the packet.

STP (1) Shielded twisted-pair: A wiring scheme, used in many network implementations, that has a layer of shielded insulation to reduce EMI. (2) Spanning Tree Protocol.

straight-through cable Type of Ethernet cable that connects a host to a switch, host to a hub, or router to a switch or hub.

stub area   An OSPF area carrying a default route, intra-area routes, and interarea routes, but no external routes. Configuration of virtual links cannot be achieved across a stub area, and stub areas are not allowed to contain an ASBR. *See also: non-stub area, ASBR, and OSPF.*

stub network   A network having only one connection to a router.

STUN   Serial Tunnel: A technology used to connect an HDLC link to an SDLC link over a serial link.

subarea   A portion of an SNA network made up of a subarea node and its attached links and peripheral nodes.

subarea node   An SNA communications host or controller that handles entire network addresses.

subchannel   A frequency-based subdivision that creates a separate broadband communications channel.

subinterface   One of many virtual interfaces available on a single physical interface.

subnet   *See: subnetwork.*

subnet address   The portion of an IP address that is specifically identified by the subnet mask as the subnetwork. *See also: IP address, subnetwork, and subnet mask.*

subnet mask   Also simply known as mask, a 32-bit address mask used in IP to identify the bits of an IP address that are used for the subnet address. Using a mask, the router does not need to examine all 32 bits, only those indicated by the mask. *See also: address mask and IP address.*

subnetting   Used in IP networks to break up larger networks into smaller subnetworks.

subnetwork   (1) Any network that is part of a larger IP network and is identified by a subnet address. A network administrator segments a network into subnetworks in order to provide a hierarchical, multilevel routing structure, and at the same time protect the subnetwork from the addressing complexity of networks that are attached. Also known as a subnet. *See also: IP address, subnet mask, and subnet address.* (2) In OSI networks, the term specifically refers to a collection of ESs and ISs controlled by only one administrative domain, using a solitary network connection protocol.

summarization   Term used to describe the process of summarizing multiple routing table entries into one entry.

supernetting   *See: summarization.*

SVC   Switched virtual circuit: A dynamically established virtual circuit created on demand and dissolved as soon as transmission is over and the circuit is no longer needed. In ATM terminology, it is referred to as a switched virtual connection. *See also: PVC.*

switch (1) In networking, a device responsible for multiple functions such as filtering, flooding, and sending frames. It works using the destination address of individual frames. Switches operate at the Data Link layer of the OSI model. (2) Broadly, any electronic/mechanical device allowing connections to be established as needed and terminated if no longer necessary.

switch block A combination of layer 2 switches and layer 3 routers. The layer 2 switches connect users in the wiring closet into the access layer and provide 10 or 100Mbps dedicated connections. 1900/2820 and 2900 Catalyst switches can be used in the switch block.

switch fabric Term used to identify a layer 2 switched internetwork with many switches. More commonly, it is a term used to identify the inner workings of a switch itself. Thus, it is the matrix of pathways that any frame or cell might be able to traverse as it is switched from input port to output port.

switched LAN Any LAN implemented using LAN switches. *See also: LAN switch.*

synchronous transmission Signals transmitted digitally with precision clocking. These signals have identical frequencies and contain individual characters encapsulated in control bits (called start/stop bits) that designate the beginning and ending of each character. *See also: asynchronous transmission* and *isochronous transmission.*

syslog A protocol used to monitor system log messages by a remote device.

T reference point Used with an S reference point to change a 4-wire ISDN network to a two-wire ISDN network.

T1 Digital WAN that uses 24 DS0s at 64Kbps each to create a bandwidth of 1.536Mbps, minus clocking overhead, providing 1.544Mbps of usable bandwidth.

T3 Digital WAN that can provide bandwidth of 44.763Mbps.

TACACS+ Terminal Access Controller Access Control System Plus: An enhanced version of TACACS, this protocol is similar to RADIUS. *See also: RADIUS.*

tagged traffic ATM cells with their cell loss priority (CLP) bit set to 1. Also referred to as Discard Eligible (DE) traffic in Frame Relay networks. Tagged traffic can be eliminated in order to ensure trouble-free delivery of higher priority traffic, if the network is congested. *See also: CLP.*

TCP Transmission Control Protocol: A connection-oriented protocol that is defined at the transport layer of the OSI reference model. Provides reliable delivery of data.

TCP/IP Transmission Control Protocol/Internet Protocol. The suite of protocols underlying the Internet. TCP and IP are the most widely known protocols in that suite. *See also: IP* and *TCP.*

TDM Time Division Multiplexing: A technique for assigning bandwidth on a single wire, based on preassigned time slots, to data from several channels. Bandwidth is allotted to each channel regardless of a station's intent to send data. *See also: ATDM, FDM,* and *multiplexing.*

TE   Terminal equipment: Any peripheral device that is ISDN-compatible and attached to a network, such as a telephone or computer. TE1s are devices that are ISDN-ready and understand ISDN signaling techniques. TE2s are devices that are not ISDN-ready and do not understand ISDN signaling techniques. A terminal adapter must be used with a TE2.

TE1   Terminal Equipment Type 1. A device with a four-wire, twisted-pair digital interface is referred to as terminal equipment type 1. Most modern ISDN devices are of this type.

TE2   Terminal Equipment Type 2. Devices known as terminal equipment type 2 do not understand ISDN signaling techniques, and a terminal adapter must be used to convert the signaling.

telco   A common abbreviation for the telephone company.

Telnet   The standard terminal emulation protocol within the TCP/IP protocol stack. Method of remote terminal connection, enabling users to log in on remote networks and use those resources as if they were locally connected. Telnet is defined in RFC 854.

terminal adapter (TA)   A hardware interface between a computer without a native ISDN interface and an ISDN line. In effect, a device to connect a standard async interface to a nonnative ISDN device, emulating a modem.

terminal emulation   The use of software, installed on a PC or LAN server, that allows the PC to function as if it were a "dumb" terminal directly attached to a particular type of mainframe.

TFTP   Trivial File Transfer Protocol: Conceptually, a stripped-down version of FTP; it's the protocol of choice if you know exactly what you want and where it's to be found. TFTP doesn't provide the abundance of functions that FTP does. In particular, it has no directory browsing abilities; it can do nothing but send and receive files.

TFTP host/server   A host or server on which Trivial File Transfer Protocol is used to send files using IP at the Network layer and UDP at the Transport layer, which makes it unreliable.

thicknet   Also called 10Base5. Bus network that uses a thick coaxial cable and runs Ethernet up to 500 meters.

thinnet   Also called 10Base2. Bus network that uses a thin coax cable and runs Ethernet media access up to 185 meters.

three-way handshake   Term used in a TCP session to define how a virtual circuit is set up. It is called a "three-way" handshake because it uses three data segments.

token   A frame containing only control information. Possessing this control information gives a network device permission to transmit data onto the network. *See also: token passing.*

token bus   LAN architecture that is the basis for the IEEE 802.4 LAN specification and employs token-passing access over a bus topology. *See also: IEEE.*

token passing   A method used by network devices to access the physical medium in a systematic way based on possession of a small frame called a token. *See also: token.*

Token Ring IBM's token-passing LAN technology. It runs at 4Mbps or 16Mbps over a ring topology. Defined formally by IEEE 802.5. *See also: ring topology* and *token passing.*

toll network WAN network that uses the public switched telephone network (PSTN) to send packets.

topology database A topology database (also called a topology table) contains all destinations advertised by neighboring routers. Associated with each entry is the destination address and a list of neighbors that have advertised the destination.

traceroute Also trace; IP command used to trace the path a packet takes through an internetwork.

transparent bridging The bridging scheme used in Ethernet and IEEE 802.3 networks, it passes frames along one hop at a time, using bridging information stored in tables that associate end-node MAC addresses with bridge ports. This type of bridging is considered transparent because the source node does not know that it has been bridged, because the destination frames are addressed directly to the end node. *Contrast with: SRB.*

Transport layer Layer 4 of the OSI reference model, used for reliable communication between end nodes over the network. The transport layer provides mechanisms used for establishing, maintaining, and terminating virtual circuits, transport fault detection and recovery, and controlling the flow of information. *See also: Application layer, Data Link layer, Network layer, Physical layer, Presentation layer,* and *Session layer.*

trap Used to send SNMP messages to SNMP managers.

TRIP Token Ring Interface Processor: A high-speed interface processor used on Cisco 7000 series routers. The TRIP provides two or four ports for interconnection with IEEE 802.5 and IBM media with ports set to speeds of either 4Mbps or 16Mbps set independently of each other.

trunk link Link used between switches and from some servers to the switches. Trunk links carry traffic for many VLANs. Access links are used to connect host devices to a switch and carry only VLAN information that the device is a member of.

TTL Time to live: A field in an IP header, indicating the length of time a packet is valid.

TUD Trunk Up-Down: A protocol used in ATM networks for the monitoring of trunks. Should a trunk miss a given number of test messages being sent by ATM switches to ensure trunk line quality, TUD declares the trunk down. When a trunk reverses state and comes back up, TUD recognizes that the trunk is up and returns the trunk to service.

tunneling A method of avoiding protocol restrictions by wrapping packets from one protocol in another protocol's frame and transmitting this encapsulated packet over a network that supports the wrapper protocol. *See also: encapsulation.*

U reference point Reference point between a TE1 and an ISDN network. The U reference point understands ISDN signaling techniques and uses a 2-wire connection.

UDP User Datagram Protocol: A connectionless transport layer protocol in the TCP/IP protocol stack that simply allows datagrams to be exchanged without acknowledgments or delivery guarantees, requiring other protocols to handle error processing and retransmission. UDP is defined in RFC 768.

unicast Used for direct host-to-host communication. Communication is directed to only one destination and is originated only from one source.

unidirectional shared tree A method of shared tree multicast forwarding. This method allows only multicast data to be forwarded from the RP.

unnumbered frames HDLC frames used for control-management purposes, such as link startup and shutdown or mode specification.

user mode Cisco IOS EXEC mode that allows an administrator to perform very few commands. You can only verify statistics in user mode; you cannot see or change the router or switch configuration.

UTP Unshielded twisted-pair: Copper wiring used in small-to-large networks to connect host devices to hubs and switches. Also used to connect switch to switch or hub to hub.

VBR Variable bit rate: A QoS class, as defined by the ATM Forum, for use in ATM networks that is subdivided into real time (RT) class and non–real time (NRT) class. RT is employed when connections have a fixed-time relationship between samples. Conversely, NRT is employed when connections do not have a fixed-time relationship between samples, but still need an assured QoS.

VCC Virtual channel connection: A logical circuit that is created by VCLs (virtual channel links). VCCs carry data between two endpoints in an ATM network. Sometimes called a virtual circuit connection.

VIP (1) Versatile Interface Processor: An interface card for Cisco 7000 and 7500 series routers, providing multilayer switching and running the Cisco IOS software. The most recent version of VIP is VIP2. (2) Virtual IP: A function making it possible for logically separated switched IP workgroups to run Virtual Networking Services across the switch port.

virtual circuit (VC) A logical circuit devised to assure reliable communication between two devices on a network. Defined by a virtual path identifier/virtual channel (really the only time "channel" is used) identifier (VPI/VCI) pair, a virtual circuit can be permanent (PVC) or switched (SVC). Virtual circuits are used in Frame Relay and X.25. Known as virtual channel in ATM. *See also: PVC and SVC.*

virtual ring In an SRB network, a logical connection between physical rings, either local or remote.

VLAN Virtual LAN: A group of devices on one or more logically segmented LANs (configured by use of management software), enabling devices to communicate as if attached to the same physical medium, when they are actually located on numerous different LAN segments. VLANs are based on logical instead of physical connections and thus are tremendously flexible.

VLAN ID   Sometimes referred to as VLAN color, the VLAN ID is tagged onto a frame to tell a receiving switch which VLAN the frame is a member of.

VLSM   Variable Length Subnet Mask: Helps optimize available address space and specify a different subnet mask for the same network number on various subnets. Also commonly referred to as "subnetting a subnet."

VMPS   VLAN Management Policy Server: Used to dynamically assign VLANs to a switch port.

VPN   Virtual private network: A method of encrypting point-to-point logical connections across a public network, such as the Internet. This allows secure communications across a public network.

VTP   VLAN Trunking Protocol: Used to update switches in a switch fabric about VLANs configured on a VTP server. VTP devices can be a VTP server, client, or transparent device. Servers update clients. Transparent devices are only local devices and do not share information with VTP clients. VTP devices send VLAN information down trunked links only.

VTP transparent mode   Switch mode that receives VLAN Trunking Protocol VLAN information and passes it on, but doesn't read the information.

WAN   Wide area network: Is a designation used to connect LANs together across a DCE (data communications equipment) network. Typically, a WAN is a leased line or dial-up connection across a PSTN network. Examples of WAN protocols include Frame Relay, PPP, ISDN, and HDLC.

wildcard   Used with access lists and OSPF configurations. Wildcards are designations used to identify a range of subnets.

windowing   Flow-control method used with TCP at the Transport layer of the OSI model.

WINS   Windows Internet Name Service: Name resolution database for NetBIOS names to TCP/IP address.

WinSock   Windows Socket Interface: A software interface that makes it possible for an assortment of applications to use and share an Internet connection. The WinSock software consists of a dynamic link library (DLL) with supporting programs such as a dialer program that initiates the connection.

workgroup layer   The distribution layer is sometimes referred to as the workgroup layer and is the communication point between the access layer and the core. The primary functions of the distribution layer are to provide routing, filtering, and WAN access and to determine how packets can access the core, if needed.

workgroup switching   A switching method that supplies high-speed (100Mbps) transparent bridging between Ethernet networks as well as high-speed translational bridging between Ethernet and CDDI or FDDI.

X Window   A distributed multitasking windowing and graphics system originally developed by MIT for communication between X terminals and Unix workstations.

X.25   An ITU-T packet-relay standard that defines communication between DTE and DCE network devices. X.25 uses a reliable Data Link layer protocol called LAPB. X.25 also uses PLP at the Network layer. X.25 has mostly been replaced by Frame Relay.

ZIP   Zone Information Protocol: A Session layer protocol used by AppleTalk to map network numbers to zone names. NBP uses ZIP in the determination of networks containing nodes that belong to a zone. *See also: ZIP storm* and *zone.*

ZIP storm   A broadcast storm occurring when a router running AppleTalk reproduces or transmits a route for which there is no corresponding zone name at the time of execution. The route is then forwarded by other routers downstream, thus causing a ZIP storm. *See also: broadcast storm* and *ZIP.*

zone   A logical grouping of network devices in AppleTalk. Also used in DNS. *See also: ZIP.*

Index

Note to the reader: Throughout this index **boldfaced** page numbers indicate primary discussions of a topic. *Italicized* page numbers indicate illustrations.

Q

R

S

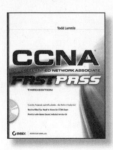

Wiley Publishing, Inc., End-User License Agreement